INTRODUCING PLANNING

INTRODUCING PLANNING

Clara Greed

THE ATHLONE PRESS
LONDON & NEW BRUNSWICK, NJ

First published in 2000 by
THE ATHLONE PRESS
1 Park Drive, London NW11 7SG
and New Brunswick, New Jersey

© Clara Greed, 2000

Clara Greed has asserted her right under the Copyright, Designs and Patents Act 1988,
to be identified as the author of this work

British Library Cataloguing in Publication Data
A catalogue record for this book is available from the British Library

ISBN 0 485 00612 X HB

Library of Congress Cataloging in Publication Data
Greed, Clara, 1948–
    Introducing planning / Clara Greed.
        p.   cm.
    Includes bibliographical references and index.
    ISBN 0-485-00612-X (pbk.: alk. paper)
        1. City planning.   I. Title.
HT166.G685 2000
307.1′216—dc21   00-038947

Distributed in The United States, Canada and South America by
Transaction Publishers
390 Campus Drive
Somerset, New Jersey 08873

Typeset by Florence Production Ltd, Stoodleigh, Devon

Printed and bound in Great Britain by
Cambridge University Press

CONTENTS

Part 4   Planning is for People?

ILLUSTRATIONS

FIGURES

TABLES

TEXTBOXES

ACKNOWLEDGEMENTS

Most of the photographs and diagrams in this edition are the author's own work. Updated maps were by drawn Paul Revelle, Faculty graphics technician, UWE.

Thanks to Linda Davies for use of Figure 12.6, and Mike Devereaux at UWE for help on Chapter 2.

Figure 6.4 is adapted from Ebenezer Howard's drawings of garden city principles, and permission was given for their use by Trustees of Ebenezer Howard's estate, Attic Publications, and the Town and Country Planning Association.

Thanks to Chauncy D. Harris, Professor Emeritus, University of Chicago, and the American Academy of Political and Social Science for the use of Figure 12.1 showing Social Ecology Diagrams.

PREFACE

My purpose is to provide an overall introduction to planning, providing a 'one-stop shop' for the busy reader, but in this third edition some more advanced material is also provided on planning theory and research perspectives in response to changing course demands and structures. The book is chiefly aimed at students studying for the various built environment professions, and will also be of interest to planning academics, practitioners and community groups.

The scope of the book has been expanded to include a wider range of current planning whilst retaining its previous urban social focus. Greater emphasis is given to environmental factors, and to the related issue of planning for sustainability within the wider context of global movements, national and regional reorganization, and European Union requirements.

Illustrations have been added, for planning is a visual subject as well as a statutory process, and the section on urban design has been expanded. The emphasis was upon choosing illustrations which highlight significant points, rather than seeking to provide a tourist guide of spectacular buildings. It was intentionally decided *not* to include detailed plans, diagrams and maps in the design and layout sections. The purpose is to widen the readers' perceptions of what constitutes planning, and to introduce the readers to key debates in planning policy, rather than to provide what may be taken as a 'recipe book' of standards on how to plan.

The book should be seen as a compendium of topics divided into four main sections, which should ideally be read sequentially, but may also be dipped into as the need arises. Further reading guidance is provided on each topic. Three categories of student tasks are provided for each chapter. First, information gathering tasks have been included to encourage the reader to get 'out and about' finding out about planning. Second, conceptual tasks are provided which comprise writing discursive essays on the nature and scope of town planning. Such essays are similar to the examination questions set on many courses. Third, reflective tasks are suggested, which involve the reader simply thinking about a topic in a structured way, or expressing their views with reference to their own experience as citizens of the built and natural environment.

Clara Greed
Bristol, 2000

INTRODUCTION

WHY PLANNING MATTERS

THE CONTEXT

Geographical Setting

Nearly 80 per cent of the population of Britain lives in urban areas, yet there are substantial areas of open countryside between the towns and cities. The United Kingdom has a population of 59 million, but 80 per cent of the total 24,410,000 hectares of land is agricultural (ONS, annual, Table 1.2). A major factor in keeping development at bay is the town and country planning system, which has sought to control development over the last 50 years.

The emphasis in this book will be primarily urban, that is upon *town* planning. But, urban and rural issues are inseparable, and are overarched by environmental concerns that affect the entire planet. Officially, the full title of the subject is 'Town and Country Planning' as enshrined in the many Acts of Parliament of that name. But, planning is more than physical land use control, it incorporates economic, social, environmental, architectural and political dimensions, at local, regional and national levels. 'Planning' will be used throughout, to describe this range.

An Atmosphere of Distrust?

The first half of Chapter 1 comprises an introductory commentary on the scope and nature of planning. Highlighted are different viewpoints, popular images and expectations of the planning system. The author seeks to allay common misconceptions and to begin to explain 'why planning matters'. Key areas of concern, will be highlighted for illustrative purposes: transport planning, for example. All topics raised will be dealt with in detail in the appropriate chapter. The final section of this chapter comprises a summary of the book's contents.

WHAT IS TOWN PLANNING?

City-Wide Policies or Local Regulations?

Many people's first contact with the planners is in relation to seeking planning permission, perhaps for an ill-fated house extension application. Planning law and its enforcement, through what is known as development control, are major aspects of town planning.

Town planners may appear to be chiefly concerned with standards and rules about the size of plots, road widths, and the layout of new developments. But these controls are only one of the means whereby planning policy can be put into effect and made a reality. One of the main aspects of the town planner's work is the production of city-wide development plans, which determine which sites can be built upon in the first place. Every time a new housing estate is built on the edge of a city for commuters working in central area offices, the cars generated by the new development will add to the rush hour congestion in the centre. The next 'little' site development may be the straw that breaks the camel's back, leading to the need for new roads and increased car parking provision within the central business area of the city. Planners therefore have to retain a broader city-wide perspective, and

Textbox 1.1   Metric/Imperial Conversion

The United Kingdom (UK) is defined as England, Wales, Scotland, and Northern Ireland. The total area of the UK is 240,900 square kilometres (93,012 square miles). Great Britain (and Britain) means England, Scotland and Wales, but not Northern Ireland, the Channel Isles, or the Isle of Man. The British Isles is all of the UK plus all of Ireland and other islands. The planning Acts and systems discussed apply to England and Wales only; Scotland has similar systems and policies under its own legislation. Official government statistics (as in *Social Trends*, annual) are normally produced for the United Kingdom as a whole.

To convert inches to centimetres multiply by 2.54; feet to metres multiply by 0.3048; yards to metres multiply by 0.9144. To convert centimetres to inches multiply by 0.3937; metres to feet multiply by 3.2808; metres to yards multiply by 1.0936. For area measurements that are used in indicating floorspace, for example for retail development, 1 square foot = 0.0929 square metres, and 1 square metre is 10.764 square feet, – that is divide or multiply by 10 approximately. Cubic measurements that are of relevance to development control, for example when assessing the size of house extensions, are as follows: to convert cubic feet into cubic metres multiply by 0.0283, and to convert cubic metres into cubic feet multiply by 35.315. An acre = 0.405 hectares, and a hectare = 2.471 acres: in other words multiply a hectare by 2.5 to turn it back into acres. There are 640 acres in a square mile.

a more critical viewpoint towards new development, than that of the private sector developer whose horizons may be limited to the boundaries of the site under development, and the 'cost factor'.

Nevertheless, nearly all development requires planning permission, as explained in Part I. The Town and Country Planning Act 1990, as modified by the Planning and Compensation Act 1991, forms the basis of the current planning system (see Government Publications Appendix). Incoming legislation and government initiatives continue to reshape the nature of planning. Some of the main recent changes to

legislation and policy have not come from the British government but are the result of the requirements of EU regulations and directives. For example, the Environment Act 1995 brought into force in the UK a wide range of 'green' planning regulations, including the need for environmental assessment of many categories of new development (Grant, 1998).

Spatial or Aspatial?

The modern town and country planning system was established under the Town and Country Planning Act 1947 as part of reconstruction planning. At the time, the primary emphasis was upon controlling land uses and development and producing actual physical 'plans'. This approach is reflected in the following definition, which was made by a prominent post-war town planner who was famous for his publications on how to build complete new towns from scratch.

Post-war reconstruction planning was based upon a simplistic 'masterplan' blueprint approach, best suited to planning new towns on greenfield sites (undeveloped land) which is no longer appropriate today. Over the last half century planning has become much more complex. The emphasis has shifted from controlling the land uses and developments themselves, to seeking to influence the aspatial (non-physical) processes (Foley, 1964: 37) such as the economic, social and political forces that determine the spatial (physical) end product of the built environment.

Arguably, the spatial and aspatial can never be separated (Greed, 1994a, Chapter 1). Nowadays planning is no longer primarily a subject concerned with a range of spatially delineated, identifiable physical land use topics or design policies; rather it should be seen as a 'process', or a 'methodology' as a tool of urban governance (Thomas, 1999). Senior town planners, in local government, are strategic managers whose skills are especially valued because their professional perspective enables them to take the broader view, to see the connections between a diverse range of issues and topics in order to initiate urban renewal and economic regeneration.

Today's town planners are more likely to work in multidisciplinary teams, liaising with other policy makers from the fields of housing, economic development, cultural and social policy to fulfil higher-level governmental targets. Planners are working alongside other professionals on policy initiatives to reduce 'social exclusion', which is one of the key 'New Labour' urban priorities as will be discussed in later chapters. As a result of these changes, planning can no longer be seen as a separate, discrete activity. Current planning policy guidance reflects the government's commitment to what it calls *joined up thinking*; that is, integration of policies from different departments towards common goals such as urban renewal and reduction in unemployment and social deprivation.

Although nowadays planning has shifted from its physical map-making origins, it is important not to forget the spatial effects of planning. Plans still to shape the built environment. Patterns of employment, investment and social well-being continue to show distinct spatial variation between regions, and so 'space matters' (Massey, 1984: 16). The relationship between land uses within urban areas, and between regions, is often already firmly established for geographical reasons, which have influenced the nature of development before modern town planning was even invented. Therefore modern town planning retains both a spatial and an aspatial perspective in the development of appropriate policy.

Old or New?

As can be seen planners are involved in a wide range of activities. Town planning is often still associated with new town building, and with new developments on greenfield sites. But much less than 5 per cent of the population of Britain has ever lived in New Towns (TCPA Annual Survey); no new ones have been started by the government since the 1970s, and most of the existing ones have now been de-designated.

Much of the modern planner's work consists of dealing with already developed older sites in which a major objective may be to incorporate existing buildings into a proposed new scheme. On such sites it may be impossible to apply exact 'standards' or precise blueprints. The planner's job is to seek to be flexible in respect of planning standards when negotiating with the developer in order to get the best solution possible within what is often a difficult situation. Emphasis is likely to be put upon retaining significant existing buildings and features where possible, rather than on demolition and total clearance.

These days planners are much more concerned with planning for existing towns and cities, with regeneration, refurbishment, conservation, sustainability and urban management, and with building upon derelict and infill sites: that is, upon 'brown land', as will be discussed further in Chapter 9 in respect of New Labour's policy targets. New construction represents less than 3 per cent net of the total building stock each year (DETR, annual, JFCCI, 1999); however, much higher rates are recorded in some regions than in others, for example, in the southeast of England. Much of the work of the other built environment professions is now concerned with existing rather than new development. For example, a chartered surveyor may spend more time dealing with the transfer, letting and management of existing property, than with putting through new development schemes (Ratcliffe and Stubbs, 1996; Seeley, 1997). Urban conservation and the preservation of historic buildings and areas have become major preoccupations of town planning. In the public sector there has been a dramatic decline in the building of council housing; most of the new-build social housing development is being undertaken by housing associations. Maintenance and refurbishment of existing stock is now a major aspect of work in the construction industry.

Physical or Social Town Planning?

In discussing land use and development it must not be forgotten that 'planning is for people' (Broady, 1968); there is still a great deal of truth in this maxim. It is important to acknowledge the importance of the needs and wants of the population in generating demand for development in the first place, and to seek to meet the requirements of 'users of land' rather than focusing on the 'land uses' in isolation.

Leisure, entertainment, sport and recreation are social issues of concern to the modern town planner, all of which generate demands for physical land use, space and design. Development plans not only include policies for all the main land uses and types of development, but also must take into account, in the policymaking process, the broader social, economic and environmental trends in the area of the plan, such as the land use demands creating by changing patterns of employment or household formation. The 'social aspects of planning' should not be seen as a euphemism for inner urban problems. Nevertheless, the 'inner city' has been a major planning issue in recent years and this has been followed by a continuing concern with urban renewal and regeneration of deprived areas. Planners need to take into account such issues as urban poverty, environmental deprivation, health standards, and minority issues in drawing up plans for sensitive urban areas. Developing good community relations and undertaking public participation and consultation are important aspects of good town planning practice.

It is important to plan equally fairly for everyone. To return to the above definition of town planning (Keeble, 1969) one must ask for whom is it important 'to secure the maximum level of economy. convenience and beauty'? The various members of the urban population do not have the same needs or requirements, and planners can only hope, 'to please some of the people some of the time, rather than all of the people all of the time'. Planning for the 'average man' may lead to planning successfully for no-one. It is important to take into account the needs of everyone in society, including women, ethnic minorities, all social classes, all age groups, and disabled people.

Conflicting Viewpoints

Having introduced the subject, it must be acknowledged at the outset that planning is not a straightforward, factual subject, but one that is surrounded by a cloud of suspicion, riven with uncertainty and contradiction, and subject to intense criticism and dissatisfaction. In spite of its achievements, many people are of the opinion that town planning policy has been ineffective and misdirected, and that more could have been achieved with better policy in town and countryside (Brindley *et al.*, 1996; Shoard, 1999).

Many take the view that town planning imposes unnecessary restrictions on the property market and on individual citizens' freedom, with little of benefit to show in return. Others consider the British planning system to be the best in the world, and argue that without it Britain would long ago have been covered from coast to coast in housing development to accommodate a disproportionately large population relative to land surface. This book will show that there have been both successes and failures attributable to the operation of the planning system, within a complex and ever changing developmental context.

The last Conservative government (1979–97) attempted to speed up the planning system; the subsequent New Labour government has sought to modify the objectives of planning. But neither government has removed the planning system. Many private developers support the need for town planning because it is seen as providing a framework within which the private property market can operate. But they may question the objectives upon which it is based, and the way in which it is administered.

The issue of transport will now be given as an example of conflicting policy viewpoints:

Planning for Transport?

One area that continues to cause great national concern is 'the traffic problem. Much of the blame is laid at the planners' feet by the media. But the powers and the culpability of the planners in dealing with urban problems should not be overestimated. Under the present statutory system, planners have considerable powers over the nature of land use and development, but they have limited powers over the transport systems that connect the land uses, and which have contributed to the outward growth of cities. There is concern nationally about the problems created by the increased use of the motor car, and by the government's attempts to limit car use. There are demands from environmentalists for more public transport, less pollution, and generally more sustainable cities (as discussed in Chapter 10).

Significantly many of these views are echoed by those concerned with the social aspects of town planning, especially those representing minority groups and those with limited access to the use of a motor car, such as women with small children. However negative controls on the use of the motor car are proving both unpopular and unworkable. For many in the suburbs, where the majority of the urban population lives, cars may be the only realistic means of getting to work, reaching out-of-town retail centres, and of taking small children to school (ONS, annual). As a result of previous misdirected planning policy there are few retail outlets or social amenities at the local district level.

There are over 22 million cars on the road. While around 75 per cent of households own at least one car, and over 25 per cent own two or more cars (ONS, 1999, Tables 12.6 and 12.7; Mawhinney, 1995), it does not follow that everyone in the household will have equal access to a car. Large concentrations of households without cars, particularly among the elderly, can also be found. Over 85 per cent of males and over 55 per cent of females hold a driving licence, but it is estimated that only about 20 per cent of women have access to a car during the day time, only 8 per cent of women use their cars to participate in the school run, and over 70 per cent of all car journeys are still made by men. In fact, it remains true that over 75 per cent of all journeys are *not* by car: that is, they are by foot, bicycle or public transport (RTPI, 1991; Barton, 1998).

To plan for the motor car as if it were the main means of transport for everyone is an inequitable approach, and a more socially aware attitude is already in evidence at the newly created DETR. There are considerable differences in the land use and transport needs of people in respect of their age, gender, income, disability, mobility, and ethnicity (Ahmed, 1989; Little 1994; Greed, 1994a; Davies, 1999). The situation is complex, with diverse groups of people with different needs and conflicting priorities all requiring attention from the planners.

Thus the transport example illustrates many of the controversies and dilemmas surrounding planning policy-making in general. Planning is not a straightforward subject in which there is one right answer or a fixed set of rules; it all depends on the answer to the question 'How do you want to live?' (DOE, 1972a). Planning is a messy, complicated, never-ending,

tedious and time-consuming process. Much can be learned from how other European countries deal with 'planning for everyday life' and meeting the needs of ordinary people (Skjerve, 1993) in a more progressive and socially aware manner, and, as explained in Chapter 2, membership of the European Union (EU) has opened up alternative ways of planning for all.

Political or Technical Interpretations?

In that planning contains within it the power to control the way in which people use their property and, nowadays, increasingly their cars, it is a highly political activity. Towns and cities are not God given or 'natural'. They are the result of centuries of decision-making by individual owners, developers, and government bodies. Although topography and geography do play a part, they do not absolutely 'determine' development. The nature of towns and cities, to a considerable extent, is dependent on who has the greatest influence over policy, and thus who has the strongest voice.

Planning is inevitably a highly political activity: first, because it is concerned with land and property. Planning is concerned with the allocation of scarce resources. It is inextricably linked to the prevailing economic system. Planning policy change inevitably reflects of the booms and slumps that are an enduring characteristic of the property market, and of capitalism itself. Planners are not free agents: they are not operating in a vacuum but within a complex political situation at central and local government levels which reflect these societal forces (Simmie, 1974). But, as Rydin has commented town planning alone, cannot externally control the market, as the forces involved are immense (Rydin, 1998: 6). Nowadays there is much talk of partnerships between the public and private sector. Indeed, whether planners are working for the public or the private sector of development, there are certain common requirements that have to be adhered to, to make a scheme work.

Second, planning is political because it has become a component of the agenda of national party politics and political ideology. Planning is a political process, informed by a range of ideologies (Kirk, 1980; Healey, 1997; Montgomery and Thornley, 1990; Rydin, 1998; Tewdwr-Jones, 1996). It has been scrutinized by those concerned with understanding 'capitalism', and class and power structures within society. Urban social theory, which influences social planning, is seldom neutral. It will be seen, that Labour and Conservative interpretations of the role of planning have differed considerably. Social town planning has, in particular, been associated with 'the Left', for example in respect of the policies of the Greater London Council (GLC) at its height in the 1980s (GLC, 1984) or as part of full-blown East European state socialism. But 'planning' has attracted interest from people across the political spectrum, and some of the most radical challenges to planning have come from environmentalists and from feminists who do not fit into the conventional right/left divisions. Thirdly the planning process is political at the local urban area planning level, where community politics and grass roots activity thrives, and where individual personalities, especially councillors, exert influence over planning decisions.

CONTENTS

This book seeks to combine the *physical* and *social* aspects of planning; reflecting the trend in existing introductory courses and increasingly in planning practice itself. The book seeks to introduce students to the *visual* urban design aspects, and the *political, legal* and *institutional* context of planning. In addition the *environmental* aspects of planning are focused upon, particularly in Chapter 10, as nowadays this aspect has become such a key factor in the whole planning process. All these factors – the physical, social, visual, legal and environmental dimensions of town planning – may be seen as floating in a sea of urban politics and governance. In practice all these elements are linked and inseparable components of modern town planning.

The book is divided into four parts, following this introductory chapter. Part I comprises two chapters. Chapter 2 describes the organization and operation of the planning system. It outlines the different levels of planning, including European Union, central government, regional and local government levels. It also covers the development plan system. Chapter 3 describes the development control system. Special controls are explained, such as in respect of conservation areas and listed buildings. Information on environmental assessment and EU requirements is given. An account of the process of property development

concludes this chapter. Thus Part I seeks to be introductory and factual in style and approach, with only a small amount of discursive commentary.

Part II recounts the story of planning from earliest times to the dawn of modern town planning in the twentieth century. Chapter 4 covers the Ancient, Classical, Medieval, Renaissance, and Georgian periods with a short section on the parallel historical development of the countryside. Chapter 5 describes nineteenth century development, at which time industrialization, urbanization and population growth called for the need for state intervention and the creation of what became known as town planning. The ensuing reaction and reforms are the subject of Chapter 6. Chapter 7 takes the story into the first part of the twentieth century. Thus Part II, seeks to be narrative and historical in style and approach.

Part III charts the successive manifestations of town planning over the last 50 years, with emphasis upon the expansion of planning horizons in the 1990s as a result of environmental and European movements. Chapter 8 outlines the scope and nature of post-war reconstruction planning, and takes the reader from the 1950s to the late 1970s, by which time the consensus of 'believing in planning' had begun to break down. In Chapter 9 the recent story of planning, as manifest in the 1980s and 1990s is recounted, covering the New Right (Thatcher and Major Conservative governments) and New Labour (Blair government) respec-

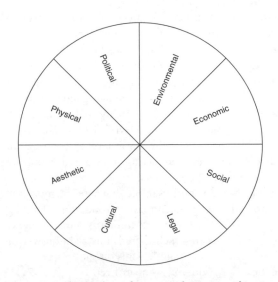

Figure 1.1 **The Realms of Town and Country Planning.**

Textbox 1.3a   Range of Planning Topics, Issues and Policy Areas

- Environment: sustainability; green issues; countryside; ecology; nature; rural conservation; landscape; green belts; national parks; areas of outstanding national beauty; minerals; energy; nuclear power; roads; pollution; waste treatment; land reclamation.
- Social issues: population; housing; inner city; race; gender; disability; poverty; social exclusion; crime; community; neighbourhoods; family; elderly; diversity.
- Economic issues: economic planning; urban renewal; single regeneration budget; urban regeneration; regional planning; enterprise zones; industrial; commercial; retail areas; employment.
- Aesthetic issues: urban design; urban conservation; landscape; public art; housing layout and design; development control.
- Cultural: arts; culture; recreation; leisure; minority issues; cultural diversity; tourism; sport.
- Legal: development control; planning gain; planning agreements; planning appeals; European law; national statutes and case law.
- Physical: land use planning; zoning; infrastructural services; highways; layout and siting; land uses residential; commercial; recreational; industrial; amenity.
- Political: national governmental policy; local authority political attitudes; councillors; national politicians; European Union; local pressure groups; NGOs and grassroots movements.

Textbox 1.3b   Plan Policy Issues

- Housing
- Employment
- Shopping
- Urban Conservation
- Countryside
- Open Space and Amenity
- Highways and Transportation
- Public Utilities and Social Facilities

tively. The contrasting approach to planning taken by these two administrations is used to highlight the political nature of planning and to illustrate the diverse range of issues and ideologies that have shaped the organization and operation of the planning system. Planning is not a straightforward, factual subject. There is never 'one right answer', there is always controversy, debate and disagreement as to what should be done.

Thus from Part III onwards the book becomes more discursive in style. The author seeks to present the reader with a representative range of viewpoints and current opinions on planning. Inevitably the author incorporates her own views and conclusions, in seeking to give an analysis of contemporary developments in planning, in order to provide an account of the evolving situation, highlighting unresolved conflicts and controversies within planning policy.

Chapter 10 is dedicated to the story of the greening of planning. The environmental movement, together with the objective of achieving sustainability, has been one of the most important factors in reshaping planning over the last 20 years. The chapter first describes the development of rural planning, with its pre-existing environmental concerns, prior to discussing modern environmentalism, which is concerned with both town and country, and the wider ecosystem. The impact of global movements for health, sustainability and equity, and the effect of European policy and environmental regulations on the operation of the British town and country planning system, will be highlighted.

While Chapters 9 and 10 have, relatively speaking, focused upon global trends and 'macro' level policies, Chapter 11 returns to the continuing concern among planners with the 'micro' level issues of layout and design. The visual and design aspects of planning were important elements in shaping towns and cities in the past, when planning was more linked to architectural, civic design, and at present a renaissance of the urban design movement is occurring within town planning circles. The discussion will be linked to the influence of higher-level policies on sustainability, the arts, culture, tourism and conservation.

Part IV returns to the issue of 'planning for people' within the context of discussing the theories and political perspectives that have informed planning. It reappraises the various manifestations of the 'social

Figure 1.2 **Conflict Between Cars and Houses.**
Car ownership has increased rapidly since the 1960s.
Town planners have moved from a pro-car policy towards
the current emphasis on traffic calming and limitation of
car use. Cars can scarcely be adequately accommodated
within historic, close-knit street patterns in inner areas.

Figure 1.3 **People Walking Through the City Centre at
Lunchtime in Bristol.**
In the final analysis 'planning is for people', who experience the city primarily at street level, for example, as they
walk through it in their lunch-hour.

aspects of planning' over the last century, and discusses
the characteristics of the planners and the planned. It
discusses the role of politics and theory in conceptu-
alizing planning, and seeks to provide a framework of
understanding, drawing out key pointers and themes
now that the story of planning has been told. The rise
of a more collaborative, inclusive approach to policy-
making as a means forward for this new century is
discussed. Part IV has a stronger research dimension,
which may be of interest to more advanced students.

Thus Part IV is discursive and reflective in style,
and has a stronger sociological dimension. Part IV is
characterized by an emphasis upon planning research,
theory, sociology and debate. Thus the final section
incorporates more advanced level material.

Chapter 11 revisits the story of planning to provide
a parallel account of the development of urban sociological issues and related 'social aspects of planning'.
Pre- and post-industrial theories are presented, and
then the nostalgia for a golden age of 'community' is
highlighted. The emphasis upon simplistic, spatially
focused urban policy solutions, such as environmental
determinism, is discussed in relation to the development of twentieth-century statutory planning. The
influence of American social ecology theory is
discussed. The gradual change towards a conflict-
based, as against consensus, view of urban society is
charted, with reference to neo-marxist tendencies in
the development of 1970s planning. Then a range of

post-modernist, post-structuralist, yet neo-weberian
theories have come to the fore, which have since
melted into a melange of diverse issues and groupings,
which will be further discussed in the final, retrospective chapter on the theory and related politics of
planning.

It is important to retain the 'gender and planning'
dimension of the previous edition and to update the
situation, and this is the function of Chapter 12.
Subsequently many of the original 'women and plan-

Figure 1.4 **People Still Waiting at the Bus Stop.**
Unless policy proposals for reduction of car use are
matched by actual provision of an adequate and reliable
public transport system little progress can be made in
changing people's travel patterns in the city.

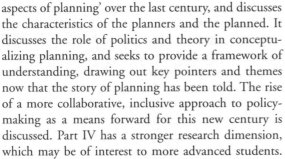

ning' policies were never implemented, and the topic has fallen out of fashion, even though the issues have not been solved. In this new edition the terms of reference have been widened to discuss the related needs of other minorities too.

While Chapters 11 and 12 are concerned with the 'planned', Chapter 13 is concerned with the nature of the 'planners'. Chapter 13 describes the role and composition of the different professions involved in the planning and development process, including planners, architects, surveyors, and construction professionals. Data on minority representation in the professions are provided. Arguably as the built environment professions become more diverse in membership, and therefore more reflective of the composition of population as a whole, then planning policy will become more in tune with the needs of society.

The penultimate chapter, 15, discusses the chances of changing the culture of the built environment professions, not least planning, in order to increase the chances of implementing the policies discussed in Chapter 13. This inevitably leads to a discussion of future planning issues. The chapter discusses measures that might resolve and implement minority policies issues by means of using the current sustainability agenda, and looks at other means of generating change, such as utilizing urban regeneration policy.

Having told the story of planning, the final chapter (16) highlights and reviews the underlying theoretical perspectives and political values, that have shaped, informed and questioned the nature and practice of planning. Thus it comprises a conclusion and plenary to the book as a whole, and a means of reviewing the different approaches to 'doing planning'. The changing persona of planning and the different manifestations of planning theory are discussed. Because of the nature of planning theory the final chapter may be seen by some readers as more advanced than introductory in content. Therefore it is appropriate that this material should be left to the end, by which time readers will be familiar with many of the concepts discussed from earlier chapters.

TASKS

Information Gathering Tasks

I: Go out and find out what the main town planning issues and problems are in your area. Visit your local library, read the local newspapers, and find out whether any local plans affect where you live. Write yourself a short essay on what you find out, and start a file on your area. (Give yourself two weeks to achieve this task.)

II: Go to the library and find the *Encyclopaedia of Planning Law* and see what you make of it. Look at the journals section and find *Planning*, the journal of the Royal Town Planning Institute which is published weekly. Look at some of the other property journals, such as *Estates Gazette*, *Property Week*, *Chartered Surveyor Monthly* and check for the planning items. Choose one topic, look through this month's journals and write a short essay on what you find, and the differing emphasis of the above journals.

Conceptual Tasks

III. Write an essay of 2000 words on either of the following:
(a) Define and discuss the scope and nature of British town planning.
(b) The planning process has been identified as being inevitably political and never neutral. Do you agree with this? Discuss giving reasons for your views.

Reflective Tasks

IV. What do you personally think about town planning? Why did you study planning? Have you had any experience of planners/planning?

FURTHER READING: Introduction

This textbook is intended to be introductory in content. Readers seeking more detailed information and depth on their chosen subject will find a range of further references given for each topic covered at the end of the relevant chapter. For example, readers wishing to pursue the topic of urban design further, should first read Chapter 12 of this book and then follow up the references given therein (such as Lynch, 1960, 1988, or Greed and Roberts, 1998). Recommended source books will generally yield a further set of sign-posts and markers to further references on specific aspects of the topic.

There are several other introductory town planning books, each of which have their own emphases and priorities.

1. *Town and Country Planning in Britain* (Cullingworth and Nadin, 1999) is a definitive source book on the British town and country planning system. The emphasis is on legislative detail, and this book assumes some prior knowledge of the scope and nature of planning.

2. *The Encyclopaedia of Planning Law*, (Grant, 1999 and annual update) is a loose-leaf, frequently updated publication, which provides the most accurate information on planning law and procedure. Readers should also consult *Planning* the weekly journal of the Royal Town Planning Institute (RTPI).

3. *Urban and Environmental Planning in the UK* (Rydin, 1998) emphasizes the economic and political dimensions of planning. It conveys the 'grand picture' of the scope, role and place of planning within modern British governance structures.

4. Work by Healey such as *Collaborative Planning* (1997) is concerned with urban governance and with high-level theory, but also manifests a concern for community issues and planning processes. Planning theory is dealt with in Part IV, see also *Urban Planning Theory* (Taylor, 1998). For the wider political context, see Tewdwr Jones, 1996; Brindley *et al.*, 1996; Rydin, 1998; and Reade, 1987.

5. Peter Hall's classic work *Urban and Regional Planning*, (1992) prioritizes the physical, and geographical aspects of town planning, and is of historical interest.

6. Chapman, D. (1996) *Neighbourhood Plans in the Built Environment*. This book deals with planning at the local community level as well as covering wider planning issues.

7. Books which give a more commercial, private-sector perspective on planning include: Marriot, 1989; Cadman and Topping, 1995; Scarrett, 1983; Stapleton, 1986; Burke and Taylor, 1990; Seeley, 1997).

8. Statistical sources include *Social Trends* produced by the Office of National Statistics (ONS), which contains information on every aspect of population, housing, transport, environment and other urban issues.

ONS data may be downloaded from 'The Source' web page at: http://www.statistics.gov.uk

Housing and Construction Statistics produced annually and quarterly by the DETR is also a valuable source of data.

9. Lists of the main planning publications produced by the DETR and other government sources are included in the Appendix: *Government Publications*.

See Central Government WEB page, http://www.open.gov.uk, and DETR page: http://www.open.gov.uk/detr

Part 1

THE PLANNING SYSTEM

2

THE ORGANIZATION
OF PLANNING

INTRODUCTION

The levels of planning are examined in the following sequence, national, regional and local in respect of the dominant system applying to England and Wales. Recent constitutional changes within the UK have created new planning powers for Scotland, Wales, Northern Ireland and London, which will be discussed as separate entities in their own right. These days, as part of the European Union (EU), the UK planning system is subject to various policy directions emanating from Brussels; therefore, the EU *should* be the first level discussed. However, the UK level is still the point of service delivery, and its powers are still arguably primary in determining policy and practice. Therefore, the European level will be discussed in the last section of Chapter 2 as this overarches all other levels and nation state planning systems.

LEVELS OF PLANNING

Central Government

The organization of the planning system is complex (see Figure 2.1) (Cullingworth and Nadin, 1997, Chapters 3 and 4). The Department of the Environment, Transport and the Regions (DETR), formed in 1997, is the main central government department responsible for town planning. The DETR is composed of the former Department of the Environment (DoE) and the Department of Transport (DoT), and controls national policy making on land use and transport. This amalgamation is New Labour's attempt at *joined up thinking* in government, being the inte-

gration of policies from different departments and ministries to create a effective whole. For example, the relationship between traffic congestion and the land use patterns which generate that congestion in the first place is now being acknowledged more fully as a key issue in planning for sustainable development.

The Secretary of State who heads the DETR, is thus the main 'minister' for the environment, and has overall responsibility for shaping and guiding national planning policy; with the final say on individual controversial planning decisions. He is advised by professionally qualified staff including town planners, surveyors, architects, and housing managers. The Secretary of State does not have to accept their advice if it is not politically acceptable to the Government. Professional town planners working in the public sector are not the final decision makers, they are employees of the government, and as such their statutory role is that of government advisors.

Not only was the DETR created but new, creative links were made with other departments, reflecting shifts in policy emphasis and priorities. A separate Department of Heritage was established by the last Conservative government. This subsequently became, under Labour, an expanded Department of Culture, Media and Sport (DCMS) which is closely linked to the DETR. The wide scope of this Department covers urban conservation, and incorporates within its structure English Heritage and the Royal Commission on Historic Monuments. The Department is responsible for policy on tourism, urban cultural issues, and the Millennium programme. The Department is therefore concerned with urban design issues both in relation to historic and new developments, and, for example,

EUROPEAN COMMISSION
Directorates-General

CENTRAL GOVERNMENT
(DETR, Department of the Environment, Transport and the Regions

Secretary of State (politician, M.P.)
Approves Development Plans.
Gives overall policy guidance.
Deals with appeals (SS assisted
by the planning inspectorate).

Advised by planning
professionals
(civil servants).

Also: range of other central government departments liaise with the DETR on
planning issues, including MOD, Home Office, MAFF, Industry, Ministry of Culture,
Media and Sport.

REGIONAL LEVEL

English Regional Development Agencies, Scottish Parliament, Welsh Assembly,
Greater London Authority, Northern Ireland Assembly.

LOCAL GOVERNMENT

Decisions are made by the politicans (elected councillors on council's planning
committee) as advised by the professionals (planners who are employed as local
government officers). Two types of development plan system are in existence.

TWO TIER SYSTEM

COUNTIES
Overall policy direction.
Structure Plans (SPs).
Minerals and waste disposal.

UNITARY SYSTEM

METROPOLITAN DISTRICTS
AND LONDON BOROUGHS
Unitary Development Plans
(UDP's combine contents of
structure and local plans).
Policy implementation.
Development control.

DISTRICTS
Local Plans.
Implementation of planning.
Development control.

RANGE OF *AD HOC* BODIES WITH PLANNING POWERS

Including: Urban Development Corporations, National Park Boards, Countryside
Commission, Social Exclusion Unit, English Partnerships, English Heritage, Single
Regenerations Budget, Social Exclusion Unit, Urban Taskforce, Audit Commission,
inter alia.

Figure 2.1 **The Levels of Planning.**

public art, and prestige schemes, perhaps imitating
the French enthusiasm for '*grands projets*' (Greed and
Roberts, 1998).

Functions of the DETR

The DETR is an overarching department within
which many other aspects of policymaking for the
built environment are carried out, such as matters
relating to housing, transportation, building and
construction, inner cities, environmental health,
conservation and historic buildings, urban regeneration, environmental issues, and many other policy
areas. The situation is confusing as some topics and
policies are also administered, in part, by other government departments and ministries, such as aspects of
nature conservancy, road traffic, and scientific matters
related to the environment.

The DETR is not responsible for producing plans
itself, indeed there is no National Plan, as exists in
some other countries. Central government has an

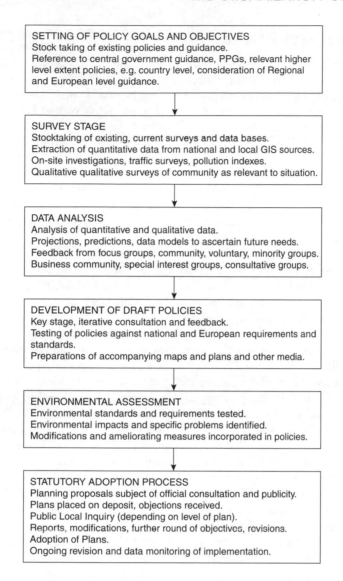

SETTING OF POLICY GOALS AND OBJECTIVES
Stock taking of existing policies and guidance.
Reference to central government guidance, PPGs, relevant higher
level extent policies, e.g. country level, consideration of Regional
and European level guidance.

SURVEY STAGE
Stocktaking of existing, current surveys and data bases.
Extraction of quantitative data from national and local GIS sources.
On-site investigations, traffic surveys, pollution indexes.
Qualitative qualitative surveys of community as relevant to situation.

DATA ANALYSIS
Analysis of quantitative and qualitative data.
Projections, predictions, data models to ascertain future needs.
Feedback from focus groups, community, voluntary, minority groups.
Business community, special interest groups, consultative groups.

DEVELOPMENT OF DRAFT POLICIES
Key stage, iterative consultation and feedback.
Testing of policies against national and European requirements and
standards.
Preparations of accompanying maps and plans and other media.

ENVIRONMENTAL ASSESSMENT
Environmental standards and requirements tested.
Environmental impacts and specific problems identified.
Modifications and ameliorating measures incorporated in policies.

STATUTORY ADOPTION PROCESS
Planning proposals subject of official consultation and publicity.
Plans placed on deposit, objections received.
Public Local Inquiry (depending on level of plan).
Reports, modifications, further round of objectives, revisions.
Adoption of Plans.
Ongoing revision and data monitoring of implementation.

N.B. This shows the general principles which might be applied to a local, borough or county
level plan. Check for current level plan. Check for current regulations on precise requirements
which are subject to frequent updating, especially in request of consultation and timescales.

Figure 2.2 **The Development Plan Process.**

important role to play in overseeing policy and plans produced by local government planning authorities, and gives policy guidance and leadership on all environmental matters. It also liaises with international level bodies concerned with similar issues such as the Organization for Economic Co-operation and Development (OECD), World Health Organization (WHO), United Nations (UN).

One of the most important roles of the Secretary of State for the Environment is to give approval to Development Plans. Following the Planning and Compensation Act 1991, local authorities were given delegated powers to approve plans themselves in some cases but overall power still resides with the Secretary of State. Development plans – including Structure Plans – are produced by the counties and larger urban

Textbox 2.1   Definition of Development

'Development' is defined in planning law under Section 55 of the Town and Country Planning Act, 1990, as **the carrying out of building, engineering, mining, or other operations in, on, over or under land, or the making of any material change in the use of any buildings or other land.**

areas. These constitute the main planning policy documents, and show the structure of future development.

In the London boroughs and large metropolitan areas, which comprise the conurbations of the North and Midlands, Unitary Development Plans (UDPs) are the main type of development plan. The UDP system is being selectively extended nationally, and is tied in with recent changes in local government administrative area organization. In 1996 local government boundary reorganization took place abolishing many of the large administrative counties which were created in the 1970s (Hill, 1999).

Thus the whole country is covered by a series of plans of various types. Theoretically the Secretary of State could put together all the plans, similar to a giant national jigsaw, ending up with a 'national plan'. It is important to ensure there are no incompatible changes of policy on either side of the boundaries of each county area, and should this arise, the Secretary of State acts as arbitrator between authorities. Although the Secretary of State does not produce plans himself, he has an overview of planning across the country through these plans and related policies, as explained in *Development Plans: Good Practice Guide* (DoE, 1992a).

This should not be confused with another publication with a similar title, namely: *Good Practice Guide on Environmental Assessment of Development Plans* (DoE, 1993a) which specifies that all development plan policies subject to environmental assesment (EA), as explained in Planning Policy Guidance Note (PPG) 12 entitled, *Development Plans and Regional Guidance* (DETR, 1998a; DETR, 1998b). This is to ensure that development plans deliver sustainable development. PPG12 emphasizes that the environment is not a 'bolt-on' extra, rather that appraisal of environmental impact should be integrated into the process of policymaking and subsequent implementation.

The Secretary of State produces policy guidelines at national level to advise local authority plan making. To do this he acts on the advice of his professional staff, and these policies are published in government white papers, circulars, consultation papers, guidance notes and directives and PPGs. PPGs generally cover strategic issues of national interest and are important as expressions of government policy and are likely to be quoted in planning appeals. They are produced in full in the *Encyclopaedia of Planning Law*, a loose-leaf system of over six volumes, which is updated every month. The PPG's are revised from time to time so they require careful checking for the most up-to-date version, as there are usually substantial policy changes in subsequent editions.

The Secretary of State carries out consultations with the local authority planners, and with relevant professional and voluntary bodies in order to set policy guidelines. The 'rules' governing planning decisions cannot be reduced to the question of sizes of road widths or precise land use zonings, but are embodied in a range of strategic policy documents which are subject to interpretation. Central government has a major role in setting policy guidelines and approving plans, but it is the local authority level of counties and districts that constitute the main plan-making level to produce plans. Arguably the present situation represents an uneasy truce – a compromise – as there has always been a considerable amount of tension between central and local government, likewise between counties and districts at local government level.

Development Control and Call-in Powers

Much of town planning is concerned with development control, as discussed in Chapter 3, with the granting or refusing of planning permission. The development control systems exist, together with town planning legislation, and related case law, to enable planners to make their plans a reality. Planning control covers two main categories of change: first, the development of new buildings and other works, and second, the change of use from one land use to another. This is a minimal, but useful definition, for as will be illustrated in subsequent chapters, there is a range of additional complex controls and special area regulations; for example, in some circumstances demolition may also count as development.

Development control is both a technical and bureaucratic process a highly sensitive political activity, in that the planners seek to control what owners can do with their land and property; often a great deal of money is at stake. If an applicant is dissatisfied with the decision made by the planning department an appeal may be directed to the Secretary of State against this decision. Alternatively, if there have been procedural or legal irregularities – as against policy discrepancies – in the way the planning application has been dealt with, then the appellant can request a judicial review and ultimately the case may be taken to the High Court.

The Secretary of State, therefore, as well as having the overall national view, has another important role, namely dealing with appeals and public inquiries on contentious planning issues and decisions. In practice, some of the decision making is delegated to the Planning Inspectorate, and many decisions are made in writing rather than coming to a full hearing. Over 500,000 planning applications are received each year by English local planning authorities. Of these under 30,000 go to appeal, and of these less than a third are allowed (see DETR webpage).

The Secretary of State has the power to take a more direct interest in any aspect of the planning system with which the applicant is unhappy, and has the power to 'call in' controversial plans and applications (Heap, 1996) if it is considered that the local authority have gone against national planning policy in their decision. Aggrieved parties may write to the Minister, via the relevant Regional Government office, and ask for a decision to be called in. There have only been around 100 'call ins' in the last five years (*Source*: DETR, 1998).

Other Central Government Agencies

The Ministry of Agriculture, Fisheries, and Food (MAFF) has a major influence on the nature of the countryside, which at times may be at odds with the objectives of the planners to conserve the landscape, and achieve environmental sustainability, and the needs of the general public as consumers.

Non-Governmental Organizations (NGO's) such as the National Farmers Union (NFU) and the Country Landowners Association (CLA) act as strong pressure groups to influence policy. In June 1999 a separate Food Standards Agency (FSA) was established concerned with food safety from 'farm to fork'; this is

not a full Ministry as it has a regulatory, rather than policy, role. It may, however, better represent the needs of consumers (i.e. the public) as against the farming interests represented by the MAFF and NFU viewpoints. Consumer groups had begun campaigning for a neutral food ministry long before the Green movement became popular and this has become even more pressing as a result of concerns about BSE (popularly known as mad cow disease) and genetically modified food (Shoard, 1980, 1999). As with many areas of planning, it is generally considered that consumer and community groups are under-represented in the decision-making process.

The siting of nuclear power stations is an environmental matter, and public inquiries to decide whether more stations should be built have been held under the auspices of planning inspectors appointed by the DETR. Since the issues involved were seen as too large and political to be contained within the planning system alone, a separate Environment Agency (EA) for England and Wales has been established which has considerable powers for controlling developments that are likely to have ecological and environmental implications. This agency should not be confused with the European Environment Agency (EEA), set up within the European Union. The various statutory bodies concerned with provision of public utilities and services and their recently 'privatized' successors have considerable separate powers of their own which may contradict DETR policies. The Ministry of Defence (MOD) although not a civilian planning authority, has a major effect on the nature of settlement patterns. It also has rights over vast areas of land used for training. The MOD is not subject to the normal planning control for its own activities, and may for example build service housing estates in the countryside without planning permission.

Regional Planning

As is explained in Part III, regional economic planning was once an extremely important aspect of town and country planning, especially following the Second World War as a means of effecting implementing both economic and physical land use planning policy. But, there has been no significant regional level of planning between the national and the local authority level for nearly 20 years under the last Conservative government.

The new Labour government, since 1997, has sought to establish a foundation to rebuild the regional level of planning. Regional Development Agencies for England were created on 1 April 1999, under the Regional Development Agencies Act 1998, with a brief to establish regional strategies to deal with economic development, regeneration and regional competitiveness. Their role is seen to complement the established Regional Planning Guidance (RPG) system. Subsequently the revision of PPG11, *Regional Planning* issued in 1999 set out principles for the resurrection of the regional level. The topics listed in this document worthy of consideration at regional level are as follows: economic development, housing, transport, retail, hospitals, leisure, and sports uses, rural development, biodiversity and nature conservation, the coast, minerals, and waste.

At the time of writing, the situation is in transition. The 'new regionalism' is a dynamic policy area to watch, both at domestic and European levels. In the foreseeable future regional bodies may be given executive powers, to produce statutory regional plans, as indicated in PPG11. There are demands for separate English national and regional elected governments now that Wales and Scotland have gained a measure of autonomy. The British Isles is also subject to European regional policy making and funding allocations as a member state within the European Union (EU) as outlined in Chapter 9.

Local government

The New Unitary Authorities

The local government system in England, Scotland and Wales, has been based upon a two-tier system, consisting of counties and districts, for the last 20 years. Long awaited Local Government Boundary Reorganization took place in 1996 (following the 1992 Local Government Act), creating a system of unitary authorities (Cullingworth and Nadin, 1997). This involved breaking up many of the large super-counties such as Avon (around Bristol), created under the last major boundary reorganization in 1974, and restoring some of the original historical boundary demarcations. Elsewhere, larger erstwhile second-tier district authorities were restructured as unitary, single-tier authorities in their own right. The map of England now constitutes a confusing mixture of single and two-

Table 2.1 **List of English Unitary Authorities**

New	Previous	Established
Isle of Wight	Isle of Wight	April 1995
Bath & N E Somerset	Avon	April 1996
City & County of Bristol	Avon	April 1996
East Riding of Yorkshire	Humberside	April 1996
Hartlepool	Cleveland	April 1996
Hull	Humberside	April 1996
Middlesborough	Cleveland	April 1996
N E Lincolnshire	Humberside	April 1996
North Lincolnshire	Humberside	April 1996
North Somerset	Avon	April 1996
Redcar and Cleveland	Cleveland	April 1996
South Gloucestershire	Avon	April 1996
Stockton-on-Tees	Cleveland	April 1996
City of York	North Yorkshire	April 1996
Bournemouth	Dorset	April 1997
Brighton & Hove	East Sussex	April 1997
Darlington	Durham	April 1997
Derby	Derbyshire	April 1997
Leicester	Leicestershire	April 1997
Luton	Bedfordshire	April 1997
Milton Keynes	Buckinghamshire	April 1997
Poole	Dorset	April 1997
Portsmouth	Hampshire	April 1997
Rutland	Leicestershire	April 1997
Southampton	Hampshire	April 1997
Stoke-on-Trent	Staffordshire	April 1997
Swindon	Wiltshire	April 1997
Bracknell Forest	Berkshire	April 1998
West Berkshire	Berkshire	April 1998
Reading	Berkshire	April 1998
Slough	Berkshire	April 1998
Windsor & Maidenhead	Berkshire	April 1998
Wokingham	Berkshire	April 1998
Peterborough	Cambridgeshire	April 1998
Halton	Cheshire	April 1998
Warrington	Cheshire	April 1998
Plymouth	Devon	April 1998
Torbay	Devon	April 1998
Southend	Essex	April 1998
Thurrock	Essex	April 1998
Herefordshire	Hereford & Worcester	April 1998
Medway	Kent	April 1998
Blackburn with Darwen	Lancashire	April 1998
Blackpool	Lancashire	April 1998
Nottingham	Nottinghamshire	April 1998
Telford and Wrekin	Shropshire	April 1998

tier authorities, whereas Scotland and Wales are primarily organized, at present, on a unitary system.

Readers are recommended to find out what the situation is in their area and to consult journals such as the *Local Government Chronicle* to discover what

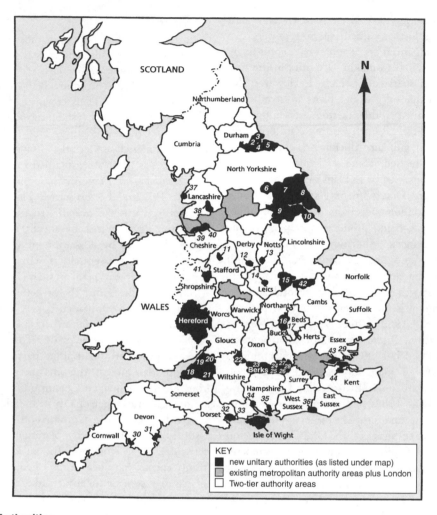

Unitary Authorities

1	Darlington	12	Derby	23	West Berkshire	34	Southampton
2	Stockton-on tees	13	Nottingham City	24	Reading	35	Portsmouth
3	Hartlepool	14	Leicester	25	Rutland	36	Brighton and Hove
4	Middlesborough	15	Rutland	26	Bracknell Forest	37	Blackpool
5	Redcar and Cleveland	16	Milton Keynes	27	Windsor and Maidenhead	38	Blackburn
6	York	17	Luton	28	Slough	39	Halton
7	East Riding of Yorkshire	18	North West Somerset	29	Southend	40	Warrington
8	Hull	19	Bristol	30	Plymouth	41	Wrekin
9	North Lincolnshire	20	South Gloucestershire	31	Torbay	42	Peterborough
10	North East Lincolnshire	21	Bath and North East Somerset	32	Poole	43	Thurrock
11	Stoke-on-Trent	22	Thamesdown	33	Bournemouth	44	Gillingham, Rochester and Medway

Figure 2.3 **Map of Local Authorities in England.**

future changes are under discussion. Also readers should be aware that within individual local authorities, some departments have reorganized their affairs, finances and structures more rapidly than others, as these changes not only affect town planning, but housing, highways, education and social services departments also. Some local authorities have even abolished planning departments, transferring its functions to estates or technical services for example, whereas others have renamed theirs, with titles including the words regeneration, enterprise, environment or urban management *inter alia*.

Many boundaries have been redrawn and local authorities have lost or gained planning powers as a result of this reorganization. Planners have accordingly had to adjust their plan-making activities to the new size and level of spatial units created. However, this does not mean that all previous plans are redundant, or that the planners suddenly stop everything, and change their policies. Rather, existing statutory plans remain the main guidance documents, until in due course, they are revised. There are two main types of development plans, Structure Plans in the shire counties, and Unitary Development Plans (UDPs), first used in the London boroughs and metropolitan districts, and now being produced for many of the new unitary provincial authorities. Both forms of plan are still current and provide policy guidance until superseded by new approved plans.

Originally it was envisaged that all local authorities would progress to a new unitary system, as suggested by the 1989 White Paper *The Future of Development Plans*. But a less drastic approach was signalled in PPG 15, 1990, which put less emphasis upon the form of plan adopted and more upon making the system more efficient. The Conservative government of the 1980s had a continuing commitment to speed up and simplify the planning system by increasing the emphasis on the local plan level, and doing away with duplicate tiers of local government. This objective has been pursued by the new Labour government which now prints on the cover of all the DETR publications the slogan 'modernizing planning' (DETR, 1998c; 1999e).

In predominantly rural areas, there has been less enthusiasm for speeding up the system or moving over to the unitary plan system, because there is a need for a strategic county-wide overview to be retained. Issues that need to be included in county-wide development plans include strategic policy statements on new housing, green belts, industrial, business, shopping and employment areas, rural economy, strategic highways and transport, mineral working, waste disposal, tourism and leisure. It could be argued that unitary authorities, covering urban areas which were previously historic urban boroughs, have gained the most from producing their own comprehensive local plans, unfettered now by a higher county planning level. For guidance on development plan practice see DoE, 1992a, b; DoE, 1996a, and DETR, 1998a.

Counties

Counties remain the top tier in those areas where the two-tier system prevails. The county planning authorities and also some of the large city authorities are required to produce Structure Plans along with their accompanying Local Plans constituted the new form of Development Plans system introduced under the Town and Country Planning Act 1971, and subsequently updated under the Town and Country Planning Act 1990. As explained in the still applicable *Development Plan Manual*, produced in 1971 (DOE, 1972b), the Structure Plan, as its name suggests, sets out the overall structure or framework for future development by means of written statements, illustrated by diagrammatic plans. In fact the Structure Plan is essentially a written policy report rather than a drawn 'plan' as such (Moore, 1999).

The plans illustrating the Structure Plan are deliberately not to an Ordnance Survey base but shown 'squared off' on a diagrammatic grid system, so that individual sites cannot be easily recognized. Although there is provision for public participation in the Structure Plan process, there has been much criticism from environmental and community groups of the remoteness, and impersonality of the planning system. Currently the Audit Commission in undertaking a survey of local authority planning departments to determine their efficiency. In particular a series of 'reality checks' have been established to determine the service they provide for local 'stake-holders' including local residents, applicants and businesses (Audit Commission, 1999).

The topics which are investigated in order to develop the plan are population, employment, resources, housing, industry and commerce, shopping, transportation, minerals, education, social services, recreation and leisure, conservation and landscape, and utility services (DOE, 1972b). This reflects the realization that for planning to be effective there is a need to understand the human activities which create a demand for the land uses in the first place, in order to make a 'pre-emptive strike' when producing plans for the future. While all these things have to be looked at with regard to potential future demands for land and development, the capacity of local authority planners to influence them directly is limited, because these matters are under the control of other local government departments or the private sector. Planners in the past have tried to do so by seeking to increase their powers, and to take on the role of corporate city managers and technocrats.

Districts

The shire counties are further subdivided, on average, into four or five district authorities, and this arrangement remains in many areas, such as in Surrey and Sussex, although in some regions the counties themselves have been reconfigured. The districts carry out the detailed daily work of local government, whereas the counties tend to concentrate more on overall policy, resource allocation and strategy. Whilst Structure Plans provide the overall policy at the county level, Local Plans are produced at the district level to show what is going to happen, for example, in a particular village, district or redevelopment area within the next 5 years, and are produced to an Ordnance Survey map base.

Unitary Development Plans

There is a move towards a more stream-lined unitary system. Change began in the 1980s with the abolition, under the 1985 Local Government Act, of the Greater London Council (GLC) and the Metropolitan County Councils (MCCs) on 1 April 1986. These were replaced respectively by 32 London Borough Councils and 36 Metropolitan District Councils (MDCs) (Heap, 1991: 38 [1996]). Each of these 67 smaller authorities is required to produce its own UDP. The process was further complicated by the redrawing of local government boundaries in 1996. The new UDPs are now coming on line, indeed some London boroughs are on their second or third revision.

The new UDPs are meant to combine the best of the structure and local plan approach from the old system. Part I of the new UDPs is devoted to strategic policy statements, like the old Structure Plan, whereas Part II deals with detailed land use issues and planning in specific areas like the old Local Plans. Details of the format were set out in the Circular 3/88 'Unitary Development Plans', and further updating of guidance emanated from the Department of the Environment as an ongoing process (PPG12). The legislation setting out the principles was consolidated in the Town and Country Planning Act 1990. Information on changes is frequently reported in the professional press, for example, in *Planning, Estates* *Gazette, Property Week* and *Chartered Surveyor Monthly* (Devereaux, 1999a, b).

Other Plans and Planning Bodies

National Park Plans

In addition to the main county and district level plans there are a range of other types of plans and governmental agencies with planning powers. National Parks were introduced under the National Parks and Access to the Countryside Act 1949. The National Parks were at first administered collectively by the National Parks Commission which became the Countryside Commission (CC) in 1968. The CC has a wider ambit for conservation management in the countryside as a whole and is still a thriving, positive body. Subsequently, National Park Boards and authorities were set up to administer each National Park. Parks took up much of the area of existing counties, as in the case of Exmoor in Somerset, therefore liaison committees with the existing county authorities were established.

National park administration was subsequently reformed by Sections 61–79 of the Environment Act 1995. As a result, each National Park has its own independent planning authority although liaison at county and district level continues. These authorities have development control and development plan making powers, both in respect of control of what are seen as negative uses such as extraction of minerals, and in terms of proactive policies to promote the use and enjoyment of the countryside both by residents and by visitors.

Non-Statutory Plans

Non-Statutory Plans are not directly part of the development plan system, but are plans produced by local authorities with the approval of their planning committee, and which express overall policy direction and which, therefore, in the past have been seen as having some validity as legal sources of policy. Successive governments have taken the view that such informal 'bottom drawer' plans have limited weight in planning appeals (Grant, 1990: 138, 299).

Developers may act proactively and produce their own plans. A private developer proposing a large scheme prepares a 'planning brief' with the planning application, which sets out how the scheme meets the planning requirements of the area. Alternatively the

Figure 2.4 Exmoor National Park, Somerset.
Much of Britain still consists of countryside, including farm-land. Many regions of Britain are underpopulated, but, in contrast there are intensely developed urban areas in the South-East and Midlands.

planning authority will produce its own developer's brief setting out acceptable planning parameters. There is likely to be considerable negotiation and joint discussion between developer and planning authority. Many local authorities prepare design guides and planning standards reports which are taken as being the definitive policy of the local authority (Essex, 1973; 1997). The subject of non-statutory plans is complicated, but it is important be aware that they may have a bearing on decision making in the planning permission process and appeals system.

Ad Hoc *Bodies*

As well as, and often quite separate from, the main central and local government structure of town planning, there are many other governmental bodies which administer various other aspects of town and country planning. There has been a tradition in this country of setting up special government bodies to deal with a particular problem or policy as and when it is needed, often to be disbanded at a later date – namely the *ad hoc* body. *Ad hoc* means literally 'to this', i.e. 'for this purpose'. Many aspects of British town planning are administered through such bodies. The New Towns were collectively administered by the New Towns Commission, and individually planned by a Development Corporation for each town. These development corporations were intended to be completely separate from the local authority and adminis-

tration of the area in which they were located, in order to concentrate resources and speed up development, without the problems of being slowed down by existing local government bureaucracy. Each Development corporation was intended to have a life of 30 years by which time it was assumed that the New Town would be thoroughly established, and could then be 'handed back' to the local authority, and the Development Corporation would be disbanded.

The present government is still creating *ad hoc* bodies, including QUANGOs. A QUANGO is a Quasi Autonomous National Government Organization, describing any of the numerous government sponsored agencies or authorities with independent powers. As will be explained in Part III and Part IV, the present government and recent governments have created a range of bodies to deal with specific policies or to tackle particular problems. These include, *inter alia*, English Partnerships, Single Regeneration Budget, Social Exclusion Unit, and the Urban Taskforce (Rogers, 1999).

CHANGES WITHIN THE BRITISH ISLES

New National Planning Systems

Radical changes are occurring to the planning systems within the British Isles as a result of devolution, independence and a range of political changes within individual countries within the UK. The devolution of power from Westminster, in 1999, to a Scottish Parliament in Edinburgh and a Welsh Assembly in Cardiff, together with arrangements for the devolution to an elected assembly in Northern Ireland, have signalled fundamental changes in the government of the UK. London has also been given its own governing body, the Greater London Authority, and there is likely to be further regionalization of functions within England. These changes have important consequences for planning.

Scotland

Scotland became part of the United Kingdom under the Act of Union 1707. It has had an Independent Scottish Office since 1939, and a separate planning

Table 2.2 United Kingdom Populations

United Kingdom Populations	In thousands
England	49,284,000
Scotland	5,123,000
Wales	2,927,000
N.Ireland	1,675,000
London (Greater London)	7.8 million
United Kingdom (rounded)	59 million

(*Source: Social Trends* (ONS, 1999).

system with its own laws as detailed below. In anticipation of independence in 1999, a consultation paper *Land Use Planning under a Scottish Parliament* set out the guidelines for a revised planning system (Scottish Office, 1998; TCP, 1999; Collar, 1999).

The new Scottish parliament, established in May 1999, is able to make laws in respect of devolved matters. Insofar as planning is concerned these matters are widespread, they include: land use planning and building control, transport, economic development, area regeneration, and financial assistance to industry. Also included are environmental protection, natural and built heritage, flood prevention as well as responsibility for agriculture, forestry and fisheries. Until now the planning system in Scotland has been co-ordinated at Central Government level through the Secretary of State for Scotland and the Scottish Office. The new powers will be exercised by the Scottish Parliament with a Scottish Executive. The executive comprises a First Minister and ministers along with law officers.

As in the rest of the United Kingdom planning in its present form began in Scotland in 1947. As Scotland has its own legal system there has been scope for planning legislation north of the border to develop somewhat separately from that in England and Wales. Nevertheless much is common, Structure and Local Plans were introduced to Scotland by the Town and Country Planning (Scotland) Act 1969 and the Planning Act 1972 formed the basis of planning in Scotland until recently. The main legislation is contained in the Town and Country Planning (Scotland) Act 1997 and the Planning (Listed Buildings and Conservation Areas) (Scotland) Act 1997. These are consolidating Acts rather than introducing anything new. Scotland also has provisions similar to those in England on permitted development and changes within particular use classes.

The Scottish Office has been responsible for issuing national planning guidance (NPGs) in Scotland since 1974. Since 1991 these have been under review and many have now been replaced by National Planning Policy Guidance Notes (NPPGs) which are similar in form and content to Planning Policy Guidance Notes in England. NPPGs are statements of government policy on nationally-important land use issues and are used during plan production, being a material consideration in determining planning applications. These are supported by a series of Planning Advice Notes (PANs) which give examples of good practice.

Local government in Scotland is organized along similar lines to that in many areas of England. After many years of a two-tier system of regions and districts, reorganization in 1996 redrew the administrative map to introduce 29 unitary authorities throughout Scotland. These exercise all the local planning authority functions (plan making and development control) in their areas. In respect of planmaking, the Scottish system makes provision for the production of Structure Plans and Local Plans. However, this is complicated by the fact that under S4A of the Town and Country Planning (Scotland) Act 1972, the Secretary of State has until now, designated Structure Plan Areas, rather than leaving it to each local planning authority to draw up its own Structure Plan. There are at present 17 such areas, but only 11 follow the same administrative boundaries as the local planning authorities. That leaves six that cross administrative boundaries and therefore require joint working between authorities in order to produce the plan. This, of course, has potential to cause difficulty. Since the passing of the Local Government Scotland) Act 1973 it has been a requirement that there be total coverage of the country by local plans. This was the responsibility of the districts until 1996, now that task falls to the unitary authorities. It is for the authority to decide whether to make one plan or several to cover its area (Devereux, 1999a,b).

Development control in Scotland is organized along much the same lines as the rest of the UK. It is therefore a discretionary system. Section 58 of the Planning and Compensation Act 1991 confirmed the presumption in favour of proposals which conform with the development plan by inserting S25 into the

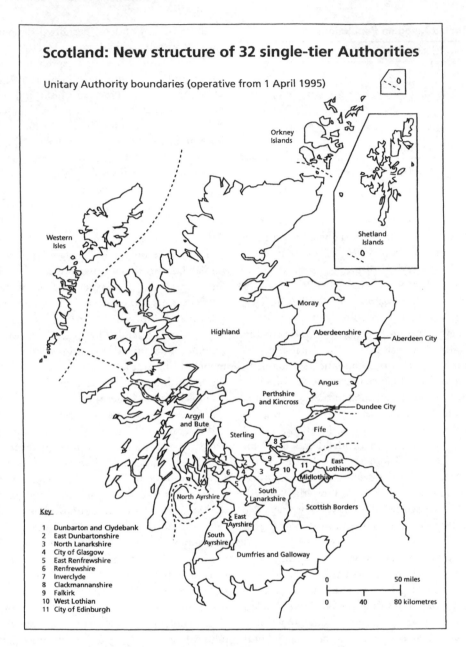

Scotland: New structure of 32 single-tier Authorities

Unitary Authority boundaries (operative from 1 April 1995)

Orkney Islands

Shetland Islands

Western Isles

Moray

Highland

Aberdeenshire

Aberdeen City

Angus

Perthshire and Kincross

Dundee City

Argyll and Bute

Sterling

Fife

8

9

East Lothian

Midlothian

1

2 6 4 3 10 11

5

North Ayrshire

South Lanarkshire

East Ayrshire

South Ayrshire

Scottish Borders

Dumfries and Galloway

Key

1 Dunbarton and Clydebank
2 East Dunbartonshire
3 North Lanarkshire
4 City of Glasgow
5 East Renfrewshire
6 Renfrewshire
7 Inverclyde
8 Clackmannanshire
9 Falkirk
10 West Lothian
11 City of Edinburgh

0   50 miles

0   40   80 kilometres

Figure 2.5 **Map of Local Authorities in Scotland.**

1972 Act in the same way as S54a was inserted in to the 1990 Planning Act in England. While steps have been taken to ensure greater neighbour consultation in England, this is something which historically has been a more important part of the Scottish system. The emphasis on publicity is still stronger north of the border.

The planning system extends to protecting the natural and built environment throughout the UK. In Scotland the main agency responsible for advising central and local levels of government on the natural environment is Scottish National Heritage (the successor to the Nature Conservancy Council in England and Wales). (Rydin 1998: 5a) (English

Table 2.3 **Scottish Structure Plan Areas**

Local authority	Structure plan area
City of Aberdeen Aberdeenshire	Aberdeen & Aberdeenshire
City of Dundee Angus	Dundee and Angus
Stirling Clackmannan	Stirling and Clackmannan
City of Edinburgh East Lothian Midlothian West Lothian	Edinburgh and the Lothians
Dumbarton and Clydebank East Dumbartonshire North Lanarkshire City of Glasgow East Renfrewshire Renfrewshire Inverclyde South Lanarkshire	Glasgow and the Clyde Valley
North Ayrshire East Ayrshire South Ayrshire	Ayrshire
Argyle and Bute Borders Dumfries and Galloway Falkirk Fife Highland Moray Orkney Islands Perthshire and Kinross Shetland Islands Western Islands	Argyle and Bute Borders Dumfries and Galloway Falkirk Fife Highland Moray Orkney Islands Perthshire and Kinross Shetland Islands Western Islands

Nature, 1994). They perform a similar role to English Nature. There have been no National Parks designated in Scotland, although Loch Lomond and the Trossachs are being proposed as such, with the Cairngorms likely to follow into this designation also. Until now the highest level of protection has been afforded by designation as one of the 40 National Scenic Areas. These were established in 1981 and have a stricter development control regime (SDD Circular 20/1980 and 9/1987). Sites of Special Scientific Interest (SSSIs) and National Nature reserves protect sites of particular natural heritage interest.

The built heritage has been the responsibility of the Scottish Office and now rests with the Scottish Parliament. Historic Scotland, an executive agency within the Scottish Office, has discharged the Secretary of State's functions and advised on policy. A parallel could be drawn with the work of English Heritage. Historic Scotland administers the listing of buildings of architectural and historical importance, and scheduling of ancient monuments as well as looking after historic property in state ownership. In Scotland a similar listing system applies as in England, although buildings are classified A, B or C rather than I, II* or II. The existence of a separate legislature has meant that there is a different framework for planning in Scotland but in general terms the laws and administration have followed a similar pattern to those in the rest of the UK. The new Parliament has the opportunity to amend and make new laws controlling planning which may take it down a new path, more removed from its roots in the 1947 Acts.

Scotland is recognized as having a more flexible planning system, strongly influenced by wider European and environmental trends towards a more inclusive, less land use based planning system (Brand, 1999). Significantly the above-mentioned consultation paper stresses the importance of public participation and a more accountable results orientated system. The new Scottish parliament and related executive provide a means to modernize the Scottish planning system, to introduce cross-cutting measures embracing economics, social, environmental and transport issues. Also the 'women and planning' movement has always been strong in Scotland and it significant that one previous adherent of this movement, Sarah Boyak became the first Minister of Transport in the new Scottish Parliament.

Wales

Welsh affairs were previously dealt with by the Home Office, although a separate Welsh Office was created in 1964 with its own Secretary of State for Wales. The Welsh Office produces its planning publications in both Welsh and English, but the planning 'systems' have been virtually the same. Welsh authorities had previously been reorganized under the Local Government (Wales) Act 1994. Now greater independence is being achieved, with the new Welsh Assembly established in 1999. At present the Assembly has only limited powers, for example it has some tax

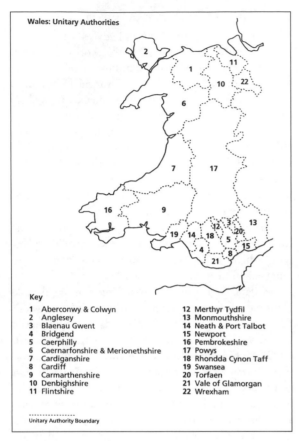

Wales: Unitary Authorities

Key

1 Aberconwy & Colwyn
2 Anglesey
3 Blaenau Gwent
4 Bridgend
5 Caerphilly
6 Caernarfonshire & Merionethshire
7 Cardiganshire
8 Cardiff
9 Carmarthenshire
10 Denbighshire
11 Flintshire
12 Merthyr Tydfil
13 Monmouthshire
14 Neath & Port Talbot
15 Newport
16 Pembrokeshire
17 Powys
18 Rhondda Cynon Taff
19 Swansea
20 Torfaen
21 Vale of Glamorgan
22 Wrexham

....
Unitary Authority Boundary

Figure 2.6 **Map of Local Authorities in Wales.**

distribution powers but not tax raising powers. The planning system in Wales has developed much more in line with that in England when compared to the situation in Scotland. Nevertheless there are some important differences in both administration and practice. The new Welsh Assembly also has planning powers which will allow for the development of planning in Wales to move forward separately from that of England in future.

Until recently planning in Wales at central government level fell within the remit of the Secretary of State for Wales and the Welsh Office. The main planning circulars were issued jointly with the DoE or DETR in England and therefore touched on the same subject matter. There were a few occasions when distinctive guidance was issued specifically for Wales, such as circular 53/88 on 'The Welsh Language: Development Plans and Development Control'. This

circular recognized the importance of the Welsh Language as part of the cultural and social fabric of Wales and allowed it to be taken into account in plan production. It also recognized that language was a material consideration in determining planning applications. This has been the subject of controversy in Wales with some authorities attempting to apply strict restrictions on house building in an attempt to limit the influx of English speakers.

Planning Policy Guidance Notes issued in England do not apply in Wales. Instead guidance comes in the form of a single document, namely: Planning Guidance (Wales): Planning Policy, issued in May 1996. It covers a wide range of issues from transport and economic development through to conservation and waste. This is supplemented by a series of Technical Advice notes (TANs). There are 16 at the time of writing (see Appendix). These are similar in content to their English counterparts.

There are three national parks in Wales: Snowdonia, Pembrokeshire Coast and Brecon Beacons. Responsibilities and powers are similar to those in England, with the Countryside Council for Wales playing a similar advisory role to English Nature and Scottish Natural Heritage. The built heritage is administered through CADW, till now an executive agency within the Welsh Office. CADW are responsible for providing advice and policy guidance, along with caring for historic sites and buildings in state ownership.

Prior to reorganization in 1996 local government in Wales was organized on a county and district/borough framework which was introduced in 1974. In 1996 this was replaced by a system of 22 unitary authorities throughout the country. Each authority is responsible for producing a district wide unitary development plan addressing strategic issues in Part 1 and detailed land use policies in Part 2. The plan should last for 15 years from the base date and does not require Secretary of State approval, but can be called in and modified. More detailed guidance is given in Planning Guidance (Wales) Unitary Development Plans. Unitary authorities are responsible for plan making and development control, but below them in the hierarchy are Community Councils who are formally consulted on many planning matters before a decision can be taken.

Following elections in May 1999, The National Assembly (*Cynulliad Cenedlaethol Cymru*) took on responsibility for 'devolved matters' on 1 July 1999. The assembly has 60 members. Subject committees have been established to deal with detailed matters. There are also four regional committees to deal with the interests of their locality, made up of members in their area. Executive powers rest with the First Secretary and Assembly Secretaries. Together they form the Cabinet, which is accountable to the whole assembly. The assembly has powers to develop and implement policy on a wide range of planning issues including: agriculture, historic environment, economic development, environment, local government, town and country planning, transport, Welsh language, tourism and culture.

The powers of an Assembly in Wales are less than those of a Parliament in Scotland at present. It nevertheless has considerable scope to influence the development of the planning system in Wales. It remains to be seen just how much the new bodies do exercise their power. Given the wide scope of their responsibilities it should not be long before the systems in Scotland and Wales differ far more than they already do from that in England.

Northern Ireland

Owing to the security problems in Northern Ireland the planning system is organized along different administrative lines from that in Great Britain. While the Local Government (Boundaries) Northern Ireland) Act 1971 created 26 unitary local authorities, their powers were limited and they do not have a strong role in the planning process. Instead that function has been the responsibility of the Northern Ireland Department of the Environment since 1973. 'The Planning Service' is an executive agency within the department set up in 1996. It is responsible for the production of development plans and all development control work. The Northern Ireland Government offices also have responsibility for agriculture, economic development, industrial development and tourism. The 'Environment and Heritage Service' within the government is responsible for historic buildings and sites along with natural environment.

Development plans are produced against the background of a 'Planning Strategy for Northern Ireland'. These plans may be one of three types: area plans, local plans or subject plans. Although not required to

be so, they do have a tendency to be zoning plans which set out requirements (e.g. access) that would enable a site to be developed. The primacy of the plan does not exist to the same extent as in Great Britain. The main planning legislation, the Planning (Northern Ireland) Order, 1991, states only that the decision maker, '. . . shall have regard to the development plan. . . .' In practice the plan does carry weight, but considerable importance is also given to Planning Policy Statements (PPS) and Development Control Advice Notes. There are six PPS at the moment, with four in production. They are similar to PPGs in England. DC Advice Notes tend to cover a wide range of issues. There are 14 in the series to date ranging from 'Bookmaking Offices' (No. 3) and 'Amusement Centres' (No. 1) to 'Hazardous Substances' (No. 12) and 'Telecommunications' (No. 14). Local authorities are consulted on all applications and on the plan making process (Johnston, 1999).

Under the terms of the Belfast Agreement (Good Friday Agreement) of April 1998, a Northern Ireland Assembly was elected on 25 June 1998 with 108 members. This is still very much in a transitional period, but it is envisaged as having full legislative and executive powers for all those issues now the responsibility of the Northern Ireland Government. Also under this agreement cross-border bodies will be established to work on transport, environmental protection and economic development issues, among others.

The precarious situation in Northern Ireland makes it difficult to foresee how the planning system will develop and the extent to which it will be operated at a local level. However, there have been unexpected initiatives coming out of it, of benefit to the social aspects of planning, such as for example the New Equality Plans required as part of the Good Friday Agreement in 1999 (Booth, 1999; Johnston, 1999; Devereux, 1999). At the time of writing a new Town Planning Bill for Northern Ireland was being drafted, but the overall situation remains in the balance.

London

The organization of planning system for London has been undergoing radical change. Greater London with a population approaching 8 million may be seen as a significant spatial unit within the UK, even as a separate 'country' ringed by the M25, and extending beyond the boundaries of the Greater London Boroughs. Significantly the M25 is the boundary chosen by many commercial companies in setting their tariffs and charges. Following the abolition of the GLC in 1986, the remaining planning advisory functions were taken over by the London Planning Advisory Body, with the London Residuary Body being responsible for administering its gradual demise. The GLC's powers were devolved to the 32 London Borough Councils (Heap, 1991: 38).

The Greater London Development Plan (GLDP) had been written in draft by 1984 and was ready for full approval by 1986 when the GLC was abolished. The GLDP's policies should still, in law, be seen as binding planning policies because they were passed as the agreed policy of the planning committee of an enpowered local government council at the time – namely the GLC – whose powers were vested to the individual London Borough planning authorities, and many of its policies have been integrated into borough UDPs. Existing policies still have the force of law if approved by the Secretary of State for the Environment as the existing development plan for the area.

There were many problems of implementation of GLC policies, particularly in relation to some of the more radical and socially orientated aspects of the GDLP. This was because of the different political complexion of the boroughs, plus cutbacks in local government finance, and the constraints of other approved policies within the boroughs themselves. The GLC was Labour-dominated in the mid 1980s, and New Left in particular, whereas many of the London boroughs were Conservative and therefore likely to approach town planning somewhat differently. In defence of the GLC it was argued it is unrealistic to produce strategic level plans for individual boroughs and districts when many of the issues in the large urban areas can only be dealt with at a conurbation wide level, for example, transportation and location policy. Many regret the passing of the GLC and its strategic level of plan making that proved vitally necessary when dealing with large metropolitan areas.

The Labour government is committed to creating a new strategic authority for the governance of London, namely the Greater London Authority (GLA) (Fyson, 1999) and see WP3897 on the governance of London). Five strategic policy areas for the GLA to

Figure 2.7 Inner London: Chaos or Creative Functionality?
All the problems associated with traffic congestion, property development and the quality of the environment bear down upon the inner city.

tackle have been identified, namely, economic development, transport, environment, culture, and land use planning. An elected Mayor and Assembly will have considerable powers to 'run London' similar to those of the North American 'city manager' (Hambleton and Sweeting, 1999).

As to town planning powers, major applications from the London boroughs will have to be referred to the GLA, and overall policy guidance given a Mayoral Spatial strategy, which will be particularly concerned with urban renewal and economic regeneration. There have been considerable concerns expressed by the community and commerce as to the workability of these proposals, not least because of fears of loss of rights of objection and public participation opportunities under the new system. A special body Transport for London (TFL), will be created which will co-ordinate the capital's transport strategy. The London Development Agency (LDA), will take on 'regional functions', in the style of the Welsh Development Agency, by promoting London from an economic and employment perspective. Also the Spatial Development Strategy (SDS) for the capital, like the former Greater London Development Plan, will provide planning policy guidelines for the capital.

In the light of such major changes, one must ask what happens to planning in the rest of the territory

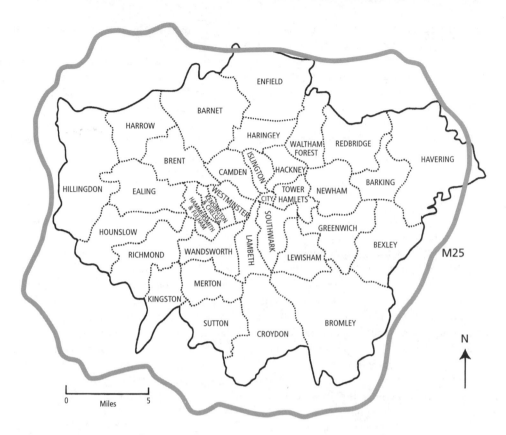

Figure 2.8 **London Boroughs Map.**

which is not part of London, Wales, Scotland or Northern Ireland. Already, people in the regions, and the other large metropolitan conurbations are arguing for greater devolution and a more federalist system of local government. All these factors will have implications for the development of planning in the future. In the next section a range of alternative planning systems in operation in other European countries is discussed as a means of showing other ways of planning and dividing up the country.

COMPARATIVE PERSPECTIVE: OTHER EUROPEAN NATIONAL SYSTEMS

Comparing planning systems is not easy. Different traditions and cultures mean that planning in other countries has developed in ways quite unlike that in

the UK. There are a number of indicators that can be used to explain just how different another system is. Most common among these are: the level at which plans are produced, administrative structures, level of political involvement and the flexibility of the development plan. In the UK plans are made only at a local or county level. In most other countries they are also made at a national (e.g. the Netherlands) and regional (e.g. France, Belgium and Netherlands) scale. This tends to allow far more integration of planning-related issues such as economics, transport and housing than is the case in the UK.

While in the UK the number of local planning authorities is relatively small, in France the number is much higher. There are over 36,000 communes each responsible for carrying out the functions of plan making and development control. In some cases they join together with neighbours, but often they act alone in planning matters. Other tiers of government, regions and departments, also have planning functions such as economic development and transport. This makes for a complicated system, but one that has evolved in response to the geography and culture of the country. As a Republic founded on a revolution, democracy is a strong element within French administration. With such a large number of communes, mayor and councillors who make decisions are well known in the community and closely involve the local citizens.

In the Netherlands on the other hand decisions on applications are made at the level of the municipality, not unlike the UK situation. As in France the decisions are made on the basis of a binding land use plan – in the Netherlands it is the 'Bestemmingsplan', in France the 'Plan d'Occupation des Sols'. These are legal documents that set out people's rights to develop. Applicants who follow the plan will be given permission, those who contravene it will be refused. There are anomalies, but they are the exception rather than the rule. These rigid systems provide more certainty and less flexibility than in the UK.

Somewhere between these rigid systems and the UK's flexibility is the system of the Irish Republic. Planning legislation in the Republic is set out in the Local Government (Planning and Development) Acts 1963–93. Ireland has a zoning approach to plan making; not only are areas zoned for particular uses but zones can be linked to policy objectives. Each of the 88 planning authorities has to produce a development plan every five years. The functions of a planning authority are divided into 'reserved functions' i.e. those matters which are the responsibility of the elected members and 'executive functions' which are those duties and responsibilities charged to officers. Like Britain, the adoption of the development plan is a 'reserved' function; but unlike Britain (and many other countries, including France), the granting or refusing of planning permission is an executive function. No material contravention of the plan is allowed when decisions are made.

France, Netherlands and the Irish Republic all demonstrate two other features that are not yet present in the UK, but may be soon. In these countries plans do not have to be made directly by the Local Planning Authority itself but can be commissioned from a private consultancy. In the UK plans are generally made by the Authority's own planners. Where consultants are used the local authority still retains primary control. In these three countries, third parties have the right to appeal if a decision is made contrary to the plan; whereas under the UK system only applicants can appeal against development control decisions, and third parties cannot appeal.

Moves are already being made to harmonize all the different European planning systems, and indeed, in parallel, progress is already underway in harmonizing building regulation control across the European Union – a process fraught with considerable difficulty and disagreement. While European integration on some environmental issues may bring countries closer together there is little prospect of harmonizing planning systems. As indicated above (and discussed by Rydin, 1998), there is a need to achieve economic fairness, in a Single Market, with systems that are equitable. Some harmonization is therefore inevitable. Different cultures, administrations and traditions will, though, always have a part to play in retaining differences. Therefore the process of harmonization is likely to be longer and more complicated than first imagined (Devereux, 1999b).

EUROPEAN PLANNING

A New Level of Power

Overarching the nation-state level of planning, the pan-European level of planning powers will now be discussed. In Part III policies and issues of that have featured strongly in European planning, such as environmental sustainability will be discussed further, whereas in this section the basic organizational structure will be presented. The European Economic Community (EEC), or Common Market as the European Community was previously known, was created by the Treaty of Rome in 1957. It originally consisted of France, Germany, Italy, Belgium, Netherlands, and Luxembourg. The UK joined in 1973. The European Community is often referred to as the European Union (EU). The abbreviation EC is used for European Community, whereas European Commission is shortened to 'the Commission' in this chapter to avoid confusion.

At the time of writing, the EU comprises 15 member states. The EU's main institutions are as

Figure 2.9 **A Typical European Street Scene in Northern Italy.**
Many European cities consist mainly of medium rise apartment dwellings in high-density districts. Urban policies, many argue, developed for such Continental cities are inappropriate to British cities where suburban houses with gardens predominate.

follows (Williams, 1996). The Commission is based in Brussels and is responsible for preparing proposals for the Council of Ministers and for overseeing the implementation of all of the EU's policies and programmes, it is not a final decision-making body but is answerable to the Council of Ministers. It is rather like the British Civil Service consisting of both professional and administrative staff, and is a supranational governmental agency (Ludlow, 1996).

The Council of Ministers is the primary decision-taking body in the European Union, acting on recommendations made to it by the Commission. The Council of Ministers comprises ministers from each of the Member States with the chairmanship rotating every six months amongst these states. It is supported by committees, working groups and support staff. Its membership varies according to the matters under discussion, whether it be, for instance, regional policy

or the environment. The European Council is a separate body consisting of other senior ministers, which has consultative powers over policy directives in liaison with the Council of Ministers.

The Commission has to consult, and is advised by, an Economic and Social Committee on all relevant matters. The European Court of Justice rules on legal questions raised by EU legislation and is nowadays seen by many as the ultimate Court of Appeal above the British system, for all law, including planning and environmental law. The European Court of Human Rights may make decisions on property-related applications. The Human Rights Act 1998 came into force in 2000 in the UK, endorsing the EC emphasis on rights of families and individuals. The implementation of European environmental legislation is overseen by the European Environmental Agency (EEA) which seeks to ensure that member state planning agencies and local authorities are actually aware of the requirements. Whilst environmental control is to be welcomed some are of the view that this may increasingly make the planners appear to the public as an environmental police force.

The European Parliament consists of over 500 elected members drawn from the member state, who discuss and debate all Council policy proposals. It acts

Figure 2.10 **Mixed Uses and Mixed Ages of Buildings in the Centre of Paris.**
Retaining the urban heritage whilst planning for modern needs is an important component of urban planning across Europe.

as a check and balance to the Council and the Commission. It has fiscal powers to supervize the European Commission Budget. Policy is implemented through a range of statutory instruments and other means, including legislation, regulation, and Directives, the latter being most relevant to town planning. Green Papers which set out policy issues and White Papers which set out details of policy implementation are produced. 'Town' planning is not widely referred to in EU documentation, rather the term 'spatial' planning is more likely to be found.

EU Planning Powers

Twenty-four Directorates-General produce policy guidance, directives, and regulations which must be taken on board by all the member states of the European Union (EU), which together have a population of over 380 million, rivalling North America (Davis, 1992; Ludlow, 1996; Williams, 1996 and Williams, 1999; ESDP, 1999). The Directorates of particular relevance to town planning are those on agriculture; employment, industrial relations and social affairs; energy; environment, nuclear safety and civil protection; regional policy and cohesion; tourism and transport.

There is a considerable amount of policy guidance emanating from the EU on regional planning, town planning, and environmental matters, but much of this is advisory in status. In contrast, there are certain EEC Directives which must be complied with, and which take precedence over UK law. Foremost, EEC Directive 85/337 on the Environmental Assessment of certain categories of new development must be complied with. This was subsequently updated and expanded as EEC Directive 97/11. In this case the regulations, which relate to protecting the environment and to achieving 'sustainability', are stricter than under conventional UK planning law, and definitely much 'greener'. In time more Directives will come into force, and the influence of European-level strategic planning policy is likely to influence UK town planners' perspective on cities more strongly. The procedures for incorporating environmental assessment within the planning application system are described in the next chapter on development control.

EU policy and law takes precedence over that of the member states, including town planning legislation.

In 1987 the Single European Act gave the EU's environmental policy explicit legal backing for the first time (Williams, 1996) and strengthened and harmonized trade and cultural links. The EU's Single Market required common environmental standards to keep the 'playing field' level (Rydin, 1998), and that meant town planning controls must not be more restrictive in one country than in another: a principle that will have far reaching implications. As the development of the internal market progressed, it became more apparent that harmonization of environmental standards was an important element in securing fair competition, and that the Community had a role in ensuring that standards were set at a high level of protection. Thus the objective of achieving monetary union has a direct environmental dimension within the machinations of the EU system.

'Subsidiarity' means the principle that policies should be dealt with at the appropriate and 'lowest' possible level for effective implementation, thus encouraging devolution of powers into the regulatory structures of the member states themselves (Rydin, 1998, p. 131). The guiding principle for town planning (Williams, 1999; Ludlow, 1996) is that the EU should directly intervene only where any required action would transcend the frontiers of Member States, or could be undertaken more efficiently by the EU than by Member States acting separately. This is particularly so in the case of environmental policies which may transcend individual member state boundaries, and urban policy issues which may have wider ramifications. Over two-thirds of West Europeans now live in urban areas with populations exceeding 300,000, and in individual Member States urbanization is clearly an issue of common concern (Fudge, 1999).

European Union policy is impinging on every aspect of British town and country planning policy and practice. Environmental controls have been strong, but also a range of cultural ideas, planning theories and urban trends from other European countries are having an impact on the way 'planning' is conceptualized and imagined, as will be discussed in later chapters. Arguably, trends and theories can prove more influential than laws and regulations in shaping future planning, and the nature of towns and cities.

TASKS

Information Gathering Tasks

I. What are the names of the present Secretary of State for the Environment, and the junior ministers who assist him, and what aspects of the environment are they currently responsible for?

II. Find out what type of planning authority exists in your area, for example, is it a MDC, a London Borough, or a shire county and district system. Find out what stage they are at in the production of the main Development Plan.

Conceptual Tasks

III. To what extent do EU powers impinge upon the British planning systems? Discuss.

IV. To what extent are the political and the professional dimensions of planning should be separated? Relate your discussion to the division of powers currently found with the central and local government levels of planning

Reflective Tasks

V. What are your personal views on membership the EU?

VI. What are the likely advantages and disadvantages of Scottish and Welsh independence for their respective planning systems? What are the implications for planning in England?

FURTHER READING

For details of the planning system see the main planning law books, namely Heap, Cullingworth and Nadin, Telling and Duxbury, Moore, V. and Grant, M. and also the *Encyclopaedia of Planning Law*. Details of local authority districts and other administrative changes are to be found in the *Municipal Year Book*, and also consult the *Housing and Planning Year Book* (Pitman, annual) which lists all local planning authorities and their chief officers.

Blackhall, J.V. (1998, 2000 forthcoming) *Planning Law and Practice*, London: Cavendish.

ESDP (1999) *European Spatial Development Perspective – Towards Balanced and Sustainable Development of the Territory of the European Union*. Brussels: European Commission, see http://www.inforegio.org

The EU level of planning is covered Davis (1992); Williams (1996, 1999) and Ludlow (1996).

For Scottish planning see Collar (1999) and Brand (1999). For Northern Ireland see Johnston (1999); for Wales see Tewdwr Jones, M. (1996).

Information on central and local government may be obtained from the following websites:

PPG 25. Development and Flood Risk.

The Local Government Association, at http://www.lga.gov.uk

RTPI at http://rtpi.co.uk

UK Government index including DETR, at http://www.open.gov.uk/detr

3

DEVELOPMENT CONTROL AND THE DEVELOPMENT PROCESS

INTRODUCTION

The purpose of Chapter 3 is first to describe the development control system, whereby planners can control development, and thus influence both land use and design, and implement their plans. Second, the chapter outlines the wider context of the property development process within which the planning control takes place. Readers should take note that the development control and planning law are highly complex legal areas. There are exceptions to almost every rule, as decisions are frequently challenged by planning appeals, and the legislation and case law is constantly changing. There is also a range of other controls on development, parallel to, but not strictly part of, the statutory planning system, that may delimit the nature of development. These are in relation, *inter alia*, to agriculture, public health, building control, water supply, toxic waste, noise, disability, nature conservation, licensing laws, military defence, and environmental requirements. There have also been areas of special control in which ordinary planning controls are relaxed, such as Simplified Planning Zones and Enterprise Zones; and some where planning controls are increased, such as Urban Conservation Areas and National Parks. Therefore readers should always check the current situation, at the time of reading the book, against official sources.

DEVELOPMENT CONTROL

Planning Applications

Before development can be carried out planning permission must be obtained by the landowner. As stated in the previous chapter;

> 'Development' is defined in planning law under Section 55 of the Town and Country Planning Act 1990, as 'the carrying out of building, engineering, mining, or other operations in, on, over or under land, or the making of any material change in the use of any buildings or other land'. Therefore development defines two main activities: first, the development of new buildings and other works; and second, the change of use from one land-use to another.
>
> *Source*: Town and Country Planning Act 1990: Section 55

A planning application form from the local planning office must be completed and submitted in order to obtain planning permission (or refusal). There are financial charges for both planning permission and building consent. These are frequently revised upwards and readers should check the cost for information purposes. At the time of writing for example, the cost is £95 for a householder application in Bristol, with much higher charges subject to a maximum of £9,500 for large developments. There are two types of planning permission, outline and full (detailed). Outline permission establishes the broader principles that development of a certain type is allowed on a particular site whereas the full application deals with all the

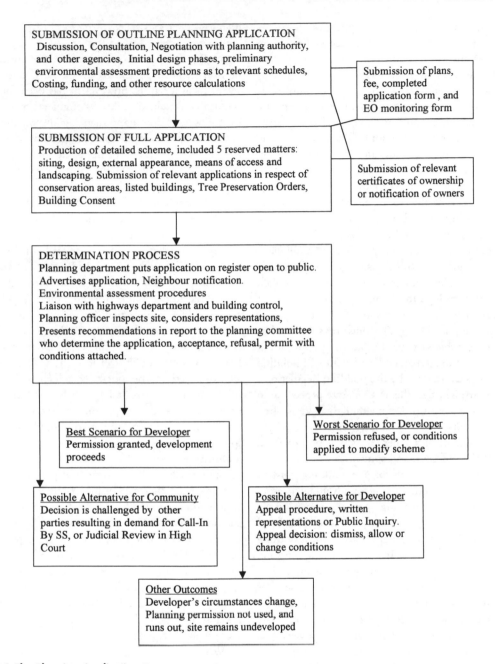

SUBMISSION OF OUTLINE PLANNING APPLICATION
Discussion, Consultation, Negotiation with planning authority, and other agencies, Initial design phases, preliminary environmental assessment predictions as to relevant schedules, Costing, funding, and other resource calculations

Submission of plans, fee, completed application form , and EO monitoring form

SUBMISSION OF FULL APPLICATION
Production of detailed scheme, included 5 reserved matters: siting, design, external appearance, means of access and landscaping. Submission of relevant applications in respect of conservation areas, listed buildings, Tree Preservation Orders, Building Consent

Submission of relevant certificates of ownership or notification of owners

DETERMINATION PROCESS
Planning department puts application on register open to public. Advertises application, Neighbour notification.
Environmental assessment procedures
Liaison with highways department and building control,
Planning officer inspects site, considers representations,
Presents recommendations in report to the planning committee who determine the application, acceptance, refusal, permit with conditions attached.

Best Scenario for Developer
Permission granted, development proceeds

Worst Scenario for Developer
Permission refused, or conditions applied to modify scheme

Possible Alternative for Community
Decision is challenged by other parties resulting in demand for Call-In By SS, or Judicial Review in High Court

Possible Alternative for Developer
Appeal procedure, written representations or Public Inquiry.
Appeal decision: dismiss, allow or change conditions

Other Outcomes
Developer's circumstances change, Planning permission not used, and runs out, site remains undeveloped

Figure 3.1 The Planning Application Process.

specifics. Normally small householder-type applications, e.g. kitchen extensions go straight to the full stage.

For larger, more complex and controversial schemes, such as the building of a new housing estate, or a new out-of-town shopping centre, it is usual to agree the principles at the outline stage. The planners and developers may meet for discussions on the scheme long before the actual planning application form is completed. It is likely that what are known as 'reserved matters' will be held over for consideration at the detailed stage. These are usually shown under five headings on the planning application forms as siting, design, external appearance, access (including car parking) and landscaping. There is no single standardized type of planning application form at present, as they vary from local authority to local authority. It is normal with larger authorities to have a separate form for small householders, compared with larger developer planning applications. These days many local authorities will include an 'ethnic monitoring' form with the planning application form pack, requesting the ethnic origin of the applicant or their agent. This may be due to a perception of a greater refusal rate being applied to applications from ethnic minority householders and businesses.

To submit a householder application, or a full planning application for other uses, the applicant is required to complete four copies of the forms supplied by the local planning office, and supply four copies of the plans. It is not uncommon for the Building Regulations application (which must be submitted as well) to be combined with the planning application, which is passed to a separate department. All building work requires consent under the Building Regulations. It must be stressed that this is a separate procedure to the planning decision process, although there is often need for liaison between planning and building officers on the details of a scheme. As will be explained in Part III the different, and sometimes contradictory, objectives of planning control and building consent may lead to user groups being disadvantaged, especially the disabled. A planning application may 'go the rounds' to different departments within the local authority. In the case of an application for a housing development for example, it is likely the application may be referred to the highways department, and to other departments responsible for providing services and infrastructure in the district, such as education and social services. Development proposals may require approval under other statutory powers and governmental agencies, for example under the Noise Act 1995, Noise Impact Assessment (NIA) may be required.

The local planning authority is not necessarily a free agent in determining the application. In a district authority within a shire county (operating under the two-tier system), highways matters may come under the jurisdiction of the County Highways Department. In some administrative areas the county delegates

highways decisions back to the local district planning department when dealing with matters such as access, circulation and layout on new infill developments, and housing estates; powers to do so have existed since 1988. In other areas, however, it has been found that traditionally-trained highways engineers may still seek to impose car-dominant road layouts on local planning schemes where the local planners want to achieve a more human scale and better urban design principles. As a result of the governmental emphasis upon environmental sustainability, a reduction in residential parking standards has been signalled by revisions to PPG3 'Housing', and these are likely to be enshrined in subsequent regulations.

The plans that must be submitted consist of a site plan, normally to the scale 1:1250, showing the buildings (proposed and existing) in and around the site, with a red line around the whole plot. An Ordnance Survey grid reference may be required and is shown as follows: first (with the north at the top), the 'easting' is given which is the number (found on the top or bottom margin) of the vertical line to the left of the site, followed by the 'northing' which is the number of the nearest horizontal line below the site (shown on the sides of the map). In other words the figures along the bottom of the map should be read first followed by those up the side of the map. The local authority will store the details of the application on computer using GIS software (Geographical Information Systems) that can display both map details and information about the application. Building plans should also be provided, indicating the floor plans and elevation of the building, plus a section through the building showing annotated details of the construction and materials, to the scale of 1.50 or 1.100. In Imperial, this is approximately 1/4 in to 1 ft, or 1/8th in to 1 ft respectively. The North point, the scale, and a key should be included on every plan or map. (See Conversion, Textbox 1.1.)

When submitting a planning application, a Certificate must be completed which records the ownership of the property. This is required under Article 7 of the Town and Country Planning (General Development Procedure) Order 1995. Complete Certificate A if one is the sole owner. Complete Certificate B if the ownership is shared with others, and then send Notice 1, which is given out as part of the application form, to each owner. Certificate C is used where the applicant is unable to discover all the names of the owners, and Certificate D where the applicant is unable to discover any of the names of the owners. Publicity of the application will be required in cases C and D. This procedure is under review, and at present 'neighbours notification' is practised by many planning authorities. In general at present certain other types of planning application are advertized by the local authority in local newspapers, and by site notices. Twenty-one days is given for inspection of the plans at the local planning office, and for objectors to submit written representations if they are unhappy with the proposal.

Written representations are taken into account at the decision-making stage when the local planning committee (the councillors) decide whether or not to approve the scheme, taking into account the professional advice of their planning officers. Under Section 69 of the Town and Country Planning Act 1990, the planning authority is required to keep a register of planning applications available to the public, which they may consult without charge. This is a separate register from the Local Land Charges Register which gives information on other matters relevant to the area, such as road widening, and planning matters affecting a piece of land. Also it is separate from the Land Registry, which records the ownership of all registered land and property covering most of the country.

It may be that the applicant does not require planning permission. Under Section 10 of the Planning and Compensation Act 1991, an applicant can apply for a certificate of lawfulness. These are of two types, the 'certificate of lawful use or development' for existing development, and the 'certificate of lawfulness of proposed use or development' for proposed development. There have been earlier versions of these certificates such as the 'certificate of established use' which have now been replaced by the above.

The planning authority makes its decisions on the basis of national planning law, that is the Planning Acts, and 'rules' of the Orders, such as the Use Classes Order and General Development Orders, deriving from the 1990 and 1991 Acts, and on various other directives, statutory instruments, circulars, white papers (command papers), PPG's and guidance notes. These are all a reflection of the Secretary of State's policy and, therefore, should a particular planning

decision go to appeal the decision may be determined in accordance with specific aspects of their contents. In addition to these ministerial documents, existing case law and appeal decisions are major indicators of current policy as to what is permissible: perhaps more so than all the other factors mentioned. The local authority also takes into account its own policy statements, which may have the force of law as enshrined in the Structure Plan and especially in the Local plan (S26, 1991 Act), and also, to a lesser degree, non-statutory plans and statements approved by its planning committee.

Many planning authorities produce design guides which set out the accepted standards of design, car parking, density and estate layout guidance, and these, too, are taken as agreed policy having considerable influence on the decision-making process. The application of planning standards and design principles in respect of a particular site should not be seen as absolutely fixed, but are subject to a certain amount of negotiation and 'trading' to get the best solution for that site, all things considered. On some small inner city sites it is practically impossible to achieve the fixed standards. The planners and developers may find their decisions are constrained by the presence of underground sewers, unstable land, soil contamination, restrictive covenants, and the height and effects of neighbouring development, also the existence of archaeological remains (PPG16).

City-wide level policy statements found in the Structure Plan or UDP are of major importance when deciding if a development should occur at all in a particular location in the case of the larger planning applications, as it must tie in with proposed development allocations for the area. Even before an outline planning permission is submitted, the developers may enter preliminary negotiations and discussions with the planners to sound them out, and either side may produce a planning brief, a document for discussion setting out how the area is envisaged developing. For the planners the location of large housing estates might have strategic implications for the future structure of the whole urban area, future infrastructure, bus routes, schools, everything. Developers stand to make or lose millions of pounds depending on the planners' decision. Thus, developers will try various tactics to speed up the planning process including discussing 'planning gain' (see section below, page 50).

Figure 3.2 Demolition, Bexhill on Sea.
Buildings that were once seen as outdated nuisances occupying valuable land are nowadays more likely to be 'listed' and converted into luxury apartments or upmarket commercial premises.

Local authorities are required to make a decision within 8 weeks of the application being received, but on average decisions are given within 15 weeks. There have been many attempts to speed up the system, by means of setting targets, undertaking audits and creating more efficient office systems (Audit Commission, 1999). If an applicant disagrees with the decision given, they have, in some cases, 6 months to appeal to the Secretary of State. Applicants also have the right to put in an appeal upon the expiry of 8 weeks, if they have not received a planning decision. The big developers have all sorts of ways of harassing the small local authority, for example pressing the planners into making a favourable decision so as to save the authority from legal costs incurred from appeals during times of restricted government spending. Likewise the local authority can create delay by means of bureaucratic procedures. This is in a quite different league from ordinary householder applications. Planning consultants and planning lawyers working for the private sector, know how to play the game and how to submit the application in the most favourable manner to get the desired result for their clients.

Planning decisions will receive one of three answers, yes, no, and yes but with conditions. Planners are entitled to impose 'such conditions as they think

Table 3.1 The Use Classes Order

The Use Classes Order is in summary as follows:

Class A1	Shops of all types including superstores and retail warehouses, also includes hairdressers, sandwich bars etc., but not car showrooms.
Class A2	Financial and professional services, including banks, building societies and estate agents and betting offices
Class A3	Food and drink including restaurants, pubs and take aways.
Class B1	Business use, includes offices, research and development, general industrial use provided it is not detrimental to the area.
Class B2	General industrial.
Class B3–7	Special industrial uses.
Class B8	Storage and distribution including wholesale cash and carry.
Class C1	hotels and hostels.
Class C2	Residential homes and institutions.
Class C3	Use as a dwelling houses (a) by a family (b) by not more than 6 persons living together as a household (including those under care).
Class D1	Non-residential institutions including religious buildings, museums, medical, public halls, creches, nurseries.
Class D2	Assembly, leisure, cinemas, bingo halls, casinos, indoor sports.

fit' (Section 70 of the 1990 Act). Circular 1/85 sets out the six tests as to the validity of conditions of permission and this was subsequently incorporated in planning guidance (for example PPG1). The basic principle is that the conditions must have been imposed for a planning reason related to the site, and not for some broader environmental or social policy reason. The local authority may accept the development in principle but require modifications, or they may choose to limit the permission to a period of years. This is a growing trend in the case of a change of use to allow the local planning authority an opportunity for future review of the situation in case of changing circumstances. In the case of new building development, matters such as landscaping, car parking and access may have to be altered; for example, tree screening might be required.

The highways authority is be concerned with traffic generation, parking, access, and road safety, and with the question of whether new road development is needed. Until recently the developers would enter into an agreement under Section 38 of the Highways Act 1980, which allows the developer to undertake the construction of the roads in return for the local authority adopting them and maintaining them in the future, or alternatively advance payments were made by the developer to the local authority under sections 219 and 228 of the Highways Act before the site was 'released' for development, with Sections 38 and 278 also allowing for an element of 'highways gain' over above the minimum to facilitate site development. The New Roads and Street Works Act 1991 modifies the legal mechanics of these methods to a degree (Section 22) but the principle remains the same. Under Section 104 of the Water Industry Act 1991 a sewage undertaker can agree with a developer to adopt the new development's sewers. Any development, however small, which requires access on to a trunk road or classified road requires permission from the county highways authority. However, if permission is given for car access, the local authority may permit access by dropped kerb on the site. The highways authority must be notified before work commences, and the householder would be expected to pay for the works involved. Classified roads are A and B roads, also C roads, which are not shown as 'special' on Ordnance Survey maps are coloured in yellow along with ordinary small non-classified roads. Most bus route roads are classified roads.

Under the Open Spaces Act 1906, a developer can agree to lay out, plant and maintain an area of public open space before handing it over to the local authority for adoption, but few new housing schemes nowadays contain even a small park or open space. They may contain 'left-over' bits of green space which the local authority may not want. Other negotiations are entered into between the developer and the statutory authorities for the provision of the other infrastructural services. There are additional hurdles in respect of public health, building regulation consent, and environmental assessment before development can commence. Work should normally start within five years of permission being granted, and in the case of outline permissions the detailed application should be submitted within three years of the initial permission, and development should commence two years after the approval of detailed reserved matters. In some cases a completion notice may be served, once building has started, if the development process is dragging on.

Sui generis: many uses do not fall into any class and are therefore in a class of their own. Theatres, car hire, petrol stations, car showrooms and various innovative uses have been seen to be *sui generis* (in a general category). This leaves the planning office discretion to decide on the basis of planning policy whether a change of use has occurred or not. They must also take into account the zonings shown on the approved plans for that area. If all changes of use were set out in the UCO, planning would become mechanical and there would be no professional judgement involved. Also the

Figure 3.3 (a and b) **House Extensions on New and Older Properties.**
Dealing with extensions forms a major aspect of development control, and for ordinary people this is what planning is seen to be.

extent and intensity of the change has to be taken into account to determine if it is a 'material' change of use or just a temporary or ancillary (secondary) use.

Not all changes require permission, the general principle being that if the change is from something 'good' to something 'worse' then it will require planning permission. If a building changes from being a house to an office that counts as development even though no actual new building has taken place. Certain minor changes, such as the painting the outside of a house, count as 'permitted development' and do not need normally planning permission. The General Development Order (GDO) sets out what counts as 'permitted development' (Grant, 1990; 1999). Readers are warned that the GDO is subject to frequent revision and the current situation should be checked carefully.

The General Development Order

The General Development Order 1988, as revised in 1995, sets out those matters which do not require planning permission. Changes are detailed in the Town and Country Planning (General Permitted Development) Order (SI 1995 No 418) 1995, and the Town and Country Planning (General Development Procedure) Order (SI 1995 No 419) 1995. But the GDO does not apply everywhere. Under Article 4 of the GDO the Secretary of State and the local planning authority can withdraw some or all of the GDO rights, and they may also be reduced by planning conditions being imposed. Sensitive urban areas may be subject to these additional controls.

Areas of Outstanding Natural Beauty (AONBs) and Conservation areas are subject to somewhat different GDO rules. Local Authorities have powers to suspend rights under Clauses I–IV of the Schedule of the GDO in cases where the development proposed would be detrimental to the proper planning, or a threat to the amenities of the area, but this direction can only remain in force for 6 months, unless approved by the Secretary of State. Article 4 Decisions remain in force indefinitely.

The display of an advertisement requires a special planning application under the Town and Country Planning (Control of Advertisements) Regulations 1984. Local authorities also have the right to designate areas of Special Advertisement Control in areas where greater levels of control are needed, for example to protect the amenity of an area. Current policy, and likely revisions to the existing situation are included in the consultation document *Outdoor Advertisement Control* (DETR, 1999a).

Class I of the GDO contains various small scale aspects of householder development not requiring permission, and are known as permitted development. For example, a porch may be built provided it is less than 3 square meters in area, less than 3 metres high and is more than 2 metres from the boundary of the road. At present householders are allowed to have one satellite dish provided it does not normally exceed 90 centimetres in diameter depending upon the location, and area designation in question (60 or 70 cm in some areas), and is no higher than the ridge of the roof (DETR, 1998d). A loft can built provided it does not increase the total cubic content of the house itself by more than 50 cubic metres, or 40 cubic metres for a terrace in terms of loft extension. This is not in addition to overall permitted house extensions but should be deducted from it. The loft extension should not be above the ridge of the roof, and normally it should not face the road.

House extensions can be up to 15 per cent of the original current cubic volume on a semi-detached or detached property or 70 cubic metres, or 10 per cent on a terrace or 50 cubic metres, whichever is larger, both up to an overall maximum of 115 cubic metres. Note that in respect of getting permission for extensions all measurements relate to the house as originally built, or as it stood at 1 July 1948, and are relevant to the external cubic volume. To come within planning law the extension should not be in front of the front wall of the house except where the house is set further than 20 metres from the boundary. Many of the rules seem to favour large houses over small. Neither should it go above the ridge of the roof. No part of the extension should be higher than 4 metres and it must lie within 2 metres of any boundary. Along with outbuildings the extended house must not occupy more than 50 per cent of the garden area. Planners are very conscious of plot ratios in some areas, with regard to how much of the site is actually covered by buildings.

Gardens and Vegetation

Subject to any special provisions, such as Article 4 Directions, any amount of hardstanding or patio is allowed, and almost anything can be planted in the garden, provided it is 'incidental to the enjoyment of the dwelling' but even these factors may be covered by special controls. Students always ask about the 'hypothetical' carport without walls in the front garden. If it is joined to the house, it is development in any case; if it is in front of the front wall of the house, and/or over the building line, the local authority are likely to act on it (if they notice it). Some local authorities have additional controls about parking caravans in front gardens, and any caravan which is permanently occupied within the curtilage of a dwelling is bound to attract the wrath of the local authority. Working or running a business from home may be construed as a 'change of use', unless the use is 'ancillary' to the main residential use. There is the principle that the 'intensity' and 'predominance' of the use should be taken into account, and a use which is ancillary or secondary to the main use is not necessarily a change of use. Planners are more concerned about external effects such as generation of car parking, noise, and disturbance, than about the turnover of a business or how much disruption it causes within the household (Thomas, 1980).

Another tricky issue is that of incidental buildings such as greenhouses, outbuildings, garages, lean-to's and conservatories within the curtilage of a dwelling. The case of greenhouses in residential areas, should not be confused with that of glasshouses which are horticultural greenhouses and permitted in agricultural areas and greenbelts. Conservatories count as extensions if attached to the house, or if they stand within 5 metres of it, and similar rules apply to garages. But greenhouses are part of the enjoyment of the curtilage of the dwelling and permitted under the GDO. In the case of listed buildings anything within the curtilage of the dwelling is subject to additional planning controls. New balconies jutting out from upper floors, even with no extension beneath them are also likely to be counted as development.

Hedges are not subject to control. A householder can plant fast growing coniferous *Leylandii* (DETR, 1995) trees which can form a high 'wall' without getting planning permission. Hedge and plant height is not controlled by planning law, but they may be the subject of other local authority controls if plants affect the public use of the adjacent pavement. Because of unsuitability, height, loss of view and light, and neighbour nuisance some countries have banned the use of certain non-indigenous species. Eucalyptus and *Leylandii*, for example, are banned in some Canadian states where there is much stronger 'tree control' in relation to private gardens, boundaries and hedges than is the case in Britain. Likewise Australia, home of the eucalyptus, exercises a range of flora (plant) planning controls over foreign species, because of the fragility of the local ecology.

There have been various attempts by means of private members bills and from consumer groups to increase the controls on trees, especially, *Leylandii*. Certainly greater tree control would be welcome, and may be allowed as a result of future EU harmonization of European planning systems. But at present, in spite of approximately 20 per cent of the population at any one time, having 'neighbour disputes', there is no 'right of view'. But there are other legal remedies such as: tort of nuisance; 'trespass' of roots and overhanging branches; and infringement of restrictive covenants that may be invoked in a limited range of cases. The problem of controlling a neighbour's *Leylandii* has been the subject of a national campaign and a consultation briefing note by the government (DETR, 1999b), signalling that stronger measures may be introduced in the future.

In contrast individual native trees may be protected under TPOs (Tree Preservation Orders) and planning permission is required to lop such a tree, and if felled, must be replaced with a tree of similar species. Article 4 Directions may be used to impose controls on planting in open plan estates, and in conservation areas trees and hedges are subject to special controls. Fences and walls are normally permitted development up to a height of 2 metres, or 1 metre if next to a classified road (except in conservation areas and other areas of special protection).

Confusion as to what is or is not allowed under planning law, arises because some local planning authorities enforce the rules more rigidly than others. Indeed, if the authority are short-staffed and no-one 'notices' an illegal development, it may appear to be all right. However, it should be pointed out that planning authorities do have powers to require the demolition of unauthorized developments, and it is a criminal offence not to comply with an enforcement notice. The Planning and Compensation Act 1991 increased the penalties and related enforcement powers. If for example, the alterations to a house would have been permitted in any case had the owners applied for planning permission, then there are means of granting retrospective permission, which may be necessary if these irregularities show up at the time when a house is being sold or in the process of conveyancing. In this age of do-it-yourself conveyancing it may go unnoticed, with dire consequences for the next owner down the line when a more vigilant planning officer tracks it down. Under the 1991 Act, the 4 year rule giving immunity to development without permission (which has not been challenged in that period), is now accompanied by a new 10 year rule which gives immunity for uses carried out without planning permission.

Caravans and Campsites

There are a range of controls over caravans and camp sites. There are over 500,000 caravans in Britain, with a substantial number actually stationery; indeed the difference between a mobile home and a caravan is a moot point. Many caravan sites are temporary and permission is often granted on a seasonal basis. The insidious, gradual use of seasonal holiday facilities as year-round housing is problematic. Mobile homes are a particular problem. Planners have control over temporary uses such as fairs, circuses, sport-related marquees, and markets. These powers are administered in conjunction with the magistrates and public health officials. There are additional problems these days concerning 'travellers' – compared with traditional gypsies or caravan holiday-makers. Traveller problems are often generated by large gatherings such as pop festivals, for example, the summer solstice in the west country. These matters are complex and controversial as they impinge upon legislation related to housing, vagrancy, gipsy sites, and anti-racism policy, and go beyond the scope of town and country planning. The legislative situation is in transition, and it is worth checking the professional press for future developments.

Environmental Assessment

EU directives require Environmental Assessment (EA) to be undertaken in relation to granting planning permission on larger industrial, toxic developments (Fortlage, 1990; Grant, 1998). This came into force under EEC Directive 85/337, subsequently updated with assessment categories extended in EEC Directive 97/11. Directions were given to local planning authorities to undertake this process in the Town and Country Planning (Assessment of Environmental Effects) Regulations, No. 1199, 1988, while the Planning and Compensation Act 1991 integrated the process into the statutory planning system. The process has also been strengthened by the requirements of the Environmental Protection Act 1990.

As indicated in Chapter 2, PPG12 requires local authorities to undertake an environmental assessment of their development plans (DoE, 1993a). Schedule 1 of the Directive lists all the types of development for which assessment is compulsory, as part of the development control process, and Schedule 2 lists those which may have environmental consequences because of size, scale location, and other characteristics (Table 3.2). A scheme which does not require assessment may be referred to as having 'Schedule 2 exemption' (Rydin, 1998: 238). The uses requiring environmental assessment range from rural uses that would not normally require planning permission under the British system, such as salmon fishing and forestry to intensive urban renewal projects under Schedule 2.

Under UK town planning legislation, Agriculture (Class VI) has been subject to less planning controls than urban development. Farm buildings come under control if they are near an airport (if they are more than 3 metres high and within 3 kilometres of an airport or 12 metres elsewhere), the trend is towards more control in view of pressure from environmentalists and the Green movement in general. Environmental assessment regulations do not, significantly, make the same sharp division between urban and rural development, or between industrial and agricultural uses, rather the emphasis is upon scale, size and likely impact of the development.

Normally an Environmental Statement (ES) (showing the results of the EA) would be required if the development was considered to fall into a qualifying Schedule. In the case of large developments it is

Table 3.2 Schedule 1 and 2 for Environmental Assessment Purposes

Schedule 1	Schedule 2
In summary this includes the following 21 categories of development:	In summary these are uses not included in Schedule 1, which may not appear to be so environmentally *problematic*, but which because *of their size*, intensity or ecological aspects require special attention. Each of the 13 sections covers many types of development. Aspects which have caused comment are given for illustrative purposes.

Schedule 1

1. Crude-oil refineries
2. Thermal power stations, nuclear power stations
3. Installations for processing nuclear fuel or waste
4. Iron and steel smelting works
5. Asbestos processing works
6. Chemical plants
7. Construction of railways, airports, motorways and express roads
8. Ports, piers, and waterways
9. Waste Disposal installations involving incineration, landfill, hazardous waste and chemical treatment.
10. Non-hazardous waste disposal installations over 100 tonnes per day
11. Groundwater extraction works
12. Water resource transfer works
13. Large waste water treatment plants
14. Petroleum and natural gas extraction
15. Dams and other large water storage works
16. Pipelines for gas, oil or chemicals
17. Installations for intensive poultry or pig rearing
18. Industrial plans for timber, paper and pulp production
19. Quarries and open cast mining
20. Construction of overhead electrical power lines
21. Storage of petroleum and chemical products

Schedule 2

1. Agriculture, silviculture and aquaculture, including fishfarming
2. Extractive industry including underground mining
3. Energy industry, including wind turbines
4. Metal processing, including shipyards
5. Mineral industry, including manufacture of ceramic roofing tiles
6. Chemical industry, including manufacture of paint
7. Food production, including brewing and malting
8. Textile, leather, wood and paper industry, including cellulose
9. Rubber industry
10. Infrastructure projects, including urban development projects, where the ground covered is more than 0.5 hectare, such as shopping centres and multiplex cinemas
11. Other projects, including knackers' yards.
12. Tourism and leisure developments, including theme parks
13. Any change or extension of the projects listed in sections 1–12 above.

likely that the developer will submit an environmental assessment as part of the initial stages of the proposal. However it must be stated that some developers, nd significantly some local planning authorities have been slow to take on board the need for environmental assessment and this has led to legal challenges in some cases.

Listed Buildings and Conservation Areas

Listed building consent may also be needed, for which there is a separate application form, in addition to the ordinary planning application. The local authority will advertise the application; usually in conservation areas. A full application must be submitted in the case of listed buildings (not outline) because the planners will want to know what the scheme will look like, in terms of façade, townscape, and also car parking, access etc.

Listed building consent may also be required in cases of alterations to the building. Conservation area consent is required for demolition of an unlisted building in a conservation area. In sensitive cases, the developers might produce a small report, in addition to the application, and include annotated diagrams and plans, photographs and further explanation of exactly what is intended, for example, whether a significant wall is going to be demolished, and how landscaping will be dealt with. The planners and developers invariably have a meeting regarding the building materials at the detailed stage at which, among other items, samples of different materials will be discussed.

The DETR provides guidance to local authorities on the listing of buildings and on control to prevent demolition or alteration without notice, also neglect by owners and to benefit the general public. English Heritage, under the DETR, is the body responsible for listing buildings (in England). Previously the Royal

Figures 3.4a and b **(a) Conservation Area, Regents Park, London and (b) Bitton Village Near Bath.**
Conservation areas vary from landmark heritage tourist areas such as Nash's Regency scheme in London to small village streets where infill of new housing must be undertaken with sensitivity.

Commission on Historic Monuments and the Historic Buildings Council have operated this role. English Heritage advises the DETR on listing, finance, conservation areas, and town schemes. The DETR co-ordinates conservation with policy related to inner city initiatives, city grants, housing improvement funds, all of which also deal with 'old' buildings. Private development companies themselves often have a conservation section and seek to liaise with the DOE, English Heritage and the relevant local authorities on larger schemes, to keep a 'good image' with the planners and the grant givers.

Buildings are listed if they are seen to be of outstanding historic or architectural interest, All buildings built before 1700, most 1700 to 1840, some 1840 to 1914 and a few 1914 to 1939 and even a small number after that, are listed. In some countries, buildings are given the equivalent of a listing 'at birth', if they are considered to be of exceptional architectural merit, although these are likely to be the least endangered. Being listed is likely to increase the value of the property but may restrict the owner's freedom of use. In England and Wales, there are three main categories of listing. Grade I must not be removed in any circumstances and are of national, even international importance: if a motorway is to be built, the motorway would have to go around it. Grade II comes in two sub-categories. Grade II* (starred) which means they have an asterisk * beside them on the list, cannot be

removed without a compelling reason, and are usually of significant regional, if not national importance and include set-piece Georgian houses in some of the main terraces and squares in cities such as Bath.

At present there are approximately half a million listed buildings, around 10,000 conservation areas and 16,000 historic monuments. Conservation is not the same as preservation. Preservation conjures up images of buildings turned into museums and put in mothballs. Conservation contains the idea that the buildings in question remain as part of the living fabric of the city in daily use, for example, as houses and offices. Conservation should not be seen, either, as just being applicable to stately homes, palaces, and tourist destinations, or simply to the 'Country Life' type up market private houses. There are many working-class areas and terraces which are conserved because they too are part of our heritage, and in such areas conservation policy can often be linked to urban regeneration programmes, and more collaborative approaches to undertaking urban renewal (Punter, 1990).

Grade II (unstarred) are more ordinary buildings such as typical Georgian or Victorian town houses of more local importance. There is also a non-statutory category, Grade III which is not actually on the central government list, but on a list composed by the local planning authority. This list is advisory, but there are powers to upgrade such buildings to Grade II if they are threatened. Conservation control is particularly concerned with the external appearance of buildings but in the case of Grade I and Grade II* there are additional controls on internal features. Of the approximately half a million listed buildings in England and Wales 5,800 are Grade I, 15,000 are Grade II*; there are also more than 6,000 conservation areas (*Source*: DETR website).

A building cannot be demolished or altered without listed building consent, but in the past some people just let their buildings fall down 'naturally', particularly if they were in the way of a new development scheme. To prevent this a Repairs Notice may be issued, if a building is not properly maintained, and two months after its receipt the owner may serve a compulsory purchase notice on the local authority. On the other hand the owner can issue the local authority with a listed building purchase notice to buy the property if the upkeep is too much. Although there are considerable negative powers associated with conservation, there are also limited positive financial incentives to encourage conservation. Also there is the questionable assumption that listing will increase the value of the property, which does not necessarily apply to all parts of the country. Nevertheless the local authority may impose additional burdens by stipulating in renovation work the use of genuine slate tiles on the roof, or traditional hard wood sash window frames, rather than condoning the use of aluminium frames or plastic double glazing.

As more and more Victorian and Edwardian areas come under conservation policy control, people on low incomes may find they are faced with impossible choices and often simply move out of the area to avoid the costs of upkeep. Further, some of the design controls on listed buildings actually contradict the rules under public health and building regulation controls, e.g. the heights of ceilings and the design of windows in relation to conversion and modernization work. Basically, there is more flexibility if it can be shown that the developer is seeking to return the building to what is agreed is its original design. A building can be listed without the owner's consent and there is no appeal procedure against this. While conservation is a worthy objective in protecting the visual quality of the townscape, many would argue that it involves greater infringements on personal freedom and rights over one's own property than ordinary planning law. Application for 'Listed Building Consent' is on a special type of planning application form, if the intention is to alter, extend or demolish a listed building; planning permission in the normal way is also required if the proposal involves wider planning matters, such as a change of use.

There has been limited financial assistance available under the Historic Building and Ancient Monuments Act 1953, which empowers the Minister to make grants for maintenance and guardianship of properties which are of national tourist importance. Under this Act the Minister can also designate 'Town Schemes', which are usually small areas such as a town square, a high street, or village green, for which the following grants are available: 25 per cent from central government and 25 per cent of the cost from local government, the rest being supplied by the owner. The current legislation on town schemes, and the limited availability of grants and loans related to conservation is set out in Sections 77–80 of the recent consolidating act on conservation, namely the Planning (Listed Buildings and Conservation Areas) Act 1990.

City grants are available in some cases under Part III of the Housing and Planning Act 1986 and are part of the 'Action for Cities' programme. Under the Local Authorities (Historic Buildings) Act 1962, local authorities can make grants and loans towards conservation but in view of the present nature of local government finance and cutbacks this is rare these days. Many listed buildings are also used as houses and therefore people have been able to claim Housing Improvement Grants under the Housing Acts (1969 onwards). In the 1970s this was easier and more money was available for a range of improvements and alterations, indeed this provision contributed towards the process of 'gentrification', although the original intention was to help poor working-class areas. The term gentrification describes the process in which middle-class people move back into the inner city and renovate property thus causing a rise in the property values in the area. In some cases, areas worthy of conservation were also designated as General Improvement Areas or Housing Action areas. There are so many listed buildings that buildings are no longer considered so 'special' and worthy of financial support just because they are listed, also housing grants are only available for a more limited range of improvements. Another bone of contention has been the question of VAT on listed building repair and/ or renovation. This is a detailed taxation and legal question. Checking the professional press is advisable for the current state of play at the time of reading this book.

In the 1990s a range of new possibilities for funding listed buildings was opened up. Conservation Area Partnership Grants (CAPS) are available for selected properties as a result of Lottery funding. Additional assistance may be available at local authority level, for example in Bristol, from the City's Wanted Homes Team which seeks to bring empty property, badly in need of repair, back into the housing stock. Also liaison with housing associations, educational establishments, letting agencies and charitable bodies all provide means of funding such property, particularly in conservation areas.

Whilst listing dealt with individual buildings it seemed more logical to plan for historical areas as a whole to enable increased control, not only on individual buildings, but on the surrounding townscape, trees, street appearance, and incidental non-listed buildings which together form the backcloth against which the listed building stands. The Civic Amenities Act 1967, established the category of 'conservation areas'. These are designated and controlled through the local planning authority. The aim is to maintain the overall visual quality and character of the area. New buildings can be constructed in a conservation area but they must fit in with the historical style of the area. Thus there has been a proliferation of neo-Georgian office buildings with modern, imitation sash windows and mansard roofs.

The Town and Country Amenities Act 1974 gave increased powers of control in conservation areas, preventing demolition of all buildings and also giving further protection to plants, trees, and other townscape and street features within conservation areas. Local planning authorities can protect trees anywhere by Tree Preservation Orders (TPOs) , making it illegal to cut or prune them without planning permission. TPOs are enforced under S198 of the Town and Country Planning Act 1990, through the recently revised Town and Country (Trees) Regulations 1999 (Statutory Instrument No. 1982).

Figure 3.5 **Off Street Parking.**
For many people the front garden of the house provides essential parking space for cars, caravans and boats, leaving the garage free for storage. Current proposals to restrict residential parking may effectively mean people lose their 'extra room'.

All the conservation legislation is now consolidated in the Planning (Listed Building and Conservation Areas) Act 1990. This has not, of itself, introduced any significant new measures but tidied up existing legislation. Many planning authorities found that the designation of conservation areas (often on the rather questionable pretence of protecting marginally important buildings) was a means of increasing development control and reducing rights under the General Development Order (GDO) for example, in respect of demolition which heretofore has not counted as 'development'. Under Section 13 of the Planning and Compensation Act 1990, the demolition of a building may count as 'development' in certain complex circumstances; it is advisable to check the current situation at the appropriate time. There are already additional powers by which the Minister can introduce special planning controls which suspend the rights under the GDO. These are commonly known as Article 4 Directions. There is a range of special controls under Section 102 of the Town and Country Planning Act 1990. An Article 4 Direction can be used to increase the level of control in an area which is not in a conservation area, by preserving the architectural features and layout of a housing estate or retaining open plan front gardens, for example. Alternatively it can be used to increase powers in conservation areas, although this has become less necessary as the legislation (and case law precedents) have tightened up the controls over the years. There is a range of Special Development Orders (SDOs) which can also be introduced to protect areas in the countryside and in other special circumstances. Compensation is payable in some cases for loss of development rights under the GDO.

When designating a conservation area, the local authority needs to be concerned about traffic movement, parking, and pedestrian circulation within the area. In some cases streets are blocked off, or one-way systems introduced to control traffic movement. The environmental effects of modern traffic have to be taken into account both in terms of the effects of attrition on the building fabric, and also the overall visual impact. Most conservation areas are localities where people live and work, and so a compromise must be reached between the need to protect the area and the need to enable people to carry out their businesses and lives in the area. In some cases conservation areas are also designated as Local Plan areas in the Development Plan, because this enables the comprehensive planning of the area on the statutory basis of the approved policies enshrined in the plan's written statement and land use plans. There has been much controversy about car parking restrictions, and through traffic controls in conservation areas. Whilst these no doubt improve the quality of the conservation area, some community groups living in nearby working-class inner areas are of the opinion that such policies can be class biased, pushing the commuter traffic and on-street parking into poorer areas where residents are less articulate. Furthermore, from the viewpoint of the suburban commuter – faced with reduced car parking space in central areas – residents of conservation areas are often seen as projecting a fortress mentality in protecting their areas from urban transportation pressures generated by adjacent central business district expansion. Yet again planning for the needs of one group may disadvantage another.

In addition to governmental bodies, there are several non-governmental bodies which have acted as powerful pressure groups in bringing about the current emphasis on conservation, and which exert a continuing powerful role. These voluntary bodies include the National Trust which, among other matters, is concerned with the fate of stately homes, large country houses, and large rural estates, and its urban relative the Civic Trust founded in 1957. Both of these bodies are entirely independent from the government. There is a series of voluntary bodies representing the needs of buildings from different historical periods, such as (in chronological order), the Georgian Society, Regency Society, and Victorian Society. In recent years societies defending buildings from the 1920s and 1930s have grown up, and 1950s and 1960s societies are now being established. There are other government bodies such as the Royal Fine Arts Commission and various other design bodies, including the Design Centre which may be consulted on visual townscape issues.

There are a number of categories of historical buildings, especially those associated with Royalty and the Church, which are not subject to normal conservation policy, but of necessity, their guardians take their custodial role in preserving Britain's heritage most carefully. Normally voluntary agreements are made in respect of Crown Land (Section 293 of the TCP Act 1990) as the Act does not 'bind' the Crown. Similar exemptions may apply to land and properties under the control of Ministry of Defence, the police, and a range of statutory undertakers, or their privatized successors, related to gas, electricity, water etc., some have a better reputation than others in respect of environmental sensitivity. Many would argue that there is a case for a complete overhaul of the powers of the planning system in relation to these bodies. However, there is provision that on the disposal of land by these organizations, planning permission can be given before the sale which enhances its value in the market, for example, in the case of property in the Green Belt.

When dealing with aesthetic issues, expert advice and local opinion both play a part, over and above the strict interpretation of planning law. Overall, the objective of preserving the 'amenity' of the area is central in many a planning controversy. 'Amenity' is an extremely elastic and much used word in the world of planning. It does not have a strict legal definition, but nevertheless carries considerable power as a material consideration in determining a planning decision.

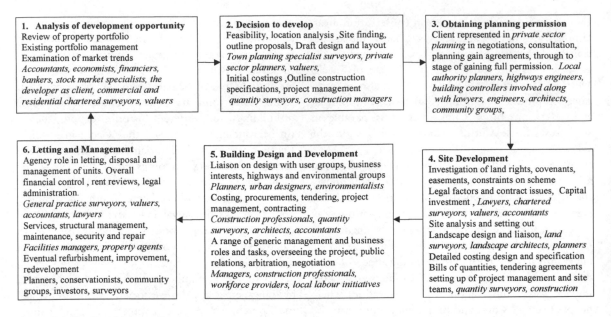

1. Analysis of development opportunity
Review of property portfolio
Existing portfolio management
Examination of market trends
Accountants, economists, financiers, bankers, stock market specialists, the developer as client, commercial and residential chartered surveyors, valuers

2. Decision to develop
Feasibility, location analysis ,Site finding, outline proposals, Draft design and layout
Town planning specialist surveyors, private sector planners, valuers,
Initial costings ,Outline construction specifications, project management
quantity surveyors, construction managers

3. Obtaining planning permission
Client represented in *private sector planning* in negotiations, consultation, planning gain agreements, through to stage of gaining full permission. *Local authority planners, highways engineers, building controllers involved along with lawyers, engineers, architects, community groups,*

6. Letting and Management
Agency role in letting, disposal and management of units. Overall financial control , rent reviews, legal administration.
General practice surveyors, valuers, accountants, lawyers
Services, structural management, maintenance, security and repair
Facilities managers, property agents
Eventual refurbishment, improvement, redevelopment
Planners, conservationists, community groups, investors, surveyors

5. Building Design and Development
Liaison on design with user groups, business interests, highways and environmental groups
Planners, urban designers, environmentalists
Costing, procurements, tendering, project management, contracting
Construction professionals, quantity surveyors, architects, accountants
A range of generic management and business roles and tasks, overseeing the project, public relations, arbitration, negotiation
Managers, construction professionals, workforce providers, local labour initiatives

4. Site Development
Investigation of land rights, covenants, easements, constraints on scheme
Legal factors and contract issues, Capital investment , *Lawyers, chartered surveyors, valuers, accountants*
Site analysis and setting out
Landscape design and liaison, *land surveyors, landscape architects, planners*
Detailed costing design and specification
Bills of quantities, tendering agreements setting up of project management and site teams, *quantity surveyors, construction*

Figure 3.6 **The Development Process.**

Electronic Plans

In terms of development control procedures, an important innovation which is revolutionizing the efficiency of the development control system is the introduction of electronic media based recording and mapping systems. Increasingly planning offices store all their information of planning applications, decisions and policies on a computerized map reference systems. There is a trend towards local authorities adopting computerized Geographical Information Systems (GIS) ((Maguire *et al.*, 1992; Allinson, 1998). By referencing spatial data to maps through the use of powerful data bases GIS is revolutionizing planning. It enables the planning officer to be better, and more quickly, informed about the site in question. While quantitative material is more readily incorporated, technological advances are enabling qualitative data to be registered too, such as transcripts of interviews and text relevant to the site, audio material and visual data such as photographs and video footage.

The use of Geographical Information Systems (GIS) and Computer Aided Design (CAD) has grown. The Ordnance Survey has extended its role beyond merely producing maps to being providers of computerized spatial information for a wide range of public and private sector users. There are a range of national GIS data bases, and readers are recommended to consult the web for further information in this ever-changing and expanding field. Indeed the explosion of the use of e-mail, and the development of the World Wide Web (www) has been taken on board by town planning authorities. Many local authorities and central government departments have their own web pages. In some countries application for the equivalent of planning permission, contributions to public participation discussions, and voting on controversial policy issues can all be done 'on-line'. However, the DETR has its own extensive web page from which one can download many current policy documents, as detailed in the Government Publications Appendix.

THE DEVELOPMENT PROCESS

The Sequence

The wider context of the development process will be described. Rather than giving a purely planner's eye view on the process, the role of the planner is set alongside that of other development professionals, within the context of the world of property development (Grover, 1989; Lavender, 1990; Seeley, 1997; Greed, 1997a). The stages in the development of a scheme by a private sector, commercial development company will be outlined (Figure 3.6, Process of Property Development). In fact whether the developer is private sector or government, as in the case of council housing, the principles and stages are very similar. As with many dynamic processes many people are involved all at once, and the different stages and events described may happen in a slightly different sequence depending on the nature of the development.

Are the planners the developers?

There is often confusion with the difference between planners and developers. They are broadly two different groups, the developers being mainly the private sector people who initiate, co-ordinate and implement new building schemes, and the planners *inter alia* are those who exercise control over these schemes to ensure they comply with the public interest (Ambrose, 1986). However, this picture is too simplistic as there are examples of private developers and local authority planners co-operating and entering into a 'partnership scheme', for example on large shopping developments, so they are not always completely separate in professional practice (Ambrose, 1986; Ambrose and Colenut, 1979). Also local authorities have acted as developers themselves, particularly in the past, in respect of housing and amenity developments.

Whilst Cadman and Topping (1995) include within the term 'developer' the property company who put the scheme together, the investor financing the scheme, and the builder Lavender (1990) argues that the term is usually reserved for the property development company itself, or the investor on whose behalf they are operating. Thus the developer is seen to be the individual or organization who initiates a construction project: and therefore does not include the builder, designer, user, or planner. As has been seen the planner often takes the role of 'development controller' although in urban regeneration schemes nowadays the planning department may take on a more proactive, entrepreneurial role too.

Prince Charles has laid much blame on architects and planners, but some would say that he should be attacking developers, whom he seldom mentions (Prince of Wales, 1989; Hutchinson, 1989). The architects in particular are heavily constrained in the designs they put forward by the requirements of their clients and the all-prevailing cost factor. The scheme may be directly financed by pension funds, insurance companies, trusts, or by the future users in a commissioned development. They will naturally be concerned that their shareholders and investors money is being invested wisely. Nowadays many insurance companies have their own in-house property advisors, these often being surveyors and valuers who ensure that the 'portfolio' of property investment is well balanced, and that any actual development project is carefully evaluated. There may be an actual human need for better facilities in an area, but the extent of need is not the main criterion, as developers are interested in making a profit from the scheme. This is why on the accompanying diagram ('The Development Process', Figure 3.6), the first box is not the decision to develop, but rather the analysis of the property investment situation, as property (to the market) is no more than a commodity, like racehorses and oil. But if they do not take into account and respond to human need they are unlikely to find themselves with a viable scheme.

Feasibility

Before proceeding, the developers might carry out a feasibility study as to the potential catchment area and turnover of the scheme and may bring in the specialist skills of a development surveyor and property researcher for this purpose, possibly using the in-house expertise of one of the large London companies of chartered surveyors, who produce property market analysis reports. They will also need to consult with the local authority planners to find out what the zoning and overall policy is for that area. It is likely that in large or controversial schemes, planning consultants for the developers will produce a planning brief setting out the proposals as a basis for negotiation. The local planning authority may have already have drawn up its own development brief or policy statement as to what is acceptable in the area: particularly if they are located in an area such as certain parts of London where there is already demand to develop, and 'site finders' are scouring every square inch of the territory looking for development potential. The planning authority and developers are unlikely to see eye to eye at their first meeting but by a process of negotiation they can move closer towards defining a scheme which would be acceptable to both parties (Grover, 1989).

Planning Gain

As stated earlier, developers may be willing to enter into a planning gain agreement to get planning permission. The phrase 'planning gain' is a non-statutory term which covers additional 'concessions' which the local authority derives from the developer in entering into an agreement to provide certain amenities in return for a more favourable planning permission. 'Planning agreements' and 'planning obligations' are entered to under Section 106 of the Town and Country Planning Act 1991. Circular 16/91 (which updates 22/83) sets out what the parameters of what the DETR considers to be 'reasonable' factors germane to a planning gain agreement. Planning gain is not a bribe, as it is done for the benefit of the community, and has to be directly related to the development in question. Typical examples might be the provision of public conveniences, a creche in a shopping centre, landscaping, seating, and street improvements. The stakes get much higher with some London boroughs who might seek to get contributions out of the developer for community centres, local schools, and sports facilities. In fairness this is one of the few means left to local authorities nowadays to make the 'social aspects of planning' a reality in view of the cutbacks in local government finance (Ratcliffe and Stubbs, 1996).

Planning Application

When considering whether or not to give the scheme planning permission (Box III) the planning authority is not only concerned with the nature of the development itself, but with the additional traffic and car parking it is likely to generate, and with the visual townscape impact. Planners do not look at a site in isolation but in relation to its effect on the surrounding area, and the impact of this new development on the existing mix of uses. Are there already too many offices in this area? Would the use of the site for shops preclude its use at a later date for more social uses and provisions of facilities which are lacking? Would the development of a particular site prevent surface mineral extraction at a later date? Planners are therefore concerned with balance and adjusting all the land uses together. The fact that it is profitable to the developer does not necessarily mean that it is right from a town planning viewpoint.

Delay in gaining planning permission can cost a development company millions of pounds in interest payments, for 'time is money'. In some cases a scheme may go to public inquiry to deal with objections from the general public; or to appeal if the scheme is refused and the developer appeals to the Secretary of State. One should not see the planners and the developers as necessarily being adversaries, in some cases the local authority and the developers will enter into a partnership scheme together. The local authority planners have powers which can help the developers such as land assembly and compulsory purchase, and the developers have expertise in getting the scheme off the ground which are of use to the local authority. It depends, to some degree, on the location, and more particularly the region, as some areas are keen to attract developers, whereas in the South East planners can afford to be more choosy as there is much competition between developers for the right to develop on different sites. It has even been suggested that the planners ought to hold auctions and sell the right to develop to the highest bidder, as in California.

Design considerations

When it comes to the design and building of the scheme a whole range of other property professionals come into play (Boxes IV and V). First there is the architect who designs the scheme, these days it is unlikely to be just one person, but a whole team of skilled people. Interior designers are also likely to have an important role, particularly if it is a shopping mall type of development to create the right lifestyle image for the consumers (Fitch and Knobel, 1990). The planners, both public and private, will be involved in respect of the overall layout and the relationship with surrounding buildings, particularly if the development is in, or adjacent to a conservation area. Car parking, goods vehicles servicing, public transport, and the overall circulation, access, and general road layout all need to be integrated within the scheme. This will involve the specialist skills of transportation planners, and also ultimately of highway engineers. The design process is likely to last for many months, because of a thousand and one constraints and the question of the 'cost factor'. Quantity surveyors in particular are responsible for costing out the 'price' of the building. The actual cost of materials and construction is only a small part of the final value of the property. There is also the cost of the land, the initial acquisition of the site, which can be a very substantial part of the overall investment outgoings. The value of the development once built is dictated more by market forces than by construction or land costs. There may be statutory requirements for public participation and community consultation on the scheme, and there is usually likely to be a level of public opposition to larger schemes.

The property lawyer will deal with easements (Rights of Way), and the restrictive covenants which are private legal controls against certain uses or types of development on the land. There may be a confusing maze of freehold and leasehold land titles to be dealt with. Separately professionals who specialize in building contract law, and 'project management' will need to sort out the contracts, tenders, and all the legal details of dealing with the large numbers of people, contractors, and suppliers involved in building the scheme.

Once the architect has worked out the design, the quantity surveyor must work out the cost, and the project manager in control must put it out to tender and bring the contractors in to build it. There is a multitude of detailed design factors and legal factors which must to be taken into account. The actual construction will involve a large team of professionals such as civil and structural engineers, heating and ventilating engineers, etc., also a variety of building trades workers and labourers, all with their foremen, managers and back up administrators. The land surveyor also has an important role both at the beginning in setting out the site, and at the end when the development is completed, at which time it is likely that the Ordnance Survey department will send someone along to check the details of the new scheme to be included on their mapping data system ready for the next revision. However, it is more than likely that they will already have been sent copies of the new layout.

Disposal and management

When the development has been built it has to be let or sold (Box VI). Following this the building and site have to be cared for, and managed. Again this is the job of the surveyor (Cadman and Topping, 1995; Scarrett, 1983; Stapleton, 1986). There are the maintenance aspects to be considered, but beyond this janitorial role there are the other financial and legal matters to deal with. A building is not just bricks and mortar but an ongoing investment, so matters such as rent reviews, dealing with existing tenants (such as chain stores or commercial office takers) and on-going letting policy have to be managed. In larger schemes specialist facilities management professionals may be utilized. At a later date questions of alterations or redevelopment of the scheme, or indeed the question of whether the original client owner wishes to sell his interest in the property and invest elsewhere. The vast majority of all office and shopping developments are not owned by the users, but are rented to them, the freehold, or headlease belonging to a variety of financial interests including insurance companies, pension funds, and investment consortiums, and sometimes affluent individuals. Thus the cycle starts again.

TASKS

Information Gathering Tasks

I. Obtain a set of planning application forms from your local authority and study them carefully. Do you find them clear and easy to follow?

II. Identify on a map of your home town or locality, Conservation areas and other areas of special planning control

Conceptual and Discursive Tasks

III. Discuss the main stages of the planning application and determination process. Identify the main points in the process at which difficulties, delays and conflicts might arise.

IV. What are the main concerns of the development control system? Do you consider that these adequately cover the range of issues of concern nowadays?

Reflective Tasks

V. Have you had any personal experience of dealing with the planners, or planning applications, appeals, protests? Describe your experience, and build up a file of relevant material and subsequent events. Some planning applications take years to resolve themselves so do not necessarily expect a final outcome. If this question is not relevant to you, chose any one current topical planning proposal in your area and keep a file of its development.

FURTHER READING

As can be seen few references have been included in this chapter to avoid distraction, as it is intended to provide a simple descriptive account of a potentially confusing area. For those who wish to delve deeper there is a vast body of planning case law which is not incorporated into this introductory text, but which is discussed in more depth in planning law textbooks. See for example: Blackhall, Grant, M.; Heap; Denyer-Green; Telling and Duxbury; Moore, V.; Cadman and Topping; Ball and Bell; Ratcliffe and Stubbs; Speer and Dade. Readers should check the edition date and make sure they use the most recently published.

The *Encyclopaedia of Planning Law*, a loose leaf publication, provides the most up to date information, but it is unlikely at this introductory level that readers would need to go into such depth, and it is more important to understand the general principles of the system. Readers wishing to pursue legal details of development control might usefully consult the *Journal of Planning Law*, the *Planning Law Reports*, the *Property, Planning and Compensation Reports* also the *All England Law Reports* – albeit with caution as these reports are all highly detailed and might overwhelm the newcomer to the subject. Readers should ask themselves first, Why do I need to consult a more detailed reference source? Is it because I want more information, or because I have not understood the basics? If the latter is the case it would be better to consult a tutor or simply read the local newspaper, also look in the local library for examples of planning applications and ongoing plans. There are a number of on-line law reporting services, such as LawLine and Lexis, but these can only be accessed through a password. Readers should check library access status.

Part 2

THE STORY
OF PLANNING

4

HISTORICAL DEVELOPMENT

JUSTIFICATION

This section traces the story of town planning from earliest times to the end of the Georgian period that is the early years of the nineteenth century (Table 4.1). The aim of Chapter 4 is to give an overview of key themes, and to identify factors of relevance for today. The main references and sources throughout the text are listed together under Further Reading and referencing is kept to a minimum with the text. Illustrations were chosen on the basis of highlighting significant details and planning issues, rather than featuring touristically famous buildings.

It is important to know about the history of planning, including the visual aspects of planning, such as urban design and architectural style, because today great emphasis is put upon urban conservation. The main emphasis in this chapter is on British town planning and the wider context of Western European architectural development, although the importance of international influences is highlighted. The following historical periods are covered: Ancient (Egyptian), Classical (Greek and Roman), Medieval, Renaissance, and Georgian.

THE ANCIENT WORLD

Architectural features and town planning principles from ancient times have been a continual source of inspiration to designers. For example, 'neo-Egyptian' influences can be seen in 1930's architecture, and nowadays in post modern architecture. In the ancient world of Egypt, town planning and architecture had

the role of reinforcing the power of the ruling elite. Public buildings often had a mystical rather than practical purpose by modern standards. Planning can be used for a wide range of political, religious and ideological purposes. In comparison it is interesting to observe that both Hitler and Mussolini favoured heavy classical architectural styles for public buildings. Totalitarian regimes whether they are political or otherwise seem to favour for megalithic architecture on a gigantic scale. Large cities, such as Thebes with great processional routes and geometrically laid out streets were designed chiefly to meet the religious and governmental role of the state. Planning does not have to have a social welfare function, or be associated with concepts of equality and democracy.

Many of the early settlements were located where there was a good water supply, accessible transport routes, and fertile ground to support the population. A river valley was an ideal location with the town sited at the narrowest bridging-point of a river. Towns and cities in modern times can be located virtually anywhere provided there is adequate technology to overcome natural disadvantages and enough money to pay for it. In Britain, the development of the national electricity, gas, and water grids and road systems reduces the geographical restrictions on location.

Most of the ancient civilizations built their main public buildings in stone or other local materials. Until the Industrial Revolution every region in every country had its own local architecture distinguished by its local building materials and its own style which developed in response to the needs of the village culture and the constraints of the local climate. This raises the classic 'geographical determinism' debate:

Table 4.1 Chronological Phases of Architectural Style and City Development

Date	Period, style, civilization	Key manifestations
BC		
5000	Ancient Civilisations	Mesopotamia, Tigris-Euphrates Valley
3000	Egypt	Cairo, pyramids, Nile
1000	Early Greek	Knossos, Mycenae
500	Greek	Athens, Parthenon, Columns
400	Roman	Rome, grid-layout towns, roads
AD		
400	Byzantine	Constantinople
500	Dark Ages	Anglo Saxons
600	Islam	Moslems, mosques, cities
900	Norman, Europe	France, churches, defence
1066	Norman, English	William the Conqueror, cities, castles
1200	Gothic	Organic towns, Medieval, churches
1450	Renaissance	Italy, Venice, Florence
1550	High Renaissance	Rome, classical, art
1666	Great Fire of London	Rebuilding London, Wren
1700	Georgian	Bath, London, Edinburgh, Adam
1800	Regency, classical	Brighton, colonial cities
1820	Victorian	Industrial revolution, neo-gothic Garden cities, arts and crafts
1900	Modern architecture	America, international, functionalism futurism, technological change
	Edwardian	Art Nouveau, Neo-Egyptian
1945	Post-war reconstruction	New towns, planning system
1960	High rise	Town centre redevelopment, flats
1970	Reaction, conservation	Conservation areas, neo-vernacular
1980	Post modernism	Out of town centres, shed architecture
1990s	Green environmental movement	Sustainable buildings

Is it the geography of the areas which makes the people the way they are, or the people who shape the built environment? With the coming of mass-produced materials and the spread of the International style of architecture, building materials have become much similar in different countries in the twentieth century, and may be supplied by the same multi-national suppliers.

These days it is often quite difficult to obtain the original materials for restoration work and maintenance has always been a major problem in respect of ancient historical buildings the world over. The present day emphasis on conservation has broadened the emphasis to not only preserving buildings as historical monuments, but also restoring the surrounding context of the buildings which form the backcloth and setting to the main attractions. In the case of more recent (rather than ancient) historical buildings the aim is to ensure that they are conserved as part of the living fabric of the city, and are used rather than being just preserved as antiquities.

CLASSICAL GREECE

The Greek civilization is the source of many of the ideas and philosophies of Western Civilization. The classical style of architecture with its use of columns, topped by 'capitals' in the three main Greek orders, Doric, Ionic and Corinthian are still seen by many as the only 'real' architecture. The Doric has what looks like a spare tyre on the top of the column, the Ionic has 'two eyes on it' (a stylized depiction of curled rams horns), and the Corinthian has decorative acanthus leaves above the column. The Greeks developed theories on town planning, many of which they put into practice in the building of their city states and colonial towns. Most Greek settlements were based on a grid layout (streets at right angles to each other) but they combined this with a flexibility of design which took into account site characteristics. Greek settlements centred on the Agora (market place) which was surrounded by the main public buildings such as the Stoa (town hall). Not only did the Greeks build

Table 4.2 **Chronological List of Monarchs with Populations**

Population	Reign	Census	England	London
William I	1066–1087			
William II	1087–1100	1100	1,500,000	17,850
Henry I	1100–1135			
Stephen	1135–1154	1500	1,750,000	20,000
Henry II	1154–1189			
Richard I	1189–1199			
John	1199–1216	1200	2,000,000	22,500
Henry III	1216–1272	1250	2,500,000	25,000
Edward I	1272–1307	1300	3,300,000	30,000
Edward I	1307–1327			
Edward II	1327–1377	1348	4,000,000	40,000
Richard II	1377–1399			
Henry IV	1399–1413	1400	2,500,000	35,000
Henry V	1413–1422			
Henry VI	1422–1461	1450	3,000,000	50,000
Edward IV	1461–1483			
Edward V	1483			
Richard II	1483–1485			
Tudors				
Henry VII	1485–1509	1500	3,500,000	65,000
Henry VIII	1509–1547			
Edward VI	1547–1553	1550	4,000,000	80,000
Mary	1553–1558			
Elizabeth	1558–1603	1600	4,500,000	150,000
Stuarts				
James I	1603–1625			
Charles I	1625–1649			
Commonwealth	1649–1660	1650	5,500,000	400,000
Charles III	1660–1685			
James II	1685–1688			
William III	1689–1702	1700	6,000,000	600,000
Anne	1702–1714			
Hanoverians				
George I	1714–1727			
George II	1727–1760	1750	6,400,000	750,000
George III	1760–1820	1800	8,900,000	950,300
George IV	1820–1830			
William IV	1830–1837			
Victoria	1837–1901	1850	18,000,000	2,300,000
Edward VII	1901–1910	1900	32,500,000	4,500,000
Windsors				
George V	1910–1936	1930	39,750,000	8,000,000
Edward VIII	1936			
George VI	1936–1952	1950	43,700,000	8,350,000
Elizabeth II	1952–			

Figure 4.1 Pyramids Mobbed by Tourists.
Contrary to the image given by many a television documentary the pyramids do not stand in splendid isolation surrounded by desert but are victims of global mass tourism and the encroachment of urban development from Cairo.

(a)

(b)

(c)

Figures 4.2a, b, c Doric, Ionic and Corinthian Capitols, Athens, Greece.
There is a constant battle to preserve antiquities, through conservation policy. But their influence lives on throughout Western architecture. For example classical capitols are to be found in Georgian and Victorian buildings in Britain (compare Figure 3.4).

magnificent streets and buildings but they took into account the need for sanitation, drainage and water supply. Lewis Mumford (1965) stated that the quality of a civilization should be judged by the way in which it disposes of its waste material. The architecture of Athens has acted as a model for generations of architects. The Parthenon (a temple) on the top of the Acropolis (a large natural hill in the centre of the city) has inspired many travellers and is considered to embody perfect harmony of proportion. It became fashionable in the eighteenth and nineteenth centuries to make the Grand Tour of Europe, and many of the features of Greek architecture were copied back in Britain adding a 'touch of class' to the new industrial cities, e.g. Birmingham Town Hall (Briggs, 1968). Some of the buildings on and around the Parthenon are being restored, and this is the subject of much controversy. People are often startled by the fact that many of the Greek temples originally had red 'Roman' tile roofs and the walls and sculptures were decorated in bright colours.

ROMAN PLANNING

Rome completes the classical period with the emphasis shifting to a relatively more decorative and ostentatious style, Greek architecture being purer and more simple. Throughout history it is noticeable how architectural styles go in cycles from pure classical simple buildings into more and more ornate styles: ostentatious styles; mixtures and novelties; over decorative; reaction; then a return to classical simplicity. Some would say the modern movement of plain abstract architecture was a reaction against the over-decorative styles of Victorian times. The present emphasis on conservation and neo-vernacular and generally more historical styles may be leading to another decorative phase of architecture. Rome was a vast empire which extended across Europe, even as far backward to the then third world country of ancient Britain – which soon became a profitable agricultural colony. The Roman Empire was a city building enterprise and 'every Roman soldier had a town plan in his knapsack', the Army did most of the construction and many of the town planners, civil engineers, and architects were military men. Roman towns were more standardized than Greek ones, and were based on a simple grid layout with a square in the Centre, called the Forum, and several other standard public amenities were provided around the town such as baths,

Figure 4.4 Architecture at Jaipur, India.
There are many influential architectural traditions outside of Western Europe. For example, Indian architectural features, from Hindu and Mogul buildings, have been incorporated in British Architecture.

latrines, an arena, etc. There was an element of land use zoning based more on the social rank differences and occupations of the residents, with distinct areas for retail (merchants) and industrial (artisans) areas. A high proportion of the population would be slaves. Likewise when the Greeks talked about the ideal city consisting of 5,000 people they meant the people that mattered, discounting slaves, women, and tradespeople.

The greatest engineering achievements of the Romans were the perfection of the Arch and the Dome. The Coliseum in Rome is of Arch construction, as are the many aquaducts and viaducts dotted throughout the Empire. Fresh water, good sewerage and drainage and good roads were all features of Roman development, and in many respects they were never surpassed for many centuries until the time of the Industrial Revolution. The Roman town was an important colonizing tool in the Empire, acting as a garrison and an administrative centre in order to subdue the local population. Defensive walls were an essential feature of many Roman settlements. Town planning was part of a military exercise to ensure effective defensive measures. The Roman towns and interconnecting roads established the national land use and settlement pattern for Britain's subsequent development. Today many main roads, such as the A1, follow Roman routes. Many of the main towns and cities (particularly those ending in chester, or cester) are of Roman origin. Some believe the Romans were

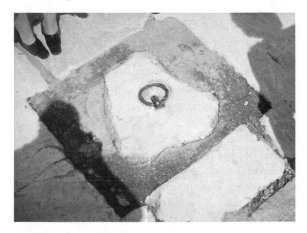

Figure 4.3 Drain Cover, Ephesus.
The greatness of a civilization may be judged by how it disposes of its sewage, according to Mumford. Many Greek and Roman cities had sewers and drains, and arguably this 'invisible architecture beneath the city streets' was centuries ahead of its time.

Figure 4.5 (a) Chartres Cathedral; and (b) Chartres Town.
The main investment of medieval times was in church and cathedral building, but often such buildings were hidden away within closeknit, tangled surrounding street patterns, designed for the glory of God rather than the human eye.

following earlier roads related to ley lines (pre-historic lines of alleged terrestrial power) and that many of their settlements were based on earlier religious or tribal centres in what was a sophisticated, but predominantly rural society that pre-dated urban civilization.

MEDIEVAL DEVELOPMENT

In the centuries after the Romans left, there were a series of invasions, for example, of Angles, Saxons, Jutes and Danes, but none of these were great city-building civilizations. Britain reverted to a rural society in which towns were market centres and local administrative nodes. The Norman Empire, which was extended in Britain by William the Conqueror in 1066 had a major effect on the land use patterns of Britain. It influenced the class structure, and feudal foundations of society. The Church was the main administrative arm of the state. The establishment of abbeys and the endowment of cathedrals led to a new spate of construction, and the development of new market places and squares and related buildings administered by the ecclesiastical powers. There were some new towns built by Edward I, and castles built mainly for defence, but in general towns grew and

expanded naturally in an unplanned organic manner (Bell and Bell, 1972). A small settlement would develop beside a river and gradually tracks would develop into roads that meandered down the valley side to a bridge. Houses would be built alongside the roads where and when the residents felt the need. Gradually other facilities, artisan quarters, houses, paddocks, and market places would develop, often centring around a well or a crossroads. Roads would follow footpaths, creating the typically irregular street pattern characteristic of medieval towns. This contrasts with the pre-designed, premeditated plan characteristic of Roman towns, and other periods of history when the design has been imposed from above by a powerful empire, military force or ruler upon the subject population.

In medieval times the main architectural styles were of two types. First there was the official architecture of the Church. The Norman style (with a rounded arch) pre-dates the Gothic style (pointed arch) which went through various phases from a simple basic style to a very decorative exaggerated style. The Gothic style was a much copied in later centuries especially by the Victorians. Local vernacular styles developed in different parts of the country dependent on availability of materials and local weather conditions. Thatch and

▲ *Figure 4.7* **Organic Street Pattern, Northern Italy.**
Whilst planned towns were generally based on a grid layout, naturally evolving settlements tended to be more random and human in scale.

◄ *Figure 4.6* **Glastonbury Abbey, Somerset.**
Likewise in England, church architecture was dominant. Church, abbey, and castle were key buildings. Note the arches shown, norman rounded and gothic pointed. Such features were widely copied in secular buildings in Victorian times.

half-timbering were not universal, indeed slate and stone were probably more common in some areas, and 'cob' in others. Nowadays neo-vernacular is a popular style. Mock Tudor, also known as pseudo-Tudor, is a variation of neo-veo (neo-vernacular) which has always been scorned by architects and loved by the people.

Towns and cities tend to evolve naturally, if somewhat chaotically, and not necessarily in the ideal interests of all the residents. In recent years, almost in reaction against 'overplan', there has been a return to enthusiasm for organic natural town forms. Paradoxically to achieve this effect today, with a new housing layout for example, requires a good deal of forethought and planning to create a genuine quaint townscape! Another effect of current planning which emphasizes the virtues of the past, and conservation in particular, has been to stop the natural change that would normally occur. Ordinary street scenes usually contain buildings from different historical periods positioned cheek by jowl; some clashing and some complementary. An emphasis on design policy controls may lead to an artificial sterilization of a quality townscape.

VERNACULAR BUILDING

Before the mass production of bricks, and their nationwide distribution by rail in the nineteenth century, each region of Britain had its own distinctive style reflecting the availability of local materials, and climatic factors, e.g. houses in areas of heavy rainfall such as West Wales had a steeply pitched roof, and the roof would be built of local slate rather than thatch. One of the most common styles in the South-East and Midlands was half timbering, This was originally introduced by the Anglo Saxons, who originated in areas where there was ample supply of wood in Central Europe. The areas between the wood were filled in with wattle and daub and with other materials which were locally available, e.g. flints. In areas where stone was available this became the main material, different qualities were given to the buildings by different building materials, e.g. hard stone and granites in the Penines (which weathered to black) as against soft golden stone in parts of the South West. The colour and texture of the materials used were important factors in creating the townscape and atmosphere. Cob a mixture of clay,

Figure 4.8 A Village Scene, Somerset.
Many a village was to grow into a town or even a city, but some have retained their rustic features and vernacular style, albeit modified by rural gentrifiers.

sand, mud, was a material used in areas such as Devon where neither stone nor wood were plentiful local materials. Walls were built to approximately 2 feet thick to create a flexible load-bearing construction which stood by its own weight, as is found in Dorset. Gable ends of cob and half-timbering were sometimes decorated by pargetting, with folk art patterns and mouldings raised in 'stucco'

Clunch consists of blocks of chalk which are used like stones. Chalk is porous, so a dampcourse of hard stone or brick was often inserted first, while tar from the boat building industry was used in some seaside areas along the south coast of England. Weatherboarding is an attractive form of exterior cladding often found in seaside areas, and apparently 'copied' from the design of ships. It consists, in England, normally of horizontal slats of wood used to clad wattle walls. However, in North America wood boarding and wooden shingles are frequently used on their own as the main structural material, particularly in New England. In Britain tile-hanging on walls was often used as another form of weather protection on the windward end of the building, often in conjunction with weatherboarding. Bricks were not a native material, but were imported from Holland, although there are early examples left by the Romans. Bricks were used for expensive public and royal buildings, Hampton Court in Kingston upon Thames in London being a classic example from Tudor times (parts of

which were burnt down and later restored). During the Industrial Revolution there was a boom in factory made bricks which replaced most of the traditional building materials. Likewise mass produced roof tiles replaced traditional materials such as thatch, and slate roofing. (Prizeman, 1975; Munro, 1979: Oliver, 1997).

THE RENAISSANCE

Toward the end of the Middle Ages in Europe the influence of the Church became less dominant in the prosperous city states which were developing particularly in Italy, where self-made business men and merchants, rather than traditional feudal powers, took control. There was a re-birth (re-naissance) of interest in the ideas and culture of the classical civilization of the Greeks and Romans, which were considered more appropriate to then modern values than the mystical emphasis of the Middle Ages. There was enthusiasm for the use of classical features in new public buildings and palaces to express the wealth of the merchant princes, e.g. the Medicis in Florence. Splendid new town planning features were introduced to Italian Cities, which were in effect major central area re-development occurred. Emphasis was put on the creation of a formal central square (along the lines of the forum, or agora), namely the piazza. Most Mediterranean settlements have squares which often act as 'outdoor living rooms' where people meet and eat in the pavement cafés, and walk around in the cool of the evening. Many Italian cities of the late Middle Ages had been built at fairly high density owing to the need for defensive city walls. It was dangerous and expensive to extend them even if population growth occurred. The layout was shaped by the need for defence. Many examples can be seen in Italy, and in the planning books for geometrically laid out military settlements with octagonal, star-shaped, and circular forms. The outdoor squares acted as important safety valves in providing communal open space, and areas for military parades and carnivals. Later Renaissance piazzas often incorporated a colonnaded walk way in the classical style along one side, and fountains and statues in the centre.

The use of perspective techniques to create space and depth in paintings was carried over into town

Figures 4.9a **A Small Square in Venice.** *b* **A Model of the Key Elements in the Renaissance Square.**
At all levels from the inner house 'patio' to the public space 'piazza' the square was the key element of Renaissance town planning, providing a social and functional focal point.

planning. Long narrow squares with a statue or townscape feature placed strategically at the 'vanishing point' drew the eye into a greater perception of three-dimensional space. Windows on a building became progressively, but imperceptibly, smaller as the upper floors were reached giving an illusion of height. Town planning and architecture had more in common with a theatrical stage set design and 'art', rather than with modern-day practical, functional land use planning.

Venice is a renaissance city of particular interest to modern planners. It had all the features of piazza planning but also served as an ideal example of complete pedestrian–vehicular segregation as there no roads in Venice, only canals. Originally Venice consisted of a series of swamps and small islands that were reclaimed by the construction of drainage canals. Each small artifically-constructed island was centred on a well in

a piazza, in which fresh water rose up naturally from the artesian basin under the sea bed. A natural 'neighbourhood unit' developed around each well. Another interesting feature of Venice is the unique architectural style, a combination of Classical, Gothic and Eastern Mediterranean Moslem influences. This style was often copied, particularly by the Victorians.

The renaissance style developed on a more magnificent scale known as the High Renaissance style quickly followed by the Baroque and the Rococo styles. Various Popes in conjunction with leading artists and architects of the time, such as Michelangelo and Bernini, progressively redeveloped the centre of Rome creating magnificent squares and processional avenues. St. Peters Basilica was rebuilt in a style that resembled a pagan Roman temple, replacing the Gothic structure which was destroyed by fire. The Baroque style of planning and architecture made good use of the space around and between buildings. An obelisk (pointed stone column monument) was often used in the centre of a square to act as a central pivot to the geometrical layout of avenues and buildings radiating from it. No expense was spared, but the purpose of this type of town planning was not to rehouse the poor, to zone industry or solve traffic problems; indeed, these matters were of little interest. The grand manner of Renaissance planning gradually spread throughout Europe. It was the ideal style to express the power and magnificence of the ruler and the state. Many European cities were replanned (some several times over) with boulevards, squares, fountains, statues and triumphal arches. Town planning was essentially a form of art aimed at meeting the aspirations of the rising merchant classes and affluent bourgeoisie.

GEORGIAN PLANNING

The development of Georgian planning and architecture resulted from the influence of the Renaissance on Britain. The style and scale are significantly different from the Grand Manner in Europe (Summerson, 1986). The Georgian style is so named as it developed at the time when a series of King Georges were on the throne between 1714–1830 (George I–IV) (Tables 4.1 and 4.2). It is a mixture of classical Italian renaissance features with other influences from Northern Europe. In particular the Dutch had developed (with their usual enthusiasm for frugality, cleanliness and puritanism), a distinctive domestic (housing) architectural style as expressed in the neat, but restrained, symmetrically-proportioned brick town houses in Amsterdam with sash windows and gabled façades. Brick, being a relatively expensive building material in Britain, was usually used only in great houses, being imported from the Low Countries (Holland and Belgium), although brick was also made in small quantities in London, Luton and Bridgwater. Following the Great Fire of London in 1666, an opportunity arose to rebuild the capital with a grand manner comprehensive master plan approach to planning, but not without much opposition from individual landowners. The monarchy did not have the power of some of its European counterparts to impose a plan from above. Individual real property rights and increased parliamentary democracy meant that redevelopment was inevitably going to be piecemeal.

A series of individual speculative developments emerged, many of which took the form of town squares with Georgian town houses facing on to grass and trees in the middle of a square. The houses themselves, intended for the new affluent middle classes, were a mixture of Dutch features and classical elements with an emphasis on symmetry, sash windows, and Greek pediments, and columns, rather than traditional gables. The squares were no doubt inspired by the Italian piazza, and had a soft grass centre rather than a hard paved surface, thus prefiguring the garden city movement's love of grass and trees. Individual front gardens were not favoured, being considered rather rural and peasant like, but there were often long walled back gardens, and separate mews at the rear for the servants and the horses. Names such as Bedford Square, Grosvenor Square, and Sloane Square bear witness to the property development abilities of the ducal landowners who possessed estates in what is now the West End, Kensington, and Chelsea. The main city churches and St. Paul's Cathedral were rebuilt by Sir Christopher Wren following the Great Fire of London in 1666. St Paul's is in the style of St Peter's in Rome, whereas many of the other Wren churches are more English, yet still classical in design.

Prior to the fire, Inigo Jones, the king's surveyor, had built the Covent Garden scheme, just outside the

Figure 4.10 Back Streets in Bath.
Bath does not only consist of the grand squares and crescents, but it is held together by all the small backstreets and incidental features which make it a 'real city', capable of accommodating a wide range of social classes and urban functions.

Figure 4.11 Trafalgar Square, London.
So much of 'tourist London' is composed of Georgian, Regency and Victorian Architecture, which is also part of the living fabric of the city.

City of London. This was designed along the lines of an Italian piazza with a colonnaded walkway and town houses facing the square. An opera house and theatre was provided for the leisure and pleasure of the residents. A small market was held on the square from time to time. Over the centuries the market became the main fruit and vegetable market for London and the area declined socially. In the early 1960s the market was relocated at Nine Elms, Vauxhall, and the area seemed threatened with demolition, eventually becoming a conservation area and an upmarket tourist attraction. Many of the original working-class residents despaired that they no longer 'fitted in' to the area and could not afford to live there any more. London continued to grow throughout Georgian times to develop as a prosperous capital and eventually in the nineteenth century as a world capital of the Empire. This role was reflected in the architecture of individual buildings in Georgian and Victorian times. Yet, there was no comprehensive replanning of the whole of London in the grand manner. In the early nineteenth century in Regency times (named after the Prince Regent) part of the Crown Estates just to the north of the centre of London, namely Regent's Park, was developed as a series of upmarket town houses by John Nash. Further developments occurred down Regent Street to Clarence House, a north–south axis on the boundary between Soho and Mayfair. Trafalgar Square, the Mall, Piccadilly Circus, Oxford Circus,

and Buckingham Palace were all part of this grand design. In fact the scheme developed over many years, with the Victorians altering and enlarging various elements of the original Regency scheme.

In Georgian and Regency times a large number of provincial towns and resorts was developed to meet the needs of the new affluent leisured classes. The early resorts were mainly inland and centred on spas where people could 'take the waters', e.g. in Bath, Cheltenham, Harrogate, Epsom complete with racecourse, Hotwells in Bristol, and Brixton in South London. Later sea bathing became the fashion, and a second series of resorts were developed, including Brighton with its Regency Pavilion, Skegness, and later Weston-super-Mare. It was not until the development of the railways that these became popular working-class resorts. Bath is one of the most famous spa towns. Its importance was established when Queen Anne 'took the waters' there for her rheumatism in the 1720's. But Beau Nash really popularized and publicized the city when he was made the Post Master for Bath. He has been compared with Billy Butlin by creating the holiday industry, in this case, encouraging wealthy people to come for 'the season'. Bath is composed of a series of terraces, squares, and crescents all designed in the Georgian style. Even the smaller houses, back streets, and mews buildings are designed in a similar style creating a totally co-ordinated 'designer' environment. Houses in those days were built to different

Figure 4.12 Edinburgh Centre.
Edinburgh incorporated Renaissance features, interpreted in local stone, giving it its own particular gritty style and rugged grandeur.

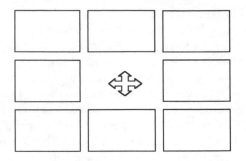

Figure 4.13a The Formal Grid Layout Settlement.
Usually military or colonial in purpose e.g. Roman towns.

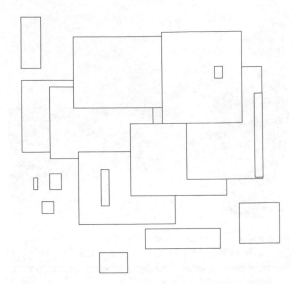

Figure 4.13d The Modern City is Characterized by the Effects of Town Planning, Zoning and Decentralization.
American cities are the most pronounced version of this, including Los Angeles where the motorcar has rendered walking distances meaningless.

Figure 4.13b The Organic Town Which Grew Naturally.
Usually with a centre around a bridge and market e.g. medieval town which grew from a village.

Figure 4.13e The Linear City.
Strung out like beads on a necklace each 'bead' having its own centre and neighbourhood, all connected by a linear transport route. The linear city can be joined to form a continuous ring or annular city.

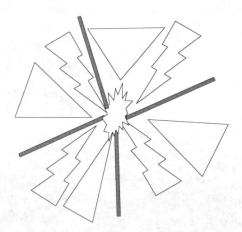

Figure 4.13c The Radial City Based on Rail and Road Networks.
Usually a nineteenth or early twentieth century city.

Figures 4.13a, b, c, d, e Summary Diagrams of Main Types of City Form.

maximum sizes which were taxed at different levels of 'rates' and this was a considerable constraint on the design and density of the housing planned. In Bath there were six main rating levels in operation. Thus the phrase, 'it's only second rate', originally meant it was not quite the best type of housing. Nash worked in conjunction with the two architects named John Wood the Elder and John Wood the Younger (father and son), who created an atmosphere of refinement and classical culture in designing a city of Georgian town houses.

All this was done through private enterprise without any major government intervention or special powers, though there were some elementary by-laws and build-ing regulations in some areas which influenced the architectural style to a small degree. There is no doubt that aesthetically Bath is a great achievement and that even today it has retained its 'classiness' as a desirable place to live, in spite of various attacks by bombers, planners, and property developers.

This chapter has concentrated on English towns, but it should be noted that both Dublin, and Edinburgh in the 'New Town' also provide magnifi-cent examples of classical development. Chapter 4 has also focused upon urban development. An account of the history of rural development is to be found in the next chapter.

TASKS

Information Gathering Task

I. What are the main historical periods represented in the town or city where you live, or with which you are familiar? Draw a map showing the extent and boundaries of the main phases of development.

Conceptual Tasks

II. What are the advantages and disadvantages of grid layout planned settlements, as against settlements which developed organically without pre-planning? Relate your answer to examples of historical settlements with which you are familiar.

III. 'Planning is for people'. Discuss the applicability of this statement to renaissance and baroque period town planning

Reflective Tasks

IV. Is there an historic area, monument or landmark near you that has become a tourist feature? What are your views on how it is managed and presented to the public? Do you consider its image is authentic or has it been subject to 'disneyfication?

V. Which architectural style do you prefer? What are your views on vernacular traditional architectural styles?

FURTHER READING

History of Planning books include: Bacon, Bor, Benevelo, Betjeman, Bor, Burke, Cherry, Dyos, Hall, Morris, Mumford, Oliver, Penoyre, Pevsner, Prizeman, RTPI (1986), Ravetz, and Summerson, which are all to be found in the bibliography. More sociological accounts which reflect upon pre-industrial and modern cities include Sjoberg and Mumford.

5

INDUSTRIALIZATION AND URBANIZATION

PHYSICAL CHANGE

Introduction

At the beginning of the nineteenth century Britain was undergoing major economic and social change (Ashworth, 1968; Briggs, 1968). There was already a long historical tradition of town planning before this period, dating back into the ancient world of Greece and Rome which provided Western civilization with the classical style of architecture and urban design (Burke, 1977; Mumford, 1965). But town planning, prior to the Industrial Revolution, was based on quite narrow objectives, such as the desire to create beautiful architectural set pieces. Nineteenth-century town planning was more down to earth in its concern with public health, sanitation and with meeting the functional requirements of industry and transportation. Georgian town planning was aimed mainly the upper and middle classes, as against nineteenth century planning which sought to meet the needs of the industrial working classes, especially in respect of housing. The demand for town planning was called forth by a combination of the effect of three main factors, namely, industrialization, urbanization, and population growth, and the related problems of overcrowding and disease. The Industrial Revolution, as its name suggests transformed Britain from a predominantly rural agricultural society to a modern industrial urban society (Ryder and Silver, 1990). Changes in agricultural methods in the eighteenth century led to greater yields produced by fewer agricultural labourers. In some areas this created a surplus of workers, leading to migration to the towns, thus providing the necessary workforce for the Industrial Revolution.

Industrialization

Development of new forms of technology, and in particular the creation of machinery which could produce manufactured goods much faster than the human hand, led to major changes in the nature of work, and the duties of the workforce. Originally, for example, textiles had been hand produced by individuals sitting at their looms and spinning wheels in their separate cottages. The introduction of mechanical forms of power which drove several machines at once required the assembly of many workers (called 'factors') and machines, all together in the same building which became known as 'the factory'. Initially industrial development occurred on a fairly small scale, fitting in with the surroundings with little disturbance, because early woollen mills and factories were powered by water power. The first industrial settlements were relatively rural being placed alongside fast flowing streams in hilly countryside.

Later coal was used to fuel steam engines which could power many more machines at once, by means of connecting drive belts running throughout the factory. New industrial settlements grew up located alongside the coalmines particularly in the North, Midlands, and South Wales. The emphasis shifted from the production of textiles in rural areas, to iron and steel, and later manufactured goods in highly urbanized areas, as a result of technological development. These were aimed at the home market, and at the expanding overseas markets which resulted from the growth of the British Empire in the nineteenth century. People flocked to the newly industrializing areas, resulting in rural depopulation and a complete regional redistribution of the population broadly from the south toward the north and across from the west country to south Wales.

In the later stages of industrialization other forms of power were developed which could be transmitted anywhere nationally, such as gas and electricity. In theory anything could be developed anywhere, provided there was the financial backing to do so. This led to the phenomenon of 'footloose' industry which went wherever it was most economically viable to locate. Nevertheless, industrial development was inevitably attracted to locate in areas which had already established themselves as business centres, because they offered high concentrations of skilled workers, the necessary infrastructure and commercial expertise to help run the businesses, and markets needed to sell the products. Nowadays access to transport routes for distribution purposes, especially the need to be near motorway junctions, or within prestigious motorway corridors such as the M4, is likely to be more important than being near sources of local power because of the ubiquity of the national grid. Modern high technology industries are different in their education and skill requirements from those of the past. Industrialists often find that suitable personnel are more likely to be drawn from the traditional office and 'quaternary' workers (see below) living in the south and south-east, than among the skilled and unskilled manual workers of the north and midlands (Massey *et al.*, 1992).

Transport Revolution

The goods produced had to be transported to their markets both within Britain and overseas. In the late eighteenth century the turnpike road system developed, which served the early years of the industrial revolution at the turn of the century, but this proved to be an expensive and bumpy way of transporting manufactured goods. It was soon overtaken by the development of the canal system, which was especially backed by the Staffordshire pottery manufacturers to ensure less breakages en route.

At its height this provided an extensive system connecting the main industrial centres, markets, and ports throughout Britain, but it was soon upstaged by the development of the railway system. Nowadays the canal system provides a valuable leisure and environmental asset which is painstakingly being restored in

Figure 5.1 Industrial Settlement with Steam Train.
Both urban and national structure were transformed by the development of mills and factories and the new railway system for the distribution of goods. The industrial and transport revolution were inseparable.

many parts of the country, mainly through voluntary initiatives which have only latterly attracted government support, as in the case of the Kennett and Avon Canal which links London to Bristol. The railways developed as a viable form of transport as a result of the invention of steam power. Watt's steam engine was stationery and revolutionized factory production, driving the machinery; but George Stephenson developed the steam engine to pull a train along metal rails. Horse-drawn rail transport had previously only been used to a very limited extent in coal mining areas. The first main passenger railway was the Stockton to Darlington Railway opened in 1825, growth continued, until at the peak in the 1870's there were nearly 16,000 miles of railway track.

In the nineteenth century Britain was a major maritime power and trading nation, and this affected the settlement pattern and nature of urbanization at home. Raw materials and ready markets were provided by the territories comprising the British Empire. Therefore new docks became an important part of development, as can be seen in the extensive dockland areas today in London, Liverpool and Bristol. Britain had been a maritime nation for nearly 1,000 years. There was already a vast amount of trade in exotic goods, including the infamous triangle of trade in sugar and slaves, between Africa, the West Indies and Europe: involving ports such as Bristol and Liverpool long before the Industrial Revolution. Today it is difficult to imagine that the London Docklands area with its marinas and upmarket housing was once a industrial and warehousing area with working-class housing and communities alongside the docks.

Urbanization

The growth in industrialization was accompanied by the growth of towns and cities, and also population growth.

Tables 5.1a and b shows the tremendous rate of urban growth occurring in the new industrial towns and cities which were doubling and tripling in size.

While there was overall growth, there was also a large movement of the population from one area of the country to another on a regional basis, and a migration to the towns from the countryside. This may be summed up in the following statement:

1801–80 per cent of the population was rural.
1991–80 per cent of the population is urban.

Not only were there changes in the quantity of people in towns and cities, but inevitably there was a decline in the quality of their lives owing to disease and overcrowding (Ravetz, 1986). Conditions and standards were not much different from the situation in rural areas at that time. Rural folk managed with fairly elementary methods of sewage disposal in small villages, but the sheer concentration of numbers in the new cities increased the likelihood of disease developing in the crowded alleyways and tenements. These problems could not be solved by personal individual efforts but required civic initiatives and national solutions.

VICTORIAN ARCHITECTURE

Victorian architecture was decorative and 'heavy' in style. It was eclectic, incorporating features from a range of historical styles, in particular the Gothic and the Classical. But also with the expansion of the British Empire, a range of features from all over the world were incorporated too, including Indian, Egyptian, and Chinese. This type of architecture fell out of favour while the Modern Movement held sway,

Table 5.1a UK Population Growth, 1801–1901

Date	Total population
1801	8.9 million
1851	17.9 million
1901	32.5 million

See Ashworth, 1968: 7 for fuller details.

Table 5.1b England: Urban Growth, 1801–1901

Date	Birmingham	Manchester	Leeds
1801	71,000	75,000	53,000
1851	265,000	336,000	172,000
1901	765,000	645,000	429,000

See Ashworth, 1968 for fuller details of many towns.

in which the emphasis was on clear-cut lines and 'honesty' in building style. It is recognized today that Victorian architecture and townscape made a valuable contribution to the urban fabric, as reflected in the listing of many buildings from this period.

The Victorians liked to build solid enduring public buildings using stone and often a range of marble, e.g. Portland stone transported from Dorset by rail for use in London. Civic pride and public building works went hand in hand with reform which often took the form of what was called 'gas and water socialism', that is investment in public works to build up the necessary infrastructure (Dixon and Muthesius, 1978). A vast amount of investment went 'under the city streets' in the form of sewers and drains (Bell and Bell, 1972). The new wealth derived from the industrial revolution was used, by the city fathers and urban benefactors, to add prestige and respectability to the new industrial cities such as Manchester, Leeds and Liverpool and to build magnificent town halls, museums, libraries and art galleries. Society was strongly divided into classes which lived in different parts of the city and had different travel routes. Working-class mill workers may never have visited the new central business district, and if they did they were unlikely to have gained entrance into the galleries.

Many industrial buildings particularly warehouses were given the full architectural treatment and there were many examples of magnificent buildings in commonplace industrial settings, among declining docklands and industrial zones, although many of these have since been renovated and incorporated in the new gentrified schemes. Railway stations and other pub-

Figure 5.2 The Law Courts, London.
The Victorians and Edwardians built a range of splendid public buildings. They also built sewers and drains and provided essential public facilities as shown in the foreground, creating the basic infrastructure for modern cities to build upon.

lic buildings, workhouses, police stations, asylums, public conveniences were all however more humble in design, but still given some architectural embellishment. In the case of workhouses and prisons the style of architecture was intended to give the inmates a sense of the overpowering fortress like strength of the buildings and the harshness of their circumstances. Also because people were unsure about travelling on the new railways it was thought that if they were made to look like great cathedrals people would be less afraid because they thought they were going to church. Toward the end of the nineteenth century a reaction was setting in to the excesses of Victorian architecture. Magnificent new structures in the form of factories, bridges, warehouses, and engine sheds (built by people such as Isambard Kingdom Brunel) were still seen as 'engineering', although they proved to be the true ancestors of modern architecture.

How Bad Was It?

A false impression is given by suggesting that the entire population at the time of the Industrial Revolution worked in factories and lived in poor housing in the north. In fact, conditions varied considerably according to people's social class and the region in which they lived.

Relatively speaking, there was an increase in overall national prosperity. There was a considerable amount of building of commercial premises, town halls, libraries, and the beginnings of modern High Street development, with large rows of individual shops and early department stores: all these buildings together creating the foundations of the modern Central Business District (CBD). There was also emphasis on the building of town parks and playingfields, which today are often seen as a luxury by both developers

Figure 5.3 Small Terraced Housing, Easton, Bristol.

Figure 5.4 Victorian Villas, Redland, Bristol.

and local authorities. Many such open spaces are in danger of development, as they are often located in what are central area sites with high land values.

Likewise not all residential development consisted of sub-standard working class housing and slum properties, but of town houses and villas. The nineteenth century was the most prolific period for house building, and this included the construction of middle-class villas, town houses, and substantial terraces which still occupy large tracts of our cities. There were also areas of better quality, skilled artisan and respectable working-class housing consisting of miles of little terraced houses built on a grid layout – much of this is ideal building stock even today. Many Victorian residential areas have been recolonized (gentrified) by the middle classes. Erstwhile 'slum' houses within the inner city such as Islington, London are now areas with some of the highest property values in Britain.

Housing problems occurred in the nineteenth century chiefly in areas where there was a concentration of large numbers of working class people in poorly built housing around the new factories and mills. They located there, because at the beginning of the Industrial Revolution, there was very little money or time for commuting and the transport systems had not yet developed, so people were huddled together

in proximity to their workplace. At first it was a matter of converting existing housing. For example, larger inner city town houses were subdivided into separate dwellings, in some cases whole families were living in one room or cellar (Ashworth, 1968). A few factory owners provided cheap housing for their workforce, although they may have deducted the cost from the workers' wages; the philanthropic factory owners were the exception to the rule.

Many local builders cashed in, building substandard tenements and terraces, which were 'jerry built' (apparently a phrase deriving from the reputation of the work of a particularly bad builder of that name). Houses were often 'half a brick thick' (i.e. thin, substandard walls) and 'back to back'. What appeared to be a terrace of ordinary houses, in fact contained *twice* the number of dwellings, because the houses were divided at the ridge of the roof and backed onto each other, creating two 'rows' of houses, one facing on to the street and the other facing onto the back-alley way.

Suburbanization and Transport

For centuries, cities had been relatively close knit because the extent of cities and the distances between

***Figure 5.5* Townhouses, London.**
Houses ranged from substantial townhouses and villas to more modest terraced properties. Many large Victorian villas, subsequently became 'inner city' dwellings, becoming rundown and were subdivided by the post-war period but they have since experienced gentrification and refurbishment.

(LNER) and Southern Region (SR). They were not nationalized and unified until the mid-twentieth century, and therefore a considerable variety of architecture developed with each railway company having its own style, as is the case of the well-conserved railway village at Swindon. Following privatization in the late twentieth century separate styles are developing again for different railway companies.

Tramway systems contributed to decentralization, and were popular for many years. In Britain they were removed by the middle of the twentieth century, but many European cities have kept their trams. The London Underground system was opened in 1863. With the invention of the internal combustion engine, public transport was augmented, particularly after 1918, by omnibuses, which were not limited to a fixed linear track and could go anywhere. The buses, and of course the subsequent development of the private motorcar, led to a veritable explosion of suburbanization, for, provided there were passable roads people could for the first time in history travel anywhere they wanted at considerable speed. The bicycle became popular in the late nineteenth century and is making a comeback today. These changes in transport technology further encouraged cities to grow and to segment into distinct land use zonings, in particular

different land uses and amenities had been governed by the distances which people could comfortably walk or go by horse. With the introduction of mechanical means of transport, people could travel further, and more quickly than they could walk, and cities began to spread out horizontally. With the development of the railway system, those who were more affluent moved further out and commuted into the town centre, starting the trend of suburbanization and decentralization which has been a major feature of urban development in Britain over the last 150 years. Many small towns owe their very existence and prosperity to the development of the railways, being blessed with a station which brought with it potential customers for local goods and services. Other towns were more directly involved as major interchange points on the railway system, e.g. Crewe, or major producers of rolling stock, such as Swindon. The railways were grouped into four large companies in 1923, Great Western Railway (GWR), London Midland and Scottish (LMS), London and North Eastern Railway

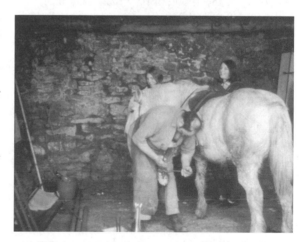

***Figure 5.6* The Oldest Means of Transport, Blacksmiths, Winford, Somerset.**
Until the nineteenth century cities' growth was limited by the scope of horse-based travel and by walking distances. Nowadays horses have become 'pets' and luxury items but in the past they were seen as 'vehicles' and as necessities.

for the industrial and residential (the work and the home) areas to be separated out (Greed, 1994a). At the same time the traditional Central Business District, that is the centre with all the offices, shops, and civic buildings remained pivotal, expanding and acquiring increased importance in servicing the needs of trade and finance which had expanded as a result of the Industrial Revolution.

The logical conclusion, in order to create maximum efficiency, was to abandon the traditional radial, circular form of cities and build linear developments along the main routes, with concentrations of housing ideally located at relatively high density, clustering around each railway station or tramway stop. It was important to have enough people living close to each stop, within walking distance, in order to make the developments viable in enabling passengers to reach them without them having to use a secondary form of transport each time. For example, in Spain Arturo Soria y Mata suggested the concept of the linear city – he visualized it stretching right across Europe from Cadiz in the south of Spain across to Leningrad (now St. Petersburg) in the north-west of Russia (Hall, 1992)! The linear form could be joined up to form an circular 'ring' city, or turned in on itself as a figure of eight, such as in Runcorn New Town Plan, near Liverpool, in the 1960s. Soria y Mata only succeeded in building a few kilometres outside Madrid (Hall, 1989: 70).

As motor cars grew in number, public transport declined. Nowadays people without cars in some areas are worse off in terms of transport than their ancestors were in the nineteenth century. The motor car soon became popular in the USA even amongst relatively low income people, thanks to the cheap mass production methods of Henry Ford. One of the main concerns for planners in the twentieth century has been with the problem of planning for the motorcar.

Frank Lloyd Wright (1869–1959) an American architect, developed the idea of a city planned entirely for the motor car, 'Autopia', as proposed for Broadacre City in the 1930s. This was to be based on a very low density grid with every house being like a homestead with a 1 acre plot in which they would grow their own food. The settlement would not have a centre in the traditional sense but the districts would be focussed around the gas station (petrol station). This vision is what some American cities actually became like, such as Los Angeles where everybody drives rather than walks. Those who do not have cars, e.g. the poor, or who are unable to drive such as the young and old, are at a severe disadvantage, and have to depend on limited public transport or the goodwill of others.

Rural and Regional Perspectives

As a result of the development of the railways, Britain 'shrank', because it was now much easier to travel, and few areas were very far from a railway station. The urban/rural division was rapidly breaking down. Some of the industrial settlements, whilst appearing very urbanized and concentrated around the mill or the mine, were in fact near to the countryside. In the Welsh Valleys, or parts of Derbyshire it is a short walk to be out of the industrial environment and into the open countryside. The effects of industrial activity, especially mining, encroached to some extent on the surrounding countryside, spewing out slag heaps and pollution, leaving behind an extensive burden of industrial dereliction. Such land is still being reclaimed for example by the Welsh Development Agency (WDA) in South Wales, and as part of projects such as the 1992 Garden Festival at Ebbw Vale. This was different from the situation in the south of England

Figure 5.7 **Forth Bridge, Scotland.**
Railway engineering and architecture represented the height of technological development at the time, yet many railway stations were designed in gothic church architecture, perhaps to allay passengers' fears.

where large amounts of manufacturing industry developed within inner city areas, often as back-street business in erstwhile residential areas. Many houses on main roads were converted into shops or businesses, as one can quite clearly see when looking down on the buildings from the top of a double-decker bus that the shop fronts were added later. Urban development spread out, in all directions with hardly a break, covering many miles in and around the London region.

Some of the most industrialized, urbanized, as well as commercialized areas of Britain were in the south, concentrated in the inner London boroughs with large working-class populations to match. In the south, the office and commercial revolution followed hard on the heels of industrial revolution, creating a new 'proletariat' made up of clerks, typists, service industry workers, and shopkeepers who were often arguably perceived as middle class and thus unworthy of special attention, in spite of their low incomes and poor working conditions.

Figure 5.8 Longleat, Mungo Gerry Concert, 1960s. Although both the Industrial Revolution in the nineteenth century and the growth of 'pop culture' in the twentieth may be seen as evidence of greater modernity and equality, landed estates still comprise a substantial component of land use and power structures within Britain.

SOCIAL CHANGE

Employment Structures

Not only were the settlement pattern and the nature of cities changed as a result of the Industrial Revolution, there were also major changes taking place within the nature of urban society itself and the patterns of daily life. The changes which occurred in the nature of social class divisions, the family, and community, and the relationship between home and work, male and female, and in people's daily lives will now be discussed. All of these were manifested in the nature of the layout and zoning of towns and cities.

'Class' is a complex word to define. A typical twentieth-century definition of a social class, is 'a number of persons sharing a common social position in the economic order' (Chinoy, 1967). For the purposes of this chapter, 'class' should be taken in the common sense of meaning of people's social position in terms of their work and way of life. As a result of the Industrial Revolution, the structure of society changed. New types of class divisions and occupations emerged as a result of new technological inventions, and wider changes in the economy itself. In the traditional rural society of the past, a relatively feudal static social system existed, the inhabitants of a typical village consisting

of the land owners and the agricultural labourers, with a vicar and a few skilled trades people in the middle, but without an intermediate middle class or large numbers of working class people, who worked in factories rather than on the land. People did not have a social class as such, but rather were endowed with a certain status, which they were born with, and all human relationships were governed by this. The static and deferential nature of pre-industrial social attitudes is summed up in the following ditty,

> God bless the squire and his relations,
> And keep us in our proper stations.
>
> (Anon.)

With the coming of the industrial revolution social structure was transformed, as large numbers of people moved from the villages and set up home in the new industrial cities swelling the ranks of the new working classes. It now became acceptable to classify people in relation to what their occupation was, rather than what they were born as. Most noticeable was the development of a new industrial working class, or rather working classes, as they were many and varied. However, in spite of all these changes, a small minority continued to own the majority of the wealth and land (Norton-Taylor, 1982).

In the modern industrial society the workforce is clearly defined. Workers may be classified as: primary workers – those employed in basic industries such as agriculture, mining, heavy industry; secondary workers – those involved in manufacturing; tertiary workers – those engaged in office work and the service industry. A further category is also recognized, namely quaternary workers who are those involved in research and development, higher professional work and the creation of knowledge. There is much debate over the use of socio-economic classifications, these occupational groupings used for government census purposes have recently undergone revision (ONS, 1998). Male factory employment was the largest growing sector in the nineteenth century. Professional, office, and service industry employment have been the largest growing sectors in the second part of the twentieth century, with large numbers of women entering the office sector in particular. Of the 16 million male and female inhabitants of England and Wales recorded by the 1841 census a little under 1 million were in domestic service. Throughout the nineteenth century, and indeed until 1914, domestic service was the largest single employment for English women, and the second largest for the population. Within society as a whole, traditional 'master and servant' social divisions co-existed alongside the new emerging industrial class structures.

Relationship between 'work and home'

As a result of the Industrial Revolution, changes occurred not only in the range of occupations, and related class structure, but in the nature of work itself with more people working outside the home. Rather than individuals working each in their own workshop or home, as was the case in the traditional craft industries, e.g. weavers living and working in cottages which had large windows up in the weaving loft to let maximum light onto the loom, as can be seen from the architecture of these dwellings. Workers and their machines were concentrated in one place – the factory, which people attended at set times each day. The ability of the steam engine to run a large number of machines was largely responsible for this. In contrast, the traditional agricultural worker's life was governed by the seasons, and by the amount of daylight. For women, 'work' had not been rigidly divided between work in the home and going out to work elsewhere, many tasks which were eventually industrialized, such as weaving, were originally carried out within the home (either working in their own home, or as a servant in someone else's home) along with everything else, such as cooking and childcare. The factories were all dependent on the same sources of power to drive the machines, and were often clustered together creating distinct factory zones, with the housing huddled around the factories. With time the early planners sought to segregate out the land uses creating separate industrial and residential areas, which, as has been explained, were increasingly located further and further away from the workplace.

Increasing numbers of women worked in factories and went 'out' to work similar to men, and as domestic service declined women were affected by these land use trends. This tended to segregate women's lives, for zoning while organized and efficient, made it very difficult for women to combine work and home, and it was also inconvenient for men as well. The approach to early town planning reinforced the fact that society itself was defined and structured in relation to work, creating a very mono-dimensional existence, compared with the traditional rural community, where work had been constrained by the natural seasons and religious festivals, or when individuals felt inspired or in the mood to work at their crafts.

Increasing separation of work from home, and greater social class gradation, has led to the building of a wide range of suburban housing although many people continue to live within the inner city, often in subdivided older properties. It would seem that the work/home divisions which dominated for around 200 years are now breaking down again, as more people (male and female) work from home, as a result, in part, of the electronic revolution, enabling people to work from a commuter terminal at home using a modem.

Family structures

The traditional rural family in pre-industrialized society was fairly large by modern standards. Most families are called 'nuclear' families, which means they consist of the nucleus of the mother and the father and the immediate off-spring, classically of 2.4 children on average and has nothing to do with nuclear war or explosive family relationships! This image may be based more on myth (as represented in the 'Cornflakes Family' seen on television commercials) than on statistical reality, as the situation has changed rapidly in recent years (Hamnett, *et al.*, 1989). In pre-industrial societies, and indeed in Third World agricultural societies today, families were more likely to be 'extended families' which meant that they consisted of the nucleus of the parents and children, vertically might consist of grandparents and grandchildren, and horizontally may extend out to include uncles and aunts, nephews and cousins. Indeed the borderline between the extended family and the concept of the tribe, and the village in which everyone is related to everyone else is a matter of degree.

During the industrial revolution it was generally younger people who moved to the new industrial towns and cities, leaving older people behind, although sometimes sending money back to support them. Birth rates were high in the new industrial towns with many families having six or more children. This was in spite of the small size of houses, which consisted of two-up and two-down terraced accommodation with high infant mortality levels (Whitelegg *et al.*, 1982; Lewis, 1984). As time went on families became smaller, and paradoxically housing for the working classes became somewhat larger.

These days there is not the same rate of population growth as in the past. Nevertheless people require more privacy and higher standards of housing, there are also many more single-person households, all creating demand for more housing. Regional movement of population, especially to the south east has created increased demand for housing around London. However, houses are left vacant and unsold in other less prosperous, previously industrialized parts of the country such as the north east, it is estimated that at any one time about 1 million will be vacant because of the above factors. Some empty houses may be in the course of being transferred to new owners but many are unoccupied for lengthy periods. Clearly, regional imbalance is a continuing legacy of the nature of nineteenth-century urbanization and industrialization.

HISTORICAL DEVELOPMENT OF THE LANDSCAPE

A parallel account of the history of the countryside will now be given (Hoskins, 1990). As the demand for greater planning control in the countryside, and especially conservation of, what are imagined to be, traditional natural features, increases it becomes vitally important to understand the historical nature of the factors which have shaped the present-day countryside. People often assume that the countryside is natural and not man-made, however there is hardly any part of Britain's landscape which has not been touched in some way by human activity, often more so than in the urban areas. There are many complaints about the removal of traditional field patterns and hedgerows, but in fact those hedgerows were not always there, and much of the land has been brought into cultivation either from forest, or from heathland. Likewise there is much concern about the natural habitat of wildlife being destroyed as a result of the draining of the wetlands in Somerset and the fenlands in East Anglia, but again these only exist in their current form because of man-made drainage schemes in the past, and which animals have adapted for occupation.

Before the Romans arrived, there was fairly limited cultivation in Britain, settlements tended to be on the higher land and lowlands were left undeveloped. Still being found are many examples of hill forts, standing stones, ancient trackways (often aligned along ley lines), and earth works from earlier times, some of which are protected as ancient monuments. The Romans had a tremendous impact on land use, urbanization, road construction, land drainage, and cultivation patterns. The decline of the Roman empire was followed by a series of invasions by European tribes, each contributing in their own way to farming and to place names and local cultures.

The Normans arrived in 1066, and established a programme of colonization and plantation development. The land and society itself was divided up and organized on the basis of the feudal system. In the Middle Ages the population was over 80 per cent rural, mainly located in small villages with agricultural activity based on what was known as the three-field system of crop rotation, typically of wheat, barley and fallow on a three-year cycle. Each peasant farmer had his own 'strips' of land in each field within this framework. Increasingly the more remote areas were brought into cultivation by the monasteries who introduced sheep to the Pennines. Other improvements were made by monks, for example, the Abbots of Glastonbury in Somerset had Sedgmoor drained. Britain was relatively peaceful and unified allowing expansion of agriculture into the more remote areas, while many other European countries were not unified, with walled cities providing shelter from which the inhabitants would cautiously venture forth to tend the adjacent farmland.

The development of rich city states in Italy provided the seedbed of the Renaissance. Formal gardens of huge dimensions, were laid out according to classical architectural principles, purely for the pleasure of their owners, and as a sign of 'conspicuous consumption' (wealth). Flowers and vegetables had little place in these gardens, and were relegated to the servants' area. These ideas spread to Britain, but had to compete with an already established traditional form of garden which was on a more intimate and functional scale, as typified by the Shakespearean knot gardens consisting of box hedges containing beds of herbs, flowers, and vegetables.

By the seventeenth century there was a gradual move towards a more 'Grand Manner' approach to gardening, which in Britain took the form of the landscape movement, with its emphasis on earth modelling on a huge scale, creating lakes and vistas, accompanied by extensive tree planting. This was linked to the growth of the English country house set in its own grounds without fortifications, also without the estate farm, kitchen gardens or tenants in sight. There had always been a great interest in arboriculture (tree cultivation) as evidenced by the cultivation of the Royal forests of oak for ships and also as hunting parks. In 1664 John Evelyn wrote *Sylva*, his book about tree cultivation, which was highly influential. Art and literature influenced people's ideas about the landscape too. Milton's poem *Paradise Lost* describes a beautiful natural wilderness. French artists, such as Claude, Poussin, Lorrain, painted 'naturalistic' landscapes, presenting an idyllic image of pastoral life. This romantic view of the countryside was chiefly for the upper class and bore little relationship to the harsh realities of farming for ordinary people. In 1720 Bridgman designed a country estate at Stowe in Buckinghamshire in which he created

'a little gentle disorder' as he put it, thus rejecting classical principles and purposely designing a more 'natural' layout.

It was possible to look out of the windows of the 'big house' at the pastoral landscape stretching into the distance with cows grazing and 'figures in the landscape' – meaning picturesque peasants going about their work. These peasants were prevented from straying up to the house by Bridgman's invention of a hidden ditch, which was called a 'ha-ha'. Other landscape architects of this time include William Kent who was it is said, 'the first to leap over the fence and to show that the whole of nature', and Lancelot Capability Brown, the most famous of the landscape gardeners responsible for schemes such as Blenheim Palace, and Longleat in Wiltshire. Humphrey Repton, created a more contoured approach and incorporated artificial grottos and 'follies' (pretend ruins). In all these estates, the emphasis was on grass and trees and features in the landscape, rather than on details of flowers and colours. Outside these developments, prior to enclosure taking place, the countryside remained a patchwork of villages with their cottage gardens, large communal fields and open woodland.

The Agricultural Revolution preceded the Industrial Revolution and was based on many innovations in agriculture by people such as Jethro Tull (1674–1741), Turnip Townsend who perfected crop rotation, and George III who was known as 'Farmer George'. These changes increased yield while reducing labour. The need for larger units for efficient rotation, and the extension of sheep farming led to the General Enclosure Acts of the early nineteenth century, further reducing grazing and common land rights for the rural population who increasingly migrated to the towns. The Industrial Revolution, and the urbanization, canal and railway building, mining and factory development which accompanied it, had a major impact on land use patterns, and created large amounts of derelict land, spoil tips, and pollution.

The Victorians were keen gardeners. The science of horticulture and cross-breeding developed, accompanied by the introduction of exotic species from all corners of the Empire. Botanical gardens and greenhouses, such as Kew Gardens, became popular. Formal Victorian parks were developed in the new industrial towns for people to enjoy. These were characterized by formal beds containing flowers in primary colours, floral clocks as in Edinburgh, and also adjacent playing fields for recreation. Domestic gardening by individual households also became popular now that most people no longer worked on the land. Those who lived in high density back-to-back houses had no gardens, but were able to rent an allotment locally. The development of the garden city movement enabled the provision of large individual flower gardens for each house.

Carefully designed cottage gardens for the more discriminating affluent members of society became fashionable, as popularized by the work of Gertrude Jekyll (1834–1932) (Massingham, 1984) who in conjunction with Lutyens, the famous architect, developed several gardens around large country houses at the turn of the last century. Jekyll's hallmark was the use of subtle blue, silver and white flowers and foliage, as at Sissinghurst, and at Hestercombe in Somerset. In contrast, in the early twentieth century there were still landscape architects, such as Jellicoe, designing in the grand manner. Jellicoe even admitted he knew nothing at all about flowers, but he was a founder of the Landscape Institute.

As the twentieth century developed, the emphasis upon the cultivation of individual domestic gardens, particularly in the suburbs continued. The develop-ment of large new public parks was less common, although there were many sports facilities, and public recreational areas. In the post-war period, landscaping was required for municipal and public sector schemes, rather than for private estates. For example land-scaping, for the new universities in the 1960s, the New Towns and modern day motorways rather than for large individual houses, became the main outlet of work in the post-war period.

In more recent years a concern with the environment and 'nature', rural estate management, afforesta-tion, and planning for recreation and leisure in the countryside are all leaving their mark on the rural landscape. Most large developments are 'landscaped', if it is done well people need not even notice. There is also a tremendous growth of interest in gardening for the masses, as evidenced these days by the pro-liferation of television programmes, books, and gardening centres. However, as a result of the environ-mental movement, and greater awareness of Green issues, there has also been greater criticism of rural policy, and of the use of pesticides, and of so-called scientific 'modern' horticultural practices. In conclu-sion, it can be seen from this chapter, that neither urban nor rural areas are entirely natural, they are all the result of centuries of human activity and inter-vention.

TASKS

Information Gathering Tasks

I. Identify examples of nineteenth century town planning and urban development in your vicinity. These might be model industrial communities, new commercial high streets, speculative housing development, Victorian formal gardens, and museums.

II. Find out to what extent the transport network in your vicinity is the result of nineteenth century devel-opment. Is there, or was there, a railway station, and what date was this built? Also investigate roads, canals, and tramway networks.

III. Emphasis has been given to social class in this chapter. Check the current socio-economic groupings adopted by the Census (ONS, 1999), see current social class classifications adopted by the Government (ONS/ESRC, 1998). Also identify growth areas of employment and and related technological change that are reshaping society (for example, care industry, electronics, banking).

Conceptual and Discursive Task

IV. Discuss the nature of social change in the nineteenth century in relation to class, work, gender, and family life.

V. With reference to examples from an area with which you are familiar discuss the extent human beings have shaped the nature of the countryside.

Reflective Tasks

VI. What are your personal impressions and images of the nineteenth century? If you had been alive in say 1890 what would you have 'been'? Imagine what your life would have been like? Better or worse? (For example, you could have travelled extensively on a much better railway network, through more attractive countryside, although work was harder and there would be no electric lighting, or television, in the evenings).

FURTHER READING

There are a range of books which cover the history of town planning in the nineteenth century, many of which have already been mentioned in the previous chapter's reading guidance. For more detailed information see Ashworth, 1968; Bacon, 1978; Bell and Bell, 1972; Bor, 1972; Burke, 1977; Mumford, 1965; Morris, A., 1972; Cherry, 1981, 1988; Ravetz, 1986; Chapter 2 of Hall, 1992; Morris, E., 1997; RTPI, 1986; Penoyre, 1990; Service, 1977.

The history of the development of the countryside and of the landscape is recounted comprehensively in Hoskins, 1990. Shoard's books on current controversial issues in the countryside are extremely valuable (1980, 1987, 1999), covering matters such as farming practices, access and the right to roam, and the visual and social aspects of the countryside. More recent material from groups such as Friends of the Earth, the Countryside Commission and the National Trust will give a wider perspective.

Material on social change is to be found in Ryder and Silver, 1990; Joseph, 1988, Haralambos, 1995; Hurd, 1990; Bilton, *et al.*, 1997.

6

REACTION AND REFORM IN
THE NINETEENTH CENTURY

INTRODUCTION

Modern town planning arose in the nineteenth century in response to the problems and conditions discussed in Chapter 5. The purpose of this chapter is to look at this response. First, the reforming legislation will be described. The early reforms simply sought to deal with the worst effects of disease, overcrowding, and slum development. This approach had much in common with the 'sites and services' approach adopted in Third World cities today: dealing with the absolute basics of sewerage and drainage. Later the emphasis moved from this necessarily negative controlling approach to seeking to create, more positively, whole new ways of living. In the second part of the chapter examples of the model communities which were put forward by various visionaries and philanthropists will be discussed. Emphasis will be placed upon the concept of the Garden City which was to have such a major influence on the nature of twentieth-century town planning.

LEGISLATIVE REFORMS

Local Government Reforms

The spread of cholera and other water born diseases made intervention necessary. There were major outbreaks in 1832 and 1849. Because cholera was a waterborne disease it was no respecter of persons. It might originate in working class districts, but could spread anywhere along the insanitary water systems of the city. In 1854, a Dr. Snow discovered the relationship between a major cholera outbreak and a single polluted pump in the Soho district of London (Hall 1992: 18). Increased state intervention to provide sewerage and drainage systems was urgently needed (Briggs, 1968; Cherry, 1988).

To implement reform there was a need for an effective, administrative structure, and a series of Acts of Parliament were passed, the main ones are listed in the Appendix on Government Publications. The Municipal Corporations Act 1835 laid the foundations for this, making possible the creation of locally elected urban councils, i.e. local authorities, which had the powers to levy rates from householders and businesses, and to use the money to employ professional and administrative staff in order to carry out these improvements and building programmes (Macey and Baker, 1983; M. Smith, 1989).

Public Health

In 1840, a Select Committee had been established, headed by Edwin Chadwick, which was responsible for the 'conditions in towns', leading to the 'Report on the Sanitary Conditions of the Labouring Population and 'the Means of its Improvement' in 1842 (Chadwick, 1842). In 1843 this was followed by the establishment of a Royal Commission on the Health of Towns, and in parallel the Health of Towns Association was founded. The Sanitary Act 1847 required sewers and drains to be provided in all new residential areas. The Public Health Act 1848 went further, being one of the first Acts intervening in *how* houses were constructed, and therefore potentially added to the cost for the developers. This Act required that all ceilings must be at least 8 feet high (nowadays ceilings only need to be slightly less than this about 7 feet 6 inches or 2.3 metres). Low ceilings had health implications as they reduced the likelihood of light penetrating the building and the circulation of air, leading, it was thought to germs and diseases lurking in the dark corners of badly ventilated rooms.

Many owners of property (especially the landlords of such substandard properties) resented the general trend of such legislation as it went against the centuries-old principle enshrined in private real property law that a man had a right to do what he wanted with his own land, and that an Englishman's home is his castle. The growth of the public health movement, and the mixed reaction it received, reflects fundamental unresolved dualisms in the development of the town planning movement itself, namely the inevitable tension in trying to solve what are essentially social problems, especially those of poverty, by imposing physical standards on the built environment. No doubt if people had had adequate wages in the first place they would have not had to live in substandard housing. Town planning has frequently been condemned for seeking to deal with the 'effect' rather than the 'cause' of urban decline, and on emphasizing 'control' rather than producing 'solution', thus not solving the problem, just moving it to another area.

The division of powers which evolved in the nineteenth century, and continued in the twentieth century, between the functions of town planning and public health departments has not been helpful. Town planners retain considerable control over the 'outside' by controlling the design and layout of the built environment, but have little control over the design of the 'inside' of the built environment. This issue has been of concern to those seeking to obtain better access and amenity provision within buildings (Greed, 1994a). The nature of the division of powers among, and between, the various professional and regulatory bodies responsible for the control of the built environment is still a key factor in determining whether a modern planning authority has the legal right to impose some design requirement upon a developer.

A Digression into Housing

Many of the newcomers to the industrial towns scarcely even achieved this level, and would live in lodging houses, and other forms of temporary accommodation, until they had established themselves and were able to rent a terraced house. The Common Lodging Houses Act and the Labouring Classes Lodging Houses Acts of 1868 were passed, introduced under the sponsorship of Lord Shaftesbury, enabled the inspection and better provision of lodging houses. From the beginning the development of town planning and housing management went hand-in-hand. The Artisans' and Labourers' Dwellings Improvements Act 1868 (the Torrens Act) increased government controls, this was followed by other acts of the same name in 1875 and 1879, which increased powers in dealing with insanitary buildings (Ashworth, 1968).

Note that all this was done in the name of public health, and was chiefly aimed at the working classes (Smith, 1989). It was considered politically unacceptable to control the design of middle class housing – indeed it was not needed, with high ceilings and large rooms – although the sanitation often left much to be desired (Rubenstein, 1974). Nevertheless these early Acts paved the way for later, wider, controls over all classes of housing and types of land uses by town planning departments. There were already some limited controls on middle-class housing, and commercial buildings in London, that had existed ever since the Great Fire of London in 1666. Private restrictive covenants were also widespread in 'good' residential areas, being intended to preserve the tone of the neighbourhood by, for example, preventing the conversion of houses into shops, the redevelopment of gardens (which would increase the housing density), or the keeping of pigs or poultry. By the end of the century many of the larger northern cities such as Manchester, Liverpool and Newcastle had also increased their controls on urban development by introducing private Acts of Parliament before the main national town planning Acts of the early twentieth century came into being. The importance of well laid out cities and town planning was widely accepted as a boost to commerce and a benefit to citizens.

Government initiatives were augmented by a range of private reforming endeavours. There were a number of housing societies concerned with improving the conditions of the working classes such as the Peabody Trust. This was set up in 1862 by George Peabody an American philanthropist. Many of his buildings can still be seen today in areas of London such as Islington,

***Figure 6.1* Peabody Buildings, London.**
By today's standards much philanthropic housing looks fairly basic, but at the time it was seen as progressive. The tenement and apartment block approach to housing never became as popular in England as it was elsewhere in Europe.

Whitechapel, Vauxhall and Bethnall Green; and most of them are in the style of walk-up tenements. There were many other schemes, many of which were based on sound commercial principles, in that subscribers to the scheme received what was then a reasonable rate of interest on their investment: that is '5 per cent Philanthropy'. Many of these schemes look fairly grim, judged by today's standards, but they were better than existing alternatives.

The attitude toward the nature of housing provision for the working classes had come a long way from the 'poor law' philosophy of the first half of the century which actively discouraged people seeking help. Official attitudes were strongly influenced by the theories of Malthus (1798 [1973]), who took the unenlightened view that over-population was caused by the poor themselves. He suggested that nothing should be done to ease the conditions of the poor, as this would only cause them to 'breed' more and thus make the problem worse. Poverty was more often caused by low wages or unemployment – rich men had large families in Victorian times, but did not become poor as a result.

Since the Law of Settlement and Removal Act 1662, the homeless and 'sturdy beggars' had been seen as a burden on the parish. The problem became greater with the movement of people generated by the Industrial Revolution, and fewer people could earn a living on the land as a result of modern farming methods, this being reinforced by the various Enclosure Acts such as that of 1801. In 1832 the Royal Commission on the Poor Law investigated the whole situation, resulting in the 1834 Poor Law Amendment Act, which actually reduced the level of help in spite of growing demand. In order to reduce numbers looking to the parish for relief (help) the view was taken that conditions should be so harsh in the workhouses that people would only seek admission as a last resort. This attitude still pervades certain aspects of council housing provision, and the housing benefits system even today, and is far removed from the value systems underpinning the creation of the garden cities and the development of the modern town planning system, in which people were more likely as being seen as having a right to good housing.

Later Developments

The Artisans and Labourers Dwellings Improvement Act of 1875 increased local authority powers to deal with whole areas, as against individual buildings, giving them compulsory purchase powers, and the powers to build schemes which provided accommodation for the working classes. This was a major step toward the modern-day powers of local authorities to carry out compulsory purchase and to take control of the building of an area themselves. The Public Health Act 1875 set minimum standards on the design of houses and also on the layout of streets, this being one of the first true town planning Acts. The implementation of these standards was achieved by giving local authorities the power to introduce by-laws themselves controlling the layout of new streets and housing schemes in their districts. These standards required that every house should have a rear access, which was meant to solve the problem of back-to-back houses, which shared a common party wall. To summarize, in these Acts the three functions of local authorities were to clear existing sub-standard housing, to carry out building works themselves and to control the nature of construction built by private builders and developers.

Normally, under the by-law regulations, the width of the street had to be at least the same dimension as the height of the building's front wall up to the eaves, this created a rather 'enclosed', reassuringly human scale to such areas. The sense of human scale in residential areas was lost with the introduction of much wider streets to make way for the motor car, and more generous front gardens on housing estates in the early twentieth century. In 1890 the Housing of the Working Classes Act increased local authorities' power to build new houses themselves, thus creating an early form of council housing. By this time developers were losing interest in building cheap housing for the working classes to rent, and were turning their attention to the more affluent emerging owner-occupied middle class suburban housing developments. Council housing was to go on to become a major feature of our towns and cities in the twentieth century. It is only since the 1980s that this sector has been in decline following various negative housing acts, and a push toward owner occupation.

MODEL COMMUNITIES

Private Initiatives

Legislation was one major response to the problems of the nineteenth century, but individuals there were also individuals who created reforms. Various factory owners, often of Quaker, non-conformist, or socialist in persuasion, sought to change society, at their own expense. Whilst some critics would accuse them of being paternalistic in their approach, others would argue that there was no compulsion on them to improve workers' conditions. There was a surplus of workers and high unemployment during much of the nineteenth century, so, presumably, they were operating out of the best of intentions and a sense of public duty. Some, however, may have been motivated by more businesslike, 'utilitarian' principles, which may be summed up in the principle that happy workers are good workers, loyal to the firm (Kanter, 1972).

New Lanark

Robert Owen (1771–1858) was one of the early 'town planners' and a socialist, who had many new ideas, and tried them out, in respect of just about every aspect of human society, including education, housing, health, trade unionism and even birth control. Like many of the reformers Owen came from humble origins. From working in a draper's shop, he rose to be manager of a Lancashire cotton mill, and

Figure 6.2 New Lanark, Scotland.
This photograph was taken in the 1970s when New Lanark was nearer it original form. Nowadays it has become a Scottish theme park in which tourists can 'experience social history'.

then married the daughter of David Dale, the owner of the New Lanark Mills in Scotland. New Lanark was already a self-contained and planned industrial village when Owen arrived, the first buildings having been completed in 1786, and by 1790 the population had reached 2,000. In 1800 the mills were taken over by Robert Owen from David Dale, who had set up the original scheme.

During the next 25 years Owen developed his schemes on community living and education. The Institution for the Formation of Character was established, which included nursery schooling, and adult education, as well as school provision for children. The town included Britain's first co-operative store. However the housing was provided in the form of tenements with minimal plumbing with shared kitchens and communal WCs. It was all rather grim by today's standards, and somewhat regimented with regular inspections of the dwellings being undertaken by Owen himself looking for bedbugs! New Lanark was set in a narrow valley along a fast flowing stream which provided water power to run the machinery. New Lanark does not have the 'look' of an industrial town. Owen wanted to spread his ideas by setting up 'villages of co-operation'. Several Owenite communities were set up by his followers, both in Britain and in North America, such as New Harmony in the USA. Also he wrote *New View of Society* in 1813 and *Report to the County of Lanark* in 1821, and his ideas spread widely.

Bradford Halifax School

The next phases of model community building occurred in the Midlands, where rapid industrialization was taking place. Colonel Akroyd, a rich mill owner built two model communties, the first at Copley in 1849 in the Calder Valley near Halifax, and then Akroydon in 1859. George Gilbert Scott the great Victorian architect was employed to design Akroydon, which consisted of fairly modest terraced and town houses for the workers, with the main family Hall of the Akroyd's set on the hillside above, so that he could look down and see his experiment at work (a common Victorian preference). This model community is now surrounded by subsequent suburban development and does not look particularly imaginative, but at that time the layout and design were seen as quite innovative.

Akroyd did not want his workers to remain tied to him, and along with other fellow philanthropic factory owners in the Halifax area, pioneered the concept of home ownership for his workers, by means of establishing the Halifax Building Society in 1845, but at the same time many existing workers who were renting their properties from the factory owners were given preferential agreements. At the time this was seen as quite radical, if not socialist, whereas later both building societies and owner-occupation became asso-

ciated more with 'capitalism', as housing provision for the working classes moved toward direct state provision and renting, rather than encouragement for workers to meet their housing needs through subsidized owner-occupation. Yet state-subsidized owner occupation has been seen as a perfectly acceptable form of housing policy in other countries, especially the United States, where tax allowances on mortgage repayments have been seen as a key aspect of social equality policy.

Another key figure in the Halifax school is Titus Salt (1803–1876) who founded the village of Saltaire in 1851, on the River Aire. His business was producing cloth from the wool of Alpaca goats, which was imported from overseas. These days Saltaire is protected by conservation area policy. Salt is famous in the history of industrial relations, for being the first factory owner to introduce an official tea break for his workers. Salt was generally seen as a benevolent employer, but he organized the housing allocation strictly according to the seniority of workers' jobs, with overseers receiving substantial double-fronted houses and factory hands modest small terraced dwellings. However no expense was spared in terms of architectural detail, a classical Italianate style known as Tuscan, being used for all the buildings including the factory, all built with soft golden stone similar to Bath stone.

Salt did not entirely understand the difficulty people had carrying out their essential domestic tasks. He banned housewives from hanging out their washing

***Figure 6.3a and b* Saltaire near Halifax.**
The town consists of small streets with back alleyways, with different sizes of houses for different levels of employee, all dominated by the elegant mill buildings.

across the backs, and apparently would gallop down the back lanes on his horse, sword drawn to cut the washing lines if they did so. However, he did provide communal washhouses, and social amenities such as libraries, canteens, allotments, schools and almshouses. Saltaire was a relatively small scheme with only 800 houses, but many public buildings and amenities. It had a strong influence, disproportionate to its size, on many subsequent model towns, in North America and Europe, especially on the Krupps model town at Essen in Germany, and on the Pullman railway towns in the United States.

THE GARDEN CITY MOVEMENT

The Ideas

There is a marked change of style from the relatively high density utilitarian developments of the early nineteenth century to the lower density, more luxu-

riant garden city schemes of the latter part of the century in which the housing consists of on traditional cottages with gable ends and front gardens, rather than tenements or plain terraces (Cherry, 1981; Hall, 1992). Designing ideal housing for the working classes became a very popular branch of architecture, although some of the schemes were so expensive that they contributed more to the development of fashionable middle-class domestic architecture, than providing a model for cheap mass produced housing, for example Bedford Park, London (Bolsterli, 1977). There had always been a tradition in the large country estates of designing quaint little cottages for the agricultural workers, often in the picturesque style, which in themselves would provide an interesting feature in the landscape when viewed from the windows of the stately home (Dresser, 1978; Darley, 1978).

Famous architects such as Unwin, Parker, and Lutyens were employed in the design of garden cities and garden suburbs, developed towards the end of the

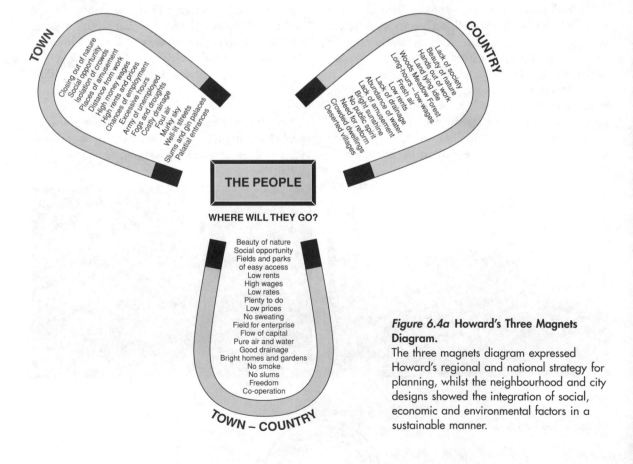

***Figure 6.4a* Howard's Three Magnets Diagram.**
The three magnets diagram expressed Howard's regional and national strategy for planning, whilst the neighbourhood and city designs showed the integration of social, economic and environmental factors in a sustainable manner.

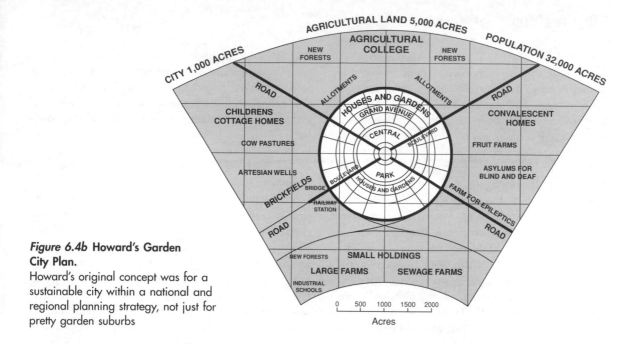

Figure 6.4b Howard's Garden City Plan.
Howard's original concept was for a sustainable city within a national and regional planning strategy, not just for pretty garden suburbs

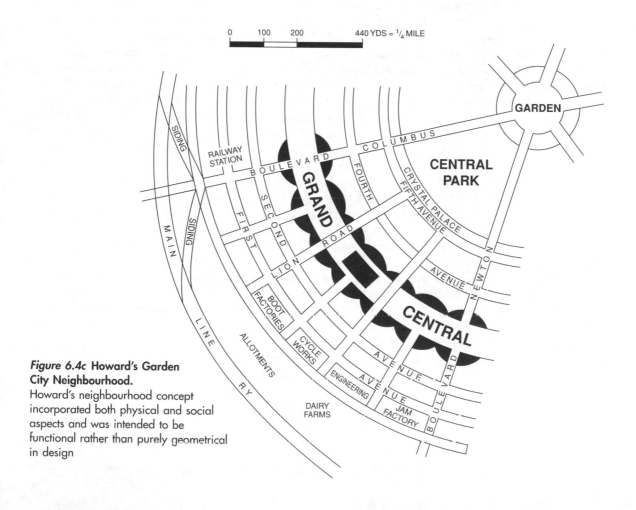

Figure 6.4c Howard's Garden City Neighbourhood.
Howard's neighbourhood concept incorporated both physical and social aspects and was intended to be functional rather than purely geometrical in design

century (Service, 1977; Dixon and Muthesius, 1978). Raymond Unwin, in particular, was in favour of low density housing with gardens and coined the phrase 'nothing gained by overcrowding' (Unwin, 1912). He sought to demonstrate in his plans that high-density grid layout of terraces was not necessarily the best way to save space, recommending 12 houses to the acre (30 per hectare) was the best solution (Hall, 1989: 55). Notable literary figures and members of the upper classes were involved in campaigning for better conditions, such as Beatrice Webb, Ruskin, William Morris, Charles Dickens, William Booth, Cardinal Manning, Charles Kingsley, and Henry George, all of whom were connected to the garden city movement, and the early town planning cause. Many women were active in the early housing movement, the most well known being Octavia Hill, who in 1875 wrote the book, *Homes of the London Poor*, and who went on to set up many housing initiatives and arguably influenced the nature of the whole modern housing management profession (Smith, 1989; Macey and Baker, 1983).

Ebenezer Howard wrote *Tomorrow: A Peaceful Path to Reform* in 1898, which was retitled *Garden Cities of Tomorrow* in 1902 in which he put forward his main town planning ideas for the creation of an ideal community (Howard, 1974 edition). Howard believed that although the industrial revolution had been accompanied by great problems of overcrowding, bad housing, and environmental problems, it had also brought many benefits. Therefore he sought to combine the best of the modern town and new industrial society, with the best of the countryside and traditional ways of rural village life, in the 'town-country' or 'garden-city' as he called his ideal community. This idea is shown graphically in the three magnets diagram, in which the garden city is seen as a powerful 'countermagnet' which would attract the people away from both the overcrowded industrial cities, and the backwardness of the countryside.

Howard was part of a wider group of men and women concerned with urban conditions in the wake of the Industrial Revolution. He had visited the USA where he had seen Owenite communities, a range of religious communities such as the Mormon settlement of Salt Lake City and various Mennonite communities founded in the land of freedom, which sought to create heaven on earth (Hayden, 1976; Kanter, 1972). Howard envisaged the creation of garden cities with a population of approximately 30,000 each, divided into smaller neighbourhoods of 5,000, acting as countermagnets to existing conurbations, and together forming larger 'social cities' linked in a complex regional network across the country. He envisaged this network as being joined together by the most modern public transport railway systems (he was truly living in the age of the train in Victorian England) with new settlements being formed as and when the population expanded.

This would result in planning on a national scale with a complete network of inter-connecting cities covering the whole country, while existing cities would return to a more manageable size and pleasant environment. Howard is often misrepresented as favouring an escapist folksy way of life based on 'green' principles. In fact he was advocating a very realistic way of restructuring the economy and community of Britain, by means of creating a complete network of garden cities which would act as countermagnets to the existing conurbations, and which would re-establish the urban–rural balance which had been shaken by the Industrial Revolution.

Howard, therefore, was not only planning cities at the macro level but had a complete regional and national land use strategy, and also had thought through how the cities would be subdivided at the micro neighbourhood level. The idea of dividing the cities into neighbourhoods of 5,000 people was realized in the neighbourhood units which formed the basic structural component of the post-war British new towns developed from 1946 onwards. The magic figure of 5,000 being seen as an ideal size for a group of citizens to engender a sense of community spirit; a questionable concept going back to the times of the Greek city state of antiquity (see Chapter 5).

Howard put forward many innovative ideas on zoning the different land uses and activities within the garden city, as can be seen from the diagram, for example, he put all the industry on the outside ring, on the periphery of the city, this being another feature which was followed in much post-war town planning. He proposed relatively low densities within the residential areas, with plenty of trees, open space and public parks, as well as generous private gardens around each house, all essential features of creating the garden city layout. But he was not just playing at creating beautiful stage sets, as some of his critics imagined, as everything had a scientific purpose to reduce disease, encourage people to grow vegetables in the gardens, and create a sense of well being, harmony and community spirit.

He proposed that there should be a Green Belt around the city, to be used for agriculture: it was not a mere buffer zone between town and country in the modern usuage of the phrase. He sought to reunite the relationship between town and country in the economy of the garden city and in the division of labour and nature of the work options which people had. Indeed he wanted to create, what today would be called, a complete lifestyle package. In order to unite town and country in everyday life, as well as on the plan, he saw the town's citizens working on and controlling the agricultural land around the city, as well as running modern industrial activities (Howard, 1974, originally 1898).

Clearly, Howard was not just concerned with the physical town planning of his developments, but had ideas for every aspect of the social and economic characteristics of the community at every level from city-wide down through the local neighbourhoods to the family level, relating to how people lived and how land and property were owned. He did not see himself as a socialist but came from a more liberal tradition which advocated communitarianism rather than communism *per se*. He envisaged much of the land being owned co-operatively where that might be the best solution, but also allowed for private ownership of shops and businesses; what these days would be called a mixed economy approach.

Likewise the idea of dividing the city into distinct neighbourhood communities' was not only a practical solution to the phasing and development of the town, and the provision of essential amenities and facilities in a logical manner. He wanted to engender a sense of community amongst the residents, and believed that by dividing his garden city into identifiable neighbourhood sectors, each with its own school and shops, this aim would be best achieved. This theme was to re-emerge in post-war British new towns. His interest in 'community' also reflected the influence of the sociologists of the day who were concerned with the 'problem' of the decline of traditional communities and the potential breakdown of society in large impersonal cities, as will be discussed in the social aspects chapter in relation to the concept of the neighbourhood unit in modern New Towns.

Unlike many modern town planners, Howard's vision was not limited to the 'big issues' of the public

Figures 6.5 Factory Town in the Garden City Style.
Both Port Sunlight and Bourneville, built at the end of the nineteenth century, utilized the mock-tudor style which was subsequently to become the dominant style in the private suburbs of the early twentieth century.

realm of life, for he did not despise the domestic and private realms of the family as trivial, arguably the whole concept of the garden city was a celebration of domestic *petit bourgeois* virtues. He was aware of the problems of the burden of domestic work and family care, which had been publicized by the feminists of the time. Therefore he sought to incorporate attempts at co-operative housekeeping into the layout and running of garden city (Pearson, 1988). At that time many men and women were looking at ways of rationalizing domestic work in the same way that production outside the home had been industrialized, and apparently rationalized. The issue had become pressing in many households as women sought greater emancipation.

The 'servant problem' was a middle class one, but co-operative housekeeping would also alleviate the toil of working class women, both in their own households and as servants in those of others. All sorts of other ideas were put forward to reduce the problems of housework, especially in North America. It was suggested, for example, that there could be a conveyor belt running round the town, from which individual households would collect their meals, then placing their 'washing up' on the same device, to be cleaned in the communal kitchen in the centre of the town (Hayden, 1981).

The garden city concept was intended to provide an alternative form of settlement for the working classes who formed the bulk of the overcrowded population of existing cities, although paradoxically it reflected many middle class attitudes on how to solve the servant problem. As will be seen garden cities later regarded as being mainly for middle class people, with disparaging images of Fabian intellectuals, and liberated women on bicycles being seen in the popular press as the main inhabitants of these rarefied communities.

Howard was not only a theorist but a man of action. In those days there was no adequate state system of town planning, so whatever was to be done had to be achieved through private investment and development. He set up the first Garden City Company Limited before the First World War and started developments in Letchworth in 1903, and later in Welwyn Garden City in 1920, both on the edge of London at the time, and now well and truly within the commuter belt. These enterprises ran into business difficulties, but the sites he had recommended for the rest of his proposed ring of garden cities were later adopted by the planners under the New Towns Act 1946 as the location of the first phase of British New Towns.

Howard's influence was greater in what he wrote than in what he built. Aspects of Howard's work continued to be very influential in the development of modern town planning including the subdivision of settlements into neighbourhoods, the creation of local and centralized hierarchies of amenities and facilities, Green Belts, land use zoning, approaches to public transport, and an enthusiasm for bicycles which were (at that time) a recent innovation. Hence the provision of cycle paths in many post-war new towns. Possibly most influential of all the aspects of the Garden City movement was the emphasis on tradi-

tional small cottage-style housing with gardens at medium-to-low density as the main form of residential development in the garden city. This contrasts with the emphasis on model tenements for the labouring classes as found in much early charitable development and some model communities within inner-city Britain and within continental Europe, such as the Peabody Building tenements in South London.

Many other aspects of Howards's ideas have been lost with time. For example co-operative housekeeping was soon abandoned by later planners. The variety of ideas about creating a new economic order based on co-operation and reconciling the town and the country were reflected, but weakly in the state planning system with its emphasis on control and sterile land use zoning. His ideas were copied in the building of many garden suburbs most of which favoured the mock tudor (half-timbered with gabled ends) garden city architectural styles. This style of housing became even more popular in the 1930s and came to represent the epitome of home ownership for the new middle classes being popularized by speculative housebuilders and estate agents' advertisements of the time. So much so, that these days mock tudor semi-detached and detached suburban houses are seen as the normal and natural form of development. In the 1990s there has been a considerable revival of this pseudo-tudor style. Many architects look upon this style as artificial and generally as bad taste, but the majority of the population now live in suburban development. It has endured the test of time much better than the so-called modern movement of impersonal functional glass and concrete, which has never been popular with the residents of such buildings.

The Communities

Howard drew encouragement from a range of like-minded people, and also influenced the work of many of the later model community builders, who built in the garden city style. For example, George Cadbury (1839–1922) moved his chocolate factory out of Birmingham to Bournville in 1879, and built the main settlement around it in 1895, at the same time as Howard was writing his book. W. Alexander Harvey, who was employed as the architect, believed in designing the layout in sympathy with the topography, stating, 'it is nearly always better to use the contour of the land, taking a gentle sweep in prefer-

***Figure 6.6* Local Facilities within the Garden City.**
Social facilities such as schools were an integral feature of such developments as in the case of this school at Bourneville.

ence to a straight line'. This contrasted with the grid-iron type layouts of many of the earlier settlements, and is a precursor of the trademark of English town planning, of meandering and curving roads and a generally 'natural' appearance. The houses were built at a very low density of seven or eight houses to the acre (less than 18 houses per hectare), with large private gardens for horticulture, lots of trees and open space, and wide roads plus adequate provision of schools and shops. Some of the houses were for sale to the general public from the beginning, but the whole settlement was strongly linked to providing accommodation for the workforce of the factory. The design was in the mock tudor, medieval cottage style so favoured by the reformers. George Cadbury was a supporter of Ebenezer Howard's ideas and was on the first board of directors for the first garden city built by Howard in Letchworth, north east of London (Gardiner, 1923; Hall and Ward, 1999).

Port Sunlight was built by Lever the soap manu-facturer, across the Mersey from Liverpool. Lever (1851–1925) (and brothers) started in business as a grocer making soap and candles in the back room of his shop. Lever bought 52 acres on Merseyside, and began building his factory there in 1888, and then started his model village in 1889 which was not completed until 1934. Again the scheme is low density with houses at 5–8 houses per acre. The houses were mainly grouped in blocks around allotment gardens without any private back gardens, much to the annoy-ance of many generations of residents. Although he employed a range of architects, he was the main influ-ence on both the architecture and town planning, and endowed the first Chair of Town Planning at Liverpool University (Cherry, 1981; Ashworth, 1968).

Joseph Rowntree (1836–1925) built a model community at New Earswick, near York. He employed Unwin and Parker as architects, developing garden city type houses grouped around culs de sac. The style and space standards of the houses were to act as models for the council houses introduced under the Housing and Town Planning Acts 1909 and 1919, and in particular the Tudor Walters standards for council housing design (later to be superseded by the Parker Morris standards in more recent times). The architec-tural style at New Earswick was to be influential in the developments of Hampstead Garden Suburb, Wythenshawe in Manchester, and the first Garden City at Letchworth, albeit in a slightly more attrac-

Figure 6.7 **Rowntree's New Earswick, near York.** The style used here was the basis of the Tudor Walters standards for council housing in the early twentieth century.

tive up-market way. There were smaller garden suburb type schemes throughout the country, but by the early twentieth century these had often become nothing more than an architectural shell used by developers to sell houses to the new middle classes, and many of the original communitarian ideals had long since been forgotten.

Model communities do not have to be built for philanthropic or utopian reasons. There were several purely commercial garden city type experiments in North America, and in the 1980s in Britain there were proposals for a ring of entirely private up-market new towns within the London Green Belt, put forward by Consortium the development group which is strongly influenced by the heritage of garden city concept. Their proposals met with considerable opposition from both central and local government, and pressure groups such as the Council for the Protection of Rural England (CPRE) that the idea was abandoned.

The influence of the Garden City movement rever-berates right through the twentieth century, influenc-ing the style and layout of interwar 'semi-detached suburbia', albeit in a debased form, contributing to the post-war New Towns programme, and informing the views of private developers on the design of residential estates. Garden city ideas spread worldwide, and schemes can be found in Japan, Australia, North America and Germany and many other countries. Indeed, it may be argued that a parallel movement in Germany pre-dated the English garden city movement.

Some have considered the garden city principle over-simplistic, with an emphasis upon architectural and physical planning solutions to complex social and economic problems. It is argued that Howard, compared with his imitators, sought to provide a holistic approach to planning which incorporates both spatial and aspatial issues. His designs are arguably environmentally sustainable, although developed at a time when industrialization and exploitation of natural resources were the rule.

Traditional Style

The desire of the garden city architects, and subsequently the speculative builders of semi-detached, half-timbered suburbia, to recreate the English village led to the revival of many of the traditional styles of domestic architecture (vernacular architecture, see Munro, 1979; and Prizeman, 1975 for more details and illustrations). The garden city movement ideas and architecture were not limited to the realms of town planning.. On the contrary they reflected a wider popular culture interest in getting back to traditional village life and architecture, no doubt as a reaction to their experiences of rapid industrialization and urbanization. Half timbering, characterized by black timbering on white gable ends, became particularly popular in new suburban housing estate developments. Some of these styles have made a comeback in recent years in executive housing estates. However many of these styles are not 'genuine', either in the nineteenth or twentieth century, and employ substitute, mass produced materials.

TASKS

Information Gathering
I. Choose a garden city or model community for which information is accessible. Identify its key features, in terms of physical layout, architecture, social and economic structure and administrative organization.

Conceptual and Discursive Tasks
II. The Garden City movement has often been accused of promoting an over-simplistic, paternalist, and essentially physical (land use and layout based) view of town planning which does not address underlying economic, social and political issues. Discuss.

Reflective Tasks
III. Which of the various vernacular styles of architecture most appeals to you and why?

FURTHER READING

The Town and Country Planning Association's monthly journal, *Town and Country Planning* is full of articles and features on garden cities, new towns and sustainable development. Also read Howard's *Garden Cities of Tomorrow*. Hall and Ward, 1999.

Books by Peter Hall and the late Gordon Cherry provide valuable background on the transition from nineteenth century utopian planning to modern twentieth century statutory planning systems. The development of housing is covered in a range of standard housing textbooks (Murie, Smith, *inter alia*).

There is a range of books on architectural styles both classical and vernacular Pevsner's guides of the different regions of Britain are particularly relevant. Betjeman, Pevsner and Oliver (1997) should be consulted.

For examples of modern architecture consult the RIBA journals, including *Architects Journal*. Also the range of construction and building journals should be perused, which are produced by various built environment professional bodies.

7

THE FIRST HALF OF THE TWENTIETH CENTURY

THE NEW CENTURY

The first part of Chapter 7 discusses the development of high-rise alternatives to planning towns, which provide a strong contrast to the English low-rise Garden City approach. The second part of the chapter traces the development of British town planning legislation to its culmination in the post war reconstruction period in the late 1940s when the foundations of the present day planning system were laid.

VISIONARIES

The New Technology

A major constraint on the development and nature of cities is the level of construction and transportation technology available. Cities can grow upward and/or outward, or they can be close-nit and compactly built, with everything based on walking distances. The Garden City approach used traditional methods of low-rise construction in the form of mock Tudor cottage-style houses, but it nevertheless, adopted the latest developments in transportation to enable the city to spread outward horizontally, utilizing trams, trains and bicycles. While the Garden City movement may be seen as going back to the past to reclaim traditional values, and re-establish harmony with nature and the countryside, the other main school of thought, the European High Rise approach to town planning, as epitomized by the ideas of Le Corbusier, saw past ideas as outdated and sought to create a new age of progress, based on the conquest of nature by

means of science and technology. Le Corbusier sought to use modern building technology to enable his cities to spread upward vertically, even suggesting the idea of mile-high skyscrapers. Rather than being seen as possessing worthwhile homely values and a well ordered sense of domesticity, the urban masses were thought of as ignorant, backward and therefore uneconomic; in need of re-education and reorganization to best serve the needs of the new industrial society, with its harsher, no-frills, streamlined view of life.

The High Rise European movement with its emphasis on clean-cut uncluttered lines and the use of pristine white concrete, glass and steel, represented a reaction against what was seen as the chaos of traditional cities (Pevsner, 1970). In the first part of the twentieth century, there were a variety of other architectural trends, such as 'Art Nouveau' which drew much from trends in art and painting, and from the broader 'Arts and Crafts' movement. This was characterized by an emphasis on the use of traditional materials in an original manner, especially ornate ironwork. Other architects sought to return to a restrained classical style, for example, Lutyens favoured a modest neo-Georgian style using traditional brick when he built many town halls and public buildings. His architecture also shows evidence of Indian influences, which he became interested in while he was designing the new state capital of India, New Delhi.

Early twentieth century architects reacted against the excesses of decoration, eclecticism, and urban chaos of the nineteenth century and sought to create a 'style-less' modern movement, which was entirely based on function and the application of science and technology in the form of new building materials and methods.

Figure 7.1a and b **Factory-built Dwellings in Moscow.**
Apartments being built in a state housing factory and the end-product high-rise Communist period blocks of flats in Moscow.

Why was the vertical extension of cities as expressed in the high rise movement essentially a European rather than English trend? In Europe there has been a need, right up until the last century, to provide defensive measures particularly city walls around individual city states because the political situation was far less unified than in Britain. It was not until the beginnings of aerial warfare that walls became redundant. The Garden City movement reflected a trend throughout English history to have undefended open cities which were fringed by low density urban sprawl and suburban villages around the main urban centres. In Europe the need for defence had led to a greater acceptance of living at higher densities, with buildings packed closer together, often consisting of apartment blocks of several storeys (Sutcliffe, 1974).

It was generally accepted that the natural limit to upward or vertical growth was about six storeys, as this was the maximum practical height the average person was willing to climb in what were effectively walk up tenements. With the development of new forms of power, namely gas and electricity, and new technological inventions and machinery, it was now possible to build higher still. Steel-framed structures enabled high rise buildings to be built, previously most building had been held up by load-bearing walls which stood by their own weight. In a steel-framed structure the wall and windows effectively are curtains hung from the steel skeleton. The invention of the mechanical lift, particularly the electric elevator in North America meant that people could live higher without walking up the stairs; in fact the sky was the limit. The social result of this, when applied to cheap state council housing, where the lifts do not work and people have to climb many flights of stairs, is another matter altogether from the situation in a cared-for for expensive block of private flats.

New movements such as functionalism, futurism, and modernism began to arise at the beginning of the new century (Pevsner, 1970). 'Form follows function', 'beauty is function, function is beauty' became the battle cries of a new generation of architects, who attempted to create a new non-decorative, honest, 'styleless style' known as functionalism, promulgated by Walter Gropius in Germany. He was an internationally famous architect and principal of the Bauhaus, a highly influential experimental school of architecture, art and design which was active in the inter-war period. After the Second World War, some of the European functionalist architects came to Britain and worked for the London County Council (LCC), contributing their designs to the post-war reconstruction planning and housing programme (Hatje, 1965). The influence of the functionalist style and the Bauhaus influence on interior design is to be found as a faint echo in Heals and Habitat furniture today.

Futurism was concerned with creating a space age society, using the new technology and materials to the full. Sant'Elia's multilevel city of 1914 looked like something out of science fiction or Star Wars film, consisting of huge apartment blocks more suitable for androids than humans. Much of this architecture subsequently proved not to function well and was in need of maintenance within a short period of being built: it was certainly unlikely to last into the future. The concrete discoloured, reinforcements deteriorated, window frames rusted, lifts broke down and flat roofs leaked. Traditional vernacular styles of building proved in the long run to be more functional but

Figure 7.2 New York Apartment Balconies.
This is the exact opposite of the garden city movement. These are high-value properties near Central Park.

had been dismissed as sentimental, old fashioned and bourgeois by the *avant garde*. Building styles that utilized local materials such as stone and slate took into consideration the local weather conditions by evolving different pitches for the roof, etc., which had often been developed by trial and error over the centuries by local builders and carpenters. Fine details, like ensuring the window sills are set out sufficiently, thus preventing water dripping off them and running straight down the wall causing discoloration, were observed by traditional master builders, but were ignored in the streamlined buildings of the modern movement.

Le Corbusier

Le Corbusier (1887–1965) (Pardo, 1965), a Swiss architect, working mainly in France popularized the ideas of the international style. He was influenced by his visits to New York. In Europe there was initial resistance to what was seen as a non-traditional, colo-

Figure 7.3 **Humans Dwarfed by Buildings in New York.**
The human-scale, traditional European city is a far cry
from the huge scale of North American architecture.

Table 7.1 **Tallest Buildings in the World**

TV Tower, Delhi, 1988	235m	(776 ft)
Eiffel Tower, Paris, 1889	300m	(984 ft)
Empire State Building, New York, 1931	381m	(1257 ft)
Sears Tower, Chicago, 1974	443m	(1454 ft)
Menara TV Tower, Kuala Lumpur, 1996	420m	(1386 ft)
Petronas Towers, Kuala Lumpur, 1996 (Tallest building)	452m	(1483 ft)
TV Tower Moscow, 1967	540m	(1782 ft)
CN Tower, Toronto, 1976 (Tallest mast structure)	553m	(1802 ft)
London Comparisons		
Canary Wharf	243m	(800 ft)
NatWest Tower	182m	(600 ft)
BT Tower	176m	(580 ft)
Nelson's Column	56m	(185 ft)

Source: The Concrete Society, 1997.

nial and commercialized American form of architecture of questionable pedigree. He did not invent a new building style; rather he made the North American style acceptable in Europe as the new-born international style. Le Corbusier had been impressed by Henry Ford's approach to the mass production of motor cars, and believed dwellings could also be mass produced on an assembly line with the components being slotted together later on site.

Living in France his concept of housing tended to centre on the apartment or flat. He envisaged multistorey living, high rise blocks of flats in which each individual dwelling unit was to be based on scientifically worked out dimension – a modular unit to meet the needs of the average man. He said, 'a house is a machine for living in' (*une machine à habiter*) (Ravetz, 1980). This is a limited view of a house and presumes that the architect can produce a standardized unit for the needs of the standardized human being.

His solution to the congestion and problems of modern industrialized urbanization was to knock it all down and start over again. He wanted to demolish and rebuild Paris, but the city authorities fortunately did not go along with his ideas. Housing, and other land

uses too, were to be piled one on top of the other to create the vertical city in high rise blocks with vertical neighbourhoods in each. These blocks were to stand on pillars, thus freeing the space at ground level for expanses of landscaped public areas of grass and trees. He even suggested that 90 per cent of the ground could be left free, by piling the people up in these blocks (Le Corbusier, 1971, formerly 1929). There are similarities with the garden city approach in the emphasis on open space, but it was to be provided communally and not in the form of individual personal gardens. Le Corbusier did allow for some low-rise housing in a few of his schemes, but not for all. Le Corbusier is often accused of being totalitarian in his views. He said 'we must create the mass production spirit' by creating a mass-produced housing environment. This is a far cry from participatory planning, rather the architect was part of the priestly caste of experts who believed, because of their superior intellect that they knew what was best for the population.

Modern architecture in general is often accused of creating impressive massive buildings from a visual and townscape aspect, but lacking sensitivity and awareness as to how individuals and families actually live in the buildings, leading to the classic problem of where to hang the washing; where to let the children play; where to spread out the bits whilst repairing the motorbike without them being stolen; to name just three normal functions of modern family life. Le Corbusier's followers would say that the high rise buildings of today are mere imitations and bear no relation to his original ideas. Whilst in Britain at the height of the 'high rise movement' the average tower block would reach around 12 storeys at most, in other parts of the world, especially North America and increasingly in South East Asia (see Table 7.1), buildings are much higher.

Le Corbusier also had a flourishing architectural practice and is well known internationally for a range of individual building commissions. The high rise element was only one aspect of a whole range of other town planning ideas put forward by Le Corbusier. Like Ebenezer Howard, he believed in the importance of land use zoning (vertical as well as horizontal in his case), and the centrality of transportation, even suggesting an early form of urban motorway to weave between his blocks to allow for the new invention, the motor car. Most of his plans remained as ideas in books rather than actual schemes, but nevertheless he greatly influenced succeeding generations. He never had the opportunity to build one of his cities in Europe. Nevertheless, somewhat inappropriately, he was responsible for designing the new state capital of the Punjab in India at Chandigargh: a fairly conventional medium rise scheme. The western architecture, with emphasis on scientific land use zoning, and ample provision of wide roads for the motor car may have been ideal solutions to the problems which existed in Europe, but the city seems out of context and out of place in India, with limited motorized traffic and a more rural way of life. Le Corbusier is probably better remembered for a much smaller scheme in the South of France, the Unité d'Habitation apartment block development built in 1947 near Marseilles, which consists of a medium-rise apartment development with the main building combining social and commercial uses, including a nursery, shops, common rooms and a roof top sports area alongside the dwelling units.

Meanwhile in British domestic housing architecture pride of place was given to the garden city mock Tudor style in the inter-war period. There were attempts by more daring local builders to apply the ideas of the modern functionalist movement to domestic housing in Britain creating 'sugar lump houses', white concrete houses with flat roofs, and functional metal window frames in the modern style. Examples of these can be found in many British cities, but these never became as popular as the vernacular style of suburban housing, such as mock Tudor.

THE DEVELOPMENT OF PLANNING IN BRITAIN

A New Century

The interests of town planners were not limited merely to housing or to working class areas, but were concerned with planning for all land uses and social classes. Relatively speaking, however, a straightforward

Figure 7.4 **Chandigargh, Punjab, India. (a) Centre; (b) Residential Area.**
Corbusier never built a city in Europe but he designed the state capital of the Punjab. Jane Drew, a woman architect, was one of his assistants responsible for the residential areas.

Figure 7.5 **Concrete House, Westbury on Trym, Bristol.**
In England such 'sugar lump' concrete houses embody the domestication and suburbanization of the new international style.

'spatial' (physical) emphasis to town planning predominated in Britain until well into the 1960s when planning became both more concerned with the 'aspatial' (social) results of the physical land use policies which it had introduced, and less self-confident and more critical of its role (Foley, 1964).

Town planning was becoming a recognized higher profession in its own right separate from surveying and engineering. The Royal Town Planning Institute was established in 1914 (Ashworth, 1968: 193). Also the Town and Country Planning Association had been founded as a major pressure group which grew out of the garden cities movement. But there were few legislative powers to make planning a reality, and it was not yet a major local government function.

By the early twentieth century it was realized that urban problems could not be solved 'once for all' by producing 'the plan', but that planning entailed an endless process of policy making, control and implementation. Patrick Geddes, a Scottish town planner had written a book stressing the importance of a methodological scientific approach summarized in the schema 'survey, analysis, plan' (Geddes, 1915 [1968]; Boardman, 1978).

In 1909 the Housing and Town Planning Act was passed. This was to set the agenda for the future path of the scope and nature of town planning in Britain. The Act, introduced under a reforming Liberal government, made possible the creation of a much extended mass council housing system, which coincided with the decline of the private rented housing sector. Under this Act local authorities were expected to produce 'schemes', as town plans were called in those days, showing the location and layout of these new developments. In the process of planning these individual schemes, they were inevitably moving toward considering questions as to the layout and design of whole towns and their likely future growth. In fact housing estates were often built out on the edges of cities, where the land was the cheapest and in areas where they were less likely to cause conflict or reduce the property values of middle-class suburban areas, storing up transport problems for the future.

The First World War

The First World War, 1914–18, was a major social and economic watershed. Following the war, partly because of the fear of social unrest, there was a demand for better housing and improved social conditions for the working classes. Society was strongly divided on class and gender lines. Many women had been drawn into factory employment, especially in munitions factories during the war. Although many women had to hand their jobs back to the returning men, new factory and office jobs gradually opened up for women. The Sex Disqualification (Removal) Act 1919, enabled women to enter the professions officially for the first time, because of the manpower shortage (Lewis, 1984). Women had previously been involved in voluntary work dealing with the issues of housing, public health reform and even town planning, but had little right to own property themselves until the reforms of the late nineteenth century (Hoggett and Pearl, 1983).

The Housing and Town Planning Act 1919 introduced a massive council house building programme specifically aimed at providing 'Homes for Heroes' for the soldiers who returned from the Great War. Under the 1919 Act, 213,000 houses were built, then the first Labour government introduced the Wheatley Act (the Housing Act 1919), which gave greater emphasis to the state provision of housing (Macey and Baker, 1983; and Smith, 1989). Standards were set based on the Tudor Walters report in 1918, the first of the big housing reports, and was influenced by garden city ideas. It was superseded by the Parker Morris Report (1961) which has subsequently been replaced by a range of other measures more related to cost cutting than pure design. The occupiers of the early council houses were chiefly respectable skilled working men and their families. Early council housing was not specifically concerned with homelessness, or housing the poor, which were the functions with which earlier charitable housing trusts and the Octavia Hill approach to housing management had been more concerned. Both then and now provision for single people, single parent families, widows, disabled and elderly groups has always been secondary to, rather than balanced with, the provision for families.

The 1919 Act required local authorities to produce schemes, that is town plans, for settlements of over 20,000 people showing the overall land use zonings and the locations of the new housing estates in particular. This part of the Act, like most of the planning Acts until after the Second World War (1939–45), was weak and difficult to administer and enforce because of lack of resources and skilled personnel. The town plan was only advisory, or illustrative, in that it was often no more than a land use map showing what had been already developed rather than what was proposed for the future, but it was a beginning. The standard of planning differed widely in different areas, with some local authorities taking the lead, and others virtually ignoring planning altogether. Although the 1919 Act was ineffective from a town planning viewpoint, it laid the foundations for a series of subsequent inter-war Housing Acts which extended the state's role in the provision of council housing.

The Inter War Period and Social Change

The 1920s and 1930s were times of extensive private housebuilding in the more prosperous areas of the south and midlands. Vast areas of private speculative housing estates were built around towns and cities and people escaped out of the urban congestion into the fresh air and sunshine of the Home Counties. Totalitarian planning schemes by architects such as Le Corbusier, arguably belonged to the nineteenth century. As more people had the resources to make their own choice as to what they wanted, many opted for the individual house with a garden rather than the flat in the high rise block. While the problems of the nineteenth century may be seen as being associated with poverty, i.e. most people having too little, in the

Figure 7.6 **Ordinary Suburban Housing.**
Twentieth century urban growth is characterized in England and Wales by vast suburbanization. The villagy mock Tudor and half-timbered styles of the model communities of the late nineteenth century were greatly imitated. Do you consider the suburbs to be part of the 'real city'? Most people in Britain live in suburbs.

twentieth century new problems, such as suburban sprawl and traffic congestion emerged, which were the result of increased affluence amongst large groups of the population. Town planning became concerned with protecting the countryside from the spread of the town, as well as controlling the quality of urban development within existing urban areas.

This process was speeded up by another transport revolution, namely the invention of the internal combustion engine. Subsequently the motorized bus (omnibus) and the development of mass ownership of the motor car gave far greater mobility. But private car ownership never topped 2 million before the war and then actually went down again after the war until economic recovery occurred in the mid 1950s, increasing ever since with over 20 million vehicles on the road today. This movement had started with the growth of the railways in the nineteenth century and grew apace with the expansion of the metropolitan railway around London at the turn of the century, spawning what was called, 'metro land' (Jackson, 1992; Betjeman, 1974).

Another economic revolution was taking place, as far-reaching in its effects on society as the industrial revolution, namely the development of commerce and office employment. This has continued to the present day. It created a new middle class of office workers, administrators and managers in the 1920s and 1930s. These were the new commuters living in the new sprawling suburbs. In 1910, 90 per cent of all housing was rented, owner occupation being limited to the more affluent classes (Swenarton, 1981). Even in the inter-war period the vast majority of people rented their housing either from the council or from private landlords, with owner occupation accounting for one-quarter to one-third of the housing tenure depending on the locality, whereas now it is approaching 70 per cent. The building society movement was growing among the new middle classes, the 'mortgagariat' who were able to buy their houses with a building society mortgage (Merrett, 1979).

This growth was mainly concentrated in the south and midlands, whereas the inter-war period was also characterized by periods of depression and high unemployment in the older industrial areas of the country. This was especially so in the north and midlands in areas of declining heavy industry. There was a demand for better government policy to counteract the effects of unemployment. Also it was necessary create a more balanced distribution of jobs, people and housing in the country as a whole, and thus to help break down the 'two nations' division between north and south which became more noticeable as the Depression of the 1930s deepened. No doubt cheap labour from these depressed areas, moving down to work in the south in the construction industry, was a contributory factor in the building boom of the inter-war years. Agricultural land was also cheap as a result of overseas food imports and so the circumstances were ripe for massive suburban expansion.

Between 1930 and 1940 alone 2,700,000 houses were built, and much of this development was occurring as urban sprawl (Legrand, 1988). The Town and Country Planning Act 1932, in an attempt to control the flood, required local authorities to produce zoning maps designating restricted areas for housing development, and requiring developers to get a rudimentary form of planning permission. In fact, many developers virtually ignored the legislation as the penalties were minimal and difficult to enforce. Local authorities were also required to pay compensation if a permission was refused which naturally discouraged them from making refusals. If there was no plan available when developers wanted to build they were

granted what was known as 'Interim Development Control' permission. In practical terms all this meant was that the planners often drew the land use zoning plan after the developers had built – hardly positive town planning!

Developers often chose to build houses along existing roads to save money, creating long ribbons of development cutting into the countryside on the outskirts of towns. Visually this housing blocked the view of the landscape although there might be fields behind the houses. Socially long spread out rows of houses made the provision of schools, shops and social amenities difficult. From the traffic aspect, as car ownership grew, a whole series of garages, and driveways going straight onto the main road caused major traffic problems. Such ribbon development is in no way part of, or comparable to, the concept of linear cities in which whole neighbourhoods and all the land uses are spread out like beads on a necklace in a linear format. The Restriction of Ribbon Development Act 1935 attempted to control this unnecessary linear development, and required developers to build in more compact units with integral estate roads off the main road. This Act covered many other aspects of land use and development and was in a sense another early town and country planning act in all but name.

The pre-war Second World War Acts were difficult to enforce and there was growing public pressure, from some quarters, for greater control. Amenity and rural preservation groups were springing up who feared the spread of suburbia and the loss of valuable agricultural land. The building of electricity pylons across the fields and extensive road building also meant that there were fewer and fewer unspoilt beauty spots. But with the coming of the Second World War, all private building ceased. Utility and function came firmly into fashion, the Anderson air raid shelter was probably the most representative architecture of the time. No homes were built during the war.

POST WAR RECONSTRUCTION

The Second World War

Unemployment and many other social and economic problems temporarily disappeared overnight with the coming of the Second World War in 1939, which required the call up of the majority of the male work-force, leaving the women to man the factories and armaments works. Back in the 1930s the government had introduced a minimal level of state intervention and regional planning in the form of the Special Areas Act 1934. This set the principle which was to be developed further in the post-war reconstruction period of designating specific areas of unemployment and economic decline for special treatment, namely the north east, south Wales, Cumberland and Glasgow districts, all of these being areas which had experienced the decline of heavy industry.

The overall policy was to attempt to take 'work to the workers' rather than the opposite of taking 'workers to the work' (the 'on your bike' philosophy). The latter was discouraged because of the massive level of population migration to the south which was putting great pressure on the housing, services and infrastructure (as it still does today). It was considered bad economics as some areas in the north were becoming 'ghost towns' as the population moved out, leaving behind empty houses, disused factories and neglected roads and public facilities, i.e. a waste of these existing facilities. These problems have continued to haunt governments over the ensuing 50 years to the present day. In spite of decades of government intervention, particularly by the Labour government after the war, the situation has not yet 'balanced' out. Following the 1934 Act, the government set up the Barlow Commission in 1937, which produced the 'Royal Commission on the Distribution of the Industrial Population Report' (Ravetz, 1986). The relationship between town planning and regional planning in the wider context of the well-being of the economy is a theme which will be addressed further in the next chapter. There was increasing enthusiasm for state planning solutions to urban and regional problems in the interwar period, particularly among leading intellectuals of the day.

The Second World War was a watershed in the development of British town planning. Relatively speaking, modern town planning only became a force to reckon with from 1945 onward. The war effort required a greater level of state intervention and state planning than was previously acceptable in controlling industrial and agricultural production, and in setting up regional and national government agencies to co-ordinate the effort. The private property market was suspended during the state of emergency created by the war. People began to become more accustomed to planning and control. Following the war there was a general acceptance that in order to re-establish the economy and reconstruct society, there was a need for as much overall government control and planning as there had been during the war effort. A series of shortages, cold winters, and political reaction against continued rationing meant that the Labour government which had been elected after the war only lasted until the early 1950s. The incoming Conservative government repealed only the more extreme aspects of the Labour government's planning legislation and continued with the town planning and state housing policies of the day, although they lifted many of the restrictions on private businesses and property development.

The extensive bombing of large areas of housing and industry, and the flattening of many historic town centres and inner housing areas made comprehensive redevelopment and planning a necessity. Planners were given extensive powers of compulsory purchase, land assembly and decision making: often against the wishes of the remaining residents who considered they suffered more from the planners than from the Germans. Many of the areas that the planners would have never been able to get demolished had been removed for them by the bombing and the opportunity had at last arisen to put planning theory into practice. Following the war there were continuing shortages and rationing of building supplies resulting in a functional 'modern' style being adopted. One feature of interest is the pre-fab (pre-fabricated housing units), an entirely temporary form of housing which has stood the test of time. Some pre-fab estates are now the subject of conservation area policy.

Reconstruction Planning 1945–52

After the war, there was again a need for 'Homes for Heroes'. As with the First World War, there was considerable unrest, and strong demands for a better society to compensate the workers for their contribution to the war effort. The Labour Party was elected to government after the war and was in a strong enough position to carry out extensive reform, implement a nationalization programme of basic industries and build the Welfare State. However, there was also

The New Towns of Britain

SCOTLAND

GLENROTHES ■
CUMBERNAULD ●   ✖ LIVINGSTONE
IRVIVE ▲   EAST KILBRIDE ■
          ▼ STONEHOUSE

WASHINGTON ✖
PETERLEE ■

NEWTON AYCLIFFE ■

▼ CENTRAL LANCS

✖ SKELMERSDALE
          ▲ WARRINGTON
✖ RUNCORN

✖ TELFORD (DAWLEY)

NEWTOWN ▲   ▲ PETERBOROUGH
              ✖ REDDITCH   ■ CORBY
              NORTHAMPTON ▲
WALES   MILTON KEYNES ▲   ■ STEVENAGE
                   WELWYN ■   ■ HARLOW
CWMBRAN ■   HEMEL HEMPSTEAD ■   ■ HATFIELD
                              ■ BASILDON
              BRACKNELL ■
                 CRAWLEY ■

■ MARK 1 TOWNS:
   LONDON RING
   NORTH EAST AND OTHERS

● 1950

✖ EARLY 1960

▲ LATE 1960

▼ 1970

N
↑

|‒ 100 km ‒|

Figure 7.7 Map of Post War New Towns.

a general consensus among all political parties of the need for more rationalization and planning in general, as was evidenced by the coalition wartime government in setting up various committees to consider the future of Britain. This was optimistic, considering that at the time the coalition government did not know when the war was going to end, or who was going to win.

The Scott Committee reported in 1942 on Land Utilization in Rural Areas and linked to this is the Dower Report on National Parks, 1947, followed by the Hobhouse Committee on national park administration in 1947. The Uthwatt committee produced a report on the vexed question of compensation and betterment in 1942. The Reith Report on New Towns was produced in 1946, being preceded by the Dudley Report in 1944 on the Design of Dwellings which had a particular bearing on the New Towns (Cullingworth and Nadin, 1997). The 1944 White Paper, 'The Control of Land Use' set out the agenda for future planning control. Also during the war in 1943 the Ministry of Town and Country Planning was set up, to be replaced in 1951 by the Ministry of Housing and Local Government, and in 1970 by the Department of the Environment. London already had a more advanced planning system than other provincial cities, because its problems were so much greater.

Other notable events were the production in 1944 of the Greater London Development Plan by the prominent planner Patrick Abercrombie, which was to form the basis of much post-war town planning in London (Abercrombie, 1945). Prior to the war London had already designated its own Green Belt under the Green Belt (London and Home Counties) Act 1938. Abercrombie's plan also made proposals for a series of inner and outer ring roads around London to cope with future levels of traffic: one of the descendants of these original ideas coming to birth 40 years later in the form of the M25. It was envisaged that new expansion would occur in a series of satellite new towns outside of the Green Belt, in locations comparable to Howard's original ideas and as part of the overall strategy for the London conurbation and the south east.

Town planning was one component of a much broader social and economic programme of post-war reconstruction aimed at creating a better more rationally organized 'Welfare State'. Though there was a strong emphasis on greater equality the aim was not to create a socialist state, and the aspirations reflected the typically British compromise of creating a 'mixed economy' of reform rather than revolution, in which both private enterprise and state intervention could play a part. Overall the emphasis was on trying to create greater efficiency, order and progress by providing modern facilities, planning having an important role in co-ordinating all this. Indeed 'planning' became the philosophy of the post-war period, the spirit of the age, being seen as the solution to all problems such as economic over-production, over-population, and of course unruly urban growth into the countryside and civic chaos. The aim was to 'Build a Better Britain' literally. Britain had industrialized earlier than many other European nations, and was now at a disadvantage in possessing much out-of-date capital equipment, plant and machinery, and had in a sense rested on its laurels depending on the support of the wealth of the Empire, much of which it was losing in the post-war period. Other European nations were also producing a solid state-funded physical and social infrastructure to provide the basic requirements for the development of their economies.

Development Plan System

Under the Town and Country Planning Act 1947 all development had to receive planning permission (Cullingworth and Nadin, 1997). Local authorities had to prepare Development Plans showing the main land uses by means of coloured zonings. The system was based on a 'master plan', or blueprint approach. The plans were to be prepared on the basis of the survey, analysis, and plan approach originally promoted by Geddes (Geddes, 1968 [1915]). The main type of plans to be prepared under this Act were the county maps which were produced to an Ordnance Survey base of 1 inch to the mile; the county borough maps which covered the main urban areas at 6 inches to the mile; and supplementary town maps showing details of smaller towns and specific urban areas. Comprehensive Development Area (CDA) plans were produced which dealt with town centre redevelopment in detail. The plans were meant to have a 5-yearly review, but the amendments system proved lengthy to implement, and the plans were seen as slow and inflexible in responding to change.

To make the new planning system work there had to be strong powers of control. In certain circumstances, compensation was given if a planning refusal deprived a developer of his natural right to develop. More political was the decision to impose betterment levy (a development tax) on developers who benefited from an increase in land value because of planning decisions or land use zoning. If agricultural land were zoned as residential land this would vastly increase its value. Originally the betterment levy was at 100 per cent, but this was later reduced and then abolished under the Conservative government of the 1950s. The 1947 system represented a half-way house between nationalization and a free market situation. It effectively 'nationalized' development value, rather than nationalizing the land itself. There has been a continuing saga over the last 40 years over the question of compensation and betterment, with Labour governments generally advocating taxation of development rights, if not land nationalization itself. For example the last Labour government introduced the Community Land Act in 1975. In contrast Conservative governments have generally reversed such policies. Nowadays any gains made as a result of the planning system are treated as capital gains through the normal taxation system. But many would argue that the present proliferation of 'planning gain' at local authority level constitutes an unofficial form of betterment levy or land tax, to get the developer to pay more towards the effects of his scheme in these days of local government cutbacks when the local authority cannot afford the costs for all the roads, community facilities and public services a new scheme generates.

Many consider, in retrospect, that town planning of the post-war reconstruction variety was unrealistic as there is no ideal single 'once for all' solution or perfect plan for everyone. Planners were unprepared for the rapid changes which occurred in the post-war period, in particular the growth of the use of the private motor car, and the increase in private house-building and owner occupation in the 1950s when the building licence controls and 'rationing' were removed. The Conservative Prime Minister Harold Macmillan summed up this new prosperity by remarking, 'You've never had it so good'. But there were hidden and enduring pockets of poverty both in inner city areas and in the depressed regions where the new prosperity was not experienced at all.

The New Towns programme

Much of the post-war housing and new development was located in the New Towns. The New Towns Act 1946 in many respects fulfilled the original dreams of the late Ebenezer Howard. The new towns were overseen by the New Towns Commission, with individual towns being run by Development Corporations which existed quite separately from the local authority in whose area they were located. The new towns were developed in three main phases, the first – Mark I – were built immediately after the war and consisted mainly of satellite settlements around London on sites which were very similar to Howard's original ones. This was followed by a much reduced second phase of Mark II new towns constructed by the Conservative government in the 1950s, and then a third extensive phase of Mark III new towns, built during the Labour government of Harold Wilson in the 1960s, which will discussed in later chapters (Aldridge, 1979).

The majority of Mark I new towns were built around London, but there were a few others in the immediate post-war period built in the depressed regions, such as Cwmbran in South Wales. Cwmbran's function was to act as a growth point for revitalization of that part of the Welsh valleys. It may be argued that concentrating investment in one new town at the expense of existing settlement is not the best way to regenerate a region, and may in fact lead to the further decline of some of the poorer settlements. New towns were seen by politicians as a tangible mark of progress that they could point to and say that they have achieved something. Piecemeal small-scale development in and around existing urban areas was far less politically attractive although arguably socially more worthwhile.

Regional planning

The issue of the location of the new towns was tied up with another cornerstone of post-war planning – namely regional planning. Major differences had developed in the economic situation between different regions, with unemployment and depopulation in the north east and over-population and congestion in the south east. In a sense the war had overnight resolved the unemployment problem for the time being, and given the government time to think. Indeed wartime munition factories were often the basis of post-war trading estates. The Distribution of Industry Act 1945 gave grants and incentives which encouraged firms to move to these areas, following the principle of taking work to the workers. However some would say that this approach penalized businesses which wanted to develop and expand in the more prosperous areas. Also even in the most prosperous cities such as London, there were distinct areas of unemployment and poverty which needed employment and could not compete with the more favoured areas (Balchin and Bull, 1987). Another related aspect of the post-war planning programme was the National Parks and

Access to the Countryside Act 1949 which was developed within the context of a national land use strategy for Britain (Hall, 1992) and will be discussed further in Chapter 12.

Did They Get It Right?

Looking back on the scope and nature of immediate post-war town planning certain issues seem to be missing, The problem of the motor car, for example, was not a major issue then, as car ownership did not rise significantly until the 1960s. Most people depended on public transport, and the 1950s were very much the age of the bicycle as well as the train, bus, motorcycle, moped and scooter. In 1951, 86 per cent of households had no car (Mawhinney, 1995).

Many of the early post-war town centre redevelopment plans were based on a total underestimate of the future needs and effects of the motor car and parking. Many housing estates had narrow roads impractical for parking and no garages or car spaces. Indeed, in planning council estates it was considered that if a family could afford a car it did not need a council house, and so provision for the motor car was minimal. This was even so when local bus services were inadequate and the estate was miles from anywhere. There were also problems associated with ribbon development, and a generally higher level of car ownership in the south east, particularly in London, where there had always been traffic problems.

There seemed to be little enthusiasm for the retention of the historical heritage of cities, either from the architectural or the social viewpoint. Indeed there was a tendency to despise Victorian architecture and to categorize many older residential properties as slums, or as awkward buildings in the way of the clean sweep of progress. It is now accepted that many valuable historic buildings were demolished just because they were old. Concern for the past expressed itself more in the preservation of archaeological remains and historic monuments rather than in urban conservation.

One of the aims of post-war planning was to solve the housing crisis. In fact several commentators argue that Britain ended up with *more* homeless people not less as a result of the net effects of clearance policies (Ravetz, 1980; Donnison and Ungerson, 1982). In some areas there was so much slum clearance, and inadequate new housing development (because local authorities ran out of money) that they ended up with a net loss of housing stock! All this activity was motivated by a desire to clear all the slums and put people in pristine, out-of-town council estates, but often the sense of community in working class areas was demolished along with the housing in the process. Some would go further and say that it was a definite policy of destruction of working class communities for political reasons, while others would say that many of these housing areas were seen as obstacles in the way of 'progress' and had to be demolished for expansion of the central business area to take place (Cockburn, 1977).

There was a shortage of suitably qualified planners in those days, so many 'planners' were likely to come from a surveying, civil engineering, architecture or public health background. These professions, in which there was arguably little emphasis put upon social issues, all had predominantly male memberships. These 'planners' may have been unaware of the wider economic, political and social complexities of town planning. But, whether or not this was the case, the new system was firmly weighted towards a physical land use approach to town planning. Planners were accused of having a naïve view of the nature of social problems and their causes. If a government does not tackle the underlying problems of poverty and disadvantage in society it is inevitable that certain areas of cities will become poor and run down and slums will develop; simply because people cannot afford to renovate their properties. Many thought that the Britain of the 1950s was, in the words of the pop star Billy Fury 'only half way to Paradise' (Wilson, 1980).

TASKS

Information Gathering Tasks

I. Find copies of old development plans from the 1950s, which are based on a simplistic land use zoning basis, and coloured in, or shaded in, using the officially approved town planning colours of the day. Compare these with modern types of development plans for the same areas, observing changes in complexity and the physical differences in terms of growth and expansion of the urban areas in question.

II. Track down the accompanying written statements for these plans and compare and contrast content and format over the years.

Conceptual and Discursive Tasks

III. Summarize the main aspects of post-war reconstruction, and identify the main aims and objectives of the legislation and policies described.

IV. To what extent was post-war town planning preoccupied with planning for housing? Discuss with examples to justify your views.

Reflective Tasks

V. What is your image of the 1950s? Where did this image come from? Television, movies, planning textbooks? Imagine a situation in which most large cities had experienced extensive bombing and subsequent redevelopment. Can you identify any parallel situations in the world today where cities have been severely affected by bombing, political upheavals, and subsequent reconstruction?

FURTHER READING

Significant history texts include Ashworth, Cullingworth, Cherry, Hall, and Burke, and others given in the previous chapter such as Mumford, which the student will find continue into the historical period relevant to this chapter too.

The RTPI Distance Learning Package, Block I, *Planning History*, Unit 4 (RTPI, 1986), gives a comprehensive background. Alternatively any good basic history book is bound to include urban issues and provide background context.

Part 3

WIDENING THE BOUNDARIES: MODERN PLANNING

8

THE POST-WAR PERIOD
TILL 1979

THE 1950s

In the euphoria of immediate post-war socialism many imagined that in the future the bulk of new development would be carried out by the State and indeed until the lifting of the restrictive building licences in the early 1950s most new development was built by the government, including council houses, public buildings, factories and public works (Hall, 1992). There was a need to rebuild public buildings and infrastructure and priority was given to industrial buildings. In the early 1950s the pent up demand of the private sector was given free play and vast numbers of new houses were constructed, testing the new restrictive planning system to the full. However, local authorities had no qualms about entering into partnership schemes with developers to build town centres.

When the bombed centre of Coventry was rede veloped, it was assumed that cars could park on the small reinforced roof which covered part of the new shopping centre (Tetlow and Goss, 1968). Shoppers complained about the unfriendliness of the design of many of these new centres, because of excessive numbers of steps, escalators which seldom worked, lack of public conveniences and a lack of sitting areas and meeting places. When the Conservative government came to power in the early 1950s they continued the national commitment to build houses, and to enforce town planning, revising the compensation and betterment tax aspects of the 1947 Act, but keeping the rest of it substantially unchanged.

THE 1960s

High Rise Development

Town planning took on a new impetus in the 1960s with an emphasis on high-rise developments (Sutcliffe, 1974), the influence of Le Corbusier and the modern movement increased. The development of a large complex of council housing at Roehampton, near Richmond Park in London, owed much to the ideas of Le Corbusier, consisting of white blocks of flats on a green landscaped slope with the buildings raised up on pillars. The high-rise movement went on to become widespread throughout the country, but the standard of the blocks varied. Less than 5 per cent of the population live in blocks of flats of six storeys or more. It was imagined that by building high it was possible to get the same number of people housed on the site in the modern blocks, as had existed in small, cramped terraced housing of the inner city areas before the site was cleared. However, this was not feasible because sunlight and daylight regulations were applied which required the buildings to be spaced out to ensure that they received adequate light and did not overshadow other buildings (DOE, 1971). By the time provision (even inadequate provision) had been made for playspace, landscaping, and increasingly the demand for car parking around the base of the blocks, the density was not that much greater than that attained by building high-density, low-rise developments.

It was argued that it was cheaper to build high-rise, but this depends on what is included in the cost. All the services, pipes and cables, had to be carried up

Figure 8.1 **Birmingham Rotunda.**
Many city centres were redeveloped in the 1950s and 1960s. This usually involved a great deal of demolition, increased access for the motorcar and less pedestrian access for the shopper. Nowadays planning initiatives such as 'Birmingham for People' are reclaiming the city for pedestrians, and revitalising the city centre.

London residential tower block, in the late 1960s confirmed their fears. A lady on one of the top floors got up in the morning and switched her gas oven on, there was an enormous explosion, and the whole of the side of the building collapsed like a pack of cards. The public outcry which followed helped swing the pendulum back towards traditional construction (Ravetz, 1986).

There were the practical problems of young families with children living in small flats, without the overflow space of a back garden, for play, storage and somewhere to put the washing. There were structural problems of faulty construction, condensation, noise between flats with thin party walls, smelly, inefficient waste disposal chutes and expensive communal heating systems. There were psychological problems of the effects of height. Socially, people felt isolated because there was no longer any street life to walk out into; simply filed away in their little boxes along each corridor. Residents felt unsafe, and unable to achieve adequate surveillance of the area around their dwelling. They could not see who was going along the corridor from inside their flats, and many of the lifts, communal areas and entrances were heavily vandalized, with strangers wandering in and out (Coleman, 1985). Most of the flats were constructed for local authorities as council housing, and built 'on the cheap'. But high-rise can work well in some situations.

into the building vertically to provide water, gas, electricity, and waste disposal for the flats, which increased the cost. Studies showed it was marginally cheaper to build up to a certain point but beyond this the cost increased, usually floor six and definitely floor ten, was when the 'threshold' was reached and costs climbed rapidly (DoE, 1993b). The Labour government of the day encouraged high-rise as the solution to the nation's housing problems by giving subsidies to local authorities to build blocks of flats, thus distorting the argument as to whether it was cheaper than conventional housing. Harold Wilson the Prime Minister was a great believer in the 'white heat of technology' and favoured the fast pre-fabricated techniques of systems building. The schemes were never popular with the residents and the collapse of Ronan Point, an inner

Figure 8.2 **Roehampton, London.**
Le Corbusier's ideas influenced the LCC's approach to mass state housing in the 1960s, first in Roehampton, near Richmond Park London. In fact this was a fairly medium rise, sensitively landscaped development compared with what was to come later.

For example, there are high-rise blocks in the upmarket area of Mayfair in central London; and along the south coast, in which the retired elderly predominate. Apartment living is also commonplace in many European cities for all social classes. Much depends upon the quality of construction, level of back-up services and the life style and income of the residents.

Many council blocks of flats built to provide an alternative to nineteenth century slums, have themselves become slums. Some local authorities have adopted drastic measures, 'beheading' them, that is turning them back into lower-rise housing or maisonettes at considerable expense. Some have simply been blown up, having become uninhabitable, whilst others have been entirely refurbished and sold to the private sector. Two of the key social questions here are, Is it the people that make the buildings 'bad'? or Is it the buildings that make the people 'bad'? Some would argue that it is the level of housing management and estate supervision which is at fault on high-rise estates which predominantly consist of rented property where nobody has a sense of ownership or belonging (Roberts, 1991).

Property Boom

In the 1960s the private property sector came into prominence again after the building controls of the 1950s, resulting in town centre redevelopments, new office blocks and high-rise housing schemes. There was a growing demand for office space, and high-rise office blocks were seen as assets valuable to pension funds and insurance companies, often being worth more empty for investment purposes than occupied, in the days when rates were not payable on empty buildings (Marriot, 1989). High-rise office blocks dwarfed historical town centres and church spires as in Manchester and in Birmingham where the city centre was circled by a ring road and pedestrians were pushed underground. This was a period of growing community discontent and urban pressure group action against the activities of the planners (Aldous, 1972). Protesters included members of early housing pressure groups such as 'Shelter' (Wilson, 1970), people protested against what was happening in the inner city (Donnison and Eversley, 1974). A multiplicity of local

***Figure 8.3* Starter Housing in the Bristol Suburbs.**
By the 1970s and 1980s the nation had recovered from the war and many were experiencing affluence. Owner-occupation was growing across the social classes with a wide range of house sizes and types being offered by the private sector.

groups were fighting the developers and planners against the demolition of their local area, such as at Tolmers Square in London. More broadly as a reaction to the market-led development of the 'Surging 1960s', the beginnings of other movements which were to become central 20 years later could be seen appearing on the horizon, such as the environmental movement (Arvill, 1969) and the Women and Planning movement (Cockburn, 1977). Town planning also appeared to be pro-motor car, and few seemed to consider the consequences. Land uses and developments were beginning to decentralize and disperse, although it was not until the extension of the motorway system that developers became attracted to out-of-town sites alongside motorway junctions (Walker, 1996).

Although the planners had immense powers they did not generally use them on behalf of the local community. On the contrary the local authority often went into partnership with the developers, using its compulsory purchase powers to assemble the site, prepare the infrastructure and generally smooth the way for the property bonanza. Many saw this unholy alliance, and tangled web of relationships between planners and developers as the opposite of what town planning was meant to be about, thus facilitating a more social and environmentally concerned approach to urban development. The property boom benefited the land use professions, creating a demand for a

***Figure 8.4* Boarded up Council Housing.**
In the economically depressed areas such as the North East, unemployment continued, poverty and social problems persist in distinct pockets of deprivation. Attempts to provide state social housing were dogged by vandalism, condensation, structural failure and decay.

greater range of property-professional specialisms and levels of expertise (Marriot, 1989).

As time went on, developments became more sophisticated. By the 1970s enclosed shopping centres were appearing, an improvement on the windswept facilities of the 1950s. From the outside these often looked like medium rise office blocks. Inside they consisted of multi-level shopping malls, the ultimate development of precinct shopping. The problem was that many of them were closed at night and patrolled on the perimeters by security guards, thus taking away the citizen's right to stroll around the centre in the evenings. Many of these centres lacked any of the cultural or entertainment facilities usually associated with town centres. Shopping precincts and pedestrianized centres were seen as dangerous, because they had no through traffic, and were completely devoid of people at night, except for would-be muggers loitering in the shadows. Ordinary people, particularly local residents who had seen their communities and houses demolished to make way for these central area developments demanded more accountability from the planners, and more planning for the benefit of the local people and less for big business interests.

New Towns

The rate of development that had been initiated in the late 1940s, under the Mark I New Towns Programme (as described in Chapter 7) was not carried through in the 1950s under the Conservative government. Cumbernauld in Scotland was the only 'Mark II' New Town commissioned, because the Conservatives favoured a policy of developing 'expanded towns', based on existing provincial towns such as Swindon and Andover to take 'overspill' from the large conurbations under the Town Development Act 1952, rather than building complete new towns. Neither Labour nor Conservative thinkers gave much attention to what today's planners would call the revitalization of the inner city, rather the emphasis was on decentralization of 'non-conforming uses' to green field sites. The Slum Clearance Act 1957 had given local authorities greater powers to carry out demolition, and this led to criticism from working class communities living in the areas affected: the very people it was meant to be 'for' had very little opportunity to decide for themselves what they really wanted for their areas.

In the 1960s there was a return to greater emphasis upon another new towns programme. The Mark III New Towns created under the Labour government consisted both of regional growth centres in depressed areas which were meant to act as growth poles for the surrounding area, and also a further phase of overspill New Towns in prosperous areas in the midlands, where they were intended to take the pressure off existing cities and provide new opportunities for investment and growth. Some would subdivide the Mark III New Towns further and call Milton Keynes, Mark IV. This is virtually a city rather than a town, and had a target population of a 250,000. In Mark III New Towns neighbourhood design and overall planning structure had become more sophisticated. For example, arrangements are based on New Towns being divided into intermediate districts of say 15,000 people, these being subdivided into smaller neighbourhoods and local areas. The assumption that people would walk to the local shops and mainly use public transport was a thing of the past. The design of Milton Keynes was conceptualized primarily as a transportation grid. It had some similarity with Broad Acre City, Frank Lloyd Wrights 'autopian' dream. Ample provision of motorway-standard roads was

Figure 8.5 **Neighbourhood Shopping Precincts.**
Every new town had its neighbourhoods replete with shopping centres and schools. The private sector followed suit, this is a picture of the expanded town of Yate north of Bristol, which was not 'planned' as such but was a private enterprise development to provide new estate housing for commuters.

provided, with pedestrians taking second place. This was a reflection of the central fixation of 1960s planning with the motor car in mind.

There have been no New Towns designated since the beginning of the 1970s. When the recession began to affect these 'artificially' created settlements, economic and social problems were amplified, particularly in the more vulnerable new towns located in the north and midlands. Many of the industries were multinational and had no 'real' local ties, and so they simply moved out to catch the next government grant elsewhere. While some of the New Towns, especially in the south, including Milton Keynes, have gone from strength to strength, others are the worse for wear. The official government New Towns policy has been wound up, there has been interest in recent years in the development of private new towns.

New Towns were financed initially by exchequer grants, but they were also intended to be entrepreneurial and financially self-sufficient once well established. They also had a strong social role, and most of the housing in the Mark I New Towns was rented. However, this gradually changed and by the time Milton Keynes was built, over 70 per cent of the housing was owner-occupied, with the ordinary large developers coming in and building virtually the same sort of houses as they would build elsewhere, the difference being that they had to be built in conformity with the neighbourhood unit principles and overall master plan of the development. These days the majority of New Town housing, nationally, is owner-occupied, tenants having had the opportunity to buy their houses from the erstwhile Development Corporations. To own your own home, on the cheap, is no bargain if the building stock is in need of repair and modernization, having been built many years ago. Currently refurbishment programmes are being undertaken in some new towns by Housing Associations to bring the stock up to modern standards.

Transportation Planning

In the 1960s, planners responded to the increase in car ownership and looked to North American transportation planning to show them what to do. It was naturally assumed that the car was obviously good and that everyone would soon have one. In fact less than 40 per cent of households had a car at that time. But there were less out of town shopping developments then and one could still go about one's daily life without the use of a car. However there had always been a problem of the lack of adequate transport for people stuck out on housing estates be they private or council. The 1960s planning strategy put great emphasis upon facilitating the 'journey to work' for the commuter, and mathematical models were developed to show trip generation, origin and destination, and trip allocation (Roberts, 1974). There has been much criticism of such models especially from non-car users.

Meanwhile cycling campaigners were suggesting better ways of planning junctions and main roads

***Figure 8.6* A Typical Flyover: Aggressive and Intrusive Transport Planning?**
New urban motorways, flyovers and car parks cut through the living fabric of the city. Are there any examples like this in your town or city?

(Hudson, 1978). Emerging environmental and community planning groups were challenging the whole basis of town planning and demanding 'Homes not Roads' (Aldous, 1972). It seemed pedestrians were seen as people who got in the way, slowed the traffic down, and were best diverted through uninviting underpasses or time consuming footbridges; it took many years for these attitudes to change. Although cyclists' needs are again being considered, policies are weak. Sometimes cyclists are allocated half a footpath or underpass route with the pedestrians which is dangerous to those on foot, halving the space they have, and unsatisfactory for cyclists too, whilst the motor car continues to take the lion's share. In the 1960s, town planning became for all practical purposes car planning, as the urban motorways, car parks, and multi-level intersections were built to meet the needs of progress, and in the process the whole nature of the structure of cities was being altered and adjusted (Bruton, 1975). In many respects this emphasis on the motor car put many people who were not car users in an even worse position than they had been in the 1950s. An added factor were the Beeching cuts to the rail network in the early 1960s, which abolished many branch lines just when growing suburban areas needed them.

Professor Colin Buchanan, a Scottish traffic engineer and planner, had produced a report for the govern-

ment entitled *Traffic in Towns* in which he suggested ways of planning for the motor car while creating the minimum disturbance for residents living in inner areas (Buchanan, 1963). He proposed that 'environmental areas' should be identified in each town; these were identifiable neighbourhoods or districts which environmentally and socially formed a unit. Road widenings and new urban motorways should be restricted to the edges of these areas to avoid traffic going through the residential area and causing conflict. He suggested that within the environmental area, roads should be mainly culs-de-sac thus preventing traffic from taking shortcuts through housing estates and causing problems to local residents. His ideas are in many ways similar to the concept of the Radburn superblock upon which many new town neighbour-

***Figure 8.7* A Typical Pedestrian Underpass: An Accessible Environment?**
While heaven and earth was moved by the planners to provide cars with unimpeded routeways, the pedestrians were relegated to going underground, through smelly, dank and dark underpasses reeking of urine; up and down innumerable steps and across uneven broken paving stones.

hoods were based. Also his ideas were foreshadowed by a traffic engineer, named Alker Tripp, a London police commissioner who in the 1930s had suggested planning London's traffic on the basis of traffic precincts (or small areas) (Hall, 1992).

Scientific Planning

In the 1960s, computers were introduced to the planning process for the first time in Britain. Consequently, much use was made of mathematical models and scientific prediction methods for developing and justifying policy, especially transportation planning which lent itself well to 'computerization' with all those quantifiable trips, and cars! Retail gravity models were very popular: and still live on in parts of the private property sector. These are used to predict the likely demand for new floorspace in shopping centres in relation to the size of the population in the surrounding catchment area and the distance shoppers travel to reach the centre, relative to the attraction that other existing centres offer. Such approaches have been much criticized, not least by women who constitute the bulk of shoppers. Not all retail space is of the 'same' quality, or of the same use value to a particular individual. Second, the calculations were usually based on assumptions that people chiefly travel by car, when many women do not have use of a car during the daytime. The frequency of public transport, the availability of facilities such as crèches and public conveniences are far more likely to act as inducements to use the centre. But, planning was now seen as a rational scientific process, with an emphasis upon objective and quantiative considerations, which contained little space for such qualitative or 'minority' considerations.

Mathematical and scientific facts are not neutral. Social and aesthetic factors cannot be measured in financial and numerical terms although the social disruption of an area might be as important as the costs of traffic congestion. It is not true to say, 'if you can't count it, it doesn't count', an opinion expressed by some planners of the time. In spite of scepticism and criticism from community interests, and transport user groups, there was also a proliferation of 'mathematical' methodologies for predicting urban change as aids to decision making, such as cost benefit analysis, thres-

hold analysis, network analysis, etc. (Mishan, 1973; Lichfield, 1975; Roberts, 1974). The mathematical techniques of this period were good at giving quantitative measurements of factors which could be easily measured, but weak on evaluating 'qualitative' social factors. These days the use of qualitative methods is increasing (see Chapter 15), enabling the evaluation of the immeasurables that make one scheme more successful or profitable than another.

This trend for 'scientific methods' was demonstrated *par excellence* by the enthusiasm that planners developed for what was known as 'systems' planning in the 1960s (McLoughlin, 1969). The city was seen as an integrated human activity system, in which it was possible to measure and track changes, so that the planner could control the future state of the city. There was a move, therefore, in the approach to plan making from a traditional survey, analysis, plan approach to first setting goals and objectives and then looking at ways in which the city might be controlled to achieve those ends. Town planners have long since become disillusioned with such ideas: although one still finds aspects of these 1960s approaches being perpetuated in some branches of urban economics and regional planning. There was a danger in treating society as a gigantic scientific tidy system, which apparently operated according to neutral scientific laws, rather than seeing it as a disorganized, somewhat chaotic, result of competing interest groups and political factions trying to get their way (Foley, 1964).

New Development Plan System

The traditional approach to plan making, based principally on simplistic land use zoning, was inadequate to deal with rapid change. The planners wished to incorporate advances in planning theory, and more public participation into the plan making process. Therefore, a new development plan system was introduced in the late 1960s, first, on an experimental basis in just a few authorities known as PAG authorities, that is those selected by the Planning Advisory Group, and later extended to all local authorities. The result was the Town and Country Planning Act 1968, later consolidated into the Town and Country Planning Act 1971, which was intended to introduce a better type of development plan, known as the Structure Plan.

Paradoxically, the nature of the new plans and the jargon they were written in were even more confusing for the general public than the 1947 version.

The 'plan' now consisted of both a written policy statement and diagrammatic plans of the policy directives as described in Chapter 2. The system was meant to be based on planners continuously monitoring change in the urban system (using their new computers) to see how, for example, economic changes would affect the demand for new industrial sites, or how changes in family structure were to affect housing demand. The planners sought to identify goals and objectives which they wanted to achieve as the basis of the plan, rather than drawing out a rigid 'once and for all' master plan. These goals, relating for example, to the expansion of a particular area or the provision of a certain level of facilities, could be reached in a variety of ways. Structure Plans were meant to be able to accommodate rather than restrict change provided it tied in with the urban goals that were set. They allowed for a more flexible approach based on negotiation and agreement, rather than preconceived land use plans. So a more 'incremental', that is a step-by-step approach was adopted in order to achieve the long term objectives. Ironically the new system proved even more long-winded and inflexible than the previous system. Many local authorities had great difficulty producing the new local and structure plans, let alone carrying out continuous monitoring. In these cases planning continued on regardless, on the basis of existing plans and non-statutory plan updates taking effect as approved 'adopted plans' of the planning committee and therefore, in the interim, having the force of law. The planners wished to incorporate advances in planning theory, and more public participation into the plan making process (Skeffington, 1969).

Disillusionment

There was considerable opposition to all these changes in the built environment, in architecture, and in the planning system itself. Conservation groups became increasingly concerned at the visual effects of high-rise 'modern' architecture (previously then the highest buildings had been church towers) and at the wanton demolition which was occurring (Esher, 1983). Many

Victorian town halls narrowly missed destruction, and many a Georgian terrace was sacrificed. The government introduced subsidies toward hotel building in the late 1960s, leading to a spate of high-rise American type 'plastic' hotels to encourage tourism. Quite what the tourists thought, who had come to see the quaint English buildings, one can hardly imagine. Towns throughout the country were becoming similar to each other with the 'same' shopping centre, high-rise blocks and traffic problems. People felt the new planning system had made the planners more remote, not more accountable.

A desire to return to more traditional values, and disillusionment with the 'brave new world' of the planners and property developers led to a great emphasis on improvement and conservation policies. The Civic Amenities Act 1967 gave powers for the creation of Conservation Areas, and the listing of buildings of historical and architectural importance became a major issue. Developers adapted to these changes. One development company set a trend, namely Haslemere Estates, specializing in the refurbishment of historical town squares and prestige buildings for offices. This form of accommodation soon became more up-market and fashionable than an office suite in an impersonal concrete block.

A period of public reaction to the 'modern movement' in architecture had set in. Traditional values, architectural conservation and appreciation of classical and historical vernacular styles were all coming back into favour. There was pressure for greater public participation in the planning process. Many ordinary people's houses had been cleared in the name of progress. Householders found their properties were condemned without prior consultation as 'unfit for human habitation', i.e. slums (as Ravetz graphically describes in relation to an actual example in Leeds) (Ravetz, 1980). People wanted greater emphasis put on housing improvement and modernization rather than on clearance. The Denington Report (1966) reflected public concern, and proposed a change of direction away from clearance towards comprehensive improvement of both older housing and the surrounding environment. All this culminated in the Housing Act 1969 which introduced General Improvement Areas (GIAs) and also increased the resources available for individual grants to renovate older property in inner areas.

This marked a turning point in government policy and the beginning of a serious concern with, and recognition of, what came to be known as the 'problems of the inner city'. While this legislation did benefit many inner city residents and working class people, it also had unexpected results such as gentrification of erstwhile rundown areas. In the process property values went up and existing working class residents were gradually pushed out.

THE 1970s

Recession and Reaction

By the mid-1970s, as oil prices increased the bottom began to drop out of the property boom, due largely to conflict in the Middle East, the economy became generally more depressed. However, in spite of increased oil prices there was still a growing demand for planners to take into account the needs of the motor car. This conflicted with the desire to plan in a way which took into account the need for conservation and the importance of local communities. The new Green environmental movement was beginning; Friends of the Earth was established in the late 1960s. Planning for the working classes had taken a back seat with many of the needs of the poorer members of society still unmet. A Labour government came to power in the mid-1970s, with its support from strong motor car manufacturing unions whose objectives were at odds with the environment movement. In the early 1970s the economy went into recession and unemployment rose due in part to the oil crisis. Traditional manufacturing industry in the depressed regions, such as steel manufacturing and ship building, declined even further, and secondary industry in other areas was also affected. Paradoxically there was growth in other sectors of employment particularly in the service sectors and in the new microchip industries. Many of the jobs in this sector were filled by women who had the required dexterity skills and were cheaper and less unionized than men.

The promise of the new leisure age as prophesied in the 1960s where everyone would work three hours a day, and play football the rest of the time (as some planners put it at the time), was beginning to wane as unemployment reappeared. However, there were other groups, particularly the middle classes in the growing quaternary sector of management, the professions and technological research, who were experiencing higher levels of affluence and seemed to have money available for luxury goods, e.g. boats to put in the new marinas created out of derelict docks. Only 3 per cent of households own boats (ONS, 1999). Two classes were developing – those with work and those without. A radical distribution of work opportunities would be required for everyone to benefit from the new age of leisure and technology. Structure planning originated in a period of economic growth and prosperity. It is a very different matter to produce a strategy for decline. The 'quantitative' mathematical emphasis in plan-making was not the most appropriate way of dealing with these sensitive 'qualitative' social and community issues.

Regional Planning

In the post-war years *economic* planning was closely linked to town planning by means of regional planning. Some of the details regarding the percentage rates of grants and incentives will be given, because much of this has now been repealed. It is more important to understand the reasons for the policies than the details.

One of the main reasons for regional planning was to reduce congestion in the south-east and create investment in depressed regions, and thus to create greater balance between regions. There have always been two sides to regional legislation. On the one hand restrictions have been introduced to prevent industry locating in already prosperous areas. On the other hand grants have been given for relocation in depressed areas, for buildings, machinery, plant, infrastructure, training *inter alia*. These grants averaged around 30 per cent of the costs, but sometimes were as low as 15 per cent or less under Conservative governments, to rise again to 75 per cent or more under Labour governments. Also incentives and perks have been given for the relocation of key workers and management from the south-east to the depressed areas. The government constructed trading estates, factory units, recreational facilities and housing, and it decentralized government departments from London to places such as Swansea in Wales (DVLC and the Royal Mint), and other departments to Strathclyde in Scotland.

The pre-war situation was discussed in the last chapter. The post-war Barlow Commission, and related Distribution of Industry Act 1945 had extended intervention so that wider 'development areas' (areas of high unemployment) covering 20 per cent of the total population. Related to this, under the Town and Country Planning Act 1947, Industrial Development Certificates (IDCs) were first introduced to restrict new development of over 5,000 square feet in prosperous areas, thus 'encouraging' industrialists to relocate to depressed areas. The system was insensitive to the fact that within an apparently prosperous area in the south-east there might be pockets of high unemployment and deprivation, particularly within inner city locations. Advanced factories were also established in the depressed areas in the immediate post-war years, which happened too conveniently to tie in with the location of the now disused wartime munitions factories, e.g. on Treforest Estate in South Wales, and with Labour constituency strongholds.

In 1958 there was another Distribution of Industry Act which extended the provisions outlined above to some non-development areas where unemployment was high. In 1960 the Local Employment Act replaced the existing system with development districts which covered 10 per cent of the country (much smaller areas) but targeted aid more directly giving 20 per cent grants on plant and machinery in these areas. The Local Employment Act 1963 gave building grants of 25 per cent on new industrial development in 'development districts', also tax allowances and 10 per cent grants for plant and machinery. A range of grants were introduced for the improvement of derelict land of up to 85 per cent of the cost, plus special grants for provision of infrastructure and the attraction of key workers to development areas.

Economic and physical planning took on a central importance under the Labour government of the 1960s. In 1965 Regional Economic Planning Boards, and related advisory Councils were established in order to create an intermediate regional planning level. These formed the institutional framework for the intended development of a much more carefully organized regional strategy, although their executive powers were fairly limited. Attempts were also made at producing a National Plan (an economic one, and

short lived) and a whole series of national economic planning bodies was created to oversee economic development in the different industrial sectors. A particular problem as perceived by the Labour government, was the concentration of office development in London. The Control of Offices and Industrial Development Act 1965 introduced Office Development Permits (ODPs) for all new office development in the south-east and midlands over 3,000 square feet, and the Industrial Development Certificate (IDCs) system was also made stricter for these areas. The Industrial Development Act 1966 tidied up what had by now become an unwieldy system, creating five large 'development areas' which covered 40 per cent of the UK, introducing a range of grants and incentives.

The Special Development Areas Act 1967 introduced another level of intervention. Wherever the boundaries are drawn, and whether the areas are large or small, there will always be some resentment that some are in and others are out. Following the Hunt Report in 1969, the Local Employment Act 1970 was introduced which designated a further series of intermediate areas with their own grade of grants and incentives. The Industry Act 1972 further developed a complex hierarchy of aid and control based on several categories of area, consisting of development areas. special areas, intermediate areas and derelict land (Hall, 1992; Heap, 1996). In addition in 1975 the Labour Government introduced the Community Land Act, which was another attempt to use the profit from property development for the benefit of the community. Under the following Conservative government, the regional aspect of planning took a back seat, and was reduced in extent. All the years of regional planning had not solved the economic problems of the UK, but would they have been worse without these provisions?

The Inner City

Traditionally depressed regions, for which the post-war planning system had been geared up to deal with under the Industry Act 1945, were not the only areas where there was poverty and unemployment. It was noticeable that the increasing level of poverty and deprivation could not be entirely explained by the rise in unemployment. Rather, they were the result of other social problems such as racial discrimination, family breakup and an ageing population. The 'inner city' became the catchphrase to describe the collection of spatially identifiable groups and problems located broadly within the poorer inner urban neighbourhoods, corresponding to what traditional urban sociologists called the 'zone of transition' (see Chapter 13).

Riots occurred in several inner city areas including Handsworth and Sparkbrook in Birmingham, Everton in Liverpool, St Pauls in Bristol and Tottenham in London. Some would say that the over-concentration on the development of New Towns, and on new development in general, plus decentralization of employment to the regions through regional economic planning policy, had taken the guts out of the cities and actually created many of the inner city problems. Others were warning, from a variety of political perspectives, of the potential problems of concentration of deprived ethnic minority groups within inner city areas. Enoch Powell, in 1968 gave his 'Rivers of Blood' speech painting an inflammatory view of the future. The Commission for Racial Equality concluded that certain racial groups were actively kept out of all-white areas by 'racist' estate agents, and biased local authority housing managers thus creating an enforced ghetto situation (CRE, 1989). Many estate agents pleaded that they simply didn't realize, and so more sensitivity was needed all round.

The Housing Act 1969 had opened up a new lease of life for many of the older housing areas, but it had not necessarily solved the related social problems, indeed existing residents often had to leave their home areas as a result of these policies. In 1968 the Home Office had initiated the 'Urban Programme' with 34 pilot local authorities to investigate the emerging problems of the inner city. This project was as much concerned with rising crime as it was with wider social issues. In 1969 the Community Development Programme (CDP) was set up. CDPs ran in 12 areas to begin with, with social workers rather than town planners taking the leading role. It was fashionable at the time to see the problems 'spatially' as a set of factors that were found in, and could be dealt with, within the framework a specific geographical area: without necessarily considering the social forces that brought people 'down' into these areas in the first place. In the 1970s, Educational Priority Areas (EPAs) had been established in areas where positive discrimination was needed, interestingly towards the white working class, rather than ethnic groups at this stage, as in the case of a scheme which was established in Everton in Liverpool.

In 1971 Comprehensive Community Programmes were introduced in a range of areas, with a broad brief to include education, health, social services and housing policy. In 1972 the emphasis shifted more towards special policies within the realms of town planning itself, and the Department of the Environment established its Six Towns Study, focussing on areas such as Lambeth in southern inner London, and at last publicly recognizing that there was poverty near at hand. The Housing Act 1974 established another category of special housing areas, that is Housing Action Areas (HAAs),. These were smaller than GIAs but in which the emphasis was upon more concentrated immediate attention.

Such schemes often seemed separate from, or insensitive to, other social problems in the areas chosen. In one black inner city area in Birmingham where unemployment was high, white workmen were brought in by the council from outside to repair black tenants' houses, causing considerable tension in community relations. In 1975 the Urban Aid Programme enabled money to be allocated to other inner city schemes including community centres, and later law centres. In 1977 the Manpower Services Commission was set up with particular concern for enabling employment in inner areas. This was followed by the Inner Urban Areas Act 1978, which established special inner urban area policy programmes, this chiefly time under the control of the town planners. Thus the tide had turned from a regionalist approach to one which put greater emphasis upon targeting specific urban areas and this policy was to be continued and amplified throughout the Thatcher administration of the 1980s.

Retrospect

The planners had done a great deal and had held great power to destroy entire sections of Britain's towns and cities since the introduction of the Town and Country Planning Act 1974. Arguably, they had solved very few problems, in fact they had created many new ones. Indeed some would blame the planners and their policies for inner city unrest. For example, after the inner city riots of the 1970s and the subsequent Brixton riots of the early 1980s, Lord Scarman implied in his report on the events that the planners were to blame (Scarman, 1982). If this is so then the planner has a major role to play in solving social problems by offering 'salvation by bricks'. Indeed, many of the nineteenth-century visionaries believed that transplanting people into model communities with plenty of grass and trees and sunshine would change them as people.

TASKS

Information Gathering Tasks

I. Identify areas of your town or city that underwent extensive change in the 1960s.

II. Make a case study of any high-rise block in your area, which may be residential or commercial in use.

Conceptual and Discursive Tasks

III. Discuss the advantages and disadvantages of high-rise development, in relation to both residential and office use.

IV. What were the factors that changed the emphasis from clearance and redevelopment to strategy of improvement and conservation in the 1970s?

Reflective Tasks

V. Looking back, it is easy for everyone to identify what was wrong with 1960s planning, with its emphasis upon clearance, high-rise development and road building. In 30 years time what policies do you consider everyone will see as wrong during the 1990s?

FURTHER READING

Texts covering this period include, Ravetz (1986) *The Government of Space*; and Cockburn (1977) *The Local State: Management of People and Cities*; Hall (1980) *Great Planning Disasters*. Both of these critique the system which gave the planners such extensive powers for slum clearance and redevelopment. Also see Hall (1980) *After the Planners*. Basic texts given at the end of Chapters 1 and 8 also cover this period.

THE EIGHTIES AND NINETIES

CHANGING AGENDAS

REFLECTING ON THE PRESENT

Chapter 9 takes the reader up to the present day. It describes new policies and measures which are as yet untested, and which in many cases are currently the subject of considerable debate. Therefore discursive commentary is given throughout, reflecting current concerns and criticisms.

THE CONSERVATIVE YEARS 1979–97

Laissez faire or State Intervention?

Whilst physical land use planning and development control continued as primary functions of local authority planning departments, by the late 1970s greater emphasis was being put on economic planning issues, by both the outgoing Labour government and the new Conservative government led by Mrs Thatcher, which came to power in 1979. The Conservative government's strategy was based on the encouragement of private business investment rather than direct state intervention. They were in favour of a *laissez faire* approach, which literally means 'free for all' (*allow [them] to do*), and thus favoured an unfettered property market (Lavender, 1990). The Conservative government saw this as the way of as creating jobs and eradicating poverty and deprivation through private enterprise, rather than through the state welfare programmes previously favoured by Labour (Thornley, 1991). But both administrations were concerned with economic planning, albeit informed by totally different images of the economy and society (Atkinson and Moon, 1993).

Arguably much of the agenda of the previous 'old' Labour government was developed in relation to the needs of traditional manufacturing industries and related working class communities, in the North, where grass roots Labour support resided. In contrast the Conservative's perception of Modern Britain was more business-orientated. Policy emphasis was put upon the revitalization, redevelopment and renewal of towns and cities, particularly in the southern part of the country, and especially London. Attention was given to the growing financial, business and service sectors of the economy (Oatley, 1998). The 'workers' were more likely to be perceived to be urban professionals, businessmen and entrepreneurial women, and those employed in offices, retail and service sectors (ONS, 1999, Tables 4.14, and 4.15). Traditional regional policy was seen as supporting 'lame ducks' thus penalizing growth in other areas. Thus emphasis shifted to supporting the needs of the tertiary and quaternary sectors of employment (q.v. Chapter 6) and away from the primary and secondary, heavy and manufacturing, industries of the past.

Factors such as the globalization of economies, international market trends, more women working, industrial decentralization, unemployment, and also a growing proportion of elderly population (9.3 million) have all redefined the nature of the available workforce and of the economy itself. During the 1980s, in the Thatcher era, town planning took on the values of the enterprise culture, inspired by monetarism and the work of the American economist Milton Friedman (1991). Under this new value system it was stated,

Table 9.1 **Governments of the Twentieth Century**

Conservative	James Balfour	1902–1905
Liberal	Campbell-Bannerman	1905–1908
Liberal	Herbert Asquith	1908–1916
Liberal	Lloyd George	1916–1922
Conservative	Bonar Law	1922–1923
Conservative	Stanley Baldwin	1923–1929
Labour	Ramsey MacDonald	1929–1935
Conservative	Stanley Baldwin	1935–1937
Conservative	Neville Chamberlain	1937–1940
Coalition (national government)	Winston Churchill	1940–1945
Labour	Clement Atlee	1945–1951
Conservative	Winston Churchill	1951–1955
Conservative	Anthony Eden	1955–1957
Conservative	Harold Macmillan	1957–1963
Conservative	Alec Douglas-Home	1963–1964
Labour	Harold Wilson	1964–1970
Conservative	Edward Heath	1970–1974
Labour	Harold Wilson	1974–1976
Labour	James Callaghan	1976–1979
Conservative	Margaret Thatcher	1979–1990
Conservative	John Major	1990–1997
Labour England and Wales	Tony Blair	1997–
Scotland, First Minister	Donald Dewar	1999

'there's no such thing as a free lunch', implying that everything had to be paid for somewhere along the line by someone, even in a welfare state. Prior to the Thatcher government, it was generally accepted by all governments that there was a need for some measure of state intervention in the economy and in the built environment. Government policy was still based on a 'mixed economy' that is of a combination of a state control and free enterprise. So there was a measure of planning but there was also private ownership of property and an active property market running in parallel.

In Britain it has traditionally been considered vital for government to take over the provision of non-profit making – but nonetheless essential – urban amenities and infrastructure, and to provide for those sectors of the population who cannot afford to meet their needs through the marketplace. In recent years there has been a breakdown in this consensus, and a more market-orientated, profit making emphasis has been applied to public services. However, although affluent people are at an individual level they still need

certain social goods and services such as roads, sewers, fire services and local facilities. These commodities are aptly described as 'social capital' (Saunders, 1979). Otherwise one ends up with a situation, as in some of parts of North America, where people have large houses but no mains drainage, and almost every house has a private septic tank. It may be more economic, and in society's and industry's interests to provide these utility services on a non-profit making basis to reap the rewards in the long run. However, the Conservative government began to change this consensus.

Acts of Parliament were seldom used (except for Consolidation Acts) to bring in changes in the planning system, as the Conservative government generally introduced change through amendments, statutory instruments and orders, and circulars, making subtle alterations in past legislation, rather than introducing clear cut new Acts of Parliament. In other words a 'non-plan' approach to planning was practised (Greed, 2000a). This tied in with the Conservatives' distaste for state intervention and bureaucracy and their preference for a *laissez-faire* approach (Brindley *et al.*, 1996). Both the Community Land Act 1975 and the ODPs were abolished by the Control of Office Development (Cessation) Order in 1979. In 1981, IDCs were completely suspended. In 1979, 47 per cent of the population had been covered by some form of regional aid. By 1982 the extent of coverage was reduced to 27 per cent of the working population. A three-tier system was established for special development areas, development areas, and intermediate areas, in which grants were available for plant and machinery at the rates of 22 per cent and 15 per cent, on a discretionary basis respectively. But in 1984, aid was further dramatically reduced, which led to a situation of less jam spread more thinly as the late John Smith, then shadow Labour trade secretary, described it. Further changes in 1984 introduced a two-tier system, with 'development areas' which qualified for 15 per cent grants towards new plant and machinery and intermediate areas which were eligible on a discretionary basis, with the areas themselves being greatly reduced. The emphasis had moved away from regional planning to inner city regeneration.

At the same time that new categories of area were being created, existing planning departments, and the local authorities to which they belonged were being reorganized. Some would allege that the abolition of the Greater London Council (GLC) and the large first-tier strategic Metropolitan County Councils (MCCs) in 1986, and their replacement with second-tier district and borough authorities was done intentionally because these big authorities were predominantly Labour-held, with the GLC carrying out what were seen as left-wing policies right on the doorstep of Parliament.

Far from reducing government controls, a great deal of state intervention and centralization of policy making was needed to sustain the free market and related enterprise culture. As the years went by the government was also faced with a range of urban problems and policy issues that required intervention and control, such as, increased traffic congestion, an 'overheated' property market and increased demand for green field site development. The latter demand incensed traditional Tories in the shire counties, who did not want the urban masses impinging on their territory. Indeed members of the new Conservative government were referred to as just a bunch of estate agents by some hereditary peers who had a more paternalistic, less commercial view of government's duty to its people.

Other forces of change and new trends were coming to bear upon planning. These factors included the environmental movement (see next chapter), and the requirements of the European Union (as described in Chapter 2). New alliances were developing between radical environmentalists and shire-county Conservatives, for example, on the preservation of green belt land and the restriction of urban growth (Shoard, 1999). But, demands for environmental sustainability sat uneasily with the enterprise culture of the 1980s.

The demand for sustainability was influencing the design of the built environment as well as the countryside. There was a reaction against much of so-called Modern Architecture, which was seen in retrospect as being ugly, energy-inefficient and socially problematic. By the 1980s contemporary architecture took two main forms. First, there was a growth in traditional, and some would say reactionary, neo-Georgian styles, which were much used in office and residential buildings in areas where urban conservation policy was in force. Second, a range of new 'high tech' styles were developed, for example, by Richard Rogers in the Pompidou Centre in Paris, and in Lloyds of

London and the Millennium Dome (cf. Rogers, 1999). Whilst conservation policy controlled the advance of 'high-tech' buildings in many provincial city centres, the development of science and business parks on the city's edges, close to motorways went unchecked, allowing free rein to the new 'shed' architecture which has developed in the name of progress and technology.

The current post-modernist mood (if not anti-modern mood) is generating a variety of styles. The Green movement is demanding 'sustainable architecture'. Disabled groups are demanding more accessible, user-friendly, buildings – with less steps. There are now a variety of energy-efficient, and ecologically-friendly styles of architecture being developed by young architects, which may yet prove to be the basis for new mainstream fashions and styles for the next century. Overall, it would seem that there is more 'space' for a diversity of styles, without the need for a slavish following of one dominant style as was common in earlier decades.

Enterprise Planning

A range of initiatives was created to bring back business to the inner city, and to facilitate urban renewal. The Local Government Planning and Land Act 1980 consolidated previous legislation and provided the enabling powers for a range of other programmes and measures. For example Enterprise Zones (EZs) were intended to attract investment to run down areas by means of reducing planning controls and suspending ordinary planning law within their boundaries. Urban Development Corporations (UDCs) were established in inner areas (Cullingworth and Nadin, 1997: 238–9). Various other grants, loans, rates holidays, and incentives were introduced, including the City Grant for the redevelopment of areas and repair of buildings which were too deteriorated to be of interest to the developer.

EZ's were relatively small areas, the size of a small industrial estate and are administered by the existing local authority, whereas UDCs are much larger areas, for example the Bristol Development Corporation area and the London Docklands Development Corporation area (LDDC). The London body was established separately from the existing local authorities in their area (much to their chagrin), and employed its own army of planners, surveyors, architects, etc. Its main purpose, however, was not so much to build new development itself, but rather to provide the infrastructure, especially roads and the famous Docklands Light Railway to encourage private developers to build and invest in the area. This is a different approach from the New Town Corporations which always took a much more active role themselves in building both housing stock and industrial units for rent.

Both the EZs nor the UDCs have a limited life expectancy, of around 10 years, when they will be de-designated, this is already happening to some of the early ones. The aim was simply to give critical areas special status whilst they are finding their feet and getting established. Considerable investment has been put into infrastructure, as in the case of the Docklands Light Railway (DLR) in London, and into road improvements. Although many firms took up the offer, as with old-fashioned regional planning, it is debatable whether new jobs and new prosperity were really created, or whether firms simply moved across the boundary in order to catch the grant, and thus deprived other areas of existing employment.

Under UDC policy, vast areas were reclaimed for upmarket residential and business use within the old London Docklands, in close proximity to the City of London, attracting a new social class to the old 'East End' and gentrifying the area (Smith and Williams, 1986). This process created considerable resentment amongst some of the original working class residents. Although the original inner city legislation was purportedly meant to be on their behalf, it has benefited the middle class groups more. Local people remember how difficult it was in the past to get the council to put on an extra bus service to get them to work, whereas now it seems no expense is spared. Meanwhile because of high house prices, and lack of council or cheap rented accommodation many working class people who also have jobs in central London (on the Underground railway, in hospitals, office cleaning and in the shops) find they have to commute further and further away, while many managers wonder why there is no longer a ready supply of working-class labour to do all the essential, yet low status, jobs on which the running of the capital depends.

In 1985 the Government introduced the White Paper 'Lifting the Burden' which placed great emphasis

Figure 9.1 The Importance of Buses.
Major cities are being clogged up with cars, while low levels of rural public transport contribute to rural deprivation. 1960s transport planners used to measure 1 bus = 3 passenger car units (pcus); in reality, one bus is worth more than 50 cars in terms of passenger carrying capabilities.

on minimizing perceived restrictions on economic growth created by planning controls. Subsequently the Housing and Planning Act 1986 introduced Simplified Planning Zones (SPZs) which supplement the EZs and UDPs, but are smaller and the criteria for their location are more flexible. Rydin notes that these were part of a move towards a blanket zoning approach to planning in which permission for development was inherent in the area designation of SPZ (Rydin, 1998: 212). There are, at the time of writing, 13 SPZs, as against 35 EZs in the UK. The need for their designation was subsequently superseded by the introduction of a range of other measures which sought to 'lift the burden' from developers. The UCO and GDO categories were revised and liberalized somewhat to enable greater flexibility between uses (especially among 'B' uses) to encourage new business development.

The principle of such initiatives was to attempt to simplify and speed up the planning system, and to create an organizational framework tailor-made for the special circumstances of a particular situation without disrupting the existing planning system. Meanwhile, in non-special category areas planning law became more complex; the Conservatives introduced planning charges for this kind of application in the late 1970s. The proliferation of *ad hoc* bodies only serves to weaken the existing planning system and increases the powers of central government.

In spite of other regeneration schemes such as 'Garden Festivals', and various inner city initiatives, unemployment continued to rise, inner city problems continued and regional disparities became even greater. Many argued that it was time to bring back 'regional planning' (Hamnett *et al.*, 1989), however, it needed to be based on more sensitive criteria than had been the case; it should, for example, take into account women's employment as well as men's, and demonstrate awareness of the great social disparities which can exist within a region such as the south-east – between rundown inner city areas and the more prosperous suburbs and market towns.

A Softening of Attitudes?

As the years progressed a gradual warming towards the traditional objectives of town and country planning may be observed within the Conservative government, although there also remained a commitment towards the needs of the developer at local level. Gradually there was a move back toward a 'plan-led' as against developer-led approach to planning. In particular, successive Secretaries of State for the Environment put their mark on the Department of the Environment. Development policy was re-affirmed as a 'material consideration' in determining planning applications, reinforcing the principles of Section 54 of the Town and Country Planning Act 1990. For example, Michael Heseltine was keen to promote a range of initiatives which incorporated a greater sensitivity to the environment, whereas in contrast Nicholas Ridley was much criticized for favouring several controversial developments on green field sites. John Gummer was generally seen as the most sensitive towards town planning issues, and became such a convert to the cause of town planning that he continues to write a weekly column for the RTPI in *Planning*.

Members of the Conservative government did not comprise a unitary group with identical values, and under John Major's administration there was a gradual softening of the hardline adopted during the Thatcher years (q.v. Table 9.1). The reason for this softening, including Major's new style of government, was his stated desire to create 'a nation at ease with itself'. The

Figure 9.2 Nibbling away at the Green Belt.
Business expansion within the enterprise culture led to pressure being put upon land use controls, especially in respect of commercial and residential development on the edge of cities.

libertarian strand of Conservatism overcame the more authoritarian strand represented by Margaret Thatcher herself and hard-liners such as Norman Tebbitt. The need to capture the 'Green vote' was also crucial, approximately 15 per cent of voters were voting Green and this was seen as a serious threat to retaining a Conservative majority. Pressure from traditional shire county conservatives to protect the countryside, along with new Green interests, plus pressure from Europe together led to a measure of 'greening' of Tory policy under John Major. The interests of conservative NIMBY voters were in uneasy coalition with 'eco-warriors', for example, in the battle over the building of the Newbury bypass in Berkshire. At an international level the government had made commitments to a range of treaties and agreements concerned with the reduction of pollution and the conservation of the natural environment such as 'Rio', which made a more environmentally-friendly and less developer-led form of town and country planning more acceptable (Barton, 1996 and see Chapter 10). Town planning was re-embraced for the traditional reasons that it actually helped the market, in creating a level playing field, and as a means of regulation and control that could be used to serve the requirements of established property interests.

Inner city problems continued, and the housing market when through a series of booms and recessions in the 1990s. Homelessness was a continuing problem, with large numbers of people sleeping on the streets. Housing issues were frequently featured in cutting-edge documentaries on the television. Anyone attempting to walk down a high street in any main town was likely to be accosted by homeless beggars. The housing situation has become increasingly topical in the light of the swing of government policy away from state provision of council housing in the 1980s. There was a greater concern with social issues in the dying years of the Conservative government, which contrasted with the harder line adopted by Mrs Thatcher, who famously had declared that there was 'no such thing as society' thus rendering valueless the work of generations of sociologists and social policy makers.

Under the Housing Act 1980 tenants were given 'the right to buy' their council houses. A series of subsequent Housing Acts, such as the Housing Act 1985, which further marginalized the role of public sector housing management and reduced the amount of stock available for people on the housing waiting lists. Little new council housing has been built over the last ten years. There had been, however, a revival of interest in the voluntary housing sector and the government favoured contributing financially toward the building and management programmes of housing associations (Smith, M., 1989). This reduced the local authority housing departments' role in the provision of social housing. Generally, the government went for more 'targeting' of special housing and planning schemes within the inner city and problem estates in terms of finance and support, arguably reducing local government's involvement in the management of their locality. The Local Government and Housing Act 1989 introduced the concept of 'Renewal Areas' which are like the old GIAs and HAAs (which they replace), but the emphasis was on partnership with the private sector in renewal, and grants to individual house-holders were means tested.

There were a series of consolidatory Town Planning Acts in the 1990's, mainly dealing with the format of the development system and the enforcement of planning control. There does not appear to have been, at first sight, any strong policy statement on national town planning policy as one would have expected from governments in the past, particularly Labour ones seeking to demonstrate their commitment to state intervention. But the spirit and the purpose of

planning had changed (Ward, 1994). The Town and Country Planning Act 1990 and the Planning and Compensation Act 1991 tidied up the system but did not introduce any new radical change to the development plan system. As the years progressed, however, there was a greater commitment to state intervention and new policy development, to 'plan-led' development, as reiterated in revisions of PPG1. Although the Thatcher and Major Conservative governments were committed to reducing state intervention and regional and urban planning, by the mid-1990s the government had created a large collection of new initiatives and programmes which together comprised a significant new block of planning policy in all but name.

New Organization and Cultures

Many of the changes introduced were more concerned with reforming the structure and culture of the local government and related service delivery bodies, rather than with policy itself; these changes were procedural rather than substantive to the planning system. Greater emphasis was put upon seeing citizens as 'clients' and 'customers' rather than as grateful supplicants of a bureaucratic planning system. A new culture based on 'audits', 'costs' and 'assessment' has been introduced across all governmental organizations. The Audit Commission (1999) was established to monitor the standards of public service provision of goods, facilities and services within local government, including everything from public lavatories and refuse collection to town planning and housing provision (cf BTA, 1999).

Commentators argue that society has moved to a post-Fordist stage. Fordism refers to large scale centrally controlled industry, whereas post-Fordism relates to the breaking up, localization and diversification of industrial and related business activity (Rydin, 1998: 118; Oatley;1996). Post-Fordism is a new mode of regulation (Taylor, 1998: 144; Oatley, 1998: 52). In this changing economic climate, welfarism and state intervention are no longer seen as viable, self-help and entrepreneurialism are dominant (Hall and Jacques, 1989). Traditional economic and political structures and 'ways of doing things' have been replaced by a range of more experimental, entrepreneurial initiatives and business enterprises

(Thornley, 1991; Atkinson and Moon, 1993: Stoker and Young, 1993: Rydin, 1998). Post-Fordism was reflected in the nature of the urban renewal initiatives, which were generally aimed at encouraging a diversity of small businesses grouped within the quaternary economic sector (professional, retail and service industries) rather than concentrating, as in the past, upon attracting one large employer with a huge workforce skilled in secondary sector industrial production (manufacturing, processing, assembly). Arguably the old divisions between left and right, Labour and Conservative, socialist and capitalist were not necessarily appropriate any more, interests in new approaches to urban governance were shared across the political spectrum.

Local authorities were increasingly being bypassed in the organization of new economic urban initiatives, with central government often making direct partnerships and linkages with the private sector: with business and property developers direct. Other means of regulation were used, over and above statutory town planning (Oatley, 1996, 1998). Emphasis was put upon positive, proactive initiatives as well as restrictive controls on property development. For example, The Leasehold Reform, Housing and Urban Development Act 1993, Part III facilitated the creation of the Urban Regeneration Agency and a more entrepreneurial approach to local government policy.

In addition to the UDCs, there were a range of other programmes and initiatives in which private developers directly dealt with central government to obtain funding as under the City Grant provisions introduced in the late 1980s. Because of the increasing diversity and complexity of government schemes, attempts were made to co-ordinate the various policies, first, under 'headings' such as 'Action for Cities', the Urban Programme and City Challenge. All these programmes were subsequently combined and reorganized under the Single Regeneration Budget (SRB) in April 1994. The SRB initially combined over 20 existing programmes, such as Estate Action, City Challenge, Urban Programme, Safer Cities, TEC Challenge *inter alia*. The SRB seeks to co-ordinate the input of different government departments, such as the DETR, Home Office, Employment Department, local authorities, and other bodies concerned with the social, economic and physical regeneration of inner city areas, through a system of integrated regional

offices. The SRB programme is continuing at the time of writing. It would seem that in order to manage such a vast initiative the government finds that it cannot do without 'planning' and 'planners' (in all but name) as nowadays these words have such negative connotations that alternatives are often used. For example advertisements in the Wednesday edition of the *Guardian* each week are for professionals qualified to undertake urban regeneration, not 'planners' *per se*.

There has been concern that such a thrust towards property market-led initiatives within the inner city as SRB presents might weaken and marginalize traditional town planning functions in some areas and unbalance the overall urban situation. In late 1999 for example, a series of 'community planning' focus groups were established in depressed areas in the north of England, which were comprised of health and social workers, local captains of industry and economists: but curiously no town planners. Clearly it should not be assumed that 'planning' necessarily means 'town planning' within the present political context. In studying 'town planning' it is always important to look at the nature of the governmental structures through which town planning policy is implemented, as well as looking at the policies themselves (Healey *et al.* 1988). The complex themes of implementation, agency, regulation, management, localism, and urban governance are developed further elsewhere by the author (Greed, 1996a, 1996b; Brindley *et al.*, 1996)

NEW LABOUR

A New Start?

The General Election in May 1997 resulted in a change of government following 18 years of Conservative administration. Relatively speaking no revolutionary changes have occurred to the town planning system, save the renaming of the Department of Environment, as the DETR (Chapter 2) and promises of future policy modifications and a general modernization (DETR, 1998c). Commitment to the SRB has continued, as has an emphasis upon partnership with the private sector, including the use of Private Finance Initiatives (PFI) to fund public projects. A new authority for London, the Greater London Authority (GLA), has been created as described in Chapter 2, to oversee the strategic planning of London. Another initiative has been the creation of elected 'city mayors' with considerable powers, following the North American model of the mayoral role (Hambleton and Sweeting, 1999). But most of these changes are concerned with the nature of urban governance, procedure, and organization rather than substantive planning policy changes.

The new Labour government has taken on board much of the agenda of the previous Conservative governments, and some pundits argue that Conservative and Labour values have now met somewhere in the middle of the political spectrum, and that it might be more appropriate simply to call the present government, 'the New Party' and drop the word 'Labour' altogether. Old Labour-type planning policies, such as the creation of subsidized development areas in depressed regions have not been at the centre of government policy to solve unemployment and related social problems. Rather the government has established the 'New Deal' to provide subsidized employment for young people across the country, all of whom are being encouraged to get into work, training or voluntary activities. At the same time there has been a vast increase in higher education places.

The government established a Social Exclusion Unit at the Home Office which has sought to co-ordinate a range of initiatives and policies. Arguably, 'exclusion' appears to equate with 'unemployment' rather than including exclusion on the basis of gender, race or disability. For example the New Deal for Communities programme (a successor to SRB) has targeted 4,000 deprived housing estates. Yet many of the government's measures are not spatially, physically linked to particular geographical areas, as was the case both in much regional and inner urban policy. Instead they cover certain categories of people, on the basis of age, disadvantage and training needs, wherever they are located, thus creating an aspatial, socially-defined approach to planning policy.

A wide range of new initiatives, groups and programmes has been introduced including an Urban Taskforce. A series of special zones have also been created to deal with specific policy areas related to health, education and housing. Education Action Zones have for example, been created within inner city London Boroughs (LRN, 1999). Also at the time of writing nine pilot 'home zone' traffic-free projects are being established, including one in Lambeth and one in West Ealing in London, which will include play streets, and in which cyclists and pedestrians will be given priority and speed limits will be set at 15 kph (approximately 10 mph). These proposals have generated a mixed reaction, with fears from local communities that the lack of through traffic may create havens for gangs of youths as has happened in some pedestrianized shopping streets. Many residents are concerned with the disturbance and noise factor from play streets, particularly these days as more people work from home. In complete contrast some private developers are offering 'child-free' housing estates for professional and older couples. New forms of residential areas, which combine work and home, are also emerging, such as the Crickhowell Televillage, in the Brecon Beacons in South Wales pioneered by the private sector.

A New Regionalism

UK Regional Policy

Consultative documents continued to be produced by subsequent governments, but with an analytical or advisory purpose, rather than policy making emphasis such as *Housing, Land Supply and Structure Plan Provisions in the South East* (SERPLAN, 1988). There were also various proposals for more regional liaison among county authorities during the Conservative government of the 1980s. A series of 15 RPGs (Regional Planning Guidance notes) have been produced for the larger regional urban conurbations, for example, *Strategic Guidance for Tyne and Wear*, (RPG 1, 1989) to ensure co-ordination of planning policies. The RPGs are currently being revised and updated.

Regional

As indicated in earlier chapters, regional planning was an important component of post-war reconstruction planning and subsequent Labour governments. In the 1960s under the Labour government of Harold Wilson, regional planning peaked, and a range of significant regional economic study documents were produced, such 'Region with a Future' for the southwest; and 'A Strategy for the South-East' produced by the South-East Regional Economic Planning Council in 1967 (Ravetz, 1986; Balchin and Bull, 1987).

Regional Development Areas in England

1 North East
2 North West
3 Yorks and Humber
4 West Midlands
5 East Midlands
6 East of England
7 Southwest
8 Southeast

Figure 9.3 **Map of New English Regions.**

Regional planning had languished under the previous Conservative government. As discussed in Chapter 2, the regional level was not prioritized and the reports and policies produced were chiefly for advisory purposes, particularly in respect of co-ordinating policies between adjacent local authorities within each region. Yet some vestiges of a strategic regional perspective remained in England, albeit at the 'sub-regional' level. Regional Planning Guidance documents (RPGs) were produced, for example, on the development of regional conurbations such as Greater Manchester and Tyne and Wear. There was also continuing concern with the congested south-east relative to the rest of the country, and this was reflected in various Regional Planning Guidance policy notes (see Government publications appendix, for example RPG3, and SERPLAN, 1988). Regional planning objectives were more strongly pursued in Scotland particularly in respect of the development strategies for the Highlands and Islands (Brand, 1999). In Wales the further decline of mining and heavy industry in South Wales led to the establishment of the Welsh Development Agency and strong regional financial support.

A new regionalism has emerged since 1997 under New Labour. A new PPG11, 'Regional Guidance' was produced in 1999, along with the consultation paper which preceded it entitled, 'The Future of Regional Planning Guidance' set out the agenda for the future. Greater responsibility is to be placed upon regional planning bodies, working with regional Government offices, and with what it describes as 'regional stakeholders'. These might include both public and private bodies which shape regional policy and investment. PPG11 states the objectives of putting greater regional focus on strategic issues, the adoption of a spatial strategy which extends beyond land use issues, and an integrated transport policy at regional level. Regional Development Agencies (RDAs) previously proposed in the White paper *Building Partnerships for Prosperity* in 1997 have been established, under the Regional Development Agencies Act 1998. Hence the emphases within the 'new' regional planning upon working in partnership with the private sector and upon developing links with business.

At present, regional level bodies remain advisory in role, and, as yet, without plan-making or development control roles. Readers are advised to check the current situation. It remains to be seen how, in the long run, the regional dimension will be integrated with the other existing levels of planning. The RTPI sees these moves as steps towards creating statutory regional plans (*Planning*, 4.6.99: 20, unattributed comment).

Concern exists, especially among minority social groups, about the focus and nature of emerging UK regional planning policy. The emphasis remains upon economic issues, specifically unemployment, and policy does not appear directly to address social exclusion issues such as homelessness, social welfare, and inequality factors, especially ethnicity and disability issues, all of which manifest great regional variation. It is argued that it might be better to take a wider more inclusive view of regional planning, as is found in the other member states in the EU, and which, with harmonization, are likely to impinge on Britain in the near future. In other words, it may be argued that, the new guidance (such as PPG11) does not go far enough in restructuring and redefining concepts of regional planning, although it is a great improvement on the definitions and approaches adopted during the last great wave of regional planning in the 1960s.

European Regional Context

UK domestic policy now needs to link in with EU regional planning strategy. The word 'regional' in EU policy documents refers to entire regions of Europe covering several countries, for example its concern with the development of many poorer southern European member states. The UK land-surface falls into three regions: the Atlantic Arc, North Sea Region and North Western Metropolitan Region under the current Inter-Regional Programme, known as Interreg III which has identified a total of 11 regions for purposes of allocation of funds from the European Regional Development Fund (Williams, 1999). For example domestic regional policy demarcations within the UK, need to be harmonized with revitalization policies and funding emanating from the EU Social Fund and Regional Development Fund in respect of planning for the north-east of England. Many EU programmes have a regional aspect, for instance, the basic theme running through 'Europe 2000+' relates to closer co-operation over territorial planning in Europe.

The European Spatial Development Perspective (ESDP), is of particular significance in respect of regional planning. It provides a forum for experts from member states to discuss policy harmonization (Davies, 1998). It seeks to inter-relate policies for environmental sustainability, economic competitiveness, and thirdly social and economic cohesion among the member states. London and the south-east is part of, what the ESDP has identified as, the core 'Pentagon' of the EU, namely an area stretching between London, Paris, Milan, Munich and Hamburg. This pentagon contains 20 per cent of the land area of the EU, contains 40 per cent of the population, and produces 50 per cent of GNP (gross national product) of Europe (Davies, 1998).

It must be stated that there is considerable criticism of the EU policy and questioning as to the value of UK EC membership. Some regions in Britain have benefited from the European Regional Development Fund, but many people are still suspicious as to whether the net amount the UK is putting in is more than the amount received from the complex system of EU finance. In the longer term, EU policy may help to alleviate social inequalities. At the day-to-day level, for many ordinary people the regional dimension is still an important part of their lives, as manifested in the great disparities in house prices which built up throughout the 1980s. Possibly with time with increased harmonization of the planning and fiscal systems of the EU member states, such local inequalities will be put into perspective, and there may be more balance across Europe as a whole.

Global Regional and Urban Perspectives

There is a wider debate about the whole question of the optimum size of regions, and indeed countries. Belgium, Sweden, Norway, Denmark, and Holland all have quite small populations of a few millions, indeed Greater London has a larger population than most of them. In fact European countries are all small spatially compared with other countries across the globe. For example, California, just one State in the USA, has a population of 32 million people and is spatially four times the size of the UK, whereas Texas is six times the size of the UK in area. Some world-class cities are larger than entire countries. Mexico City, the largest city in the world is estimated to have a population of around 25 million ('only' around 20 million if the outer squatter districts are excluded), covering 18,000 square miles. Tokyo has a population of 19 million, and is close to 25 million if the Tokyo-Yokohama conurbation is taken as a whole. Sao Paulo, Brazil, also has a population of over 19 millions. New York, Los Angeles and Shanghai have maintained their place in the world's 10 largest cities list, but increasingly the greatest rate of urban growth is to be found in the southern hemisphere.

It was announced in a BBC news bulletin that the world's population had reached 8 billion in October 1999. However, the total world population is given as 5.9 billion, in the 1999 Edition of *Social Trends* produced by the Office of National Statistics (ONS) whereas the population of the United Kingdom is put at 59 million – a tiny percentage of the world population! (Source: ONS, 1999, Table 1.2). Clearly global figures are based on informed 'guestimates' because of the disparity in accurate of census data received from different countries and the huge problem of counting large mobile populations.

Table 9.2 World Populations

Global urban growth Millions		Millions	
Largest cities 1950		Largest cities 2000	
New York	12.3	Mexico City	25.6
London	8.7	Sao Paulo	22.1
Tokyo	6.7	Tokyo	19.00
Paris	5.4	Shanghai	17.0
Shanghai	5.3	New York	16.8
Buenos Aires	5.0	Calcutta	15.7
Chicago	4.9	Mumbai (Bombay)	15.4
Moscow	4.8	Beijing	14.0
Calcutta	4.4	Los Angeles	13.9
Los Angeles	4.0	Jakarta	13.7

Some European countries' populations
in millions for comparison

Belgium	10
Denmark	5
Finland	5
France	59
Germany	82
Italy	57
Netherlands	15
Norway	4.5
Spain	40
Sweden	9

By comparison, three Swedens would go into one Mexico City!

Largest British cities (% growth)	%	Fastest growing world cities (% rate per annum)	
Greater London	7.8	Dhaka	6.2
Birmingham/West Midlands	2.3	Lagos	5.8
Greater Manchester	2.3	Karachi	4.7
Leeds/West Yorkshire	1.5	Jakarta	4.4
Newcastle/Tyneside	0.88	Mumbai	4.2
Liverpool	0.84	Istanbul	4.0
Glasgow	0.66	Delhi	3.9
Sheffield	0.64	Lima	3.9
Nottingham	0.61	Manila	3.0
Bristol	0.53	Buenos Aires	2.5

(*Source*: ONS, 1999, Table 1.7)

Overall Sources: New Internationalist, May 1997 and June 1999; Greed, 2000a,b; ONS, annual

JOINED UP THINKING

Current Agenda

The final section which critiques New Labour's attempts at 'joined up thinking' in policy making, is intended to provoke and encourage the reader to think about the future course of planning policy in Britain

Figure 9.4 **Urban Development in Singapore.**
Global urbanization is underway. South east Asian economies and societies are particularly dynamic, and have generated vast new urban cities at a rate unprecedented in the slower Western world.

Figure 9.5 **Everywhere Flyovers.**
Transport planning mistakes are being repeated globally. For example, this is just one of the many flyovers in Singapore (q.v. the flyover photo in Bristol, Figure 8.6).

with reference in particular to transport, housing, urban regeneration and the environment, the latter being the subject of the next chapter.

Transportation Planning

The new Labour government has given high policy priority to dealing with the problems created by the increasing levels of traffic. Traffic congestion and increased vehicle flows are, arguably, not just the result

Figure 9.6 **The Demise of the Traditional Shop: Demolition.**

Figure 9.7 **The Commonplace Shopping Parade.**
It's all very well seeking to restrict car use now and penalizing people for travelling too much. But what can they do? Many traditional local shops have been demolished, or have changed use. The days of the taken-for-granted shopping parade, once found along every arterial road, are numbered. Years of decentralization and out of town development leave people with limited options.

of increased car ownership. One must ask why people are travelling in the first place? An inevitable result of 20 years of developer-led urban expansion has been the growth of out-of-town development and decentralization. Suburban development continues apace, following the North American model, where now, over 50 per cent of citizens live in the suburbs. Increased suburbanization requires increased motorization. Britain along with other parts of Europe is experiencing what may be described as the 'Americanization' of urban land use patterns. These trends have been accompanied by a decline in public transport, and indeed the privatization of much public transport. The private motorcar is often the only practical way to get around in the time available. Growth in leisure and recreational pursuits have also added to road usage and traffic volume.

The former Conservative government introduced various measures concerned with controlling traffic, for example the Traffic Calming Act 1993. Under New Labour local authorities are now required to produce 'Integrated Transport Plans' which seek to link public transport and planning policy. Revised PPG12 on Development Plans stresses the need to integrate transport planning and the land use policies which contribute towards the generation of traffic in the first place. As stated in Chapter 2, the merger of the DoT and the DoE to create the DETR was intended to bring these two aspects together, thereby creating an environmentally-sustainable transport policy. Arguably, the proposals do not acknowledge the major obstacle to implementing this new inte-

grated approach, namely the existing division of power between highways departments and planning departments at local authority level. This is a particular problem in shire county authorities, where district councils give planning permission, but the County Highways department, not the district planning department, make the final decision on key road, access and layout issues that might fundamentally affect the design and planning of local policy areas and new site developments. Although (since 1988), the County Highways authority has been required to consult with the district authority and there are powers for delegating transport functions to the districts, there is a wide variation in the take-up of this opportunity among different authorities. A consultation paper produced in 1997 by the DETR *Transport: The Way Ahead* (DETR, 1998e) included suggestions for bringing trunk road planning in England into the regional planning guidance system, making strategic transportation policies a regional level matter above both county and district level. Subsequently this change was embodied in the White Paper 'A New Deal for Transport' (DETR, 1998f) (see Government Publications).

Concern has been expressed by many planners that in its rush to create new policies, initiatives and

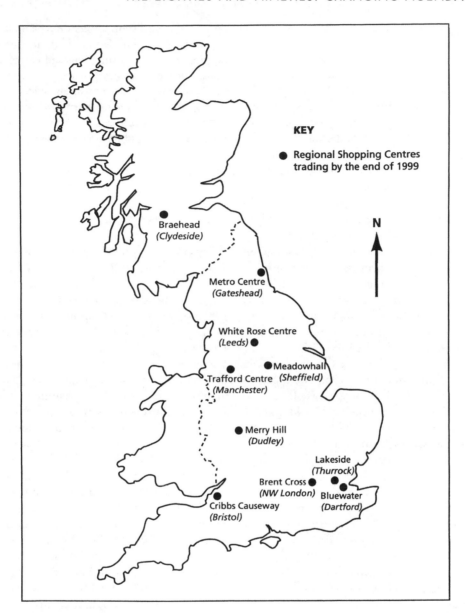

KEY

● Regional Shopping Centres
trading by the end of 1999

N

Figure 9.8 **Map of New Regional Shopping Centres.**

bodies, New Labour has failed to integrate its new ideas, policies and agencies with the existing structures of local government. Fundamental problems within the existing system have not been addressed, and it is argued that tacking on new levels of initiatives and agencies only adds to the confusion. Therefore, in order to carry through the spirit of integration from DETR level to local government level, such issues as that described above require urgent attention. To achieve sustainable development policies this issue needs to be addressed, particularly if social and economic topics are also to be included within the ambit of the definition of sustainability and within the process of environmental assessment as proposed in the document.

Housing Policy

In spite of the commitment to transportation planning, the 'cause' of much traffic generation, namely house building continues unabated. In 1995 the Government predicted that 4.4 million new houses would be needed by 2016 (DoE, 1995 and DOE, 1996b). This figure caused a great deal of controversy. Subsequently the figure was revised down to 3.8 million by New Labour, with the proviso that 60 per cent of new homes would have to built on 'brown land' that is previously developed land, within existing cities and on infill sites, rather than on new greenfield sites on the edges of cities. These principles were further set out in the revision of PPG3 'Housing' in 1999. Predicting future demand is a complex process. In 1999 there were 24.80 million dwellings (including flats) already in the United Kingdom (ONS, 1999, Table 10.1). Thus, housing remains an important issue for planners, as 70 per cent of all urban development is residential, so it is by far the largest land use.

Much of the housing debate has revolved around the question of what sort of dwellings were needed and for whom, and where people would live as discussed in the White Paper, 'Household growth: where shall we live?' (DoE, 1996b). It was argued that much of the increase would be in the form of single person units, rather than family dwellings, because of changing demographic trends and lifestyles. The 1995 National Household Survey reported that single person households constituted over 28 per cent of housing occupation. This sector is growing, mainly because of increased numbers of elderly people and also young people setting up house on their own. Planning on the basis of providing family houses at low density is less inappropriate nowadays. Families with dependent children only constitute 24 per cent of households (ONS, 1999). Thus it is important to take into account the social and qualitative aspects of land use as well as the quantitative when making projections upon which policy are to be based.

As to 'where' people should live, there is greater emphasis upon 'inner city' regeneration and encouraging people to live nearer to city centres. But development of the 'outer city' that is suburban expansion has continued apace. In the future traditional town planning problems of urban sprawl, and land availability are likely to predominate. Arguably the greatest mistake of late twentieth century planning has been the emphasis upon decentralization, particularly of housing, out-of-own shopping and employment locations. Such policies have increased traffic, eaten into the countryside, are unsustainable, and socially impractical. Introducing restrictive measures against the motor car, without addressing underlying causes, such as lack of public transport and badly designed cities achieves only resentment toward the planners from the general public.

Urban Regeneration

Policy emphasis is shifting from new build to renewal and regeneration of inner areas, but this has also generated criticism particularly from the very deprived groups the policies are meant to be helping. The new Labour government has continued its commitment to the Single Regeneration Budget, but has considerably revised the highly competitive nature of the funding system to give local authorities a greater level of involvement. Meanwhile, many inner city community groups and minorities who were intended to benefit from the urban regeneration programme became increasingly disillusioned, as they found decision-making powers were wielded by boards and committees on which they had little representation. It appeared to some community activists that SRB was just another excuse for large-scale property development, albeit, ostensibly in 'partnership' with local organizations. Ethnic minority groups (Grant, 1990) and women (WDS, 1997, No. 24) felt particularly excluded, a matter of great concern in areas where SRB agencies effectively constitute the main 'town planning' bodies (LRN, 1997). Clearly statutory town planning continues to have a major 'problem' in seeking to develop strategic plans, which combine land-use and transportation policies with one hand tied behind its back in terms of limited control over strategic transportation policy as against specific highways and road layout policy, which is also limited by division of powers with highways departments.

Likewise, environmental planning is moving toward fuller integration. The Labour Party Manifesto claimed it would place 'concern for environment at the heart of policy making. Therefore it was not to be seen as an add-on extra, but a core issue that informs and suffuses the whole of government, from housing and energy policy through to global warming and international agreements' (paraphrased quote from Labour Party, 1997). Central and local government is seeking to integrate environmental policies with other aspects of government policy. For example the New Deal, includes both the Welfare to Work Programme and the creation of an Environmental Task Force, in conjunction with the Social Exclusion Unit to 'help all our people to share in the development of more sustainable communities' (DETR, 1998g). However, significantly, the emphasis in such documents appears to be upon business opportunities rather than equal opportunities.

It has been argued that 'the pursuit of a sustainable future for our society has become a common goal across all parties' (Sewel, 1997: 2). The new government's agenda includes a commitment to cross-cutting policies, social inclusion, welfare to work, sustainable development and best values issues. In a speech in June 1997, John Prescott, the then Secretary of State for the Environment, pressed for local government to deliver on five priorities – integration, decentralization, regeneration, partnership and sustainability. These are all inter-departmental and all need a local dimension to be implemented in liaison with existing departments. These days the demands of environmental and sustainability movements sit uneasily with an old-fashioned land-use spatially-based planning system which is still more concerned with 'land use' than with 'how people use land'.

People's use of the built environment, and their access to buildings and facilities is another issue which has become more topical in the 1990s not least because of dissatisfaction among many user groups. Also the gradual implementation of the Disability Discrimination Act 1995 has highlighted the inadequacies of existing buildings and environments. The introduction of this act was the result of constant campaigning by disability groups, however, many of their original demands remain unmet (see Chapter 12). There has also been a renaissance of the urban design movement, which incorporates a concern for both aesthetic and functional issues (discussed in Chapter 13).

A whole range of related issues such as access, safety, crime prevention (Crouch et al., 1999), sustainability, minority demands, and also a greater enthusiasm for the arts, have all contributed to the new urban design agenda. As stated in Chapter 2, a separate Department of Heritage had been created by the former Conservative government – this subsequently became, under Labour, the Department of Culture, Media and Sport (DCMS) – which is closely linked to the DETR. This department has a wide ambit covering urban conservation, tourism, urban cultural issues, and the arts and thus there are strong links between the DCMS and the DETR, particularly in respect of design and planning issues.

Chapter 9 has sought to explain the changes which have occurred in the scope and nature of planning over the last 20 years, and to give discursive commentary. Environmental planning and urban design are both such large topics that they will be dealt with in separate chapters, namely Chapter 11 and Chapter 12 respectively, whereas social issues are returned to in Chapters 12 and 13.

TASKS

Information Gathering Tasks

I. Check the sizes, in population and area, of the following countries, Norway, Belgium, Uzbeckistan, The Netherlands, Mexico, Australia, the United States of America and Idaho, California and Texas therein.

II. Check the most up to date figures on the sizes of the following cities, London, Mexico City, Los Angeles, New York, Berlin, Capetown, Brussels, Bogata, Oslo, Bombay (now called Mumbai) and Tokyo.

Discursive and Conceptual Tasks

III. Compare and contrast Conservative and Labour approaches towards town planning in the last twenty years.

IV. To what extent do you consider that New Labour is practising 'joined up thinking' in respect of developing integrated planning policies?

Reflective Tasks

V. To what extent do you think that planning theory, conferences, affects actual policy, look at the advertisements for conferences and academic topics, and compare with what is going on in government.

FURTHER READING

Texts that convey the huge cultural and ideological changes towards town planning under the Tories include the following, all of which emphasize economic planning issues:

Stoker, G. and Young, S. (1993) *Cities in the 1990s: Local Choice for a Balanced Strategy*; Atkinson, R. and Moon, G. (1993) *Urban Policy in Britain: The City, the State and the Market*; Thornley, A. (1991) *Urban Planning Under Thatcherism: the Challenge of the Market*; Oatley, N. (1996) 'Regenerating cities and modes of regulation' in Greed, C. (1996b) (ed.) *Investigating Town Planning*; Oatley (1998) (ed.) *Cities, Economic Competition and Urban Planning*; Ward, S. (1994) *Planning and Urban Change*; Chapman, D. (1996) *Neighbourhood Plans in the Built Environment*.

A good starting point for sources on Euro-planning is the work of Williams, 1996 and 1999, CEC. Also check EU literature, and webpages. A vast amount of free information is available from Brussels, in all the main European languages.

For information on relative sizes of different countries, states, regions and cities therein check any good Atlas, also Encarta 1999 (Microsoft CD ROM), and Third World development literature such as *The New Internationalist*, which frequently publishes special editions on urban issues (such as No. 313, June 1999).

ENVIRONMENT, EUROPE AND GLOBAL TRENDS

SETTING THE AGENDA

Reinventing the Wheel?

Chapter 10 traces the rise, and discusses the agenda, of the environmental movement, and the related demand for 'sustainability' which has so reshaped the scope and nature of British town planning over the last 20 years (Blowers *et al.*, 1993). Town planning policy now puts great emphasis upon achieving 'sustainable development' compared with 'development' which is considered harmful to the environment. The topic will be approached in the first part of the chapter within the context of a preliminary account of the development of rural planning. Arguably, British town and country planning has been concerned with environmental issues for many years, long before environmentalism became fashionable. In the second part the broadening of the planning agenda will be charted as it has progressively taken on board the wider urban, economic and social dimensions of planning for sustainability, not least because of the influence of European and wider global initiatives and trends. Again discursive commentary will be included reflecting controversy associated with aspects of current environmental policy.

Definitions of Sustainability

At the broadest level, sustainability may be defined as the process of reaching a state where global ecosystems are capable of absorbing human impact without deterioration (Barton, 1996). There are two main perspec-

tives on the significance of sustainability. One perspective is human-centred: we must be kind to the earth so that the earth is kind to us. The other is nature-centred: we must respect the earth because the earth and its creatures have as much right to exist as we do. The health of the biosphere, and the health of humanity, are indivisible, meaning one is nature orientated and the other is concerned with the social aspects of planning (as described by Barton and Bruder, 1995).

Internationally, sustainability is normally taken to have three main elements, into which all the different dimensions will fit, namely, social, economic and environmental. But in Britain the emphasis has generally been upon the last, upon green issues. Arguably this depoliticizes the agenda and leads to a predominantly physical, land-use based approach to environmental issues, which conveniently fits in with the traditional spatial emphasis within UK town planning (Brand, 1996 and 1999).

In Britain environmentalism, and especially 'Green issues' are more likely to be associated with countryside issues and 'nature', than be applied to addressing the problems of urban areas, such as the excesses of the property development market, and the social, political and economic processes that shape the way in which the environment is used and exploited. Indeed 'planning for the environment' has been conveniently slotted into the pre-existing 'country dimension' of 'town and country planning'. This gives it 'space' on the existing UK planning agenda, but also creates limitations.

More fundamentally the Green Movement has challenged the basic assumptions which have informed much socialist Red Movement thinking, in respect of

Textbox 10.1   Definition of Sustainability

Sustainability, according to Blowers (1993) is generally accepted as having four recognized elements: conserving the stock of natural assets; avoiding damage to the regenerative capacities of ecosystems; achieving greater social equality; and avoiding the imposition of risks and costs upon future generations.

According to Brundtland (1987) and the subsequent Rio Declaration (Rio, 1992) sustainability comprises three components: summary social equality, economic self-sufficiency and environmental balance. Brundtland defines 'sustainable development' as follows, 'development that meets the needs of the present generation without compromising the ability of future generations to meet their own needs. Reference is made to this definition in PPG1 on general planning principles (DETR, 1997).

the emphasis upon 'production' and thus upon the centrality of economic growth and employment policy in planning policy. But environmentalism has drawn attention to the hidden costs of 'production' and 'consumption' and the costs and benefits of 'decomposition'. Decomposition is the next essential stage towards restoring environmental assets and balance through 'recycling' that is decomposition and recomposition of natural materials. The importance of dealing with the entire eco-system and thus with all these three components in the cycle have been stressed particularly by those working in the fields of ecology, rural planning and landscape design (Turner, 1996: 30).

The Relationship Between Sustainability and Planning

Traditional boundaries between the town and the country has become blurred with the rise of car ownership, suburbanization, the demand for out of town sites, and growing pressures on the Green Belt and open countryside. The Green Movement has drawn attention to the fact we all live on a fragile planet and from this wider perspective, town/country divisions become meaningless. Whilst the European Union and national levels are important, the globalization of economies coupled with an increasing awareness that we are all thrown together in the same 'Spaceship Earth', has led some to argue that the nation state (such as the UK) is no longer the key level at which to plan. Many of our economic, environmental and social problems require international co-operation and global solutions.

The ecological movement has stressed that we are all part of the same ecosystem, breathing the same air: and the atmosphere is not subject to land use zoning. Concerns about global warming and the discovery of holes in the ozone layer have united the world's population across national boundaries, for example to limit CFC gas emissions which are believed to be a causal factor in the creation of these holes. Whilst these insights have led to a more holistic view of planning for the environment, they have also led to criticisms of what has been seen as the more narrow and less enlightened agenda of British town planning. But many planners would argue that town planning has 'always' been aware of these wider issues. All that has happened is that the wheel has been re-invented by a new generation, and a new eco-language is being used to describe the age-old, and well-acknowledged problems, which inspired the founding fathers of the modern town planning movement. Ebenezer Howard's concept of the garden city was for example, in its original form, a sustainable settlement (Chapter 6). Although it is also important to maintain this wider perspective, it is argued that many town planning issues are best dealt with at the local detailed level.

Town and country planning has always been concerned with the countryside as well as the towns, and in particular with protecting the countryside from the spread of the towns. This perspective has inevitably involved holding a wider environmental perspective. But there is also an anti-urban theme which runs right through much of British town planning which sees towns and cities (and the town-dwellers) as 'bad', and the countryside and farmers as 'good'. This is an attitude which the modern environmental movement challenges in questioning farming practices, including the way in which agricultural land is used. When the post-war planning system was established it was assumed 'the farmer knows best' and it was considered that there was little need to control his activities.

Initially, the European Union (or Common Market as it was then) made no mention of environmental issues. Indeed, the Treaty of Rome in 1957, upon which the European Union was based, appeared to be more concerned with sustained industrial growth than sustainable growth (Cullingworth and Nadin, 1997). The primary rationale for the union of European states was commercial, to develop a common free trade area. But as the years have rolled on a range of other policy initiatives have become dominant, especially concerns about regional economic equality and the environment. Neither of these concerns have been particularly compatible with the former EECs objective of supporting and protecting agricultural interests through the notorious Common Agricultural Policy (CAP).

The EU and the Common Market before it has been plagued by negative images of butter mountains, wine lakes and unequal subsidies to farmers none of which is particularly sustainable, and all of which have heightened concerns over 'the politics of food' and with the nature of farming policy and thus with rural

planning. Several major public health scares in Britain have heightened concern about food quality and production, including, *inter alia*, the spread of bovine spongiform encephalopathy (BSE), *Escherichia coli* (*E. coli* is several distinct virulent strains of food poisoning), Creutzfeldt-Jakob disease (CJD), and the introduction of genetically modified food (GMF).

This heightened awareness about food-related issues has increased interest in farming practices and thus in rural planning issues, and has cast doubt on existing attitudes that 'the farmer knows best'. The reconciliation of the demands for conservation, agriculture, recreation, and development in the countryside is a major task for planners (Countryside Commission, 1990). But, over the last forty years there has been a remarkable move, both at European and national level to a more environmental approach.

THE HERITAGE OF RURAL CONSERVATION

State Intervention in the Countryside

National Parks

Post-war reconstruction planning was more concerned with keeping the town out of the countryside, and protecting remote and scenic areas from development, than with worrying about extending development control to cover the activities of farmers. The provisions of the Agricultural Act 1947 were based on the assumption that the farmer knows best, and that he should not be hindered while increasing agricultural production. There were demands from the urban population, and from pressure groups such as the Ramblers Association, to open up the countryside more for recreational purposes. The National Parks and Access to the Countryside Act 1947, as its name suggests, opened up a number of National Parks and a whole series of footpath networks throughout the countryside. At present there are 82,000 miles of footpaths and 18,000 miles of bridleway open to the public.

The National parks were administered by *ad hoc* bodies, mainly joint boards and committees and overseen by the National Parks Commission. In 1968 this became the Countryside Commission with a broader role, including within its terms of reference concern

***Figure 10.1* Planning for Society and for the Biosphere are Indivisible.**
The BSE crisis focused attention on the fact that human, animal health, and the wider plant biosphere are all connected within the same food chain, as highlighted by the beef crisis. Demands for reform of modern farming and a return to more organic methods are bound to have effects on agricultural land utilization and thus for rural planning policy.

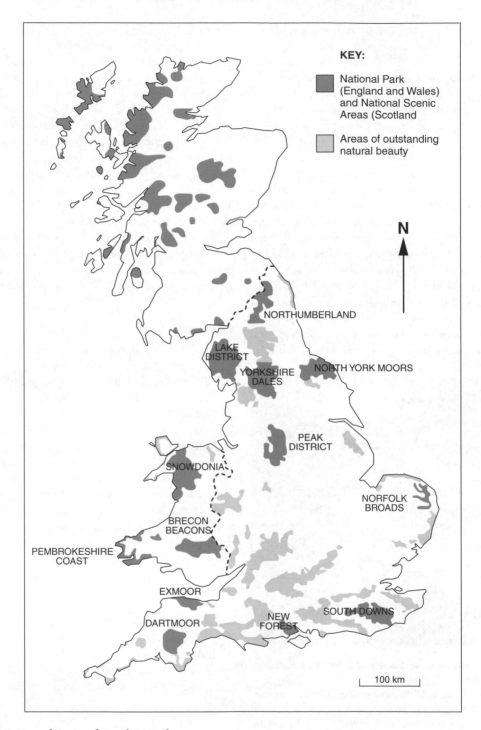

Figure 10.2 **Map of Areas of Rural Control.**

for agriculture, leisure, recreation, and landscape, as well as the National Parks. In the post-war period, car ownership was low and some areas were still fairly inaccessible by road, so the Bank Holiday traffic jams found on Dartmoor or the Lake District were not even a consideration in those far off days. The aim of the National Parks was to preserve the natural beauty of the countryside and provide access for the general public, along the lines of recommendations in the Scott, Dower, and Hobhouse Reports, and were part of the overall national land use planning strategy of the post-war period described in Part II (Hall, 1992). Since the initial designation in the 1940s, the Norfolk Broads achieved National Park status in the 1990s. It is proposed that two new National Parks be created for 2000, namely the South Downs in Sussex and the New Forest in Hampshire.

AONBS

The 1949 Act also established Areas of Outstanding Natural Beauty (AONBs), which are smaller, more accessible areas than the National Parks, e.g. the Quantock Hills in Somerset. 75 per cent grants were available to the local authorities whose job it was to administer them for maintenance and improvement of amenities. Both in National parks and AONBs there are strict planning controls on new and existing development. This is comparable to the situation in urban conservation areas. For legal details see Heap (1996) and Cullingworth and Nadin (1997).

Country Parks

Continuing pressure for rural recreation, combined with growth in car ownership, led eventually to another category of special area being introduced in 1968 under the Countryside Act. This followed the recommendations of the White Paper, 'Leisure in the Countryside', which marked a change of attitude in putting more emphasis on non-agricultural uses and ecology in the countryside. This was also the time when Friends of the Earth was establishing itself as a pressure group. Environmental issues were first coming to the fore in the media, and journals such as *The Ecologist* were established. In 1972 *Blueprint for Survival*, a foundational environmental document, was published (Goldsmith, 1972).

Figure 10.3 Trees in the Quantocks, Holford Beeches, Somerset.
It is easy to take the countryside for granted. A great deal of work, maintenance and planning goes into sustaining woodland, moorland and pastures.

The Countryside Act 1968 established Country Parks, which were created to enable people to enjoy the countryside without having to travel too far, to ease pressure on remote and solitary places and reduce risk of damage to the countryside. This was achieved by creating small, managed park areas near to urban concentrations with ample provision of car parks, toilets and amenities such as picnic sites and transit sites for campers and caravans. Local authorities received 75 per cent grants from central government to create country parks which were seen as 'honey pots' drawing people away from a more dispersed use of the countryside.

SSSIS

Greater emphasis was increasingly put upon the need for protection of smaller 'special' areas within the countryside, for example, where a rare wild flower or species of butterfly was found. Under the 1949 Act provision had been made for the identification of Sites of Special Scientific Interest (SSSI). But it was not until the 1980s that greater awareness of SSSIs developed among both the public and affected landowners, as a result of the environmental movement, and they came under the control of the Nature Conservancy Council. (subsequently under English Nature). Many of these sites were right in the middle of farm land and it was difficult to enforce these controls, indeed a site could be ploughed up before anyone even realized. Farmers were, however, given compensation for the loss of their right to farm parts of their land where SSSIs were located. Such sites could also be endangered by careless tourists according to the Department of the Environment (in 1991) by the increasing popularity of war games! Greater controls were introduced both for SSSIs themselves and also Nature Reserves and a range of other ecological issues under the 1981 Wildlife and Countryside Act.

Green Belts

Around the edges of urban areas there are additional controls within the ambit of the Green belt legislation. Green belts were given a new impetus in the 1960s by Duncan Sandys the Conservative minister then responsible for town planning under Section 4 of the Town and Country Planning Act 1962, and have gone from strength to strength ever since. Green belts are not designated for their landscape value, but to prevent urban sprawl in areas of development pressure, but, more broadly, they have also been seen as the 'green lungs of the city', and as having recreational and agricultural value. In fact, substantial parts of approved greenbelts are not really very green, more 'brown' with a whole diversity of gravel workings, glass houses, and infill sites, and yet they still contain 20 per cent of all agricultural land.

Certain facilities are seen as being suitable for Green Belt location, such as golf courses, hotels and leisure facilities, hospitals and similar government institutions. Ebenezer Howard located 'asylums' in his Green Belt circling the Garden City, but in general he envisaged the Green Belt to be much more agricultural than the present day version. Although Green Belts are intended to be permanent, occasionally bits are chipped away on their inner circumference, and extensions to the Green Belt are not infrequently made on the outer edge (Elson, 1986; Herrington, 1984).

White Land

White land, as Grant (1982 [1990]: 309) explains is a term with no legal significance. It just means land that was not designated a particular land use under the old style of development plan. It is often on the inside edge of the green belt. Developers saw these areas as ideal for housing, and in some cases the government appeared to go along with this presumption in the past. Nowadays most white land areas have subsequently been covered by Structure Plan policy. In addition there are often wedges of white land marooned on the urban–rural interface which would cut into the countryside if developed. For example, awkward little bits are often left between the edge of an urban area and a passing motorway: a prime site for development if there is also a motorway intersection nearby. Motorways cut right through established Green Belts often attracting a corridor of planning applications alongside their path. Some would argue that Green Belts do not prevent development in any case. All that happens is that development, 'leapfrogs over the Green Belt' leading to a second ring of housing, and greater commuting distances for its inhabitants further out into the countryside (Pahl, 1965; Newby, 1982).

Conflicts and Problems Arising from State Intervention

Different Ministries

There has always been a major division between the aims of the Environmental ministries (DoE and now DETR) and those of other government departments such as the Ministry for Agriculture, Fisheries and Food (MAFF). As stated in Chapter 2, in June 1999 a separate Food Standards Agency was established concerned with food safety from 'farm to fork'. But this body is not a Ministry and has a regulatory, rather than a policy-making role. But it may be seen as representing the needs of consumers, that is the public, as against farming interests.

The MAFF has for example given grants for ploughing up the moorlands, and for the grubbing out of hedgerows, as was common, for example, in the 1970s, contrary to the policies of other government departments (Shoard, 1980). There has been considerable concern about the effects of other subsidies to industrialized farming methods which have led to the creation of prairie-like, flatscape created in some lowland areas and the subsequent demise of various species of wildlife. All this has been done in theory to increase food production, but there are actually food mountains within the EU. Planning has little control over the countryside itself, but many people believe that there should be controls on the use and development of farm buildings, field patterns, ponds, and farm related businesses, particularly in respect of industrial-type agricultural buildings such as silos and battery hen units. But planning has nevertheless been powerful in a negative way, in forbidding non-agricultural building in the countryside, because of the historical need to conserve agricultural land.

Rural Deprivation

The 1980s marked the culmination of the effects of many forces which were changing the countryside. In 1981 the Census showed for the first time that rural villages were actually gaining population rather than suffering from migration. In the 1960s because of the decline in rural population some county planning authorities, such as Durham, had designated villages to 'die' as Category D villages, the view being that it was better to concentrate resources in the more populated Category A villages, and not invest further in Category D villages. The process of rural decline had been precipitated by the Beeching cuts in the 1960s when many branch railways lines and stations in rural areas had been closed.

Many people have since moved back into the countryside, either to retire, or because with the development of the motorway system some people are happy to travel longer distances to work. Ironically, by the time this happened, many of the local facilities and shops in villages were in decline. While many villages have subsequently experienced 'rural gentrification' as new affluent householders move in, those without cars in the countryside are suffering from 'rural deprivation' because of lack of public transport, local shops and community facilities which can be as devastating as the deprivation experienced by their urban cousins. Many low-income people in rural areas felt compelled to move out, particularly young couples who could not possibly compete with the newcomers in the housing market.

Housing in the Countryside

New residential development has not been allowed in the countryside unless it is built specifically for agricultural works in relation to a farm. On the other hand all manner of other agricultural buildings are allowed. People have spent years trying to find ways

around the controls on residential development in the countryside. There being several examples of spurious agricultural workers, and people building rather large 'stables' complete with horse which can easily be converted into a house, thus getting around restrictions on housebuilding on farmland. A more commercial example was the pyramid-shaped central stage which was used for many years at the Glastonbury Pop Festival. The pyramid was used as a cowshed and thus was classed as an agricultural building, when arguably it might better have been classified as a leisure and entertainment facility.

Availability of housing was reduced by the planners' policies of restricting growth in rural settlements to limited infill. There had been no provision in planning law for specifying the tenure or category of occupants of housing developments. However, in Circular 7/91 'Planning and Affordable Housing' for the first time the DOE stated the provision of low cost rural housing for *local* needs should be taken as a 'material consideration' in development control. This has proved a mixed-blessing, as cheap housing is only part of the equation in creating sustainable rural settlements. Even if people can get low-cost housing in the countryside they still need shops, schools, and jobs. Employment, for some, might consist of working the night-shift in the local chicken processing plant, which hardly ties in with the romantic view of agricultural life. Subsequent PPG3s on Housing have further elaborated this aspect of tenure control and the issue remains controversial.

Playing the System

The Conservative government (1979–97) sought to free up the planning system in the interests of the developer both in the town and in the countryside. Yet, paradoxically it was often Conservative voters out in the shires who objected to these changes, as they feared that their areas would be swamped by 'townies'. Circulars 14/84 on Green Belts, 15/84 on Land for Housing, and 22/84 on Structure Plans and Local Plans set policy directives, and were lenient by allowing development in the urban–rural fringe. It was calculated that less land was now needed for agricultural production, because of the enormous surpluses of farmland which had built up in the EU. In the United Kingdom 2.5 million acres, that is an area the size of Devon and Cornwall, were seen as no longer

Figure 10.4 Mountainside in Southern Europe.
Nowadays Britain's countryside policy is subject to the same EU guidelines and environmental controls as those being applied to the different mainland European rural landscape areas. In mountainous areas, winter sports, hydro-electric power generation, forestry, and pasturage are key 'rural' planning considerations.

needed for agriculture. Environmentalists challenged these figures and the unsustainable farming methods which generated such 'over-production'.

The emphasis shifted from seeking to protect the countryside for the sake of agricultural productivity to protecting it for its own sake as an environmental resource. Farmers felt they were being expected to take on the role of park keepers rather than food producers, and increasingly entered into land management agreements in relation to the preservation of certain sites for which they were compensated. Related to this 'set aside' policy, derived from controversial EU policy, enables farmers to take land 'out' of agricultural use, but with the proviso that interim uses should not in the long term negate the return of land to full agricultural use. UK and EU taxation and agricultural subsidies policies affect what the farmers grow, or whether they grow anything at all. Today the 'green and pleasant land' of the countryside may appear far

from green, as farmers grow whatever crop will catch the subsidies, such as an 'inland sea' of blue linseed in early summer, preceded by yellow 'deserts' of rape seed in late spring.

In the 1980s further relaxation of controls was proposed to enable farmers to carry out countryside related businesses to assist them to stay on their farms. Circular 16/87 'Development Involving Agricultural Land' and PPG7 'Rural Enterprise and Development' reflect this new philosophy and farmers were encouraged to diversify within the rural economy. Business activities still had to be related to agriculture. There is a fine dividing line between selling home produced jams in a farm shop, and setting up an industrial plant on the farm: although some saw the latter as a logical progression and argued that such industrial activities would also ease rural unemployment.

The Countryside Commission

There are many other governmental and voluntary government bodies which have a continuing impact on the nature of the countryside, but are 'above' or separate from the main planning system, but which still have an input to the process of property development and upon economic and employment policy in the countryside.

For example, the Countryside Commission, which has operated under the auspices of the DoE, produced two significant documents reflecting a new more entrepreneurial strategy toward development in the countryside, namely 'Shaping a New Countryside' in 1987, and 'Planning for a Greener Countryside' in 1989. The Commission believed that the old reason for adopting a negative restrictive approach to development in the countryside, namely shortage of agricultural land, no longer held good in the light of changing economic circumstances. There was a need for acceptance of the principle of some development in the countryside provided it was done in a constructive and controlled manner. This approach raises the question of whether development in the countryside can actually enhance the rural scene with suitable landscaping. The Countryside Commission proposed that Green Belts should be seen as having a wider purpose and be viewed more positively in their own right. The government produced a consultation paper early in 1991 with proposals that less limitation should be put on the re-use of redundant buildings such as mental homes and hospitals in the Green Belt. Business uses would be acceptable provided the development fitted in to the 'footprint' of the existing building stock and site layout.

The Countryside Commission also recommended that the idea of new settlements in the countryside should be viewed more positively and has been, to a degree, in favour of accepting more 'urban' development in the countryside, provided adequate design and landscaping measures are guaranteed. But it has also emphasized the importance 'greening of the city' in the sense of bringing the countryside into the town, thus breaking down the urban/rural dualism further. The creation of new 'countryside' on derelict land is suggested and also the development of new urban forests on the edge of cities Special areas for horses might also be considered, indeed there is already a thriving unofficial 'horsiculture' sector on the edges of many cities, providing grazing and shelter for ponies and horses. Many of these proposals and issues have remained on hold under the New Labour government. Increased pressure from environmental groups and demands for creation of sustainable agriculture and rural communities have all further politicized the situation. By the late 1990s rural communities, farmers organizations, and pro-hunt groups were mobilizing to protect what they saw as the 'traditional rural way of life'.

Forestry Commission

The Forestry Commission which owned two million acres of land has had a powerful role in protecting the countryside, but is currently subject to being broken up for privatization. However, the Forestry Commission's preference for coniferous, rather than native broadleaf trees has been the cause of much criticism from environmentalists in the past, especially since native species provide habitat for indigenous wildlife. On private land, tax incentives encouraged land owners to plant coniferous rather than deciduous trees. Much reafforestation consists of miles and miles of unnatural standardized plantation only relieved by linear fire breaks.

Statutory Bodies

Various statutory undertakers, including electricity and water authorities in the past, have had the right to develop in protected rural areas. Water authorities have been infamous for 'screening' their reservoirs with trees, and painting everything 'green' which draws even more attention to the developments. The situation has not improved markedly with privatization of utilities, and, for example, there has been a decline in the attention to the clearing out all the little water courses on the Pennines in the North; and to 'keetching the rhynes' on Sedgemoor, in the lowlands of Somerset. Lack of such maintenance contributes both to falling water levels in reservoirs and unseasonal flooding.

The electricity companies are now routing many cables underground, particularly in environmentally sensitive areas, but in the days of nationalization the Electricity Board was notorious for building pylons right across the landscape. As stated in Part I, the Ministry of Defence (MoD) owns over 90,000 acres of forestry and also they own vast amounts of land, in fact over 10 per cent of Wiltshire is MOD property.

Voluntary Bodies and User Groups

Landowners and Farmers

The Country Landowners Association, which was founded in 1926, is a powerful pressure group supporting the needs of its members which no doubt influences legislation through its historic links with the House of Lords, and with the National Farmers Union (NFU). In 1986 it produced 'Land: New Ways to Profit: a handbook of alternative enterprises' which echoed many of the government's own proposals. The emphasis in this document is more on clay pigeon shooting and golf courses than on small farm shops or crafts.

National Trust

The National Trust, founded in 1895 (Gaze, 1988), is completely independent of the government but has a powerful role in countryside matters, and in the protection of both individual Houses, and areas of landscape. Nowadays the National Trust, and other such groups, have become much more politicized, for example over the question of the abolition of fox hunting. In 1999 a huge demonstration march took place in London, composed of members of a wide range of countryside pressure groups including farmers, and landowners, to protest against what they saw as increasing pressures on their livelihoods and the rural community.

Enterprise Neptune is a branch of the National Trust which offers protection to over a third of the coastline. The Council for the Protection of Rural England (CPRE) was founded in 1926 and seeks to campaign for the preservation of rural amenities and scenery. There are many other local voluntary bodies which all play their part in influencing policy at both the central and local government level. In recent years, urban bodies concerned with food production and prices from the shoppers' viewpoint have also had an increasing influence on rural matters, and in particular the National Consumers Association (which produces *Which* magazine).

Access Groups

Ramblers groups are constantly vigilant concerning the maintenance and extension of access to the countryside through a national footpath system. The Open Spaces and Footpaths Preservation Society, founded in 1865, the Youth Hostels Association, and, of course, the Ramblers Association continue to press for better access. Farmers, on the other hand, express concern about the damage that dogs can do to flocks and seek to control the general public walking over standing crops.

Environmental Groups

Many environmental groups such as Friends of the Earth, and the Soil Association, are concerned about the use of chemical fertilizers and pesticides on crops. Animal welfare groups, including the long respected Royal Society for Prevention of Cruelty to Animals (RSPCA), are concerned about factory farming methods, and the quality of life of farm animals in general, especially battery hens. Also, in respect of pet animals, welfare groups are concerned that the increasing trend to ban dogs from public parks and beaches. This policy contributes to the likelihood of dogs being locked in hot cars on family outings, a potential cause of death. Whilst this is understandable because of perceived health hazards to young children, it reduces domestic animals' access to the countryside. (Farmers have already put increasing numbers of farm animals inside.) If there is meant to be a surplus of agricultural land it would seem logical to solve the

growing problem for dog owners of where to exercise their pets, by introducing 'dog only' exercise fields and areas of public open space, as are found in other countries. Planning must take into account the needs of all users, human and otherwise, and introduce policies which provide for greater differentiation between types of open space area, for specialist use by potentially incompatible groups, rather than having a blanket 'open space' or 'countryside' policy.

It is estimated conservatively that there are 7.5 million cats and 6.5 million dogs in Britain. Yet there are 'only' 5.1 million dog-owning households, and 4.9 million cat-owning households in the United Kingdom (ONS, 1999, Table 13.12). In some North American and Australian states (especially Victoria), because of fears about conservation of local wildlife, domestic cats are subject to a night-time curfew. In some areas under zoning planning regulations cats are only permitted if kept inside the house, and can legally be shot if found out on the street. Heated debate has ensued. A similar, but less emotive, situation has arisen in Britain in respect of grey squirrels. These were originally introduced from North America and are defined as pests and competitors to the indigenous brown squirrel. However, they are much loved by many, and are a major tourist attraction in the London parks. Likewise mink and other non-indigenous small mammals which have escaped from fur farms may be seen as causing a threat to native fauna, or as exercising their hard-won freedom. Another so-called pest, the pigeon, is a major concern to those concerned with the conservation of historic buildings. But pigeons are what many tourists go to Trafalgar Square to see and feed them. These are important issues that local authorities have to face, hardly the glamorous side of town planning, or indeed of environmentalism. But a holistic view of sustainability includes concerns for animals as well as humans, indeed for all flora and fauna.

VACANT AND DERELICT LAND

Land in Transition

There are vast areas of spoilt and underused land both in urban and rural areas which is increasingly the subject of a range of planning initiatives. The government, and indeed the EU, appears to favour the use of existing waste land within cities for new development, rather than spreading out new green field sites, as set out in the European Commission Green Paper on the Urban Environment (CEC, 1990). There is a range of policies, incentives and grants to encourage the re-use of derelict land. The use of brown land (q.v. Chapter 9) rather than greenfield sites for new development is now a major governmental objective. Brown land, generally comprising derelict inner urban land or disused previously industrial land, can be redeveloped as an alternative to using new green field sites. As stated in Chapter 1, the revised PPG3 recommends that 60 per cent of new housing should be built on such land.

The DoE kept a Register of publicly owned underused or under-utilized land under the 1980 Local Government, Planning and Land Act, and this role continues under the DETR. This particular register is not to be confused with other registers such as the register of planning applications, or the Land Registry which records the ownership and transfer (e.g. house conveyance) of land. On average per year there are 100,000 acres on around 8,000 individual sites, of under-used and vacant land, identified on this register, and this level has been maintained (*Source*: DETR Web Page). Around 25 per cent of this land has been vacant for over 20 years. Interestingly, much of this land is owned by statutory undertakers, local authorities. Nationalized industries and their privatized successors have a particularly bad record, especially in respect of railway land.

Under Section 215 of the Town and Country Planning Act 1990, local authorities have powers to require the proper maintenance of land by private owners, and there are additional powers under the Public Health Acts. If the owner considers his land has been blighted by adverse planning decisions he has the right to serve a Blight Notice for the local authority to purchase the land under Section 150 of the Town and Country Planning Act 1990. Some areas can get into a terrible mess, just through lack of management and neglect without any actual mining or industrial activity taking place.

Under the Derelict Land Act 1982, money was made available to improve such areas, this money being augmented by urban development grants, and urban regeneration grants under the Inner Urban

Areas Act 1979 and Local Government, Planning and Land Act 1980. In 1988 these grants were replaced by one category of City Grants. Money is also available within the ambit of the enterprise zone, urban development corporation legislation, Single Regeneration Budget programme, urban conservation, and EU programmes, as discussed in earlier chapters.

Mining Controls

The National Land Utilization Survey originally undertaken by the geographer Sir Dudley Stamp and continued by Professor Alice Coleman has shown, in spite of the introduction of town planning over the last 40 years, that the rate of loss of agricultural land to development has not been reduced, indeed it has continued to grow. In order to prevent at least some types of dereliction increasing in the future, the government has sought to increase controls over mining activities, especially opencast mining which causes some of the most visible problems. Mining counts as a form of development, and is therefore subject to control under the planning acts. County councils are required to include policies on mineral extraction, a county function, in the Structure Plan. The planners are concerned about how extraction will limit other future uses, for example, opencast mining can 'sterilize' wide areas for future development, while underground mining may burrow beneath surrounding sites which will subsequently be unsuitable for development because of the threat of future subsidence. Both types of mining will also create major environmental problems, as does quarrying. Heavy lorries create wear and tear on local roads and are a danger to local communities.

Planners are concerned with ensuring long term supervision of mining activities. A site will need to be re-instated after mining has ceased, perhaps in 30 years time, and planning conditions may be made to this effect with varying success. In the past some successful agreements were entered into with the National Coal Board, which were subsequently honoured, ensuring a measure of landscaping and environmental control. The Town and Country Planning Act 1947 first introduced controls over mining. Guidance on the control of minerals was found in what were known as 'The Green Books' produced by the (old) Ministry of Housing and Local Government in the 1950s and 1960s, whose influence is still to be felt. From the 1970s minerals control became the responsibility of counties and other first tier authorities. The Town and Country Planning (Minerals) Act 1981 increased planning authorities' powers of enforcement. An important feature is the need for 'after-care' of the site.

Where local government re-organization has taken place, for example in Wales in 1995, the new unitary authorities are now responsible for minerals. In Wales this is by virtue of the Local Government (Wales) Act 1994, but further changes are envisaged as a result of creation of a separate Welsh Assembly and related governmental restructuring. All minerals authorities are required to prepare Mineral Subject Plans alongside their other statutory development plans. Under the Town and Country Planning (Minerals) Act 1981 powers were increased, especially in respect of restoration and aftercare of sites, and limitations on the duration of planning permission. Typically mining permissions will contain far more 'conditions of permission' than other planning permissions, and generally take longer to go through the system. In 1988 Minerals Planning Guidance Notes (MPGs, which are similar to PPGs) were introduced. See Government Publications list). In the same year controls were increased because of European Directive 85/337 (see list of Government Publications) requiring environmental assessment of minerals applications.

Although there has been an improvement in modern controls, there still exist many pre-1947 permissions, with estimates of over a thousand nationwide. Such permissions were meant to be registered formally with the local planning department by March 1992, for consideration of imposition of modern conditions on the permissions, or they would cease to exist. In fact, in spite of considerable pressure from environmental groups, the process has not been straightforward as there are legal complexities involved in determining whether a permission is still extant or can be extinguished, and in some cases reliable records no longer exist. Such sites, nowadays, find themselves alongside gentrified rural settlements or in what are nowadays seen as environmentally sensitive areas. Such environmental considerations must be weighed against the importance of ensuring adequate provision of raw materials for industrial and construction purposes.

Minerals planning is discussed in detail in Senior (1996).

Not only is the nature of minerals planning changing so is the type of person going into minerals surveying and planning. Previously this was a field which attracted mainly men, and chiefly those of a scientific engineering bent. These days a wider range of students interested in environmental issues, including more women, are applying for minerals-related courses. For example, when research was undertaken in the late 1980s there were only six women minerals surveyors most of whom were students (Greed, 1991). In 1998 there were 36 women minerals surveyors and more women planners were specializing in minerals too (Palmer, 1997). Women were entering this field because of the popularity of the environmental movement, perhaps re-interpreting the mineral surveyors role as one of custodian and earth-carer, rather than as exploiter and planet-penetrator. A similar impact, and reinterpretation of professional roles and objectives has been found across the built environment professions as a result of the environmental movement. In fact the women's movement was in the vanguard of the original ecology movement, particularly in respect of the negative effects of aspects of science and technology, and the potentially polluting and carcinogenic effects of manufacturing practices (Carson, 1962; Griffin, 1978; Parkin, 1994).

ENVIRONMENTAL MOVEMENTS

The Influence of International Policy Trends

By the early 1990s, concern with the environment was moving from matters related to the countryside towards anxiety about the total eco-system. Concern with sustainability had became a higher governmental priority as a result of international influences such as the Brundtland Report *Our Common Future* (Brundtland, 1987). The agenda of the new 'green' environmental movement was beginning to have an impact on the scope and nature of town planning. Friends of the Earth and other pressure groups had drawn attention to deficiencies in policy and legislation in Britain, and internationally groups such as Greenpeace alerted people to the global implications of the greenhouse effect, holes in the ozone layer, pollution, and diminishing natural resources. By the 1990s environmental issues were appearing upon the governments' agenda. Early signs included the content of the revision in PPG9 1992 on Nature Conservation which now went beyond a limited concern with local, 'special site' related issues, to consider wider ecological issues.

The green intentions of the first Conservative government were expounded in the White Paper 'This Common Inheritance: Britain's Environmental Strategy', Cmd. 1200, (DoE, 1990a). This document set out the problems of unsustainable development and committed the Government to do something (not every specific) about it. The Government was already concerned about controlling pollution, but this was a rather different matter from taking proactive positive measures to create a more sustainable environment. The Environmental Protection Act 1990 consolidated and expanded the pollution controls introduced under previous public health and clean air acts such as the Clean Air Act 1974, it also increased controls on land fill and disposal of waste. Nuclear waste was subject to additional controls under Her Majesty's Inspectorate of Pollution (and see PPG23 on Pollution Control). Subsequently, the (original) Clean Air Act 1956 was repealed in the mid 1990s, by which time coal fire derived pollution, and many of the traditional heavy industries which contributed to London Smog had long since declined. There was not, as yet, an integrated approach to environmental issues, because, historically, different issues were dealt with by separate and diverse departments.

Nevertheless, increased traditional pollution control provided the gateway to a greater concern with the wider environmental agenda. Tighter controls and penalties raised the political profile of environmental issues among developers (Rydin, 1998: Chapter 11). This was because of the application of the principle 'let the polluter pay', a concept which rested uneasily in the entrepreneurial climate of Thatcher's Britain. High fines for pollution under the Environmental Protection Act 1990. Environmental taxes on landfill which were introduced in 1996 proved very unpopular with developers.

Many would argue that pollution is just one small part of the total environmental cost paid by the Planet. Whilst traditional economics recognizes the costs and profits from consumption and production it does not, as yet, recognize the economic value of the subsequent stages of decomposition and recycling of goods (Turner, 1996: Chapter 8 and p. 30). Over the last 20 years there have been moves to make the developer contribute more towards the true cost of development. For example the Water Act 1989 enables water companies to levy an infrastructural charge on developers of new housing estates. Such measures may be compared to earlier attempts to 'tax' the developer, for example by betterment levy in the post-war years (Chapter 8) or under planning gain (Chapter 3) nowadays.

Such regulation was influenced by the German-derived concept of the 'precautionary principle'. This sought to prevent pollution at source, whatever the cost to the producer, to avoid society and the environment paying greater costs later. The precautionary principle may be equated to the sentiments embodied the saying 'a stitch in time saves nine' (Cullingworth and Nadin, 1997: 170). Subsequently in 1999 the EU Directive on Integrated Pollution and Prevention Control Directive Number 96/61 came into effect, extending the precautionary principle. In the process the traditional role of British town planners was being extended, along European lines, towards that of 'environmental police'.

Meanwhile, in 1992 the Earth Summit on 'The Environment and Development' took place in Rio de Janeiro. Following this the policy document 'Sustainable Development: The UK Strategy' (DoE, 1994a) was produced by the government, which covered a range of topical issues such as global climate, air quality, and discussed policy in relation to non-renewable resources such as water, earth (soil) and minerals. Setting a future agenda for – Government, business, Non-Governmental Organizations (NGOs), and individual men and women – it stresses partnership approaches (DoE, 1994a). This strategy is paralleled by equivalent documents in other EU states, which have all been produced within the framework of the EU's Fifth Action Programme on the Environment (CEC, 1992).

Much was being learned from what had been achieved in other European countries, and from already established EU environmental policy programmes. Partnership opportunities have developed within European Union initiatives on the environment

Table 10.1 **Chronology of Sustainable Development Events**

Chronology of sustainable development events	
Early 1900s	Ellen Swallow Richards, a MIT academic is credited with developing the concept and coining the word 'ecology'.
1962	Publication of '*Silent Spring*' by Rachael Carson.
1969	Photographs of the earth from the Apollo spacecraft gave us a consciousness of planet earth as an eco-system.
1970	European Conservation Year.
1972	'Blueprint for Survival' (published by *The Ecologist* magazine).
1972	'The Limits to Growth' ('The Club of Rome').
1972	'The UN Conference on the Human Environment', Stockholm, (UN)
1973	First Environmental Action Programme (from EU).
1976	'The UN Peoples Habitat Conference' (community involvement).
1980	'The World Conservation Strategy' (species and habitat) (WWF).
1980	'The Brandt Commission' was concerned with the North South Divide.
1983	'Our Common Crisis' (Independent Commission on International Development Issues ICID)
1987	'Our Common Future' – 'The Brundtland Report' (WCED).
1990	'This Common Inheritance' first comprehensive UK government White Paper on the environment (DoE, 1990a)
1991	'Caring for the Earth, a Strategy for Sustainable Living' (IUCN, UNEP and WWF)
1991	Europe 2000 (European Union Programme).
1992	'Towards Sustainability' Fifth Environmental Action Programme.
1992	Planning Policy Guidance 12 (UK) includes environmental concerns.
1992	Rio: UN Conference on the Environment and Development (UNICED), (The Earth Summit) and Agenda 21 and Local Agenda 21.
1993	Good Practice Guide on the Environmental Appraisal of Development Plans (UK, DoE).
1993	DoE, Scottish Office and Local Government Management Board (LGMB) publish the Eco Management and Audit Scheme for local authorities, and the Framework for Local Sustainability.
1994	'Sustainable Development: the UK Strategy', 'Climate Change', 'Sustainable Forestry' and 'Biodiversity' (UK government).
1994	Report of the Royal Commission on Environmental Pollution (UK).
1995	The Berlin Conference on Climate Change.
1995	Environment Act.
1996	UN Habitat II Conference, Istanbul.
1997	Kyoto Climate Treaty (must be implemented by 2010).
1997	Labour Party Manifesto 'concern for the environment' at heart of policy.
1998	Revised UK Strategy for Sustainable Development (UK Government).
1998	Our Healthier Nation (UK Government, Green Paper).

(Expanded from Barton, 1996, and Brand, 1999)

(CEC, 1990; CEC, 1991; and Williams, 1999). A main goal of the Fifth Environmental Action Plan produced by the EU (CEC, 1992) was to raise awareness of environmentally friendly behaviour amongst three identified groups of actors – government, consumers and the public. A major objective of the European Union, 'is to achieve sustained and non-inflationary growth respecting the environment . . .'

Initiatives such as the European Spatial Development Perspective (ESDP) (as discussed in Chapter 10) seek to develop policy perspectives that relate the needs of specific cities and regions needs in the EU, to wider environmental policies from the global and pan-European level arena (Morphet, 1997: 265–7).

New advisory bodies, such as the UK Roundtable on Sustainable Development (UK Roundtable, 1996)

Table 10.2 **Key Environmental Issues**

The main issues are widely documented (see in particular DoE (1992c, 1994a, b, c) Sustainable Development: The UK Strategy and The Royal Commission on Environmental Pollution (1994).

The problems were identified as follows:

Global warming and climate change, as a result of high levels of greenhouse gas emission from fossil fuel burning and land use change (including deforestation and draining of bogs). As a direct result of the above, an unacceptable risk to low lying coastal cities and villages from rising sea levels as oceans expand and polar ice melts. This would reduce the amount of land available and is taken seriously in relation to coastal defences and town planning (PPG25).

Biodiversity, reduction in the range and extent of wildlife habitats both at the world scale and within the UK specifically, due to the impact of development and human activity. Loss of endangered species. The global 'gene-bank' is thus being impoverished. At the same time mad scientists doing genetic modification of crops, human and animal cloning and generally mucking things up. Not really a town planning issue except for development of land with endangered species living on it. Also links across the nature conservancy.

Air Quality, particularly poor air quality in urban areas as a result of traffic and industry pollution, led to health problems – e.g. the increase in asthma, acid rain, and atmospheric pollution.

Water, declining ground water levels, with consequent problems for water supply; increased run off, with consequent risk of flooding; water contamination in both urban and rural areas.

At a local level, the National Rivers Authority has recommended no further urban growth in parts of Kent because ground water levels and the quality of drinking water are threatened.

Earth loss of soil through increased erosion rates; loss of nutrients and soil fertility; problems of land contamination/dereliction.

Minerals high rate of extraction of non-renewable mineral reserves, and sterilization of potential renewable sources.

In summary, sustainability is about maintaining the health of the biosphere and husbanding key resources of air, water, land and minerals (Barton, 1996)

and the House of Lords Select Committee on Sustainable Development (House of Lords, 1995), were established in the mid-1990s. A number of existing quangos were given enhanced statutory duties in respect of environmental responsibilities. The Environment Act 1995 tightened and extended environmental controls (Ball and Bell, 1999; Lane and Peto, 1995; Grant, 1996). It increased local authority powers to control pollution, strengthened recycling measures and increased grants for Conservation (Brand, 1996, 1999).

The 1995 Act introduced measures relating to abandoned mines and contaminated land, and a new regime for reviewing and updating longstanding mineral permissions. The Act introduced changes in the responsibilities of National Park authorities, strengthened control over water resource management, flooding and pollution, and established a National Environment Agency (NEA) for England and Wales, the Scottish Environment Protection Agency, and separately the Alkali and Radioactive Inspectorate

in Northern Ireland. It should be noted that the Environment Agency incorporates the previous National Rivers Authority (NRA).

Sustainable policies were being reflected in revised PPGs such as PPG12: Development Plans and Regional Planning Guidance – produced in 1992, which highlighted the importance of taking into account the relationship between climatic change and landuse and transport policy. Most subsequent PPGs at least mention the word 'environment' and make some attempt to relate their subject matter to achieving sustainable development. PPG 12 is recognized as being particularly strong, with PPGs 1, 6 and 14 also touching upon sustainability. In general the emphasis in planning has shifted from the old adage of 'project and provide' in respect of meeting demands for more roads, houses and commercial developments, towards a more cautious approach to permitting new development, where other more sustainable solutions might be implemented. Likewise there has been a move away from the previous 'announce and defend'

Figure 10.5 **Can Recycling Cans make a Difference?**
While recycling measures are popular with the shopper,
they do not address more fundamental issues of retail location, and non-reuseable packaging, such as metal cans
and non-returnable bottles.

approach to policy making toward a more collaborative, consultative approach, particularly in environmental sensitivity situations where there is likely to be
considerable opposition.

There have, however, been marked inconsistencies
in policy as not all approved plans, and planning
permissions have embodied pro-environment objectives. Since consideration of sustainability is a new
component in the statutory planning system it is
proving difficult to determine its 'materiality' (legal
relevance) and 'force' in planning appeal situations.
This is in spite of the fact that Environmental
Assessment procedures are now required on many
categories of development. In particular throughout
the Conservative government's administration (1979–
97) encouragement continued to be given to out-of-
town retail developments and to decentralized and
dispersed urban settlement. In the meanwhile the
environmental movement was becoming popular
among the general public and a new 'green consumer'
movement was created. It was disconcerting that environmentally aware shoppers often seemed more
concerned about wanting recyclable carriers rather
than plastic bags from their local hypermarket, than
about questioning its out-of-town location and the
farming methods involved in producing its goods
(FUN, 1998).

Local Application of Sustainability Principles

Greater sensitivity to environmental issues was in
evidence at local government and community level.
The Rio Declaration on sustainability arising from the
1992 United Nations Conference provided the basis
for the establishment of the Agenda 21 programme.
This required all signatory states to draw up national
plans for sustainability. Agenda 21 is a lengthy document, with 40 chapters split into four sections,
which has been extensively analysed and critiqued
(Blowers, 1993; LGMB, 1993). In summary, emphasis
is placed on social and economic dimensions, the
need to combat poverty, strengthening the role of
major groups (including women, local authorities, and
NGOs) and the process of implementation, including
partnership (Brand, 1996: 60).

Chapter 28 of the Agenda agreement required local
authorities in each state to produce 'Local Agenda 21'
initiatives for their areas. Local Agenda 21 provides the
basis for a comprehensive programme and framework
for action into the twenty-first century for governments and development agencies (UNCED, 1992;
Keating, 1993). Chapter 28 calls upon each local
authority to undertake a consultative process with its
citizens. It is as much concerned with the process of
'planning' as it is with policy. It puts the onus upon
local authorities, with their communities, to design
and deliver (DOE, 1994a, b, c). Throughout Agenda

Figure 10.6 **Wood Storage on a South-East Asian Street.**
Sustainability is a global issue. Many 'developing poor'
countries practice sustainability as a matter of necessity.

21 there are calls for new approaches to decision-making, emphasizing inter-sectoral co-operation, local consultation and greater democracy within the community. This may be described as a collaborative approach to planning (Healey, 1997 as discussed in Chapter 16).

Subsequently, a UK Local Agenda 21 Steering Group was established and the Local Government Management Board took on the role of disseminating guidance throughout the UK (LGMB, 1993). Within the context of their national strategies for sustainable development, central governments may help the local process. Given the complexity of Agenda 21 and the need for the commitment and co-operation of UK local governments for its fulfilment within the Local Agenda 21 process, various national bodies have responded by offering guidance to the more local level.

Local Agenda 21 assumes it is not only desirable but possible to achieve a high degree of collaborative action in a 'community' by voluntary agreement. There is a strong emphasis upon the process of involvement (collaborative planning) rather than upon rules. It is a question of building up cultures and changing attitudes. LA21 committees involving the public, private and voluntary sectors would enable a discussion of sustainability issues to take place, to produce jointly an integrated plan. The UK Government required every local area to produce such a plan by the end of 1996. The process and requirements presented a challenge to those involved, and the process is by no means complete. The holistic approach of Local Agenda 21 offered a cultural and organizational challenge to authorities, which are traditionally organized on sectoral lines. Several authorities have developing cross-cutting departmental arrangements. All have appointed a Local Agenda 21 co-ordinator. They are to be found in various departments, with the Chief Executive's Office, Environmental Health, and Planning Departments being the most common locations.

The hope is that by involving different interests – e.g. the local Chamber of Commerce, utilities, environmental pressure groups and the local authority – insights will be shared and a co-ordinated strategy will emerge. This is an idealistic adventure, and has given a culture shock to many of those involved, as international level 'top down' influences impinge upon the

Figure 10.7 **Cities are for All God's Creatures.**
Cities are for all God's creatures, great and small, and should be planned accordingly. While pet cats predominate in Northern Europe, feral felines constitute a major component of the urban fauna.

various British town planning systems. Yet it needs to be successful if the deep-seated issues of unsustainability are to be addressed. It remains to be seen if government has the mettle to pursue its goal of sustainable development with the strong commitment that is required (Brand, 1999).

The environmental movement is having a growing effect upon the operation of the day-to-day statutory planning system in the UK through development control. As stated in Chapter 3, because of EU regulations the production of Environmental Statements (ES) indicating that Environmental Impact Assessment has been undertaken, are now an integral part of the development control process. As set out in Chapter 3, certain categories of planning application must now be accompanied by an Environmental Statement. These measures were progressively introduced during the 1990s and gradually began to take effect. In addition, permitted development rights under the 1995 revision of the GDO were amended to ensure environmental assessment proofing. Likewise development plans must also be environmentally appraised, as must any major planning policy document, such as the Structure Plan or Unitary Development Plan. In other words environmentalism has become embedded and mainstreamed within the national planning system.

Figure 10.8 **An Empty Motorway: A Rare Sight!**
Road to nowhere? Is the present road programme sustainable? Will the motorways become empty derelict monuments to the twentieth century?

CONCLUSION: IS SUSTAINABILITY SUSTAINABLE?

Unless there is a tremendous shift in central government attitudes, funding, and regulation towards public transport, motor car usage, pollution control enforcement, building design, energy policy, and waste disposal practice, planners alone have inadequate powers to achieve sustainable cities. To achieve sustainably planned settlements the planners would need increased powers to achieve the fundamental structural shifts in land use patterns, densities, traffic management and layout patterns (Barton and Bruder, 1995). At present, environmental principles are influencing society's attitudes, to a degree, rather than totally revolutionizing town planning or city form. Also the emphasis has now shifted from facilitating motor car movement to impeding progress, for example, by the 1993 Traffic Calming Act. Greater emphasis and value

is put upon public transport. In the 1960s, incredibly, a bus was calculated to be the equivalent of three passenger car units (PCUs), a figure which was based upon bus length, now it is acknowledged that one bus might be the equivalent of around 70 pcus, based upon the number of car trips saved.

If there is no public transport available in many areas, or if bus journeys are slow, indirect, complex, and unreliable then they do not provide a realistic alternative in terms of personal time management, accessibility and practicality then people will resort to using their cars. It is estimated, on average, that less than a quarter of car journeys are work related, but all are no doubt seen as essential by the drivers concerned, with the school run, and the trip to the supermarket competing with the journey to work as vital expeditions. In comparison in North America journeys to work comprise less than 10 per cent of total journeys, such is the aversion to walking.

Of the 650 million cars in the world, a third are within the United States of America, and another third are in the six main industrialized countries including Britain. Globally only 4.4 per cent of all cars are in Britain, and for comparison 6.9 per cent in Germany. Because Britain has one of the highest amount of road mileage per hectare, it has one of the lowest percentages of cars per kilometre of road in the world (*New Internationalist*, 1999). There are 27 million vehicles on the road in Britain (including all types of vehicles) and 68 per cent of people over 17 years of age have a driving licence. But, less than 1 per cent of the world's population own or have use of a motorcar, or for that matter a computer, telephone or flush lavatory (cf. current issues of *New Internationalist* magazine; and Lappé, 1998).

There have been a variety of fiscal and physical measures to control the motorcar. For example, fuel and vehicle duties have been increased in recent years, but the proportion of this revenue reinvested in the road system has been reduced. The average price of unleaded petrol in mid-1999 was 3.18 per gallon (70 pence per litre). Of this 82.2 per cent is taken in tax. It has been calculated that 32 billion pounds per year is raised from vehicle and fuel tax but only 20 per cent of this or 8 billion pounds is actually used for road improvements, and the Arab oil producers are conveniently blamed for the rise in fuel prices. Proposals for motorway tolls, more bus only lanes, and penalties for single occupancy cars further fuel the debate. *Ad hoc* solutions, and glib sound bites are not the answer, rather a fully integrated, and carefully structured land use transportation planning strategy is needed. Clearly revenue might be more efficiently spent both in respect of the overall transportation infrastructure and in respect of providing viable public and private modes of transport to get people to work, to school, or shops, and to undertake the thousands of other necessary tasks essential to the improvement of the economy and society.

As with most urban policies, change is likely to be gradual and long term, as it is no simple task to change urban structure, provide people with a viable alternative to motorcars, and deal with all the related social and economic effects of environmental change. Nevertheless, British town planning's encounter with the international sustainability movement has led to culture change, if not shock. In particular it has opened up the door for more collaborative approaches to the planning process, and it has challenged the physical land use basis of British planning.

It has also created new synergies and connections in respect of defining the ambit and boundaries of what might validly count as part of 'town and country planning'. Awareness of the inter-relationship between the urban environment, and thus town planning, and health issues has been marked both within the sustainability movement, and increasingly within central government policy statements from New Labour (cf. Fudge, 1999). For example, 'Our Healthier Nation' (Department of Health, 1998) recognizes the relationship between health and the quality of the environment and the social and environmental causes of ill-health. It offers a commitment to targeting inequalities in health, proposes a UK strategy to tackle poverty and social exclusion and has clear implications for urban policy and local transport policy.

Likewise the original Agenda 21 document acknowledges poverty and health issues, and states, 'good health depends on social, economic and spiritual development and a healthy environment, including safe food and water' (Keating, 1993: 11). Previously, the World Health Organization (WHO) established the Healthy Cities Project internationally (WHO, 1997). This was designed to promote good health and prevent disease, and was 'seen as a means of legitimizing, nurturing and supporting the process of community empowerment' (Brand, 1999). It is noteworthy that Mrs Gro Harlem Brundtland, the author of the 1987 Report, is now chair of the World Health Organization. The WHO covers 51 nations and 870 million people. Significantly health, along with social equity, were key themes in the subsequent United Nations Conference, Habitat II, held in Istanbul in 1996. The human element, and thus the 'social aspects of planning' is being given greater attention in the international sustainability debate, as well as the natural environment component, that has dominated British town planning. If 'predict and provide' is no longer to be the guiding principle in town planning and transportation policy, more proactive, and better funded alternatives must be found to meet people's needs to go about their daily round of work, home-making and other essential activities.

TASKS

Information Gathering Tasks

I. Find out what stage the Local Agenda 21 programme has reached in your area, and what organizations have been involved in the consultation and discussion processes.

II. What are the main environmental issues of concern in your vicinity?

Conceptual and Discursive Tasks

III. Define and discuss the concept 'sustainability'.

IV. To what extent has the sustainability agenda been taken on board by the UK planning system?

Reflective Tasks

V. What do you personally think about environmental issues? How do you travel? If you drive a car would you be willing to give it up?

VI. To what extent do you consider the scope and nature of town and country planning is likely to change by 2010? Imagine a scenario of the future role of the planner.

FURTHER READING

Concern for the environment, and subsequently for sustainability, came from a range of diverse sources, including those traditionally concerned with recreation and leisure (Arvill, 1969); with farming (Shoard, 1980, 1987, 1999); with transport, cycling and public transport (see Sustrans, Cyclebag and Earthspan publications); and with ecology and environment (on which there are countless books and groups, start with Blowers, 1993, then investigate Elkin, Glasson, Gore, McLaren, Meadows (2 books), Simonin, Theniral and Whitelegg. Check recent government publications including DoE/SS, DoE/DoT, LGMB, LRC, CPOS, CEC, WHO, guide to eco-management (DoE/SS), reducing transport emissions (DoE/DoT), climate change (DoE, 1992c), Hall, P., 1997), and from women and environment groups, from North America, Europe and Third World countries (Mies and Shiva, 1993; Braidotti (ed.), 1994; Warren, 1997, Parkin 1994). Rachel Carson's book, *Silent Spring* is a foundational text in the very creation of the Green movement. The wider European, global, and health dimensions are considered in Fudge, 1999, and Brand, 1999. Readers should not be at a loss in seeking information on environmental issues as there is a plethora of television documentaries, exhibitions, newspaper articles, journals and books on this topic.

ESDP (1999) *European Spatial Development Perspective – Towards Balanced and Sustainable Development of the Territory of the European Union*, Brussels: European Commission, see http://www.inforegio.org

URBAN DESIGN, CONSERVATION AND CULTURE

MORE THAN DRAWING

Fixed Standards or Flexible Policies?

The purpose of Chapter 11 is to familiarize readers with key themes, principles, and changes at the local design level of planning. It is not the intention to provide a primer on 'how to design' or 'how to create a housing layout', as these are topics beyond the scope of this book. Those readers who wish to pursue these aspects in more detail should consult the Further Reading section for guidance (for example Greed and Roberts, 1998). The first part of this chapter outlines the considerations involved in designing at the local level. Second, the effect of increasing social awareness and attempts to design more for user needs are discussed; third, the implications of a wider cultural agenda within urban planning are considered.

The local design level is the area of planning that many newcomers to the subject assume is the 'real planning'. They may imagine the planners' work to be centred upon drawing boards, and upon detailing road widths and housing layouts. Students often imagine that there must be one correct technical answer to the question of how a housing layout is prepared. As with much of town planning, 'the right answer' depends on what the planners want to achieve, and where the development is located. For example, if an estate has been designed with wide roads to speed the traffic up it is also likely to reduce the level of safety within the estate.

Relatively speaking different planning authorities adopt different standards for the purpose of development control. Once adopted these standards do have a legal status in the area in question. Sites and circumstances vary considerably so there always a requirement for flexibility. Some local planning authorities produce design guides, such as the popular text produced by Essex Planning Authority which has achieved cult status (Essex, 1973), this *Essex Design Guide* has been subject to criticism over the years. Much of the guidance contained in a subsequent, long-awaited revision, produced by Essex in 1997 contradicts the previous edition's standards, particularly in relation to road design (Essex, 1997). There have recently been major changes in policy direction, and therefore in required standards. For example, environmental policies have sought to restrict, rather than cater for, traffic flow (Department of Transport, 1990).

Roads and Sewers Or Art and Design?

Two strands of local planning may be identified. First, a functional and highly prescriptive form of estate planning developed within the context of the local authority planning system. Great emphasis upon setting standards regarding road widths, densities and building styles (DoE, 1990b). This was accompanied by a practical concern for the provision of sewers, drains and other infrastructural services. The focus was upon residential estates, and traditional Garden City principles guided the approach. Keeble's books on planning provided the Bible for much post-war reconstruction planning. These publications provided instant recipes and layout patterns on how to plan new towns, new housing estates, town centres and industrial estates (Keeble, 1969). Sewers remain important. The privatization of many public statutory undertakers has led to increased costs for the developer, for example, the Water Act 1989, enables water companies to levy an infrastructural charge on developers of new housing estates.

The second tradition was more architectural and aesthetic in perspective. It had had its roots both in the grand urban designs of the past and in a more visual, design-orientated cultural approach to planning, with significant influences emanating from both Continental Europe and North America. The 'Grand Manner' tradition of European planning, manifest in the great squares, boulevards and avenues of many capital cities was essentially an artistic rather than functional exercise. Yet this form of planning was also concerned with sewers and drains. For instance, in the late nineteenth century Hausmann's magnificent street plan for Paris was 'mirrored' underground by an extensive system of modern sewers. There has also been a highly influential North American urban design movement concerned with townscape and the image of the city (Lynch, 1960 [1988]).

Nowadays these two streams have come together within the context of a modern reconstructed urban design movement. Traditional concerns with the aesthetic, visual aspects of townscape and architecture have been pursued alongside more functional concerns within the scope of urban design. This is a new socially-focused approach to functionality.

PLANNING STANDARDS AND DESIGN PRINCIPLES

Understanding the Basics

It is important to be aware of the main, practical considerations that need to be taken into account in the process of planning at the local estate design level, before embarking upon a discussion of the wider urban design agenda. Therefore in this section the main considerations are summarized with reference to the development of a new housing estate. Housing constitutes 70 per cent of all development, and three quarters of all new development, however, many of the same principles could be applied to other types of development. Some additional material will be provided, where appropriate, in relation to other sorts of land uses. Commentary on how the situation is changing as a result of the renaissance in the urban design movement, environmental assessment requirements, sustainability policy, and community considerations will be provided en route. Also key changes in government guidance which shapes the main planning standards will be highlighted.

Site and Client Considerations

Private house building firms, and some local authority housing departments still have a standard pattern of house type and estate layout which they will seek to impose, whatever or wherever the site, right across the country. But good design should take into account the special characteristics of the specific site in question and seek to meet the needs of those who will live there. First, 'who' the development is aimed at should be considered carefully. In the private sector this question is directly linked to calculating the type of people, it is envisaged, who will buy the houses – in terms of class, income, and family size, and age group. For example, in a desirable area near a golf course, it might be advisable to build a few really expensive houses on the site at a low density and get a good financial return. On a suburban infill site the best solution, to capitalize on market trends, is to build for young married couples wanting starter homes at the cheaper end of the price range, and so the developer will build more houses at a higher density. Alternatively, in a fashionable inner city area that has already been gentrified, new development may be ill-advised, and instead conversions might yield more return.

Whilst private developers are concerned with getting the best return from the site, the planners have wider policy considerations to take into account. They are concerned with factors such as likely traffic generation, density, accessibility, social mix, employment opportunities and sustainability. The planners may look more favourably on a planning application for the development of the site which includes a local shop or pub, or a scheme which does not develop the whole of the site but leaves some land undeveloped for amenity purposes. All of this would have to be negotiated and may be the subject of planning gain agreements. How far the developer will go all depends on how desperate he is to develop, and whether he also has his eyes on another comparable site elsewhere where the planning authority is less fussy. Clearly financial, rather than aesthetic or social considerations often predominate in this branch of planning, but good design can make a development more attractive to potential purchasers.

Whatever the nature of the development, or the funders, certain basic 'physical' factors need to be taken into account. In designing a scheme for a site, an initial site analysis must be undertaken of its main natural and man-made characteristics. The slope and aspect of the site needs to be noted, not only with regard to drainage constraints, but also to see whether there are any good 'views out' of the site that might be capitalized upon. The planning authority may be more concerned about 'views in', because they do not want a development stuck on the skyline or half way up a hill, which might constitute an eyesore. In the past developers used to be unwilling to build on slopes of more than 1 in 7 gradient, but these days much of the remaining available infill land is sloping and therefore a range of styles of split-level housing has emerged on this type of land. The level of the water table should be investigated and whether there are any areas liable to flooding. Attention should also be paid to the micro-climate of the site, in particular whether there are any frosty hollows to be avoided, also areas which receive more sun where houses might be better situated.

It is used to be said, in more leisurely times, or in respect of building for more affluent clients, that houses should be designed so that the bedrooms face the sun in the mornings, and the living rooms and the garden at the back of the house get the sun in the evenings. This is virtually impossible to achieve on more than half of the houses on an estate if the houses are built along roads facing each other (unless the internal layout is reversed). However, reasonable levels of sunlight and daylight penetration should be sought where possible (Littlefair, 1991).

Wind direction is another important factor that should be taken into account, especially on high, exposed ground. This affects the orientation of the road layout in residential areas and passage-ways which might become mini wind-tunnels. The power of the wind is an even greater problem in central area commercial developments of high-rise office blocks, which can increase the effects of wind eddies and air streams around the buildings. Most pedestrians have had the experience of fighting their way through the elements along the pavement at the bottom of a high-rise building on a windy day. This principle also applies to council high-rise blocks of flats, which are notorious for being windswept, with accompanying swirling litter. When such schemes have been privatized wind buffers and subtle planting has often been introduced to deal with this problem (Roberts and Greed, 2000).

Legal rights over the land must be checked, including ownership and title. A 'Local Search' would be undertaken with the local authority in question by the purchaser's or developer's solicitor before the land was bought. The search will reveal any existing 'charges' on the land such as unexpired planning permissions, listed building designations, etc. An 'Additional Enquiries' form would also show up wider planning issues related to the structure plan, such as sewer availability, road widening, that may affect the site.

A typical site is likely to be criss-crossed by a range of public and private rights, footpaths and other rights of way. There may be private rights over the land, such as easements which give people, cables and drains and even animals, the right of passage over the land. The tenure situation of the land must be established as to who owns what rights, and whether there are any outstanding restrictive covenants over the land, over and above any zoning controls the planners may have on it. For example, some Victorian houses with large back gardens, which look like ideal sites for infill development, are still governed by restrictive covenants which prevent an increase in density, a condition put on when they were built to preserve the quality of the area. Application can be made to the Lands Tribunal for the extinguishment or modification of such covenants. Even if the application is granted, the applicant may be required to pay compensation.

A technical survey of the site will need to be undertaken to ascertain soil type, the load-bearing qualities of the site and the likelihood of subsidence. This is important in mining areas. A special legal 'search' can be made with the relevant Coal Authority to establish the whereabouts of old tunnels and shafts. A wary eye should be kept on nearby spoil tips where imperceptible solifluction (soil creep) can threaten a development. The Welsh Development Agency has done a commendable job greening the valleys and covering much of the dereliction and slag heaps. Much of this land is unstable and unsuitable for construction purposes at present. In industrial locations, possible noise and smells from adjacent sites should be considered. The location of cables, drainage pipes, and sewers should be established in consultation with the relevant companies or statutory undertakers.

Site development potential may be limited by the availability of adequate sewerage and storm drainage facilities, all of which costs money to install. The developer will normally pay substantially towards these services, but even so, if a site is miles from the next phase of proposed main sewer extension then it is unlikely to be built on. Likewise water does not flow up hill unless it is pumped, and therefore the cost of developing a site may be prohibitive simply because of the lack of services. These days it is important that there is adequate cabling for television reception and internet communication.

The existing visual qualities of the site and of the surrounding area need to be investigated. The vegetation of the site should be recorded. Today many local authorities require the retention of existing trees and hedgerows on new housing developments, and many would-be buyers are thrilled at the idea of real country hedges in their back gardens. Much greenfield site development on the edge of the city is on erstwhile farmland. Trees may have Tree Preservation Orders (TPOs) on them and therefore cannot be removed, if they are another tree of similar species must be put in its place.

As to new planting, fashions vary, the traditional principles found in books such as Keeble (1969) are still to some extent applicable. Ash, beech, blackthorn and spruce were in the past recommended as windbreaks (but take decades to grow). Ash, elm, oak, yew, poplar, and willow are good for open spaces, but require a wide radius for their roots and should not be planted near walls. Cedar, chestnut, lime and walnut are good for town squares, but are unsuitable for small gardens. Acacia, birch, horsechestnut, plane and laburnum are suitable for wide roads; likewise almond, cypress, holly, lombardy poplar and rowan for narrower roads. Trees with flowers and berries, especially flowering cherry are often seen as rather kitsch or suburban in taste. Trees that are likely to drop leaves on cars and pavements should not be used. Many developers prefer 'instant', fast growing, maintenance-free trees. Local authorities like to use vandal-proof trees, or prickly bushes that keep residents on

Figure 11.1 **The Importance of Access Visibility: Railings.**
Railings, or walls of spaced bricks or blocks that can be seen through are preferred where possible, provided this does not reduce privacy within gardens.

the footpaths and off the gardens, also dense plant cover which discourages weeds and dogs. On the other hand, as stated earlier, women's groups and crime prevention groups advise against putting tree cover, high walls, or screening near to footpaths which may obscure visibility.

There are wider issues of the protection of wildlife, wild flowers, etc., which may be located in some out-of-town development locations. Science parks and other commercial developments have had to be relocated a short distance from the preferred location to allow rare species of frogs and newts to remain undisturbed in their ponds. Drainage of development sites without a preliminary ecological analysis is seen as a thoughtless approach to development. As stated in the Chapter 10, environmental assessment is now required on larger schemes, including some residential schemes, under Schedule 2.

Additionally, planners are unwilling for developers to develop on high grade agricultural land. But such development is often inevitable nowadays. There are five grades of agricultural land classification running basically from very good to very poor, with Grades I and II being seen as the most in need of protection from development. The highest grade land is known as 'blue land' because it is shaded blue on the MAFF maps. But many farmers are keen to sell such land because of the current decline in the agricultural industry.

The characteristics of the local building materials, style and colour, should also be investigated to ensure that the new scheme blends in with the surrounding area, especially in urban infill sites and rural locations. In many instances the use of materials will be controlled by the planners in any case, especially in conservation areas. Existing gates, fences, walls and other townscape features may be incorporated in the design to good effect.

Design and Density

Once all these factors have been mapped on to the site plan, a possible design solution to the layout might already be proposed taking account of the constraints of the site (such as gradients or the requirement to retain protected trees). The house-type required by the developer or the planners may itself determine the likely layout of the site. To save time, preliminary discussion with the planners is advisable, with the presentation of a draft 'brief' of what is in mind, before an application is made in the case of larger-scale developments. In the opinion of some designers it is important to start the design process by sketching in the roads (taking into account their relationship with any existing sewers, etc.) and then arrange the houses around them. Others block in the main areas of housing first, and subdivide them to the density required and then add the roads. A few designers will go for the 'creative intuitive leap' and cannot explain quite how they arrived at the final design.

Residential densities measure the number of dwellings, in other words the number of habitable units per hectare (or per acre), not just the number of buildings. These two criteria may coincide in a new suburban housing estate, but do not in the case of older houses, which have been subdivided into flats. In fact, crude density is not always a good measure of actual plot coverage, which may need to be measured by other criteria for design purposes. For example, the planners may stipulate that not more than 50 per cent of the site is developed. A particular awareness of these factors is necessary in respect of tall residential buildings where there may be an apparently high net density but low plot coverage because all the dwellings are built close together. Nor is density, in itself, a measure of the quality of the area, as some conservation areas

Textbox 11.1 Densities

N.B: An acre = 0.405 hectares and a hectare = 2.471 acres. Both the persons per hectare (pph) (or persons per acre (ppa)), and the dwellings per hectare (dph) (or dwellings per acre (dpa)) are given but for simplicity's sake after the first few examples only the dph will be given. Pph (or ppa) is normally three times dph (or dpa). If there are going to be houses at 30 dwellings per hectare (dph) that is 12 dwellings per acre (12 dpa), there will be house plots of about 12 metres (40 feet) wide with a total plot depth of around 36 metres (120 feet). This will be composed approximately of a 15 metre (50 feet) back garden, 10.5 metres (35 feet) depth of house, 6 metres (20 feet) front garden, 2 metres (6 feet) pavement and say 3 metres (10 feet) to the white line in the middle of the road. Housing plots are usually measured to include half the estate road width, with pavement. These are 'typical' dimensions, it should be stressed that housing layouts are seldom this regular, as there is likely to be considerable variation in plot size across the estate because of topographical factors and other constraints.

consisting of Georgian town houses and mews may have a high density.

Relatively speaking, controls on commercial development are more concerned with the intensity of development on a particular site than overall density. For commercial development Floor Space Index (FSI) gives the relationship between the size of the plot (usually including half the width of the surrounding roads) and the total floor space. FSI has been used in the past in central London, particularly in relation to office building development. Plot ratio is also used for both commercial and residential development to determine how much of the site can be built over. The same FSI can be achieved in a variety of ways, for example, by building one tall building on a small part of the site or by spreading many buildings over the whole site, or again by 'stepping' the building back (like a staircase in tiers) as is done in New York. There are also height restrictions in many areas, as is the case in many enterprise zones, which have a height limit. Skyscrapers, generally defined as buildings over 150 metres (500 feet) tall, have been making a comeback in the UK, for example at Canary Wharf, London. Tall residential buildings, unlike commercial buildings in Britain, are required to receive a certain amount of natural daylight so they cannot be built too closely together. Guidelines were provided by the Sunlight and Daylight Regulations (DOE, 1971) which have since been superseded by Building Research Establishment guidance for both high-rise and low-rise buildings (Littlefair, 1991).

There are two main types of residential density net and gross. Net density is based on the dimensions given above that is the width of the houseplot times the length of the total plot made up of the house standing within its front and back garden plus the distance up to half way across the estate road. If all these blocks were put together they would cover the whole area of the housing estate. Gross density includes all the above, plus the land taken up for local shops, schools, amenity space and distributor roads. In other words it is a neighbourhood density, and therefore is likely to appear lower than the net density. It is important to check which type of density the planners require in respect of a particular site.

There are a variety of other types of density which might be encountered, ranging from measurements of the town density of the urban area as a whole, i.e. it is not solely a residential density, down to the very detailed accommodation densities which deal with the numbers of rooms or even bedspaces in an area, the latter being used by housing management officers working out how many council tenants they can fit into an area. Density, in this wider context, can be based on the number of dwellings or the number of people. On average it is assumed that there are three persons per household, although, in reality, there may be one person in one house, and six in the next. It follows that person densities are usually three times greater than dwellings densities. The word 'dwellings' rather than houses is usually used, as this includes not only houses, but also includes flats and bedsitter accommodation.

This is an important distinction for planners seeking to estimate the number of people that will live in an area for whom they will need to provide a certain level of shopping or school provision. This is particularly important where there are areas of large Edwardian houses which may only be 4 houses per acre (10 per hectare). When all the subdivided flats

have been counted then the number of actual dwellings might run into five times that figure, i.e. 50 dwellings per hectare (50 dph) which is approximately 20 dwellings per acre (50 dpa). Some planning authorities operate density controls to stop an area being too built up, and may refuse an extension to a house or the subdivision of a house into more than two units. This can be most insensitive to the actual residents of the house who might want a granny flat for a relative. The planners have to take into account the fact that once granted the 'permission runs with the land'. This means that it attaches to the property rather than the family in question who might move later on, and they can't take the extension with them! An answer might be: make sure that the flat is 'linked' to the house without its own separate entrance so that it does not count as a 'new' dwelling (i.e. development), fire regulations permitting. The 1998 Human Rights Act, in force from late 2000, has increased the rights of the family, and potentially given new legal rights to family dwelling extensions which are currently being established through case law.

Here are some illustrations of the sort of densities which are likely to be found in different types of housing area. Large detached houses in big gardens on the edge of the city are likely to be built at 2.5–10 dph (1–4 dpa) which is the same as 8–30 pph (3–12 ppa). Typical inter-war detached houses come out more like 20 dph (8 dpa), whereas semi-detached suburbia was normally built to around 30 dph (10–12 dpa). Council housing was formerly built to approximately this figure, but the densities became higher on new schemes as the years went by.

Moving further into the city, terraced housing averages around 37 dph (15 dpa), as does patio housing, which was much used in some New Towns and inner city locations where there is little garden space; the house forming an L-shape around an internal courtyard. Three-storey terraces and maisonettes are usually 50–70 dph (20–30 dpa). A maisonette comprises one self-contained dwelling above another, but unlike flats, each has its own separate entrance. Maisonettes are known as duplexes in the USA. Six-storey blocks of flats cover an area of 90dph (40 dpa), and may be termed, according to British usage, as medium rise development. Levels of 200 dph (80 dpa) can be achieved for a high-rise development of 10–15 storeys, provided little ancillary space is allowed around the base of the blocks. However, in Britain, unlike Hong Kong where densities go far beyond this, it is impossible to achieve really high densities by going high rise because of the sunlight and daylight regulations which require that space must be left around the block, so little is gained by building higher. Very high densities are also achieved in older areas where there has been a great deal of subdivision into individual bed-sits or studio flats, in what are termed moderate medium rise buildings, such as six-storey converted Victorian town-house mansions. Using linked and clustered forms of low-rise dwelling forms, such as patios, quite high densities can be attained without going high rise. It is important, therefore, not to confuse or conflate high-rise and high-density as they can exist separately.

Roads, Parking and Circulation

Whereas the physical factors identified in the above sections remain relatively immutable and indisputable, the standards relating to the motor car have undergone significant changes, particularly during the last five years. When assessing a site's potential, access and circulation within the site needs to be considered, in respect of existing road and other transport connections. There are some sites which look ideal on a map, but on closer investigation they prove to be completely landlocked (surrounded by other properties). Sometimes there will be just one possible access point through a strip of land, which because of the exorbitant price the owner is likely to ask, it is known as the 'ransom strip'. In these times, lack of motor car access is not necessarily a major deterrent to development, in the light of government guidance on the need to restrict motor car usage. More attention is being given to providing adequate footpaths, and bicycle path access, details which were often given secondary importance in the past when it was assumed 'everyone' would have a car (DoT, 1990).

In the past developers used to build alongside available roads creating ribbon development as was discussed in earlier chapters. It is unlikely today that a through road will go right across a new housing estate because of road safety considerations. Likewise, planners and highways engineers do not want too many cars coming out of access roads, or driveways from individual houses on to a main road and thus slowing down the through traffic. These days a road

Figure 11.2 **Cycle Path Dissecting Public Space: College Green, Bristol.**
Cyclist route provision needs to be integrated visually and the separation of pedestrians and cyclists needs to be safe and clear.

layout emphasizes the use of culs-de-sac and the safety of pedestrians. The roots of this format are to be found in the Radburn concept which is described below.

Radburn Layouts

In the 1920s in America, the town of Radburn was designed as a series of neighbourhoods each of which was ringed by an external peripheral road, from which a series of culs-de-sac penetrated into the neighbourhood providing access for residents but preventing through traffic from finding a short cut through. This is also very similar to the idea of environmental areas, proposed by Buchanan (see Chapter 9) in the 1960s, in respect of reconfiguring road systems in existing urban areas in Britain (Buchanan, 1963). Within the Radburn neighbourhood the pedestrian footpath system was designed to be completely separate from the road system. People coming to the house by car would arrive at the 'back' of the house, and park in a garage or garage court and approach the house through the 'back' door. Pedestrians would walk along the landscaped footpaths which run between the houses on the 'front' of the house. Front and back are in inverted commas, because once it is realized that pavements do not need to run alongside roads, and that houses need not face on to the street, the concept of front and back becomes almost irrelevant. Indeed, these changes to the external access to the houses did

Figure 11.3 A Radburn Footpath.
Pedestrian–vehicular segregation needs to be thought through carefully to ensure the creation of high quality townscape and a functional environment.

mean a major rethink of how the inside of the house should be planned.

The Radburn principle was adopted in many of the post-war British New Towns in combination with the neighbourhood unit concept. Such schemes often proved unpopular, for while they were meant to increase the safety from traffic by separating the paths from the roads, many pedestrians were unhappy with the remote, cut-off nature of some of the paths, especially women walking home alone after work in the evenings. This was particularly the case in towns where footpaths were routed through dark underpasses beneath peripheral roads. Contrary to the original scheme at Radburn the pedestrians' needs became secondary to those of the motor car. It was often expected that bicycles should share the footpaths with the pedestrians, an arrangement which was unsatisfactory for both groups. Residents were also confused and unhappy about not having a clear front and back to their houses, and housewives got fed up with people tramping through the back garden and then walking with muddy feet across the kitchen floor. The layout was unsafe, as children often used the garage court areas to play football, and inevitably accidents happened as motorists reversed their cars into parking spaces. Cars were often vandalized too.

Purists would say that if the true Radburn design had been adopted rather than cheap and nasty imitations, known as pseudo-Radburns then many of these problems could have been avoided. Most local authorities accept 'Radburnization' in some form or other as a basis of their design principles, with particular emphasis on the use of culs-de-sac to provide car access to houses and the provision of footpath systems. However, there are usually also pavements alongside the roads as well. The whole idea of separate front and back accesses for pedestrians and car drivers died a natural but slow death.

The concept of the 'Radburn' peripheral road can still be seen in some larger scale developments. But on smaller schemes it is common to see the reverse, a branching 'tree' layout, with a spine road giving access into the centre of the estate and then a series of smaller distributor roads branching off from this. They, in turn, subdivide into smaller roads in the form of culs-de-sac which serve 'clumps' of houses, with each drive way giving access onto the cul-de-sac. In the immediate post-war period the turning arrangements at the end of culs-de-sac used to look like 'lollipops' that is the road went around a little circular traffic island with a touch of greenery in the middle. Culs-de-sac these days normally end with a hammerhead or 'T' shaped turning space which provides adequate room to reverse. In some instances the planners have tried to 'soften' this arrangement by creating more of a court-yard effect in which the change from road to private driveway is marked by a change in the style of paving

Figure 11.4 Attention to Detail: Sidewalk Paving.
A creatively designed and well-maintained pavement surface arguably makes pedestrians feel valued in our car-dominated societies, and can be a valuable townscape and tourist feature in its own right.

stone. However, whilst this might look impressive, and create an urban 'mews' atmosphere when used in inner urban infill sites, many pedestrians find this arrangement ambiguous and therefore potentially dangerous.

Once traditional street patterns are abandoned, a range of layouts can be developed which set out the houses in different arrangements. For example, garage courts, play spaces, and communal gardens were often incorporated into local authority schemes at the expense of traditional gardens, pavements, and garages. Some architects believed that this freeing up of the estate layout created a greater sense of space, and also a relief from, what they saw as, the restrictive nature of individual houseplots. Such experiments were often combined with the use of open plan formats for front gardens, and separate 'no-man's-land' landscaped areas. Most people, however, prefer a private exterior zone for each house. Indeed, as mentioned earlier, people prefer a sense of what Oscar Newman calls 'defensible space' (Newman, 1973). It has been found that vandalism and graffiti are reduced by measures such as clearly defined front gardens, as the vandal will think twice about stepping onto a dwelling's curtilage.

In the original *Essex Design Guide* (Essex, 1973) it was suggested that every house should have a minimum 100 square metres (about 30 square feet) of back garden with high walls around each plot. This gave the residents a sense of private external space, but proved intimidating for pedestrians, especially women, forced to walk on footpaths between the gardens because of Radburnization. More subtle solutions are to be found in the 'new' *Essex Design Guide* (Essex, 1997), which illustrates many examples of design such as shared public areas and surfaces integrated within housing, in the form of small squares, boulevard walkways and playspace. Practical standards have to be integrated to ensure fire engines can reach every house, or enable the dustcarts to get through, without dustmen having to walk more than a certain distance as regulated by their trade union, normally a distance of 25 metres (80 feet).

As a guide it is normal for local authorities to specify varying widths of road according to their capacity, desired speed and function. Local distributor and residential spine roads will be in the region of 7.3 metres wide (24 feet) with a maximum intended speed of 20 kph (30 mph), whereas smaller access roads and culs-de-sac may be down to 6 metres (19 feet) or less.

Roads and driveways giving access to small groups of houses are likely to be down to around 4 metres (13 feet). But in the new *Essex Design Guide* widths as low as 2.7–3.4 metres (8–11 feet) are stipulated. Such narrow access roads are combined with a mixture of chicanes (zig-zags), road narrowings, speed bumps and other traffic calming devices to reduce the velocity of vehicles in residential areas. Such devices are also interspersed on the wider distributor roads, to narrow the carriageway, and thus slow the traffic. It is not envisaged in the *Essex Design Guide* that the traffic speed will reach above 50 kph (30 mph) even on peripheral and distributor roads within the neighbourhood.

Traditionally footpaths and pavements have been 6 feet in width, this being based originally on the fact that it enables two prams to pass. Nowadays 2 metres (6 feet 6 inches) is taken as the minimum. 3 metres width is often designated for paths that are shared by cyclists and pedestrians with a white line drawn down the middle. This arrangement has proved both dangerous for pedestrians and unpopular with cyclists, and in an ideal situation the two should be provided with a separate 2 metre wide path each.

A range of design devices are used to increase safety and space for the pedestrian, and to separate pedestrians from vehicles. They include the use of distinctive paving setts (pavé) to signal pedestrian zones, restrictive bollards, ramped kerbs, *inter alia*. But pedestrians may still find that cars are parked on shared areas, or that they have to contend with bicycles and skate boards in car-free areas, such as miniature 'town squares' provided as an 'interesting townscape feature' within some new housing estates. Indeed the division between footpath and carriageway is becoming increasingly blurred, as a result of the introduction of complex surface paving schemes. The introduction of dropped kerbs and other grading devices which reduce the number of steps and changes of level which pedestrians have to tackle, can, if thoughtlessly designed, actually encourage cars to mount the pavement when cutting corners or looking for parking spaces. Also such devices can confuse pedestrians, especially children, who may innocently walk into the road wrongly assuming the area is pedestrianized.

Highways engineers also set standards with regard to the radius of the curve on all roads, and the dimensions of junctions, turning spaces, and hammerheads,

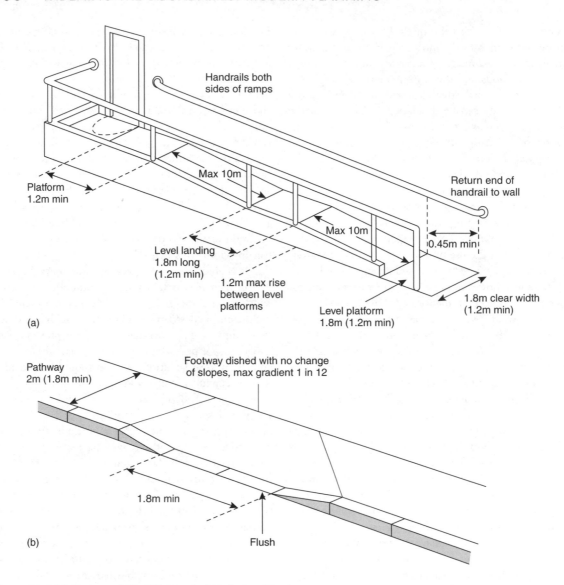

Figure 11.5 **(a) Ramp and 11.5(b) Dropped Kerb Specifications.**
Small design elements can make the whole built environment much more accessible for all. Many dropped kerbs are neutralized because a storm drain cover has been placed directly beneath it, presumably to collect pavement run-off. Drain gratings set at right angles to the kerb impedes wheel chair access.

which again vary from area to area, but 6 metres (20 feet) to 9 metres (30 feet) radii on the inner turning bends of hammerheads are common. However, standards have generally been revised down in order to achieve higher densities and to impede rather than facilitate motor car movement within residential areas (Essex, 1997: 72; DoT, 1990).

Likewise, for many years, it was general policy to provide extensive visibility splays with generous dimensions. Visibility splays are also called sight splays. These are triangles of land kept free from development on the corners of junctions to enable drivers to have unobstructed vision along the main road. For example a Pythagoran triangle of 30 feet (9 metres) by 40 feet (12 metres) by 50 feet (15 metres) comprises a typical visibility splay. This is set out so that the 30-foot side runs along the white line in the centre of the side road out to where it meets the white line of the main road, creating a right angle with the 40-foot side which runs from this point along the white line of the main road to the right. The 50-foot hypotenuse side of the triangle slices off part of the right-hand corner plot to ensure visibility, as described in *Roads in Urban Areas* (DoE, 1990b). Subsequent updates, such as described in *Residential Roads and Footpaths Design* Design Bulletin 32 (DETR, 1999a) and the *Essex Design Guide* (Essex, 1997) propose smaller sight splays on residential access roads, putting greater emphasis on pedestrian safety. For example, the *Essex Design Guide* recommends a visibility splay for residential streets formed from a right-angled triangle of 2.4 by 3.6 by 4.3 metres. A further suggestion is a smaller 1.5 by 1.5 by 2.2 metre right-angled triangle, which cuts off the corners to increase pedestrian, as well as vehicular, visibility on smaller roads that give immediate access to groups of houses.

In all cases vegetation should be limited to avoid impeding visibility. Ground cover should not be higher than 6 centimetres. The calculation of exact visibility splay dimensions is a complex issue generally undertaken by traffic engineers in consultation with the planners, taking into account local road conditions, and likely traffic speed. The addition of traffic bumps and other traffic-slowing devices on the approach to junctions can reduce the need for extensive splays.

Revised Planning Policy Guidance Statement (PPG3) on 'Housing' (DETR, 1999b, as explained in Design Bulletin 32 (DETR, 1998h; DETR, 1999a) specifies that car parking standards in any new development should not exceed 1.5 to 2 car parking spaces per dwelling off street, and that it should be significantly lower where possible (para. 42). Design Bulletin 32 also recommends that densities should be raised to above 25 dwellings per hectare. This is vastly different from 10 years ago when the principle 'predict and provide' ruled in all aspects of transport planning. However, it is most important to check the current situation, as requirements still vary according to area and the type of development in question.

The revised PPG13 Transport, issued in 1999, specified more lenient standards on non-residential uses related to gross floorspace for retail and office development. PPG13 abolished minimum parking standards and introduces a set of maximum parking standards for the different types of development. Foodstores above 1,000 square metres in gross floorspace will be permitted a maximum of one parking space per 18–20 square metres of gross floorspace. Critics argue that this guidance undermines the objectives announced in other recent PPG revisions, for example PPG6's attempt to encourage developers to relocate in town centres. Meanwhile life goes on, and in the absence of realistic local provision of shopping facilities in many areas, the weekly food shop continues to be done by car at the out-of-town centre, because this is the cheapest, quickest, most practical solution for many households.

In social housing, e.g. housing association dwellings for single people, the elderly and the disabled, the minimum of one parking space per dwelling is often permitted. At present, there are 35 orange badge holders (designating disabled drivers) per 1,000 population (ONS, annual, Table 12.13). Ordinary car parking spaces are 2.4 by 4.8 metres, that is approximately, 8 by 16 feet, while disabled parking spaces

Figure 11.6 Dual Provision of Ramps and Steps.
It is important to provide alternatives, as not all of the disabled have the same needs. Many of the elderly and disabled much prefer steps as a means of tackling changes of level, especially those with arthritis.

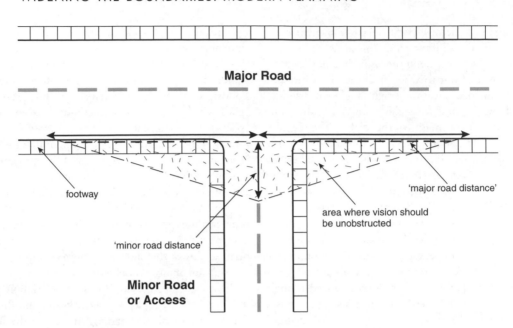

Major Road

footway

'minor road distance'

Minor Road or Access

area where vision should be unobstructed

'major road distance'

Figure 11.7 Visibility Splay Specifications.
An example of the many rules, standards and requirements set by highways engineers in planning the road system. Such elements can be used to speed up or slow down the traffic depending on the dimensions used, but all are townscape features, albeit often taken for granted.

should be 4.8×3.6 metres (12×16 feet). Alternatively, an additional strip of 1.2 metres should be provided between each two standard parking spaces, even if this means redrawing the lines and losing spaces overall (Palyfreyman and Thorpe, 1993: 3). When calculating for larger urban car parks, allowance must be made for space for aisles between the rows and for the provision of access roads. So the amount usually allocated is 19 square metres (200 square feet).

The question of how much parking space is to be allowed on non-residential development, such as offices, industry and retail developments is dependent on what the developer wants to achieve. For example, where there are no space restrictions one parking space per 200 square feet (19 square metres) of office space may apply, e.g. on a purpose-built business park. In schemes where one parking space per 200 square feet of office space is permitted, the total space taken up for parking will be as much as the original office space itself!

In a central area location where the planners seeks to discourage greater congestion, and land is limited, figures of one parking space per 3,000 square feet

(284 square metres) or even 5,000 square feet (475 square metres) of office space apply. There are currently proposals to charge for workplace parking, ostensibly to encourage employees to use public transport. As stated earlier such an alternative is not viable as many commuters living in areas poorly served by public transport.

The imposition of parking standards may appear to be a disincentive to developers, they do not want to use up potential valuable site space on parking in place of actual office development, and are willing to let office workers park on someone else's land or side roads elsewhere. In an ideal world if there are restrictions on parking there should also be good public transport, but this is seldom the case. Planners have allowed, even encouraged suburban development in the past, therefore many ordinary people wonder why it now appears that planners want to penalize suburban commuters who have little choice but to use their cars?

Whilst the factors identified above such as density, road layout, and general layout are key components of planning at the local estate level, there are several other overarching issues which today are increasingly being taken into account, namely, environmental factors, social aspects and aesthetic considerations, none of which can simply be reduced to 'technical standards' but require professional judgement.

In particular the influence of the Green Movement and the desire to create sustainable cities is reshaping traditional assumptions about layout principles (Barton, 1996, 1998). Policies to control levels of motor car circulation and penetration within an area, including traffic calming, are these days an integral aspect of street design (Hass-Klau *et al.*, 1992). Environmental issues, together with social and aesthetic aspects, have been discussed in this chapter, and readers are reminded of the need for environmental assessment of new developments.

SOCIAL ASPECTS

User Needs

The social aspects of design and design have become increasingly important. Many of the traditional assumptions and tenets embodied in foundational texts such as the *Essex Design Guide* have been challenged by those who are concerned about reducing crime, and increasing safety and convenience on housing layouts. Meandering paths across open ground away from buildings, high fences alongside paths and close planting might, according to some designers, create an element of 'suprise' and 'excitement' but many ordinary people are more concerned about lack of visibility and the dangers of being mugged. A whole new design industry has developed around the topic of 'crime and design', for example, see Circular 9/94 'Designing out Crime'. Likewise other users, such as women, children, the disabled and other pedestrian groups have long campaigned for more practical, and accessible layouts and some of their ideas are gradually beginning to penetrate the psyche of the designers themselves. See WDS, current publications for a range of alternative design solutions.

Disability

The disabled and those disenabled by the design of the built environment have had a considerable influence upon restructuring urban design (Fearns, 1993;

***Figure 11.8* Traffic Calming, Bristol.**
After over 30 years of transport planners and highways authorities demolishing, widening and altering street layouts to increase traffic speed and provide for the motor car, at the expense of the pedestrian and cyclist, the pendulum has now swung in the opposite direction, however the principle of control remains the same.

Palfreyman and Thorpe, 1993; Oliver, 1990). Disability has become a valid issue on town planning and related urban design agendas, because of conceptual changes in how society views disability. To summarize, there are three main models of disability, the medical, the charitable and the social model; the latter demands action (Swain *et al.*, 1993). The medical model views disabled people as long-term sufferers who 'should' be confined to 'special' hospitals and homes, and therefore are unlikely to venture into the built environment. However, cost-cutting 'care in the community' policies have resulted in many previously institutionalized people being 'let out' to contend with the harsh realities of modern urban society. The charitable model is based upon seeing the disabled as a group to be pitied, and unable, possibly, to look after their own affairs or lives, or unsuitable to be out 'alone'.

The third model is based on the premise that people with disabilities are equal citizens with human rights. They may be people who were previously 'abled' who as a result of accident or illness became disabled. It also allows space for a greater range and types of disabilities, takes into consideration that the disabled are not a unitary group. The emphasis is shifted toward understanding society's attitudes and thus the design of the built environment as disabling and 'making' people disabled. According to this model town planners have a major role to play. Disability groups argue that people should be able gain access to buildings, streets and spaces as workers, shoppers, theatre goers, students or in any other capacity without fuss, on their own and with no special assistance. It is argued that the whole structure of cities, employment, education and society needs rethinking. Dezoning of cities, the provision of accessible public transport, more local centres, shops and employment, and changes in the internal design of all types of buildings are advocated (Imrie, 1996).

After many years of lobbying, a series of Acts has been introduced which are intended to increase access for disabled people, and thus have implications for town planning and urban design (Davies, 1999). The Town and Country Planning Act, 1990, Section 76, requires that local authorities give attention to the question of the level of accessibility for the disabled when determining a planning application. This particularly relates to access to individual buildings, especially offices, shops and other public buildings, by virtue of the Code of Practice for Access of the Disabled to Buildings (BS 5810: 1979) and Design Note 18, 'Access for Disabled People to Educational Buildings' published in 1979 by the Department of the Environment. In 1995 the Disability Discrimination Act was introduced which is meant to increase access to new buildings. New access requirements began to come into force in respect of shops and public buildings in late 1999 under this Act. But it is not retrospective on existing buildings, unless they are the subject of substantial alteration, and enforcement powers are limited.

Increasingly local authorities are putting wider controls into their plans and design guides, on the unnecessary uses of steps and changes of level and the need for dropped kerbs in all layouts, to help the disabled, the elderly and also mothers with prams and pushchairs. All these groups may find steps an insurmountable barrier to getting about, or even to getting in and out of their own front door. Gradients on ramps should not be more than 1 in 12 slope, but ideally there should be no steep areas throughout the housing scheme. To achieve such an objective is indeed a challenge, but one which is being tackled even in

historic housing areas, for example, in urban conservation areas in hilly locations within London (CAE, 1998). Related to this, it is now considered good practice to ensure adequate lighting and visibility within public footpath systems. Many of the principles that have been established and adopted in respect of inner city regeneration projects, in which there has been a strong emphasis upon collaborative, participatory planning with the community, are now also working their way into new developments. In particular, the concept of 'Lifetime Housing' is becoming widespread (Rowntree, 1992).

The 1997 revision of PPG1 (DETR, 1997) on general planning principles included a new section (S55) on the disabled which states, 'the development of land and buildings provides the opportunity to secure a more accessible environment for everyone, including wheelchair users, and other people with disabilities, elderly people and people with toddlers or infants in pushchairs'. Therefore this is a consideration that local authorities must take into account in determining a planning application (Manley, 1999). Thus such external and internal pressures are reshaping the nature of urban design, and the creation of accessible environments both in respect of new and old areas of cities (Palfreyman and Thorpe, 1993; CAE, 1998).

CULTURAL PLANNING

The Renaissance of Urban Design

As stated in the introduction there has always been a tradition of urban design in town planning, drawing both on European civic design traditions and the North American townscape movement. In the postwar period in the USA a new breed of 'urban designers' emerged who were concerned with 'image' within the context of the modern, brash American city (Lynch, 1960 [1988]). This aesthetic view of the city contrasted sharply with the scientific, technocratic perspective current in much Anglo-American planning in the post-war era. Lynch produced a set of intellectual tools for visually analysing the city. For example, he stressed the importance of identifying centres, nodal points, edges, paths and image quality as key townscape components. Such classifications may seem simplistic in comparison with today's computerized analysis. But, Lynch was one of the first in the field to re-introduce the question of the 'imageability', and the discussion of the visual qualities of the city into professional town planning departments.

The urban design agenda has also been influenced by the demands of community and minority groups who spoke out against the inaccessibility and threatening nature of much of the planned built environment. This has undoubtedly contributed to this sea change. Those concerned with the disability, women's issues, childcare, cultural diversity, and crime prevention have all had a strong influence (Fearns, 1993). Thus the new urban design movement incorporates a concern for aesthetic issues with a new awareness of social needs and practical user realities. The requirements of the Disability Discrimination Act 1996 are likely to put even greater emphasis upon accessible environments. Although the Report of the Urban Taskforce places strong emphasis upon urban design and renaissance, it has been much criticized for the apparent low priority put on accessibility manifested in its designs (Rogers, 1999).

This realignment has not resulted in the abandonment of concern with the visual aspects of urban design. It is often argued that an attractive, aesthetically pleasing design may itself increase the suppression of crime in the area in question and deter anti-social behaviour (Crouch, *et al.*, 1999). The general atmosphere and feel of an area (Lynch, 1960), the satisfaction of the residents, their sense of security, and indeed the saleability and commercial attractiveness of a development may be influenced by quite small but significant details, such as the colour of the brick. Red brick buildings, for example, may look more homely than dingy yellow London brick, and worst of all, grey slate roofs look very dull and chilly on a wet day (Prizeman, 1975).

Traditional architectural detail, ornament and well-finished construction can create a sense of well being, whereas functional concrete slabs can be stark, unfriendly, and invite graffiti. The original Corbusian idea of white and pristine towers rising under a blue Mediterranean sky, from which rain seldom falls is inappropriate in Britain. Le Corbusier's flat roofs, which were a practicality in such climates, are a constant maintenance problem in Britain. The space around the buildings is equally important. Sympathetic planting can soften hard layouts, add colour and interest, and trees increase privacy and shelter, creating a cohesive 'townscape' of buildings and their surroundings.

Definitions

Slogans of the modern movement, coined at the beginning of the twentieth century, such as 'form follows function' 'beauty is function, function is beauty', are being given new meaning at its close. For example, nowadays 'function' is interpreted as meeting user needs, providing accessibility and creating a sustainable built environment. Modern urban design theory and practice in these times puts great emphasis upon a more comprehensive approach which incorporates social, economic and political aspects into the design process. Indeed, because of the failure of statutory town planning to address ordinary people's needs some would see 'urban design' by default as the 'new planning', strongly aligned both to sustainability and social minorities' agendas. Robert Cowan describes urban design as 'everything that is not covered by the town and country planning acts' (Greed and Roberts, 1998: 5).

The definition of urban design used by the Urban Design Unit at the University of Westminster, developed as a result of teaching the subject, is as follows:

> Urban design is concerned with the physical form of cities, buildings and the space between them. The study of urban design deals with the relationships between the physical form of the city and the social forces which produce it. It focuses, in particular, on the physical character of the public realm but is also concerned with the interaction between public and private development and the resulting impact on urban form.
>
> (*Source*: Current University of Westminster MA Urban Design Course Documentation)

Urban design nowadays is generally accepted to include factors such as: city design, pedestrianization and traffic schemes, hard landscaping and a mysterious process called 'design'. It incorporates the concepts of management and stewardship and calls for an understanding of the processes of land assembly and building procurement. It is concerned with existing areas and old buildings as much as with new developments. The socially, environmentally and aestheti-

Textbox 11.2   Urban Design Group Objectives

The Urban Design Group: *The forum for debate, ideas and action for civilized places*

1. OBJECTIVES OF THE URBAN DESIGN GROUP

The Urban Design Group (UDG) promotes the creation of high quality urban environments. Seeing beyond the narrow perspectives of individual disciplines, agencies, ideologies or styles, it demonstrates practical alternatives to the type of design that pays no regard to context, and decision making which is driven by bureaucracy. The objectives of the UDG are:

- To promote the understanding and appreciation of cities and towns and how they work (urbanism).
- To promote and engage in research, debate and collaboration between citizens, professions and institutions.
- To influence and guide decision-makers at all levels, and to educate both practitioners and the public.
- To encourage best practice in urban design.

2. GUIDING PRINCIPLES FOR URBAN DESIGN

The UDG promotes principles of:

Empowerment: building the sense of identity of the people who live and work in a place, and their involvement in caring for or changing its fabric or character.

Diversity: encouraging the variety that enlarges the interest or choices a place can offer.

Equity: making places (and their facilities and amenities) accessible to people beyond the owner and immediate users.

Stewardship: taking a broad and long term view of the costs and benefits of any change.

Context: building on the best of what already exists.

3. APPROACHES TO URBAN DESIGN

The UDG believes that successful urban design depends on:

Identifying common interests: taking account of the interests of the city as a whole, not just a development's immediate client or users.

Collaboration: bringing together a wide range of disciplines, expertise and experience throughout the design and development process.

Creative thinking: drawing on the creativity and imagination of professional and citizen alike.

Sharing visions: using graphic, written and spoken media as well as three-dimensional design to communicate and share ideas.

Learning: making the shaping of the environment a learning process for everyone, from school children to communities and decision-makers.

4. PROCESSES OF URBAN DESIGN

The processes of successful urban design include:

Analysis: understanding and defining the character of a place, its history and development, its physical and social structure, its routes and landmarks, its strengths and weaknesses.

Vision: setting goals for a place that relates to its three dimensional form and planning objectives.

Strategies: developing urban design strategies for cities or areas, establishing principles on which local design decisions can be taken in the wider context of issues such as transport, the public realm, building heights and the location of landmarks.

Guidelines: drawing up urban design guidelines to show how local action can support strategic policies. The guidelines will cover issues such as building heights, principles of frontage design, access points, open space, tree planting, street design, floorscape, safety and security.

Briefs: preparation of more detailed urban design briefs for particular sites.

cally conscious mood of urban design is reflected in books such as Bentley *et al.*, 1985, revised 1996.

Urban Designers

An Urban Design Group has been established to promulgate the ideas of urban design. Significantly, as yet, this is still a learned society or support group. It is not a professional body, and no attempt has been made to go it alone or achieve chartered status, possibly because many of its members are architects who wish to remain so.

The New Cultural Agenda

The current enthusiasm for urban design may be seen as part of a wider trend toward a greater awareness of the importance of cultural issues, and especially aesthetic factors, within town planning. It is significant that when PPG1 (DETR, 1997) was revised in 1997, a new section was added on urban design, and this aspect has subsequently been amplified (DETR, 1999f). Urban design is now a 'material consideration' that should be taken into account in deciding planning applications. However, there is much debate as to what is 'good urban design', and what 'rules' should be applied and the whole topic remains controversial.

More broadly, an interest in 'urban culture' and greater links with 'the arts' are now beginning to be found in the world of town planning. In recent years there has been a new interest in 'public art' in partic-

ular. This trend was accelerated by preparations for the Millennium, with an emphasis upon public art, national events, festivals, urban spectacles, and massive commemorative schemes such as the Millennium Dome in Greenwich, London. Other towns and cities have received Millennium funding, for example for lighting schemes. Croydon, South London received over £2,000,000 to light up its high rise 'mini Manhattan' buildings using laser technology.

Undoubtedly much of this activity is also influenced by a desire to create the 'European City' with images of lively town squares, and street cafés reminiscent of the Italian piazza or the Parisian boulevard. Linked to this is the popular concept, among planners if not local residents, of creating the '24 hour city' (Montgomery, 1994), as discussed within the context of 'time planning' in Chapter 14. London in the 1990s was considered to be one of the 'coolest' cities for tourists and residents (*Time Out: 1997 London Visitors' Guide*), and there is a whole youth culture, of urban fashion, clothes, food, media, nightlife and music which goes with this image. The Department of Culture, Media and Sport, nicknamed the 'luvvy ministry' because of its strong links with the worlds of the arts, media and showbusiness, has sought, in conjunction with the DETR, to capitalize upon these aspects. Arguably, its objectives are not purely cultural, but also strongly commercial, not least its efforts to promote tourism as a major source of income.

One result of the growth in tourism has been the commercialization of much of the historic built environment. There is vast 'heritage' tourist industry in Britain in which heritage, royalty and quaintness are sold to tourists. Also there has been a growth in theme parks and other leisure activities, all with their own architectural 'stage set' styles. The ultimate manifestation of this is Disneyland, an entirely 'artificial' creation, but one in which the 'architecture' draws on centuries old folkoric, and fairy tale images of what cities, castles, ginger bread cottages, and main streets 'ought' to be like – produced by a nation which has no history of any length of its own. Disneyfication is just part of a wider Americanization of European culture, which is 'everywhere' (ubiquitous) manifest in films, television and fast food outlets. It is anathema to many architects, especially when 'theme park architecture' influences attitudes as to how genuine historic buildings 'ought' to be restored. However, anything that relieves the boredom of life is very popular among many ordinary people trying to escape the drabness of urban Britain.

The heritage industry is linked to traditional values and nostalgia for the past. This aspect finds a reso-

nance with more traditional concepts of urban design. There has long been a British tradition of aesthetic urban design, as evidenced in the work of Trystan Edwards, Clough Williams Ellis (of Port Merion fame) and Osbert Lancaster before the Second World War (Edwards, 1921). This movement was characterized by a concern with detailed design issues, and sensitivity to the environment, rather than with the knock-out schemes found in mainland Europe. This tradition was overshadowed for many years by the modern movement, and by architecture and planning based on science rather than art.

By the 1980s, a post-modernist phase had set in, and the cause of 'good urban design' was taken up again. Prince Charles (Prince of Wales, 1989), has continued to draw attention to the deficiencies of modern town planning and architecture. He has concentrated on the visual aspects rather than the functional or social aspects of planning in the model village of Poundbury in Dorset (Hutchinson, 1989). Prince Charles set out 10 principles which were to be taken into account in the urban design process,

Table 11.1 Differences: Planning and Building Control Process

Planning control process	Building control process
Local policies and planning variations (this may result in varying provision and uncertainty for users)	National objectives and standards (people know what to expect)
Standards measured against approved plan	Measured against national criteria
Applies to most types and ages of land use and development	Only applies to new build, rebuild and major extensions. Various Exemptions
Developers/builders need to find out planning requirements	Developers know what is expected as nationwide
Long approval process before work starts	Once plans are deposited work can start or start with simple provision of notice
Work in progress seldom inspected	Work in progress inspected
Public can inspect plans and plan register	Plans are not open to public
Clients, and public involved and think they know about planning	Decisions seen as technical and unlikely to be understood
Consultation and public participation	No such outside liaison
Councillors must approve decisions	Officers make final decision
Planners must consult with many groups	Only consult with Fire service
Concerned with physical, and various social, economic and environmental factors and other on and off-site issues	Structural factors, fire and safety
Mainly land-use control and external design control.	Mainly internal and structural design control
Must advertise major (changes)	Can make changes, relaxations
Can approve phases of plan	Must approve whole scheme
Some control over future provision/fate of conditions	Cannot control future management or maintenance of access features

namely: place, hierarchy, scale, harmony, enclosure, materials, decoration, art, signs and lights and community. The Prince has remained silent on the question of the effect on peoples' activities of town planning in terms of the generation of traffic, car parking and pedestrian flows (Hutchinson, 1989). Instead he has promoted a form of architecture that is concerned with reviving traditional styles of both classical and vernacular architecture, which seem to be backward looking.

The shift away from new development and 'modern architecture' nationally has been accompanied by a new enthusiasm for older buildings, and for urban conservation, which was discussed in Chapter 3. Urban conservation may be seen on the one hand as an important component of the urban design agenda, for the movement has sought to show equal concern with both old and new aspects of the built environment. But it may also be seen, on the other hand, as a servant of the heritage industry, and in this there are potential conflicts. In developing policy there needs to be a balance between preserving the city as an architectural artefact for the tourist, and making it the venue of vibrant urban culture and modern life.

Heritage and urban conservation are by now well established trends across the western world. It is significant that an international architect, rather than a public sector, local town planner, namely Richard Rogers, was selected by the government to head an urban task force charged with revitalizing London (Rogers, 1999). Urban design has become an international issue. Each nation's historical sites are being ranked in global importance by international bodies, for example, Bath has been designated a World Heritage Site and is visited by tourists from all over the world. Vastly increased numbers of people are travelling nowadays, air traffic has increased 75 per cent in the last 10 years. Clearly urban design, tourism, sustainability are all global factors which are impacting upon British traditional concepts of local planning.

THE LIMITED POWERS OF PLANNING

While there has been a move towards creating better designed and more sustainable urban environments in recent years, progress has been slow. The planners and urban designers are not entirely free agents with total control. Highways engineers also have a substantial input at the local design level. Building regulations also shape (Chapter 3) the design of the built environment. This problem is particularly evident when trying to implement provisions large covered areas such as shopping malls, which fall outside the jurisdiction of traditional planning law, but which affect people's access to and use of urban space.

A distinction must be made regarding the power of the planners as compared with architects and developers (Burke, 1976). Planners are concerned with the overall design and appearance of the townscape of our urban areas, they can only influence the design of individual buildings within the limited parameters of their development control powers. Architects are the first to take umbrage if the planners attempt to limit their 'creativity'. Developers, architects and the clients for whom the building is designed, often have a far greater role in determining the design of the building than do the planners. For the developer the cost factor, and the aim of achieving the greatest possible amount of lettable floorspace are far more significant factors in the real world than the outward appearance of the design of the building.

More positively the community, that is 'the planned', are also having an input to the design process. A collaborative, communicative, community-based approach is in evidence in the design process in respect of inner city urban design projects, in which the designer takes on the role of 'facilitator' rather than that of 'expert'. Indeed there is considerable debate as to the role of the urban designer, and whether he/she is needed at all. It is generally accepted that the urban designer, particularly the architect–designer is essential in offering to the community the benefit of seven years of specialist study, knowledge of the statutory context and understanding of the system. Ordinary people and community members, as the recipients and users of urban design, must also be fully involved. How to achieve this in a meaningful manner is a complex issue. Emphasis must be put on sustained, continuing participation, rather than 'hit and run' approaches. Also cultivation of the people's own skills, and provision of education about the planning system and building design are also key issues which cannot be rushed. A variety of approaches such as 'Planning for Real', 'Plan Away Days' and 'Focus groups' have been used to elicit people's views and to develop community-sensitive policies. Clearly the way ahead is for planners and planned to work collaboratively to create better urban design.

TASKS

Information Gathering Tasks

I. Go and find out what design guides, planning standards, and guidance documents are available in your area.

II. Choose one example of a new housing development in your area and trace through its history in terms of design and layout requirements.

Conceptual Tasks

III. Compare and contrast the agendas of the new urban design movement and that of traditional estate layout design control.

IV. To what extent do you consider that British urban design and planning is influenced the objective of attracting more tourists?

V. In what ways has a social model of disability affected town planning and urban design practice? Can its demands be reconciled with wider aesthetic objectives?

Reflective Tasks

VI. What do you personally think about the quality of urban design in the residential area and/or local town in which you live? What are its main problems? Can these be resolved through planning policy?

FURTHER READING

Key texts on disability include Imrie, Imrie and Wells, Oliver, Swain, Adler, Palyfreyman and guides produced by the Centre for Accessible Environments, Nutmeg House, 60, Gainsford Street, London SE1 2NY. Tel: 0171 357 8182.

For urban design issues and concepts see: Lynch, Greed and Roberts (1998), Turner, and Punter (1998), Crookston, Elkin, Greed and Roberts, Roberts and Greed and for official guidance see PPG1 and accompanying document *By Design* (DETR, 2000).

For urban design primers, which take the reader through the design process or recommend standards and design guidance see: Bentley *et al.* (1985; 1992); Roberts and Greed (2000), *Essex Design Guide*, and other current local planning authority design guides.

The *Essex Design Guide* (1997) covers many of the issues summarized in this chapter, and is thoroughly recommended as further reading. Readers should retain a critical perspective on its policies and consider carefully the implications for ordinary people living within the designs proposed. Readers should check whether there is an urban design guide for their area too. Great value may be gained from looking at examples of plans and layout designs.

Web page http://www.towns.org.uk, gives access to the Resource for Urban Design (RUDI) web pages which cover urban design and urban conservation.

Part 4

PLANNING IS FOR PEOPLE?

SOCIAL PERSPECTIVES ON PLANNING

INTRODUCTION

Chapter 12 discusses some of the main social theories which have influenced town planning policy in order to provide a background to the study of the social aspects of planning. The order is broadly chronological. The whole of Part IV is more discursive in style. It incorporates research-based material and presents the reader with a range of theoretical perspectives in respect of planning and urban issues.

Pre- and Post-Industrial Perspectives

The Industrial Revolution was a major turning point in the development of modern society and town planning. It called forth a new academic discipline, namely 'sociology' which sought to explain what was occurring. Comte (1798–1857), a French academic, is generally credited with inventing the word '*sociologie*' (Brown, 1979). Many of the early sociological theories were based on highlighting the differences between the pre-industrial city (usually seen as good) as against the industrial city (usually seen as bad). Other countries in Europe were experiencing a similar process of industrialization, and for example Tönnies (1855–1936) a German sociologist wrote about the differences between what he called *gemeinschaft* and *gesellschaft*. He defined *gemeinschaft* as community, based on traditional rural village life where everyone knew everyone else, social relationships were based on kith and kin ties and traditional values and duties. *Gesellschaft* community (the German word for 'business') is where everything is based on formal and impersonal relationships, bureaucracy, law and order.

Nobody knows anyone else, and people deal with complete strangers in their daily life and work.

Durkheim (1858–1917) a French sociologist identified the new urbanized society as being characterized by a sense of 'normlessness' and 'namelessness', that is *anomie* (literally, without a name) because, in coming to the city from their local villages, many people had lost their individual identity and sense of belonging. Note that this is a societal state, people do not 'get' anomie, like anaemia! Nevertheless it affected individuals' behaviour within society, for he observed that this condition led to increased levels of suicide, and to social unrest. Fascination with the study of the contrasts between the pre- and post-industrial ways of life continued well into the twentieth century. Of the more famous, often cited, is an article by Wirth 'Urbanism as a Way of Life', published in 1938 (reprinted in Hatt and Reiss, 1963). Also the work of Sjoberg on the pre-industrial city is relevant (Sjoberg, 1965).

Many of these theories expressed the view that something had been lost as result of industrialization, especially the stability and security which apparently had existed in close-knit traditional villages. It was argued that traditional controls over 'deviance' (crime and social unrest) were lost, such as the role of the village elders in 'seeing what was going on' in the neighbourhood. One of the factors behind the popularity of the Garden City movement was the desire to re-create the village community of the past, in order to re-establish the social structures which were destroyed as a result of the Industrial Revolution. Many of the ideas of the early town planners reflect a somewhat negative anti-urban attitude; a yearning to go back to an (imagined) idyllic rural past may be seen as somewhat 'conservative' or even reactionary politically. Town planning could be used as one of the means of seeking to re-establish a sense of order in new urban areas, through well planned districts and zoning controls, which it was believed, would reduce the high levels of crime, disease and overcrowding.

Even today town planners have been seen as the 'soft police' of society, because of their attempts to stabilize people's behaviour in new towns by 'social engineering'; and in the inner city by means of environmental controls. Town planners have often been criticized by those who adopt a more radical or even revolutionary perspective, and are of the opinion that it is not possible to contribute toward the creation of a better society through redesigning towns and cities. Such critics argue that more drastic political and economic measures are needed to remove the inequalities in society which, it is alleged create the conflict, crime and disease in the first place.

The idea that social change can be achieved through 'salvation by bricks', by replanning the built environment is still prevalent and will be discussed below in relation to the planning of the New Towns. Town planning does indeed have a specific role to play in contributing towards solving societal problems by means of making physical changes to the built environment. But that does not preclude the need for other social, economic, and political measures too.

SOCIAL ASPECTS OF NEW TOWNS

Community and Neighbourhoods

The effect of these ideas on New Town development in the twentieth century will now be discussed. Following this, the account of the historical development of urban social theory will be resumed. Many of the New Towns were planned on the basis of being divided into neighbourhoods, or 'neighbourhood units' as they were called. This enabled the development to be phased logically and facilitated the physical provision of shops and schools with ready-made catchment areas. Forty years ago many people did not have cars so the plan worked realistically. However, the neighbourhoods had a second more mystical objective of trying to create 'community spirit' and to solve a range of social problems. Clarence Perry

(1872–1944) devised the concept of the neighbourhood unit as a way of effectively planning new towns and communities in the New York area during the 1920s and 1930s. Perry's ideas were copied in England by Parker at the garden suburb of Wythenshawe in Manchester, and were incorporated in the Dudley Report (1944) on New Towns.

Perry proposed that if around 5,000–6,000 people were located in a neighbourhood at 37.5 persons per acre, that is at approximately 12 houses per acre allowing for three people on average per house, this would result in a neighbourhood unit of 160 acres, that is an area half a mile by half a mile or a quarter of a square mile. These figures are given in imperial because that is how they were first presented and imperial is still used in the USA. For conversion see Textbox 1.1.

Everything was to be based on walking distances of between a quarter to a half of a mile, with a community centre in the middle of each neighbourhood and shops on the edges, at the four 'corners' so they could be shared by up to four different neighbourhoods (Hall, 1989). A local junior school would be located in the centre, 5,000 being considered adequate population to generate the number of children to make it viable (as mentioned in Chapter 12). The neighbourhood unit concept had many practical aspects to it, but it was more questionably associated with a mystical desire to recreate a sense of community, by influencing people's behaviour, and 'making' them mix by means of the constraints put upon them by the layout, e.g. designing the footpaths so that they ran past everyone else's front door, and putting the local community centre alongside the school. Many of these ideas were mirrored in the British New Towns. Various studies were carried out on both sides of the Atlantic, monitoring people's behaviour in new housing estates (Carey and Mapes, 1972; Bell and Newby, 1978). Not surprisingly it was found that people who lived nearer the centre of a cul-de-sac, or by a lift-shaft in an apartment block were likely to have a higher level of contact with their neighbours that those who lived at the end of the main thoroughfare.

Not only was there a lack of a natural community at the beginning but planners were concerned about the imbalanced nature of the community population, who were predominantly young families with children, all of a similar social class. The lack of age balance meant pressure on facilities as the children grew up and went through the stages of school, working and retirement all together. Once these first generations had passed, the facilities provided for such large numbers subsequently proved uneconomic for later smaller cohorts. British New Towns later attempted to encourage a wider age range and family mix among applicants. Socially it was seen as 'dangerous' politically that there were so many working-class people all together, so attempts were made to attract more middle-class people, and for employers actually to live in the New Towns to provide 'leaders' in the community. At the neighbourhood level there were attempts to create a 'social mix', that is mixing social classes, by combining house types and tenures; which did not work well.

There are many other factors which are involved in community formation. It may not be the shared locality (the fact they all live in the same neighbourhood), but the extent to which the people themselves have other interests 'in common' which determines the level of identity and sense of community. In the case of the New Towns, the fact that most of the population was made up of young families with school-age children who played together, inevitably drew the families together.

Sociologists have pointed out the importance of communities of interest, i.e. non-place related as against place related concepts of community, e.g. communities based on the work, hobbies, sporting interests of individuals rather than where they live. Some people are loners and do not wish to form a community with others. Many residents felt their community developed in spite of the planners. Residents found a sense of solidarity in adversity, in fighting the planners to obtain better facilities and amenities, or in seeking to rid themselves of some of the worst aspects of the 'plan' and achieve what they really wanted.

Environmental Determinism

The planners of the new towns were criticized for going much further than just seeking to provide adequate practical facilities in the neighbourhood, but indulging in social engineering, by means of 'environmental determinism': seeking to control people's behaviour (for their own good) through the nature of the layout (built environment). Environmental deter-minism (also known as architectural or physical determinism) has been an enduring theme in justifying planning *if* the layout of plans can really help solve the problems of society, and bring about 'salvation by bricks'. Critics of this theory argue that many of the problems of society derive from the nature of the economic system underpinning society: typically the development of modern industrial capitalism is cited as the root of all evil (Bailey, 1975; Simmie, 1974).

There has been much criticism from the Left, particularly as a result of the popularity of neo-Marxism in recent times, that planners are only the 'lackeys of the bourgeoisie' who spend their time 'tinkering with the superstructure', which basically translates as 'rearranging the deckchairs on the Titanic'. It was argued that more radical economic measures are required such as the abolition of capitalism, as was tried in the Soviet Union. Would these critics produce a better built environment? Many of the problems which are related to physical land use, design practicalities, and the need for different types of facilities and developments always exist in society and have to be dealt with. This is so whether the planning is taking place in a capitalist or socialist society. For example, road widths are not going to change substantially just because a country moves from say a Marxist to a market economy, sewers and drains are also still required.

Likewise, it does not follow that if a country has a radical or neo-Marxist government which has 'all the answers' for running the economy and abolishing inequality in society, that its new masters would be sensitive and conscious of all the 'little' design issues which dramatically affect the quality of people's lives in urban areas. This would be particularly so if the people in charge had no training in, nor understanding of, the built environment professions and urban issues.

Maurice Broady, a sociologist disquieted by the apparently magical powers attributed to such theories stated, 'architectural design like music to a film, is complementary to human activity, it does not shape it' (Broady, 1968). But this does not invalidate the importance of design. Often all that is needed is quite small improvements, rather than the development of high flown theories and complicated ideas. Most would agree that practical improvements are important, such as more lighting, less planting and thus more 'visibility' around buildings, and re-orientation of pedestrian routes to make them safer and potentially reduce crime. Others would go much further, such as Alice Coleman in her book, *Utopia on Trial* who makes much of the manner in which modifications in the design of the environment can alter the behaviour of the residents (Coleman, 1985). Also Oscar Newman (in *Defensible Space*, 1973) stressed the importance of the quite simple strategy of ensuring that there is a distinct demarcation between public and private space around buildings in large housing estates, so that people think twice before crossing such boundaries and indulging in graffiti or vandalism. Des Wilson, one of the founders of Shelter, the housing pressure group, wrote a book entitled, *I know it was the place's fault* (1970) showing the effect that poor quality environments and substandard housing conditions could have on people's lives and misfortunes. There is undoubtedly some truth in the theory, but many other factors have to be taken into account.

CONSENSUS OR CONFLICT?

The Context

The two main schools of thought regarding the nature of society will now be discussed, namely the consensus and conflict viewpoints. It is important to appreciate these theories, because the way in which the nature of society is perceived and the imagined cause of urban social problems will determine policy directions in seeking to ameliorate the situation. If social problems are seen as being the result of oppression, then it may seem meaningless to play around with town planning: a revolution might be more realistic. If on the other hand social problems are seen as a temporary, and as a resolvable result of unexpected social change, then a gradual policy of reform in which town planning can play a part would be seen as the ideal solution. In societies where town planners have little interest in social policy and lack social awareness, then their actions and plans, by default, are bound to contribute to the continuation of urban social problems.

Functionalism and Consensus

To return to Comte: basically, he was what is known as a functionalist. Functionalists take the view that society was like a big machine which operated mechanically, and in which different processes and groups of people had different functions, ensuring its smooth running and the maintenance of the *status quo* of authority and social order. This should not be confused with the style of 'functionalism' in modern architecture (Chapter 8), although that movement, too, was inspired by similar sentiments. The Industrial Revolution was seen as a major 'upset' to the natural order of things, which had all sorts of economic and social effects and temporarily put the system out of synchronization; it was believed that this could be put right. Society would put itself back into balance again, provided the various social institutions and value systems were reconstituted to re-inspire people's trust in the system, so that business confidence, stability and law and order could be maintained. Consensus people tend to favour bringing the system back into line and re-establishing equilibrium, by means of gradual reforms, improvements and adjustments, in which town planning as a form of 'social policy' might form a part. It was imagined this might be achieved by re-creating a sense of community, which was apparently lost in the Industrial Revolution, by the construction of model garden cities and new towns. Functionalists therefore see social problems as being temporary occurrences, with the subtext that there exists a natural consensus of what society 'ought' to be like which could be nurtured back again.

Other functionalists who, broadly speaking, favoured a consensus view of society include such famous sociologists as Spencer (1820–1903), and more recently in the twentieth century Talcott Parsons (1902–79) and Merton (1910 onwards). Durkheim (1858–1917) was also part of this movement, and Max Weber (1864–1920) (Weber, 1964) to some extent. Reference to their works is occasionally found in town planning books to justify an emphasis upon planning for community, particularly in relation to Weberian theories of power within society.

The main rival to the consensus view of society, was the view that society was in a constant state of conflict, and that it held together, not because of agreement, but because of one group actively oppressing the others. The classic example of this is expressed in Marxist theory, which centres on a perceived clash between the interests of the capitalists (factory owners) and the proletariat (workers). There is a range of other non-Marxist, conflict viewpoints too as discussed elsewhere in this chapter. Marxist theory will be discussed later in the chapter, when the resurgence of neo-Marxist ideas in the 1970s is considered, because of its influence on urban sociological theory for many years and thus a major impact on some branches of town planning.

The functionalists showed an element of cynicism in their writings on the nature of society, fully realizing that although an ordered, consensus-based society was meant to be 'natural' in fact there was a strong element of conflict within the elite groups at the top of society as to who ran it, and a fair amount of 'social engineering' and pulling of strings behind the scenes to make the *status quo* appear 'normal'. The new urban entrepreneurial (business) classes had replaced the old feudal landowners as lords and masters of the working people. These new leaders of society needed to grasp the reins of society and take control. Feudal landowners had developed stable relationships with their workers over many generations, and now business managers had to do so too. Both Durkheim and Weber (separately) talk about the need to legitimate the new power structures which emerged, 'legitimation' being defined as, 'the process of transforming naked power into rightful authority'. Such notions should not necessarily be seen as oppressive, as it was considered that a return to a stable situation was good for society, as well as being good for those in authority. Note, the word 'legitimation' is also used in relation to town planners who seek to 'legitimate' their somewhat questionable policies on the basis that they are planning 'for' the good of society or 'for' the working class.

The functionalists accepted the need for a limited amount of conflict and unrest amongst the masses, as being 'functionally' necessary (as a safety valve) to ensure the well-being of society. What Merton was later to term 'dysfunctions' were simply seen as healthy signs that change was occurring which required adjustment and solution on the part of society. But, unlike the Marxists, they did not see society as being divided into two main camps, but saw 'healthy competition' existing between a plurality (range) of 'power groups' at different levels of society. In other words they took a 'pluralist' viewpoint. Compare Bottomore (1973). Parallels to this may be seen in the theories which were developing in the natural sciences in the nineteenth century, for example in Darwin's theory of evolution. In this natural selection, as a result of continuous competition, was seen as 'normal' and 'functional' in the sense that it led to progress and further evolution. These ideas were to have a profound effect on the development of urban sociological understanding.

Tables 12.1–6 The Changing Composition of Society.
As can be seen from the following tables modern British society is ageing, is predominantly female and is increasingly diverse

Table 12.1 Population: by Age – UK

| | All ages: percentages | | | | | | | | |
	Under 16	16–24	25–34	35–44	45–54	55–64	65–74	75 and over	=100% (millions)
Mid-year estimates									
1961	25	12	13	14	14	12	8	4	52.8
1971	25	13	12	12	12	12	9	5	55.9
1981	22	14	14	12	11	11	9	6	56.4
1991	20	13	16	14	11	10	9	7	57.8
1997	21	11	16	14	13	10	8	7	59.0
Mid-year projection									
2001	20	11	14	15	13	10	8	7	59.6
2011	18	12	12	14	15	12	9	8	60.9
2021	18	11	13	12	13	14	11	9	62.2

Source: ONS, 1999. Adapted from *Social Trends*

Table 12.2 Households by size: UK

	Percentages				
	1961	*1971*	*1981*	*1991*	*2001*
One person	14	18	22	27	28
Two people	30	32	32	34	35
Three people	23	19	17	16	16
Four people	18	17	18	16	14
Five people	9	8	7	5	5
Six or more people	7	6	4	2	2
All households (=100%) (millions)	16.3	18.6	20.2	22.4	23.6
Average household size (number of people)	3.1	2.9	2.7	2.5	2.4

Source: ONS, 1999. Adapted from *Social Trends*.

Table 12.3 Economic activity rates: by ethnic group, gender and age, 1997–82: UK

	Percentages							
	Males age ranges			All ages	Females age ranges			All ages
	16–24	*25–44*	*45–64*	*16–64*	*16–24*	*25–44*	*45–59*	*16–95*
White	79	93	78	85	71	76	70	73
Black Caribbean	68	92	72	82	65	78	72	75
Black African	57	85	76	77	–	62	–	56
Other Black groups	68	85	–	78	–	71	–	71
Indian	54	94	73	81	53	70	48	61
Pakistani	54	88	60	72	41	28	–	32
Bangladeshi	58	90	–	70	–	–	–	21
Chinese	40	87	75	71	–	63	–	60
None of the above	54	84	83	76	49	58	63	56
All ethnic groups	77	93	78	85	69	75	69	72

Source: Adapted from *Social Trends*, 1999.

Social Ecology

In North America the early twentieth-century development of sociology was influenced more by 'conservative' functionalist views of society, than by 'socialist' conflict models as was the case in Continental Europe. Sociology reflected ideas from scientific theory, which could be used to justify the *status quo*, in particular the ideas of Darwinism and evolution theory. The inequalities between 'man', and even the class system itself, and the competitive and aggressive nature of the American market economy (and related political system) could be justified by the application of 'scientific' theories to human society. In fact, Darwinism and the theories of evolution that developed in the nineteenth century were not 'value free' but reflected the changing political, philosophical, and religious attitudes of the time: it is a chicken and egg question as to what caused what first. Social Darwinists were not against change or competition which they saw as inevitable and progressive, reflecting the principles of freedom and the market. Social Darwinism, legitimated the power of the ruling classes, justifying it as a result of the natural process of the 'survival of the fittest'.

Table 12.4 **Participation in the most popular sports, games and physical activities: by gender (UK)**

| | Percentages | | | | | |
| | Males | | | Females | | |
	1987	1990–91	1996–97	1987	1990–91	1996–97
Walking	41	44	49	35	38	41
Snooker/pool/billiards	27	24	20	5	5	4
Cycling	10	12	15	7	7	8
Swimming	–	14	13	–	15	17
Darts	14	11	–	4	4	–
Soccer	10	10	10	–	–	–
Golf	7	9	8	1	2	2
Weightlifting/training	7	8	–	2	2	–
Running	8	8	7	3	2	2
Keep fit/yoga	5	6	7	12	16	17
Tenpin bowls/skittles	2	5	4	1	3	3
Badminton	4	4	3	3	3	2
At least one activity	70	73	71	52	57	58

Source: General Household Survey, Office for National Statistics.

Table 12.5 **Journeys per person per year: by mode and journey purpose, 1995–1997 (UK)**

| | Percentages | | | | |
	Car	Bus and coach	Rail	Walk	Other
Social/entertainment	26	18	18	20	27
Shopping	19	32	10	24	13
Other escort and personal business	21	11	8	14	10
Commuting	18	18	47	7	26
Education	3	15	6	11	11
Escort education	4	1	1	8	1
Other, including just walk	–	–	–	15	–
Business	5	1	6	1	4
Holiday/day trip	4	2	4	1	8
All purposes	100	100	100	100	100

Adapted from Social Trends, ONS, 1999
Source: National Travel Survey, Department of the Environment, Transport and the Regions.

The Chicago School of Sociology and its theories of urban social ecology were strongly influenced by Social Darwinist thought. Such theories were originally part of, what is known as, social ecology (Bulmer, 1984; Hatt and Reiss, 1963, Strauss, 1968). 'Ecology' is a term most likely to be used in relation to concern for the natural environment and sustainability. Ecology is the study of plants and animals in relation to their environmental setting, and in particular with the process of competition for living space and territory. After the initial fight, a state of equilibrium is apparently reached, with each plant or animal attaining its own little patch. It then seeks to maintain its numbers from generation to generation.

Such concepts were applied sociologically to the urban human situation, and to each 'different' group

Table 12.6 **Households with regular use of a car (UK)**

	Percentages			
	One car only	Two or more cars	Without	All
1961	29	2	69	100
1971	44	8	48	100
1981	45	15	40	100
1991	45	23	32	100
1997	45	25	30	100

Source: Department of the Environment, Transport and the Regions.

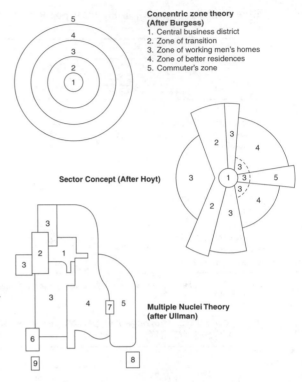

Figure 12.1 Social Ecology Diagrams.
The concentric zone theory was developed in the 1920s and the key 1–5 corresponds to the zones shown. The Sector theory developed later and the key corresponds again, with '5' being located on high ground where the air is better. The more recent multiple nuclei diagram shows that 'anything goes' because of the effects of decentralization, modern transportation systems and technology. The zones correspond again to 1–5 but 6,7,8, and 9 comprise a range of in-town, out of town, retail, industrial and business centres that are a feature of modern zoned cities.

of humans maintaining their own locality and distinct neighbourhood within the city. Social ecology has been widely adopted and modified by geographers and town planners, and much of the original background to the theories has been discarded over the years. Studies were first undertaken in Chicago in the 1920s because of public alarm at the high levels of gang warfare in the inner cities (as depicted by Al Capone in films of that era). The aim of the original study was to consider the inter-relationship between the crime wave and the high levels of immigrant groups (mainly white southern and central European) moving into the poorer areas looking for housing, creating intense competition for 'space'. The research team included Robert Park and Ernest Burgess both of whom were functionalists. Deviance and crime were analysed as symptoms of the process of the city trying to regain equilibrium after the influx of large numbers of immigrant groups, not because of underlying class conflict. It was assumed that with time the groups would assimilate and move 'up and out' to the suburbs, fulfilling the great American dream of success.

The model is not static, but dynamic, because the concentric zones should be seen like ripples on a pond continuously moving outwards (Chapin, 1965: 12–25; Chapin and Kaiser, 1979). The city was growing outwards and expanding as each of the zones within it were growing owing to immigrant pressure in the centre causing the inner area to expand and thus putting pressure on the next zone. Burgess described the outward movement of the zones of residents into the previous territory of another zone as 'invasion and succession' and believed this process was one of the reasons for urban unrest. Chapin describes the processes of 'sub-dominance' and 'dominance', in which the incoming colonizing group gradually takes over from the previous resident group. This process may be described by the residents in phrases such as 'the area is gradually going down', or 'the area has got a lot better in recent years'.

The concentric zones model *is* only diagrammatic as Chicago is built alongside Lake Michigan and thus takes the form of a semi-circular city. It is not intended to be a land use plan of how cities should be, but rather a diagram to illustrate a theory of what cities have been observed to be like. The zone of transition around the central business district is of particular interest. This is the area where the older rundown cheaper housing is found, but it is also the area where the CBD is expanding, leading to rapid changes in land values and types of development. Many British cities possess an historical central area and inner ring of housing, some of which has declined and may fit the description of the zone of transition, but other areas might consist of higher class housing and are designated as conservation areas. Such differences can readily be identified by looking at house prices in the area. The zone of transition has become virtually synonymous with the inner city and is often associated nowadays with high concentrations of ethnic minority populations. Many other European cities are quite different from British or North American ones, and have much higher concentrations of people of all classes living in the centre (and less suburban development), but different 'districts' still have very distinct class connotations. Meanwhile in North America's large cities, particularly in New York the ongoing conflict for 'space' between competing groups can still be observed. These days it is made more visible by the use of graffiti to mark territories between street gangs.

The other zones on the diagram are fairly self-explanatory and broadly applicable to the British situation. The zone of working men's homes might consist of small terraces around older factory areas. In Britain because of state intervention in housing and town planning, working-class council estates are also located out on the edge of the city where the land is cheaper, or where industry has been decentralized and re-zoned. The zone of better residences is where the 'normal' average family is meant to live, in a deviant-free area. In reality, the suburbs have proved to be the source of many problems especially for people without cars, as they are separated from the rest of the city by land use zoning and poor transport links. Further the suburbs and zoning generate traffic commuting and parking problems back in the centre of the city. The next circle, the commuter zone is meant to be the 'best' area in the model, and is entirely dependent on the motor car (note it has no outer boundary). In Britain a planned Green Belt may have been around the edge of the city, and so the suburbs leapfrog the Green Belt and form a secondary ring.

The ideas of Burgess and Park (see above paragraph) were modified by a series of subsequent models.

The sector concept developed by Homer Hoyt in the 1930s put emphasis upon the importance of transport routes, and upon parallel linear wedges of development superimposed over the concentric structure. Sectors of better development can develop on one side of the city because of the direction of the wind (from the east in this American diagram, from the west in Britain) as more affluent people prefer to live in less polluted areas. The working classes are seen as being more likely to have to live down wind from industry with smoke and other pollutants drifting over them. Many cities have a distinct east and west end, but these days all areas are probably equally polluted by gases and sediments in the atmosphere. Other geographical factors such as the existence of an attractive hillside, ideal for development of better housing, or the presence of a river or valley will also create natural sectors. Roads and railways can also act as barriers. In North America working class people are often described as living 'the wrong side of the rail-road tracks'. Lastly, the multiple nuclei concept was developed by Harris and Ullman in the 1950s. This theory reflects many of the realities of contemporary metropolitan land use allowing for decentralization, land use zoning and state intervention. There has been a variety of further developments of these theories over the years, by sociologists such as Mann in Britain, and the alternatives are endless (Bulmer, 1984).

URBAN PROBLEM AREAS IN BRITAIN

Empirical Studies and Social Reform

Whilst in Europe there was an emphasis on 'grand theory' in the development of urban sociology, there were two other strands particularly strong in British urban sociology in the nineteenth century. First there were 'empirical' social studies of the poor based on statistical evidence and extensive 'field work' such as that of Lady Bell, a social reformer who made a study of factory workers lives in Middlesborough, *At the Works* (Bell, 1911). Rowntree, factory owner, town planner, and builder of New Earswick, was a pioneer in social research and wrote a study entitled, *Poverty, a Study of Town Life* based on York (Rowntree, 1901). He was a key figure on many government committees set up to deal with the social problems of the time.

Charles Booth, philanthropic businessman and 'amateur' social researcher, undertook extensive studies of inner London (Booth, C., 1903 [1968 edition]). He is not to be confused with General William Booth, founder of the Salvation Army who also wrote widely on urban problems (Booth, W., 1890).

Second, there was a flourishing social policy and reform movement, supported by figures such as Octavia Hill, and the Webbs in respect of housing and town planning reform. Quite apart from the work of the famous social reformers there was considerable political pressure from the population for social change in the forms of Chartism, early trade unionism and in Europe actual revolutions. The working classes were not passive recipients of theory or reform, but were active in pressing for change themselves.

Community Studies

In the first half of the twentieth century, British urban problems and urban sociological studies often appear overshadowed by the wealth of American studies both at local and city wide level. These run across the full spectrum of urban communities from studies of inner areas and 'deviant groups' such as the gangs described in *Street Corner Society: The Social Structure of an Italian Slum*, by Whyte (1981, originally, 1943), through to studies of more middle class, affluent, suburban areas such in Gans' (1967) study of Levittown, a speculative private housing development (a classic, and excellent reading). Generally the problems of the inner city appear 'worse' and more violent in American cities, an image still projected today on television programmes. Likewise the suburbs always seem claustrophobic, monotonous and more distant from the rest of the city in American studies, than in Britain where the scale is less spread out.

In Britain, right up until the late 1950s, the emphasis continued to be on demolishing 'problem' areas rather than studying them, with few exceptions. However there were ongoing studies of poverty, often carried out in conjunction with housing, education and health authorities (but note, not with town planning). Post-war reconstruction planning in Britain had no real concept of the inner city as a potential major issue for the future, and the concerns of mainstream sociology itself were somewhat different. It was assumed that all the slums could eventually be cleared and the social problems would go away in the process, and this was expressed in the town planning of the time. The 1944 Greater London Development Plan already identified and named certain areas 'inner urban' [*sic*], and recommended demolition. The problems of the zone of transition were still seen as essentially American and connected with racial tension. The question of ethnic minority issues, or 'race relations' as they were called back in the 1960s did not become topical in Britain until the beginning of immigration in the 1950s of people from the West Indies, and subsequently those from the Indian subcontinent from the 1960s. These groups were encouraged to come to Britain to help solve the post-war Labour shortage, and recruitment and training programmes were established in their countries of origin. It should be pointed out that everyone belongs to some ethnic group or other, and 'ethnic' should not be used only in relation to minority groups. For example, most people in England are Anglo-Saxon in terms of ethnicity. Yet globally Anglo-Saxons comprise a small minority, and 'white' people number less than a third of the world's population.

In the immediate post-war period, planners were obsessed with the idea of creating 'new communities' in 'new towns', rather than seeking to preserve existing working class communities or addressing the difficulties encountered by newly arrived ethnic minority communities within the inner cities. A series of studies was undertaken of how residents were relating to their new housing estates, linked to empirical work on the question of environmental determinism and the creation of 'community spirit' (Carey and Mapes, 1972; Bell and Newby, 1978).

There were a few sociological studies of inner areas emerging in the 1950s. Under the growing influence of the American social ecology theory with its emphasis on 'deviance' it became fashionable to identify 'the criminal area', as in Morris's study of that name, based on an analysis of an inner city area in South London (Morris, 1958). Most urban social studies of the time were related to studying the effects of slum clearance and the decentralization of the population to new housing estates and the New Towns. Vast amounts of demolition were undertaken in the name of slum clearance, although many saw it as a convenient way of justifying the removal of housing that were in the way of new road development, or the expansion of central area schemes. In the process many really good working class communities were destroyed (Ravetz, 1980).

Young and Willmott (1957) highlighted these problems in their study of Bethnal Green in the East End of London. They studied the residents before and after they had been 'cleared', when these residents had been moved out to a new council estate on the edge of London. Before the clearance the sociologists observed a close-knit community based on strong networks of kith and kin, which was demolished along with the buildings. When the people were rehoused no attempt was made to keep them together, many were placed among complete strangers from other areas. As a result greater attention was given to the nature of working class communities. Frankenberg's book, *Communities in Britain* (1970) gives an interesting account of a range of studies from the period. This book includes urban and also rural studies as yet again people sought to analyse the ingredients of community that made village life so different from the modern urban situation. (See Rees and Lambert, 1985, for further accounts of community studies.) Many sociologists would question the whole idea of defining problems in relation to 'areas' rather than in relation to specific groups of people (as victims or aggressors), while others would argue that 'society' itself, rather than 'space', i.e. the built environment should be taken as the starting point for change.

Ethnic Minority Issues

By the 1960s, the Inner City became more newsworthy and visible because many of the people suffering from poverty and unemployment were of ethnic minority origin, i.e. 'black', adding an urban dimension to the problem of racial discrimination. It is common to see the ethnic minority groups themselves as 'the problem', but many of them would comment that they find it is the white majority which is the problem for them because of discrimination. As the saying goes, 'we are here because you were there', Britain, over the centuries, built up a vase overseas Empire, and many of these ethnic groups originate from its former colonies (Birmingham University, 1987).

Over the centuries, Britain and other European countries had promoted the idea of the need for their 'excess population' to settle in their overseas territo-

ries. The writings of Malthus the economist, such as *Principles of Population and Colonization* (Malthus, 1973 [1798 originally]) had legitimated the need for such measures. It was believed that the population of Britain was growing at such a rate that there would always be poor people as the land could not support them. This resulted in a punitive approach to 'poor law relief', deterrent workhouse regimes (because it was thought that 'charity' only 'encouraged them') and an emphasis on migration to the colonies (even compulsory transportation). Between 1871 and 1931 outward migration from Britain was, on average, at the rate of half a million emigrants per year. After the First World War the levels dropped, but gradually inward migration became more pronounced. Between 1931 and 1951 there was a net gain of 60,000 people per year. Many of these were European migrants coming for a variety of economic and political reasons. Needless to say most of these people were 'white' Europeans, and therefore less 'visible', although there was still a certain amount of racial tension in some areas of London.

Between 1951 and 1961 immigration rates continued to grow with around 30,000 to 50,000 people coming in per year, but outward movement was also high with a net outflow of 5,000 people. Three-fifths of incoming people were 'ethnic dark-skinned' (as the *Telegraph* newspaper put it in the 1960s). Many migrants arrived from the West Indies having been 'invited' to Britain owing to shortages of labour in the post-war period. For example, London Transport ran a bus driver training programme in Trinidad to prepare people for the move and guaranteed them jobs. Likewise, various hospitals and other public institutions sought to attract skilled staff from the West Indies, also from India and Pakistan. Others simply exercised their right of British citizenship and decided to make the move, mainly because of economic necessity, often sending money back home. Later there were migrations of relatively affluent Asian business people displaced from Uganda and other parts of the old Commonwealth.

'Black people' are not a unitary group, they are made up of many different nationalities, language groups and religious affiliations. They are also varied in terms of social class, ranging from urban professionals, through to people from underdeveloped rural areas. Not all can be categorized as 'working class' as is sometimes done in inner city planning studies (Smith, S., 1989). In recent years there has been an increase in immigration from Eastern Europe of those seeking asylum, travelling across from France by train. Asylum seekers number 1,500 per year in the 1970s whereas the figures reached 68,000 in 1998–9.

Town planners began to get more involved in 'ethnic' issues, because minority groups tended to be strongly concentrated in certain urban areas. Seventy per cent of ethnic minority groups are concentrated in 10 per cent of urban areas, with inner city locations in London and metropolitan areas of the Midlands being the main centres, as an example, over 25 per cent of Leicester's population is of Asian origin. It is necessary to be cautious in talking about ethnic 'minorities', in some London boroughs, people of ethnic origin constitute over 50 per cent of the population. Also, over half of the people in Britain of Afro-Caribbean origin were born in Britain, some describing themselves as 'Black–British'.

It is estimated that around 5 per cent of the population of the British Isles is of black ethnic minority origin. New Commonwealth immigration has now declined, as a result of a growing restrictive trend in immigration legislation, expressed in the Commonwealth Immigrants Act 1962, Race Relations Act 1965, Immigration Act 1971 and the Nationality Acts of the 1980s and further controls in the 1990s. The trend seems to be away from encouraging people to come and live in Britain, as citizens with rights to bring their dependants, towards a more European model in which ethnic minority groups are seen as migrant works or 'guest workers'. Indeed 'harmonization' with the rest of the EU in 1992 is seen by many black groups as creating a 'Fortress Europe' (EC = European Castle) mentality towards outsiders, including British Commonwealth citizens. Although the terms 'ethnic' and 'ethnic minority' are commonly applied by white sociologists to black groups, arguably everyone belongs to an ethnic group, and British Anglo-Saxons, from a global perspective, are also an ethnic minority. In the 1990s 'ethnic cleansing' has taken place in several European states, creating population displacement and new groups of immigrants and asylum seekers.

There were approximately 3.3 million people of ethnic minority origin in Britain in 1999, but over half were born in Britain, of this total it is estimated over half are female. Thus both *the planned* and potentially *the planners* are changing in social composition. But, as indicated in Chapter 4, only a small number of built environment professionals and students are from ethnic minority backgrounds. Arguably, various exclusionary factors are at work, whilst other 'inclusionary' factors seem to trap people in certain occupations for which it is assumed they are 'suitable' – both being manifestations of racism. Many black people do not have the contacts or background to break into the professional setting. While it may now be relatively 'easier', because of increased access to educational courses, it is still difficult to be accepted for employment in the construction industry (Greed, 1998).

One of the spatial problems is that many black people feel restricted by where they can move to, and what jobs are available to them. The Commission for Racial Equality (CRE, 1989) identified the problem of 'red-lining' whereby some estate agents have discouraged ('sorry it's gone') black applicants from buying houses in white areas, because they perceive this as leading to a drop in property values. Likewise, local authority housing officers may 'encourage' black tenants towards 'residual sink estates' (as in the case of Broadwater Farm in London) and seek to keep them out of 'nice' areas. In the early 1980s a series of 'riots' flared up, including St Pauls in Bristol; Brick Lane, Notting Hill, Brixton and Southall in London; Toxteth in Liverpool; and Handsworth in Birmingham. Since then a 'race relations industry' has emerged, and planners and other public bodies have become more aware of the issues. Erstwhile ethnic minority areas such as Notting Hill have been gentrified and have become predominantly white, although the area is still the location for one of the largest annual carnivals in Europe. In spite of this, there are still very few black town planners, surveyors or architects (excluding overseas professionals), and many ethnic areas are as rundown and deprived as ever.

SUBSEQUENT DEVELOPMENT OF URBAN THEORY

Urban Conflict Theory

Ethnic issues cannot be separated from the wider economic and social context of inner city society, and are an important dimension of urban politics. Both black and white groups suffer high levels of unemployment and environmental deprivation often with rundown services and public amenities. Further, these groups suffer by commuter traffic coming through from the suburbs, and also find their streets filled with parked cars belonging to office workers from the central area. Inevitably conflict emerges between deprived groups, the 'poor whites' blaming the newcomers for taking 'their' houses, and the newcomer groups feeling unwanted and discriminated against by the white population. Other deprived groups such as elderly people and single parent families on low incomes are concentrated in the inner areas, and are composed of both black and white individuals. Race criss-crosses with gender, age, class and income; it is never straightforward. Increasingly urban sociology became concerned with answering the question: 'who gets what, where and why?'; that is the allocation of scarce resources within the urban context and the role of the controlling power elites in society in this process (Pinch, 1985).

The theme of conflict between groups for scarce resources was first incorporated in urban social analysis in Britain in the 1960s, by Rex and Moore (1967), who made a study of Sparkbrook (Birmingham) an area with a high concentration of ethnic minority groups. Rex and Moore identified a process of conflict over the allocation of the scarce resource of housing, which they saw as leading to the development of distinct housing classes and social unrest. They drew

Figure 12.3 **Seating: A Welcome Resting Place.**
Seating which is an integral part of the townscape can provide valuable relief for the elderly and add an element of visual interest in its own right (Gilroy, 1999).

on Weberian concepts of the role of power elites in shaping society. Weber made much in his writings of the concept of 'life chances', the idea (simplifying it for clarity's sake) that different types of people had access to different levels of resources, opportunities, and 'chances' according to the level of 'power' and 'status' they had in society, and ethnic groups came fairly low in the pecking order (Dahrendorf, 1980; Weber, 1964).

Rex and Moore (1967) identified seven housing classes which may be seen as 'class positions' or indications of the levels of life chances and therefore the relative power which each group enjoyed. They concentrated on housing rather than on race as the subject of conflict. Different groups found their access barred to certain types of housing, because, for example, building societies would not lend them a mortgage, or local authorities decided they did not have enough 'points' to merit a council house. Ethnic groups could be disqualified on several grounds, including low income, inadequate residency qualifications, and lack of a conventional breadwinner or 'respectable' family structure, none of which were technically racial discrimination.

Increasingly the attention shifted in urban sociology from looking at the groups on the receiving end, to investigating the political role of the urban professionals who decided the fate of the inner city residents. There was already a substantial body of

Figure 12.2 **An Elderly Person's Dwelling in the Roehampton Estate.**
'Planning for the future' and for the exciting Corbusian age of functional planning scarcely included the elderly.

theory in America on the role of 'power elites' such as the work by C. Wright Mills in shaping society (Mills, 1959). In Britain, Pahl developed the idea of 'urban managerialism', by which he suggested that the urban managers such as public council housing managers and local authority planners acted as political 'gate-keepers' and influenced the distribution and allocation of scarce resources thus affecting people's life chances (Pahl, 1977; Dahrendorf, 1980). Instead of seeing the planners and other professionals as benevolent beings working for the good of the people, they were increasingly being cast in urban sociological research, as biased conspirators working in collaboration with other business, governmental and professional elites actively keeping the people 'down' and under 'control'. This may not have been intentional, as studies have shown, but some members of the land use professions have a very limited view of social issues, and generally do not think in terms of the social implications of their actions (Joseph, 1988); Howe, 1980 (on town planners); Greed, 1991).

Town planning policy was not seen as impartial or value-free but highly biased by many of the planned. Although many urban sociologists at this time broadly subscribed to a consensus 'liberal' pluralistic view of society, inevitably there was a movement towards a more conflict-orientated perspective. In the late 1960s, students, community activists and aggrieved groups were turning to radical politics and socialist theory for

Figure 12.5 Vandalized Public Toilets, Bridgwater, Somerset.
The day-to-day realities of the social aspects of planning are for many people the sight of yet more public toilets closed because of vandalism, not the intellectual athletics of post-modernist, post-structuralist urban theory. Yet such issues are outward physical manifestations of urban conflict which theory seeks to address.

explanations of what was wrong with their cities, and with town planning itself.

Neo Marxist Urban Theory

The subsequent development of urban sociology in the 1970s and 1980s was strongly influenced by Marxist theory. See McLellan, 1973 for a full explanation of Marxist ideas. Marxism is more than an academic theory, it has also been seen as a programme of political action to intervene in history and bring about the ideal new society of the future. In this respect it is unlike most other sociological theories. Academic Marxist theory (of which there are many versions) should not be confused with what is sometimes called 'pub Marxism'; even Marx said of himself, 'I am not a Marxist'. Marxists argue that many of the problems and inequalities of society derive from the nature of the economic system underpinning society. In particular the development of modern industrial capitalism as had emerged in the nineteenth century is often cited as the root of all evil. Basically Marx saw only two classes, the capitalists (bourgeoisie), i.e. the owners of production and the factories, and the workers (proletariat) the producers, who he saw as having a fundamental conflict of interest. Until this was resolved by

Figure 12.4 Shuttered Shops, Bristol.
In many cities the effects of traffic calming, pedestrianization and urban design have reduced through traffic and arguably created more dangerous streets for pedestrians having to walk through such sterile areas.

Figure 12.6 Ramp Access to a Cash Machine in Swindon.
Planning for the disabled has manifested itself both in practical access measures; and in the development of theoretical development of models of disability which have implications for mainstream urban sociology.

revolution, there would always be problems in society. Simply seeking to change the nature of the built environment was seen as superficial. As stated, the planners are thus seen by his followers as the 'lackeys of the bourgeoisie tinkering with the superstructure'. Marx described the economic base of society as the substructure of society, and 'above' this is the superstructure which consists of the social and cultural institutions, the built environment and everything else that makes up our civilization.

Marxist theory is strongly determinist in that it says that the superstructure takes the form it does in order to facilitate the continuance and maintenance of 'social relations' and 'means of production' which enables the capitalist class to get the most work out of their workers at the lowest wages possible. Therefore, it was argued, there was little point in carrying out improvements to the built environment if people could not afford to benefit from them. If their wages were too low (because of the structure of society) they would simply move elsewhere, rather than pay higher rents for the improved property. As Engels, Marx's colleague said, 'You don't solve the housing problem you only move it', alluding to fact that there would always be slums until people had the means to afford better housing.

The solution therefore was to deal with the cause rather than the effect, namely to change society, rather than changing the built environment. Marx believed that society could only be transformed by adopting a socialist mode of production in which the private ownership of capital and indeed all private property, were abolished. If the people themselves were running and owning the system (on the basis of the principle, 'from each according to his ability and to each according to his need') then no one would be poor again: indeed there would ultimately be no need for money or profit in a truly socialist state. But, as has been seen in respect of eastern Europe, it is easier said than done, because of 'human nature'. Followers of Marx believed that 'the revolution was too important to leave to the workers'. There needed to be an elite cadre, 'the Party leaders' who would take the lead in creating the new society (parallels with some British town planners?). Like any elite group, with time they lost touch with the people and pursued their own interests at the expense of the masses, without even being answerable to the requirement of accountability, which democracy gives.

Post-Modernist Developments

Urban sociology went through a neo-Marxist revival in Britain, being strongly influenced by French

Figure 12.7 Wheeled Pedestrian Transport of All Kinds.
This shows an assembly of wheeled vehicles brought together as part of an access-awareness exercise in a secondary school in Finland. Readers might consider how easy or difficult they would find it to get around their local streets pushing such contraptions.

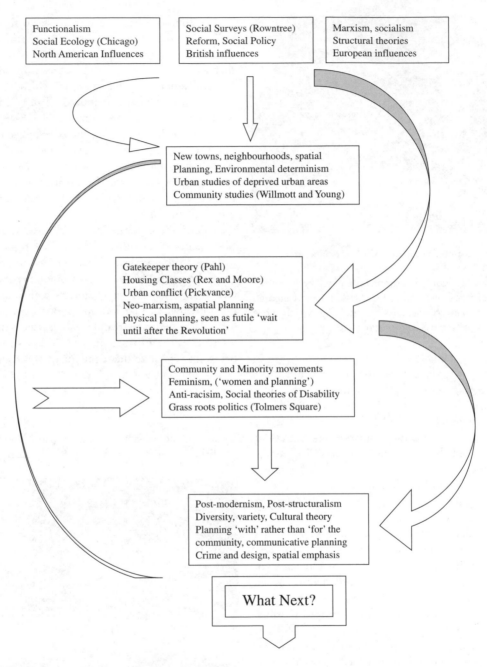

Figure 12.8 **The Phases of Urban Sociological Theory.**

urban sociological thought in the 1970s. There were attempts to apply neo-Marxist explanations to real urban situations as in the work of Saunders (1979, 1985) on Croydon, the largest London borough, and by Bassett and Short in Bristol (1980). But many of the ideas seemed to work better in the abstract. Indeed in dismissing the built environment as merely part of the superstructure of society and giving extreme importance to underlying economic forces. As Harvey pointed out earlier, it was as if people were living in a spaceless vacuum (Harvey, 1975). The urban sociologists had dug themselves into an impasse. There was much criticism of the idea that economics determined everything, it did not, for example, adequately explain why black people and women were more disadvantaged than white male workers if all were 'equal' units of labour. If women workers complained about their needs being marginalized they were likely to be told to 'wait until after the Revolution' or to 'go and make the tea'. Neo-Marxism adequately explained (from its perspective) what was 'wrong', but had little to offer as a basis for solving practical planning problems.

The emphasis in Marxism on the importance of industrialization and production as the path to societal transformation, seemed more and more out of date in the light of modern social and technological change. It did not fit well with the post-industrial emphasis within society on Green environmental issues, and Third World and other global issues (as described in Chapter 11). The over-emphasis in Marxist theory on 'production' as against 'distribution', and 'consumption' gave only a partial view of urban economic systems. Indeed Saunders (1985) and others subsequently adopted a more rounded sociological viewpoint in which urban issues were looked at from the perspective of the urban resident actually living in the area, who 'consumes' goods and services such as 'housing', infrastructural services, schools and shopping provision within the community, rather than concentrating on the world of the worker and capitalist involved in production in the workplace away from the home.

Many community groups felt that Marxist and other 'grand theory' socialist ideas could not help them, seeing the whole movement, like traditional town planning itself, as another elitist top-down attempt to 'help' the working classes. As will be seen in Chapter 13 many disadvantaged urban groups started thinking and working for themselves to press for the sort of cities and society they wanted, rather than accepting the views of academics and professionals as to how they 'should' live. Indeed the importance of their activities as pressure groups within urban politics, eventually registered with urban sociologists, who sought to acknowledge the importance of these groups in their academic theories. Neo-Marxism eventually went out of fashion, and the whole 'paradigm' (conceptual framework, way of looking at the issues) shifted again into what is known as the post-Marxist, post-modernist phase. 'Post-modernism' is also used in respect of architecture, reflecting a similar return, to more traditional values. Interestingly, Weber's ideas are now coming back into favour, and people describe themselves as neo-Weberian. The current resurgence of interest in the study of the professions and other decision making groups reflects a neo-Weberian interest in the nature of 'power' in society. This also reflects a longer sociological tradition of studying the 'culture' of different occupational and professional groups, which had become somewhat obscured in neo-Marxist times, because of this traditional sociology emphasized 'softer' participatory empirical observation and 'people issues' rather than 'hard' aggressive grand theory (Greed, 1991: Chapter 1).

There has been a retreat from the emphasis on 'heavy' deterministic theories, and a greater acceptance of the variety and complexity of factors, over and above economics and 'class', which has influenced people's life experiences since the late 1980s (compare Hall and Jacques, 1989; Hamnett et al., 1989). Indeed nowadays the words 'culture', 'discourse' and 'diversity' are frequently used by sociologists. This is because the pendulum has swung from emphasizing large-scale, and often generalized, divisions within society, towards studying the minutiae of individual difference and variation among and between groups within society. Likewise there has been a greater acceptance of the diversity of individual's experience of the urban situation, and the effects of their own personal characteristics (such as race, gender, and home locality) on their 'status' and 'power' in society. This has led to the flowering of a rainbow politics where there is a plurality of interest groups, minority issues and assorted isms.

Conversely, but often mixed together, 'New Right' values have come in under the influence of the enterprise culture created by the Conservative government of the 1980s, and there is a greater emphasis on 'self-help' and private sector solutions to urban problems. Co-existing uneasily with this ethos, there has been an on-going commitment in many local authority areas to equal opportunities policies for ethnic minority groups, women and the disabled: rather than a demand for more radical structural change in society as was the case with the erstwhile 'New Left' of the 1970s. In the next chapter the effect of demands on town planning on one such 'minority' group – women – is discussed, and leads on to an examination of other so-called minority needs in respect of disability, race and lifestyle.

TASKS

Information Gathering Tasks

I. Is there an area or community in your town or city that has been the subject of a sociological and study and subsequent publication? This is more likely in large cities. If not choose one of the studies given in the above account and find out more about it.

Conceptual and Discursive Tasks

II. To what extent do you consider that urban sociological theory has influenced town planning policy? Discuss relating your answer to at least three instances.

III. Compare and contrast the sociological perspectives of Marx and Weber.

IV. Define and discuss the concept of 'community' in relation to at least three examples of planners' attempts to create and/or preserve it.

Reflective Tasks

V. Can you relate, at a personal level, to the theories and concepts described in this chapter? For example are class and community important to you in your daily life?

FURTHER READING

Any basic introductory sociology book provides a good introduction, especially those which incorporate an urban and minority dimension such as Bilton *et al.*, as mentioned in the Bibliography (check most recent edition).

Social ecology is covered in Bulmer, 1984; Hatt and Reiss, 1963; and Strauss, 1968. For a fuller account of urban neo-Marxism read Pickvance, 1977; Castells, 1977; Harvey, 1975; Dunleavy, 1980.

For social and community planning, consider Chapman, Frankenburg, Taylor (village in the city) and check the sociology shelves. For social class classification read ONS, 1998, and ONS/ESRC, 1998 and check government census data, market research surveys and other current analyses and media viewpoints on this complex issue.

There is a range of classic texts which critique the failed social dimensions of planning, such as Simmie, J. (1981) *Power Property and Corporatism*, London: Macmillan. Books which cover the political context of social town planning include Simmie, 1974; Kirk, 1980; Healey, *et al.*, 1988; Montgomery and Thornley, 1990). Race issues in the built environment professions are covered in CRE, 1995; Grant, 1996; Harrison and Davies, 1995. Cockburn (1977) and Aldous (1972) portray the nature of urban politics at the grassroots.

It is difficult these days to define books which deal specifically with 'urban sociology', although there is a variety of social geography books that continue with familiar themes up to the present day, such as Sibley, D. (1995) *Geographies of Exclusion*, London: Routledge; and McDowell, L. (1997) (ed.) *Undoing Place? A Geographical Reader*, London: Arnold. Urban social political issues are well illustrated in Brindley, T. *et al.* (1996) *Remaking Planning: The Politics of Urban Change*, London: Routledge.

13

WOMEN AND MINORITIES PLANNING

THE NEXT STEPS

INTRODUCTION

Alternative Perspectives

In order to highlight the fact that there is no one right answer in town planning, and that it all depends on 'who you are and what you want to achieve', Chapter 13 will first reconsider the 'social aspects' presented in the last chapter, and second re-evaluate the nature of cities, from a 'women and planning' viewpoint. This perspective has arisen as a major challenge to conventional town planning in recent years as more women become town planners, and are concerned with community environmental issues. This chapter is more discursive, gives opinions and is research-related in style. The viewpoints expressed are intended to encourage debate among readers. Planning is a political process concerned with the allocation of scarce resources within society, and therefore in this case women and men do feel strongly about the issues concerned, particularly if insensitive policy limits their accessibility to the built environment and their rights as citizens and taxpayers.

This chapter presents the arguments for 'planning for women', and discusses the issues in respect of different land uses and urban needs. Gender studies are concerned with both men's and women's position in society. While it is not denied that women and men are different sexually, in particular because most women can give birth and men cannot, such biological differences should not necessarily determine cultural differences, as to how people live their lives, with regard to who does the childcare, who goes out to work and who is paid more. The word 'gender' is used to describe this package of cultural differences and roles that are given, respectively, to women and men in society, whereas as 'sex' denotes the biological differences between them.

Why Women?

Women comprise 52 per cent of the population (ONS, 1999, Chart 1.4) and since 'planning is for people', over half the attention of the planners should, reasonably, be focused on the needs of women. In the past 'planning for people' has arguably 'meant' by default 'planning for men', for gender considerations were not consciously taken into account in the days when the vast majority of town planners were men. However, is it really necessary to plan 'specially' or 'differently' for women than for men? It is argued that women's urban needs and, the way they use the city, are different from men's.

In summary, this is because women are more likely to be responsible for childcare, shopping and a range of other caring roles, all of which generate different usage of urban space. Less women than men have access to the use of a car, and they comprise the majority of public transport users in many areas. Women's daily activities and travel patterns are likely to be different and more complex than men's, as many will be combining work with childcare and other commitments. Therefore the classic mono-dimensional 'journey to work' upon which so much transportation planning policy has been based in the past, does not fit in well with women's lives and needs (RTPI, 1988, 1999). Women also form the majority

Figure 13.1 Walking Through the Arcade of Life.
Will the future be sustainable for the next generation of young women in terms of equality of opportunity? Will this be backed up with a user-friendly built environment designed for women and men of all ages?

(variously) of the elderly, disabled, low paid, single parent families, carers, urban poor and total ethnic minority population.

Almost worse than disregarding the social aspects of planning is wrongly defining the needs and nature of the groups the planners are seeking to meet. In the past some planners involved in slum clearance were keen to justify their power by stating that they are planning *for* the working class. Yet local working class communities remained unconsulted, or at best only the 'head of the household' was contacted, thus ignoring the needs of the rest of the household and

family. Similarly, traditional images of women as just 'housewives' are outdated.

The number of people working in the newer service industries and high technology areas is increasing, and many such workers are self-employed, part-time or on short-term contracts. For example, the care industry has the highest rate of growth investment and employment of any sector, and most of its workers are female (Gilroy, 1999, RTPI, 1999). This growth has been the result of the pressures of caring for an ageing population, demands for increased childcare provision, and a reduction in state provision for the disabled. Creating accessible environments, which are user-friendly for all age groups, is a key town planning issue. Over 80 per cent of single person pensioner households are carless and 75 per cent of these carless pensioners are women (Age Concern, 1993). By way of comparison only 40 per cent of pensioner households have automatic washing machines and generally they lack many of the items that the rest of the population consider to be vital to 'normal life' (cf. Gilroy, 1999). Clearly 'the planned' are a complex and varied range of human beings.

WOMEN AND PLANNING

Reappraisal of the Social Aspects Literature

Women are scarcely visible in much of the nineteenth century literature. If working class women are mentioned, they are likely to be seen as those who caused the problem of 'overpopulation' because of low morals and poor hygiene (Richardson, 1876). If upper- or middle-class women are mentioned, they are either presented as angels on a pedestal; or paradoxically as neurotic and contributing to the breakdown of society (Durkheim, 1970). Women and their needs are presented as supporting cast to the main actors, not as people with problems and needs of their own in the new industrial society. Women were not entitled to own property for much of the nineteenth century, and so they had limited access to the world of property and planning, although many were active in the early housing reform movements (Atkins and Hoggett, 1984).

Tönnies in defining his two models of society, the old and the new, as either *gemeinschaft* or *gesellschaft* (cf. pp. 179) left women in the awkward position of not quite fitting into either category. Women's lives and work activities do not divide into 'public' and 'private' realms in quite the way men's do, particularly if they are full-time housewives. Marx appears to have ignored women altogether, or perhaps he assumed they were included as 'workers' (Hartman, 1981). Marx's whole world view was founded on an arguably sexist emphasis on 'male' work and production, with little regard of women's role in production, reproduction and consumption, as homemakers, mothers, shoppers and carers (Kirk, 1980; Markusen, 1981): all of which are forms of work necessary to the creation and sustaining of life itself. Such attitudes had planning implications, for in the more 'socialist' areas of planning in the past women's needs were often seen as not related to production, and therefore as a subject not worthy of urban policy making.

The first wave of feminism at the turn of the last century had a strong emphasis on the built environment (Gilman, 1915; Boyd, 1982; Greed, 1991) which was reflected in model communities, and in co-operative housing ventures pioneered by women (Hayden, 1976, 1981; Pearson, 1988). 'Material feminism' existed in quite a different form from today, often tied up with utopianism, evangelical reformism, and the public health and housing movements. Ironically, notable individual women from this first wave, such as Octavia Hill (Hill, 1956; Darley, 1990) are often disparagingly seen nowadays as only a housing manager. Her ideas were influential over a wide range of land management issues, including rural planning, and regional economic policy (Cherry, 1981: 53), and she played a major part in the setting up of the National Trust (Gaze, 1988).

Some of the early urban social studies were by women (Bell, 1911), but later as urban sociology became more formalized women were more likely to be assistants as in Moore's study of Sparkbrook (Moore, 1977) with some notable exceptions (Stacey, 1960; Aldridge, 1979). Women's influence on the subject might be seen as somewhat stronger in North America. It is notable that some of the Chicago sociologists did allow for the possibility of women being workers as well as mothers, as reflected in the urban questionnaires used by Zorbaugh, one of the main researchers (Bulmer, 1984: 103). In Britain women appear in studies of working class communities as a variety of over-simplified stereotypes, which are based on observing them as mono-dimensional residents tied to the area, rather than as people with jobs, interests and aspirations beyond its boundaries. Young and Willmott gave some emphasis to women in their study, but their fondness for seeing them in the role of 'Mum', as virtual tea machines, and almost as wallpaper to the main action of life, is open to question. Their later work on the symmetrical family (Young and Willmott, 1957) is seen as nothing more than wishful thinking by urban feminists (Little et al., 1988: 86).

The studies of deviants within the 'criminal areas' of cities, in the genre of the Chicago school in Britain (e.g. Morris, 1958), were extremely moralistic toward young women, and tended to blame juvenile delinquency on the mother's influence and perceived lack of responsibility. In contrast in North American studies of the suburbs, women were presented as bastions of respectability, but as apparently idle, thus reinforcing the popular male image of the 'stupid housewife' (Gans, 1967; compare with Betty Friedan's early feminist book written in 1963 (Friedan, 1982 edition). This is one of the early foundational texts of the second wave of feminism, in which she talks about women in the American suburbs who were profoundly dissatisfied with their lives and environment, experiencing what she called 'the problem without a name'.

Identifying the inner city as a place of danger and conflict (Lawless, 1989) created a threatening 'macho' image of the inner city, although over 52 per cent of inner urban dwellers are women. Studies of race tended to concentrate on black 'men', whilst studies of crime and deviance often seemed to have more interest in, even admiration for, the aggressors, usually young males, than in the victims who are usually women, children and the elderly. Children are another 'minority' whose experiences of the built environment are often neglected (Adams and Ingham, 1998).

The emphasis on impersonal macro sociological forces in neo-Marxian sociology, combined with an occasional reference to an abstract 'working class' often gave the impression that there was no place for real people as individuals and families within the new urban theories. The urban sociologist Castells gave the impression that he saw the city as nothing more than 'a unit of labour power' (Castells, 1977); not as consisting of the homes and lives of the inhabitants.

In these debates the place of women was somewhat ambiguous, as they were neither 'land' or 'society'. Sometimes it seems in literature that they are 'land', just as the suburban housewife seems to be plumbed into the house along with the washing machine in much neo-Marxian theory on housing classes (cf. Bassett and Short, 1980).

It was considered 'bourgeois' and 'trivial' to raise community issues in this setting, let alone to mention 'women', with the prevailing emphasis being on political issues and urban structures rather than on individual people. There was considerable animosity from the male Left towards feminism in the 1960s, and women were likely to be told that they were 'selfish' and should be concerned with more 'serious' issues, such as the trade union movement. Pioneer women who went into town planning in the 1960's and 1970's reported high levels of hostility, sexual harassment and open aggression. They were certainly not made welcome or seen as valuable people who had a unique insight to offer on how women in the community experienced the built environment. Ethnic minority planners – some of whom were women – experienced similar problems. However, gradually greater tolerance was being given to the needs of so-called minorities and equal opportunities policies were beginning to take effect; even in town planning departments, although these attitudinal problems are by no means solved completely (Mirza, 1997, Faludi, 1992).

Later neo-Marxism put a greater emphasis on consumption, albeit defined in 'male' terms (Saunders, 1985: 85). This opened the way for women to redirect attention to urban politics with particular reference to the domestic realm and the residential area, also to redefine production and consumption and their inter-relationship from a feminist perspective (Little *et al.*, 1988: Chapter 2).

It could be argued that men were only 'catching up' with women urban sociologists, such as Cockburn (1977), who had already produced a key book on the importance of community politics. Some would suggest that the second wave of urban feminism had grown as an offshoot from the radical politics of the 1960's and early 1970's, urban feminist theory being seen as a sub-set of post-Marxian theory. But much more of the impetus for change came from ordinary women who had been involved in various grass roots community groups fighting the planners; some being concerned with design issues related to their traditional role as carers of children. As more women students entered higher education in the 1960's onwards they could not help but question much of what they were being taught in planning schools.

North American women architects and sociologists had not entirely lost the heritage of first wave urban feminism (Jacobs, 1964). Elaine Morgan's book (1974) may be seen as one of the first attempts in Britain to look at urban issues from the 'new' feminist perspective. A series of valuable books from North America dealing with a wide range of urban feminist issues past and present were appearing (Torre, 1977; Hayden, 1981, 1984; Wekerle *et al.*, 1980; Keller, 1981; Stimpson, 1981), all of which appear remarkably up-to-date in addressing still unresolved issues.

Urban feminist studies were developing internationally, the ideas and current literature of British feminist geography being encapsulated in the work of the Women and Geography study group (McDowell, 1983; WGSG, 1984, 1997). A Canadian periodical entitled 'Women and Environments' was established in the 1970s and is still going strong (WE, 1999). Feminist academics were producing their own community studies of the inner city to rival some of the earlier male classics, for example Campbell's study of working class girls (1985) made the link strongly between class, location and gender.

Many more women were entering professional and business areas in the 1980s (Spencer and Podmore, 1987; Greed, 1994a) as explained in Chapter 14. This was to have an impact on the nature of professional practice and policy priorities. Concerns have been expressed both about 'women in planning' – i.e. women as fellow professionals; and 'women and planning' – i.e. the question of how to plan in a way that takes into account the needs of women in our towns and cities, as well as accommodating the needs of men. It would seem that ethnicity, and disability to some extent, were stronger initially than gender as factors which legitimated the need for the development of 'special' urban policies for groups who are 'different'. The issue of 'Equal Opportunities' was gaining prominence among local authorities, affecting their role as employers and policy makers, especially in London. In spite of this apparent progress black women urban feminists have pointed out that they are often squeezed out of the debate, commenting that many white people still assume that (as the saying goes) all black people are men, and all women are white (SBP, 1987; Mirza, 1997). It is illegal to discriminate against people in the provision of public services on the basis of race (S20 of the Race Relations Act 1976) but research has shown that discrimination still exists (Graft-Johnson, 1999).

By the early 1980s, women and the planning movement were emerging more visibly (Foulsham, 1990). This trend was greeted with complete misunderstanding by many men planners and surveyors, who made comments like, women? that's not a land use issue and therefore were of the view that women's issues were *ultra vires*, that is outside the scope of planning law. Meanwhile the Greater London Council (GLC, 1984) women's committee was producing a series of Women and Planning reports including the most comprehensive, *Changing Places* (GLC, 1986). Women's committees were beginning to have a major influence in several cities in getting things done (Taylor, B., 1988; and Taylor, J., 1990). 'Women and the Built Environment' became a fashionable topic and several mainstream journals devoted a 'special' issue to the topic (*IJURR*, 1978; *Built Environment*, 1984, 1996; *Ekistics*, 1985; *TCPA*, 1987). By the late 1980's a series of conferences were held, and working parties were established by the various built environment professional bodies, looking at women's needs as fellow professionals, as clients and members of urban society.

Some women set up in practice on their own or in groups. Matrix (1984) an all-women collective of architects built, *inter alia*, the Jagonari Asian Women's Centre in Whitechapel, London. The RTPI produced a Practice Advice Note (PAN) on 'Planning for Women', (RTPI, 1995) which was circulated to all members, and which gives advice on policies and procedures. Since then there has been considerable pressure to see the principles put into practice and further conferences have taken place (RTPI, 1999). But those who voice such views are likely to be told, 'oh, we've done women, you should be concerned with the environment'. A second wave of books, conferences and articles appeared on the needs of 'women and planning', often more likely to be linked to environmental, European and disability issues. For example, a special issue of *Built Environment* journal in 1996 (Vol. 22, No. 1, editor Dorie Reeves) reviewed the situation in the mid-1990s. Students often appear

curious about what 'planning for women' might entail, therefore the implications for the main land uses and types of development are discussed in the next section. A broader geographical perspective on the gendering of 'space' is to be found in McDowell and Sharp, 1997.

WOMEN AND LAND USE PATTERNS

The Context

The purpose of this section is to reconsider the development of main land uses in cities from a 'women and planning' perspective and to suggest future trends and alternatives. While at present much of 'women's planning' seems to be pre-occupied with traditional women's issues such as childcare facilities, or with the problems of 'safety' and local design principles, to plan effectively for women would in the long run require the restructuring of our cities at the macro, city-wide, development plan level, in order to realign the relationships between the different land uses, and to introduce major changes in transportation systems.

Planning theorists such as Geddes, Abercrombie and Le Corbusier saw the main components of the city as consisting of 'home areas, work areas, and leisure areas', and this tradition still influences attitudes today. In contrast, many women would argue that this viewpoint makes the fundamental mistake in equating work with what is done outside the home, and ignoring all the 'home-making' and child-care work which occurs inside the home and the local neighbourhood. From this attitude flows a whole series of flawed approaches to town planning. It seemed logical to planners to further encourage the separation of work and home by means of land use zoning, which was intended to lead to greater efficiency, and less pollution from a public health viewpoint.

However, this disregarded the fact that increasingly women were adopting two roles, that of homemaker and also worker, as these days over 60 per cent of married women work outside the home. The separation of work and home, and the associated separation of business related land uses and facilities from domestic work, associated land uses such as food shops, schools, and community facilities increased the travel burden of women, the very ones who are far less likely to have access to a car in the daytime. To compound the problem, much transportation planning was based on the assumption that the 'journey to work' in the rush hour by car was the main category of journey in the urban area. The reality in some areas, is that the majority of journeys are undertaken by women, at times spread throughout the day, and chiefly by public transport, and (of necessity) by walking, as shown in a survey under taken by the GLC in London (1983) 'On the Move'. The three categories of home (residential), work (employment) and leisure will now be discussed from a women and planning perspective.

Residential Areas

The inter-war period was characterized by the growth of mono-land use suburban housing estates at relatively low density, consisting of both speculative private estates for the new middle classes and decentralized estates council housing. There was a preference for green field sites, where land was cheaper, there was also an extensive system of public transport and urban life was geared to the fact that few people had cars. Transport was mainly by bus, trams, cycles, and suburban railways, and relatively speaking, people without cars were better served then than they are today. Many food supplies were still delivered to the home by the butcher, baker and greengrocer, whereas all that remains is home deliveries of milk and dairy goods. There was a greater number and distribution of local shopping parades and other community buildings within the new housing estates: often erected by the builder himself to attract buyers.

In the immediate post-war reconstruction period local authorities continued the building tradition of low-rise houses, in the form of dispersed council estates, often miles from anywhere. Many housewives preferred the 'pre-fabs' built on a temporary basis near existing centres on bomb site land. 'Pre-fabs' had all the 'mod cons', such as fitted cupboards and modern kitchen equipment. By the 1950s private house building was back in business and many people aspired to own their own home. Building societies played a major role in offering finance and in perpetuating the 'image' of a home of your own, with

publicity aimed at the 'breadwinner', encouraging the concept that 'an Englishman's home is his castle'. However, few wives really 'owned' their own houses jointly, as was to become painfully evident when the new more liberal matrimonial laws in the 1960s led to a growth in the divorce rate and subsequently more 'homeless' wives and single parent families resulted. The housing stock and planning policy was not suited to providing for such groups, nor for the post-war growth of single young people seeking houses.

The quality of accessibility and transport to suburban areas and to cities, was declining for those without cars in the 1960s because of the overemphasis by the planners on the motor car. There were railway cutbacks on urban branch lines and rural routes, just at the time when outer suburban residential estates were growing. The growth of new large supermarket chains were putting smaller local shops out of business and making it more difficult for people without cars to shop locally (Bowlby, 1989). There were other insidious trends towards greater 'efficiency' (for whom?) in the siting and concentration of new health, school and social services facilities. The age of the out-of-town comprehensive school campus and hospital complex had arrived. Car drivers might prefer towns to be spread out with high-level provision of roads, car parks and out of town centres, but for pedestrians and those dependent on public transport, life would be better if towns were close by with facilities close together and within easy walking distance. Again, it comes back to the question, 'How do you want to live?' (DOE, 1972a).

As public transport became worse and essential social facilities became decentralized, more people bought cars until it no longer was considered economic to provide services or shops at the local community level. There was much criticism from consumer and women's groups and (even before the rise of 'feminism') in the 1960s about the fact that planners gave planning permission for new developments with little consideration of how people would get to and from them.

Many propose that because many land uses are far less 'noxious', and more compatible than they used to be, the arguments behind separating the land uses are out of date. Office development in particular could easily be decentralized back into the residential environment. The decentralization of shopping and other community facilities to out-of-town locations reflects outdated land use ideas about 'thinning out' cities and reducing congestion. Therefore, it is not surprising that many women planners nowadays press for strong policy statements on the provision of shops at the local residential area level, and greater controls on out-of-town shopping centres, and a revitalization of the food shopping component of central business area retail units for women office workers who can only shop in the lunch hour.

Many women consider that recent attempts to make the city more sustainable by restricting traffic flow and reducing access to town centres are ill-thought out as they lack a gender-perspective and therefore discriminate against women who are the ones most likely to have to use town centre shopping facilities. For example, women may find they have to cross the pay-toll cordon several times in one day. There is much need for further research on the gender aspects of the sustainability movement in respect of every aspect, including transport policy, waste disposal, shopping, cycling and house design.

Changes in architectural design and housing provision affected women badly, as they spent more of their time at home trying, with difficulty, to carry out household chores and childcare. The 1960s were marked by the relatively short but disastrous phase of the high-rise movement, which was far worse than traditional housing, although some estates were more central. Women, especially those with children do not like high-rise blocks, nor the small size of rooms in such schemes. If the flat is away from the ground floor all sorts of problems regarding supervision of children, disposal of rubbish and drying of washing arise. However, as Roberts (1991) explains in her book about London County Council housing, policies to meet the needs of women should not 'just' comprise childcare and homemaking policies. These activities are likely to take up only a limited number of years until the children have left home. Rather 'women and planning' policies should be concerned with the outside world of work, travel, safety and the environment too.

Many women combine work and home duties and find that blocks of flats are located miles from employment areas. Having an address on a 'bad' estate can reduce their chances of employment, even if they are not the perpetrators of the activities that gave it a bad name in the first place (this applies to men also). It is often suggested that families with children should be taken out of high-rise flats as this kind of accommodation is more suitable for single people. Many women living on their own feel particularly vulnerable in blocks of flats where there is no escape except onto a corridor or dangerous lift shaft system.

There have, in recent years, been some fairly drastic suggestions and action taken to 'solve' the high-rise problem including the demolition of a few estates, also the 'beheading' of high-rise blocks, returning them to a more human scale. A whole industry of environmental sociology, community architecture and high powered designers have evolved to deal with 'problem areas'. Many women architects and planners in contrast would suggest that really quite simple solutions, such as increasing the level of lighting, improving visibility, etc., would help a great deal. Most important of all, listening to the people who actually live in the flats and who on a daily basis encounter all the 'little' problems and acting on their advice would solve some of the problems without creating the need for major upheavals. As with horizontal housing estates, many women are still concerned about the mono-use of the blocks, as well as their condition.

To his credit, Le Corbusier originally designed in his Unité d'Habitation block, an integral play area, community and nursery rooms. It is not uncommon in other countries to find communal lounges, hobbies rooms, and launderettes integrated within the scheme. In North America there are quite up-market residential high-rise blocks which often incorporate restaurants, sports facilities, and childcare facilities for residents, particularly in private sector condominiums. There really is no point in putting people close together if there are no practical community facilities and nowhere for them to meet. Many women favour the addition of caretakers and security staff, and a *concierge* system such as exists in France, someone who can take in their parcels, keep an eye on the place, and 'screen' visitors as is common in France. Some women would like to see more communal facilities within low-rise housing estates too. For example the designation of, say, one in twenty houses as a community area with a built in crèche and community centre, would be very useful. Dolores Hayden in her book *Redesigning the American Dream* (Hayden, 1984) shows ways of converting existing estates in this way. Again the emphasis on detail and the importance of giving individual buildings multiple use and the question of internal house design is seen as being directly related to effective town planning. Hayden's ideas arguably prefigured the 'new urbanism' from a feminist perspective (Rothschild, 1999).

The development of the new towns has been much commented upon from a 'women and planning' perspective (Attfield, 1989; Morris, 1986). There are many problems associated with the concept of the 'neighbourhood'. It is based on the assumption that it is chiefly a women's zone separated from the 'real' world of work into a world of community and children, in which men who are presumably away at work, have little involvement in the day time. In fact many of the women in New Towns are employed; cheap female labour was one of the factors which attracted the light engineering and assembly industries to these areas. While the planners might put the shops and school in close proximity within the neighbourhood, they were likely to put the factories outside it creating major transport problems, and much 'rushing to and fro' between the different land uses (as Attfield describes).

The 'safety' of the neighbourhood concept and the separation of pedestrian footpaths from main roads has been much criticized. In Milton Keynes for example, it was found that many women were unwilling to use the footpaths and cyclepaths in the evening (Deem, 1986). Many of the footpaths were designed in such a meandering manner that people made their own short cuts or risked straying onto busy main roads. Many women prefer straight footpaths, with good visibility on all sides, preferably in full view of houses and other buildings. This problem is not just a characteristic of the new towns, but a feature of many 'design' guides (Chapter 12). In their desire to create an 'interesting townscape', architects and planners unintentionally created a threatening environment for women, with blind corners, narrow alley ways, footpaths away from the houses, pedestrian underpasses, poorly lit back routes and 'varied textures' of paved surfaces which ruin women's shoes and make the manoeuvring of push chairs and wheel chairs difficult.

From the late 1970s there was a return to the importance of conservation and historic development, with the related phenomenon of gentrification. It may be imagined that there is little mileage in discussing the gender aspects of all this. In this topic, 'class' may be a more important factor, as working-class areas have been colonized, and house prices have gone beyond the reach of the original occupants. However, many women see the importance placed on urban renewal as gender biased. The emphasis on marinas, and the needs of the boat owning fraternity in revitalizing dockland areas has not passed unnoticed, especially when it has been at the cost of 'sterilizing' water frontage which might otherwise have been used for public enjoyment. Of course some women participate in water-based activities too, and revitalization schemes do attract tourists, around half of whom are women, and docks do lend themselves to water-based leisure development. Many women would welcome the re-use of redundant buildings in central areas as crèches or as useful food shops rather than as trendy shops and pubs.

Employment Areas

In discussing the issues of employment, both in respect of industry and office development, the illogicality for women of the separation of work and home becomes apparent. Yet this division is reinforced through zoning and a whole range of other public health, building, and office and factory related legislation. Large numbers of women work in the retail industry, although they are often marginalized in the debates, or their work is relegated to the realms of 'leisure' for 'pin money' (despite the fact that they may stand up for eight hours a day, and work extremely hard). Vast numbers of women work in factories, in routine office jobs and in these times in (telephone) call centres. They have, however, frequently been excluded from the official figures and from the image of the working class in sociological literature. The post-war trend in town planning, towards both rezoning and decentralization of industry on to green field sites, created major problems for working women. This trend continues today as industry seeks to locate near motorway intersections on the edges of urban areas, and affects both up market high-tech science parks and the more mundane light engineering and warehousing facilities.

Women office workers have constituted the largest single employment group in Britain for more than 10 years (Crompton and Sanderson, 1990; ONS, 1999: *Social Trends*, Table 4.14); Bilton *et al.*, 1997). Are the planners planning for the workforce on the basis of outdated stereotypes? And how does this affect transport policy, land use and location decisions, and the level of accessibility to the built environment planned into new developments? Many are concerned about the changes which are occurring in the nature of office work, especially its 'proletarianization' because of technological change. There has been an increase in the number of work-related illnesses and disabilities associated with computer use. Women in particular are at risk in terms of miscarriages, and ophthalmic and physiological disorders brought on by radiation from VDUs (computer screens) and the poor design of equipment, facilities and office chemicals.

The separation of work and home creates major problems for women with children, indeed the whole ethos of the business world is unwelcoming to them. Much transport policy is still based upon 'the journey to work' which is assumed to be by car, an uninterrupted journey from home to work. But women workers often undertake intermittent broken journeys, rather than radial journeys straight to and from the city centre. Such journeys were often undertaken outside the rush hour if they work part-time. For example, a woman's daily journeys might be as follows; home → school → work → shops → school → home, and may not necessarily be by car. Those women who work full-time and have cars are likely to break their journeys in a similar manner, and have to contend more with the pressures of achieving it all within the rush hour.

Many women experience problems because of lack of childcare, or simply in juggling office hours with school hours, and food shopping trips. Although on average 60 per cent of all workers in offices are women, and 80 per cent of all workers in the central area, including shop workers, are women, there is very little provision of childcare either in the office buildings themselves or out in the central business district (Avis and Gibson, 1987; Gale, 1994; Law Society 1988). Many women planners argue there is a need for more childcare spaces than car parking spaces. A whole series of other policies would flow from this reallocation of spcae, further integrating work and home, and inevitably other land uses and facilities would gradually shift and realign in relation to this.

But the central business district and its offices may be doomed for the future, as more offices decentralize, and central areas become more congested and inconvenient. While the traditional argument still holds good that there has to be face-to-face contact in business, this only holds true for more senior people. In the future the trend may be to keep a central area headquarters but to decentralize office accommodation elsewhere, and this would be an ideal moment to suggest that it should be moved into the suburbs, rather than into the green field, out of town sites that are difficult to reach for those without transport and miles away from shops, schools and other facilities (Herrington, 1984).

Retail development areas are both work areas to large numbers of women and essential areas to carry out shopping. But planners and developers often give the impression they see shopping as 'fun' and 'leisure' and have little idea of the difficulties and time pressures which women operate under. The famous Lewis Mumford (1965) in his epic work on the development of the city in history, made much of the importance of man the noble hunter and food gatherer at the dawn of history. The same Mumford, in another setting had said, 'the daily marketing (shopping) is all part of the fun' (Mumford, 1930) when commenting on women undertaking the same process of food hunting and gathering in modern towns. It is now becoming popular to build leisure facilities next to out-of-town shopping centres such as the Wonderworld at Merry Hill in Dudley, and Bluewater near Dartford, London.

Shopping policy has been bedevilled by the emphasis on retail gravity models which have emphasized quantitative factors, such as the 'attraction' of large centres to the car-borne shopper, as against qualitative factors, such as accessibility and provision of facilities such as public toilets, which may be a greater 'attraction' factor for women with small children and the disabled (BSI, 1995; BTA, 1999).

Leisure and Play

There has been relatively little specific consideration of women's leisure needs in contrast to the immense amount of land, money and effort which have been devoted to playing fields and sports centres primarily used by men. Women's needs tend to get subsumed under the needs of their children for 'play areas'. Provision specifically designed by men planners for 'women and children' have come in for much criticism from women planners. The fixation with providing generalized grassed open space and 'playing' fields for, apparently the needs of all age groups and types of people, within both old and new neighbourhoods has been questioned for many years (Jacobs, 1964). The problems of 'open space as unpaid childminder' reflect deeper problems in society itself, indeed Britain has one of the lowest levels of childcare provision in Europe.

Town and country planning has always been imbued with a reverence for the importance of lots of grass and trees to improve areas. Some local authorities have painted the walls of flats in problem estates, green, presumably because of its associations with the countryside. It is often assumed that 'streets' are bad and 'open space' is good for children to play in. In fact unless open space areas are adequately supervized they can rapidly become vandalized, and the potential location (or 'turf') of gangs of youths, and dogs that frighten smaller children. The provision of children's play areas, or even play streets within housing estates can cause problems. It assumes that the mothers, and other residents, have little to do but 'keep an eye on the children'. Some planning guides suggest that kitchen windows should overlook the street or play area for this purpose. It takes no account of the noise and disruption that children make, which might be disturbing to people seeking to work at home. The assumption is that childcare is a woman's job as the mother in the home, although men who are also parents and fathers, do not appear to see childcare as part of their role.

To solve some of these problems many women planners suggest that what is needed is a clearer definition of the different types of open space with alternative uses and more supervision. Traditional parks with keepers and a range of activities within them are more useful than windswept unsupervized play areas. Many would like to see better back-up facilities such as public conveniences, clearly defined supervized, play areas (WDS, current), with suitably safe surfaces, instead of hard asphalt and muddy grass around play area equipment. To digress, the issue of public conve-

Figure 13.2 'They Can Always Use a Nightclub'.
Modern cities are profusely provided with clubs and pubs, mainly frequented by men, and by young single people. But is there any equivalent provision of facilities for women and children, are men still welcome when accompanied by a toddler?

niences is another national problem. As explained in 'At your Convenience' (WDS, 1990) facilities for women and children are underprovided; in fact, men have three times the amount of provision compared with women according to an official survey of London (WDS, current). Many male planners do not see this as a problem as they can always use a pub or club, and are unlikely to have childcare responsibilities. Greater provision of purpose built crèches and childcare facilities are needed nationally, integral to residential and employment 'zones' away from home (BTA, 1999).

What are the open space needs of women themselves, assuming only some of them want 6 acres of playing field per 1,000 population? First, most women, are not accompanied by children, and those with dependent young ones form a relatively small proportion of the female population. Many women on their own are wary of public open space, but welcome the existence of parks and green areas. However, in any landscaping or park scheme attention should be paid to security and surveillance factors. For example, the use of open railings rather than hedges around inner city park areas enables women to see into the area they are walking into. Public conveniences and seating areas should be prominently positioned, not hidden behind bushes. Sports facilities should provide crèches, and playing fields should be equipped with adequate changing facilities for women as well as men, although the 'sports pavilion' is usually seen as male territory. Many women feel intimidated by the 'Body Beautiful' image of the new leisure centres, or may have religious and ethnic objections to mixed facilities. It is not enough to say these centres are there for everyone if they want to use them, careful programming and organization of the complex, is needed to cater for women as well men.

Research has shown that young women, and for that matter ethnic minorities are less likely to use open space in the countryside for leisure compared with men (Greed, 1994a). Arguably, there exists a rather macho youth culture in the world of rural planning, and rural estate management, in which the emphasis on rock climbing, adventure sports, and fell walking, rather marginalizes women, although some women do undertake such activities. Policy attitudes often appear imbued with contempt for and disparagement of people in cars and the provision of tourist facilities for the urban masses. In fact many women who do visit the countryside do so in the family car bringing their childcare responsibilities with them in the back seat! Elderly people too, in coaches and cars, may want to look at the countryside through the vehicle window but have no inclination to do a twenty mile walk, although in their youth they may have been hikers too. The needs of all groups need to be respected.

Implementation of the Social Aspects of Planning: The Problem

Thus women's use of the built environment is different from that of men, because of different lifestyles, daily activity and travel patterns; and because of a range of diverse cultural, class, ethnicity and age characteristics too. In seeking to change the nature of the built environment, and the planning policies which shape it, minority groups have found the UK planning system somewhat unyielding.

Whether one is concerned with gender, race, homelessness, or any other social issue, it is not feasible to use planning legislation directly to implement social policy. For example, it is not possible generally to control the tenure or characteristics of the occupants of new housing through planning. The one exception is in rural areas where there is a need for cheaper housing for local residents, as introduced in Circular 7/91 and explained in PPG 3 'Housing'. Any conditions put on a planning permission must be for a 'genuine planning reason' (Morgan and Nott, 1988: 139; Morgan and Nott, 1995). Legally, town planning is strictly speaking to do with physical not social issues. However, there have been instances of planning authorities putting conditions on planning permission to achieve provision for women. Such instances, although relatively minor, are precedents which further confirm the argument that women's issues, are material considerations in the granting of the planning permission, and are valid with the guidance set by Circular, 1985/1, 'The use of conditions in planning permissions'.

Many would see the distinction as to what counts as 'social' as against 'physical' land use based planning law as gender biased. The need for sports facilities used predominantly by men for leisure are often accepted without question as being within the ambit of 'physical land use planning', whereas the provision of crèches used by working women are frequently seen as a 'social' matter, although this issue might have major implications for central area office development. Planners happily accept the National Playing Fields Association traditional standard of providing 6 acres of open space per 1,000 population in urban areas as one of the goals of their development plans, but few would accept the idea of providing one crèche space per 500 square feet of office space as part of 'normal' planning. Many women want decent public conveniences, baby changing and sitting areas in shopping centres, and would argue this is a material planning matter as it affects their access and use of retail development.

Women's needs do not fit into the existing classifications of land-use and development as embodied in planning law, and development plans; although crèches, for example, now fall into Use D2. This use class covers 'non-residential institutions' and inappropriately includes day nurseries, day centres, as well as museums and libraries. Some would see crèches as a potential element in the mixed 'B1' 'Business' Use Class (Use Classes Order 1995) (LPAS, 1986).

Permission is not normally needed for the use by a householder of a room within a domestic house for childminding unless the use becomes 'dominant' or 'intrusive'. The requirements of the Children Act 1989 have to be met with regard to childcare ratios and standards, over and above planning law.

However, the local authority or other relevant statutory authority is required by law to take gender issues into account in the provision of public facilities under the Sex Discrimination Act 1975. It is illegal to refuse or deliberately omit to provide goods and services because of the recipients' sex, and this may be construed as applying to town planning matters. There is no Circular or White Paper which specifically gives guidance on gender issues in town planning, and those which give indirect support are now somewhat dated. For example, Circular 22/84 (updated by PPG 12) stated that the unitary development plan system will 'provide authorities with positive opportunities to reassess the needs of their areas, resolve conflicting demands, and consider new ideas and bring forward appropriate solutions'. Many argue that 'women' *are* a material consideration in planning, because women and men use space in different ways, (Taylor, J., 1990: 98). The Royal Town Planning Institute, Code of Professional Conduct 1986, makes it illegal to discriminate on the basis of race, sex, or creed and religion, and this alone should govern individual planner's conduct, it should also be his/her duty to enlighten his/her local authority on these matters. This is another evolving, constantly changing area of planning law and policy.

Planners have sought to use planning gain (Chapter 3) to get additional community facilities. But planning gain agreements must only be used for the purpose of 'restricting or regulating the development or use of land' and must be 'reasonable' (Circular 22/83 and 16/91 and see PPG1). An additional problem is that even if developers are willing to build social facilities, someone has got to pay for their maintenance and management. Local authorities themselves cannot afford to pay for this with government cutbacks.

Provided there are clear policy statements as to what is expected on a site written into the relevant statutory plan developers will be reasonably expected to provide related social facilities in order to obtain

Figure 13.3 'Where's the Nearest Toilet?'
An APC Superloo'. In discussing planning issues with ordinary women the comment is often made 'It all comes down to toilets in the final analysis'. Can it really be said that equality has been achieved when toilets are not adequately and accessibly provided in modern towns and cities?

planning permission, without the need for complex planning agreements. The DETR appears to prefer this approach than leaving it to the *ad hoc* imposition of complicated 'conditions of permission' at the planning permission stage, or to complex 'planning agreements'. Many of the London Borough Unitary Development Plans (UDP) contain 'women's policies' either as a separate chapter in their Written Statement. Many of these were based upon the model Chapter 6, *Planning for Equality: Women in London* of the Draft Greater London Development Plan (GLC, 1984). Other London boroughs have included women's issues throughout the whole UDP document, adding relevant sections to each subject chapter. As accepted and approved policy these 'women and planning' statements have the force of law when determining the planning application, but they have to be durable enough to stand up to a planning appeal, the fact they are 'good' is not enough. It remains to be seen how, and whether, the new Greater London Authority (GLA) will address women and planning issues.

Subsequently by the mid-1990s many of the UDPs had gone through the approval stage. In several instances the planning inspectors required some of the

Figure 13.4 'Life's a Lottery'.
A strong element of luck is needed to achieve 'women and planning' policies. Nowadays funding for 'women's issues' is often only likely to be obtainable through Lottery and Millennium grants as 'special funding' rather than as a basic mainstream right.

'women and planning' policies be removed. This is a fate which several other more socially orientated policies suffered, such as those related to the needs of ethnic minority groups, disability and social deprivation. There appeared to be some inconsistency between the decisions of different planning inspectors, indicating lack of gender-awareness and training on these matters (WDS, 1994).

Generally, the reason for removal was that the policies in question were seen as *ultra vires* (outside the scope of planning law) meaning they were seeking to impose requirements that were unreasonable and not land-use matters. Requirements for the provision of crèches, toilets, baby changing facilities, and other such social facilities were likely to be seen as 'imposing quotas' and setting detailed space standard require-

ments which were not seen as being appropriate at the development plan level. Such decisions may be seen as somewhat biased, from a gender-perspective point of view, as many development plans include car parking standards and these have never been seen as inappropriate. It is argued that the provision of such facilities is a 'land use' matter, as it affects the way people 'use land', having sway on accessibility, and influencing the nature of development itself (Cullingworth and Nadin, 1994: 251).

Although there has been a spread of good policy statements in development plan documents (as surveyed and detailed by Little, 1994) there is not at the end of the century, as yet, a commensurate level of approval and implementation. The situation is very variable between different areas, and, at the 'coal face' of development control, in some local authorities 'women and planning' conditions on a planning permission go through without question, whereas in others they are overturned. This again reflects an *ad hoc* approach brought about by lack of strong central government guidance. In the final analysis what happens in a particular local authority, depends on the willingness and perspective of the local planners and whether they are co-operative or negative in their support of such issues. There is a need for training of professional planning staff to be aware of the issues. The existence of senior women officers, or at least sympathetic male officers is essential, and support from councillors is essential (RTPI, 1988). It is to be seen whether the creation of a new pan-London planning authority, the Greater London Authority (GLA), will follow the GLC's lead in providing planning for women. In the next chapter the nature of the built environment professions will be discussed. In Chapter 15, alternative means of overcoming some of the obstacles towards implementation of socially relevant planning policy will be presented.

TASKS

Information Gathering Tasks

I. Find out whether, and in what form, your local planning authority has stated policies specifically for women, ethnic groups and other minorities? Are these contained within development plan written statements, separate policy documents, or other formats?

Conceptual and Discursive Task

II. Do you consider 'gender' to be a land use issue relevant to town planning? Discuss relating your answer to examples of different land uses and facilities

Reflective Task

III. What do you personally think of feminism? Is it relevant to today? What other minority needs can you identify?

FURTHER READING

Foundation books on women and the built environment, deriving mainly from North America, include *Built Environment* (1996), special issues on women and planning; Hayden, 1981, 1984; Keller, 1981; Roberts, P. (1988); Stimpson, 1981; Torre, 1977; Wekerle *et al.*, 1980; and Wilson, 1980, 1991.

Publications concerned with the situation in Britain include, Greed, 1994a; Little, 1994; Booth *et al.*, 1996; Wilson, 1996; Wilson, E. (1991). The European perspective is found in Eurofem publications.

There is a range of conference reports, local authority reports, research studies, and European policy documents on women and planning. Many of these are referenced in the above texts. Consult the most recent RTPI publications and local authority planning department reports, in particular RTPI (1995a) and RTPI (1983).

The situation is constantly evolving as the lawyers define precisely what the parameters of the current legislation are through the planning appeal system and the resulting case law. It is important to read the professional journals to keep up with the current state of play.

14

THE BUILT ENVIRONMENT
PROFESSIONS

THE CONTEXT

Changing Perspectives

Having discussed the 'planned' in the last two chapters, Chapter 14 discusses 'the planners'. The nature of the town planning profession will be set within an explanation of the context of the changing characteristics and composition of the built environment professions, of which planning is arguably one part. Emphasis will be placed on comparisons between the planning and the surveying professions, and upon the wider construction industry context drawing on previous research (Greed, 1991, 1994, 1997a and b, 1999b). This will help highlight the specific nature of the planners, because many general practice surveyors are involved in planning and development activities, but their role is somewhat different from that of the predominantly public sector based town planner. This chapter is inevitably more discursive as the built environment professions are in the process of change, and are the subject of much criticism, particularly from minority groups. Thus the chapter includes commentary and analysis of the situation.

The world of the planning professional has been overtaken by some major cultural changes during the last 20 years. Arguably all the professions have become more commercially-minded, although a sense of public service and responsibility to the wider community is still to be found in the codes of professional ethics produced by the professional bodies. In the 1980s, dynamic economic growth occurred in which property figured as a major commodity. The landed professions have subsequently expanded in the 1990s, and become more diverse and entrepreneurial in membership.

The 'Big Bang' (deregulation of financial services) in the mid-1980s altered the financial world, sweeping away generations old restrictions and barriers. This provided new opportunities for the landed professions in the private sector, but it also meant that they were now undefended from invasion of part of 'their' territory, in the areas of property portfolio management and investment analysis, from a range of other professionals, not least accountants, and from worldwide competitors. These included Japanese interests, and American banking and investment companies with substantially different corporate cultures. The 1980s 'enterprise culture' faded in the recession of the early 1990's, to be replaced by the present entrepreneurial era of 'New Labour', and also by the 'environment culture'.

Office technology and telecommunications have advanced, and now the Stock Exchange operates by dealing from computer terminals. Much of the population is generally more literate, numerate and better informed, not least because of the expansion of higher education. People communicate instantaneously across vast distances by means of fax machines, e-mail and mobile telephones. In the opinion of some modern office blocks will become redundant like Victorian warehouses and factories. Large scale commuting will decline, and more people will work from terminals at home, with only the managerial and professional staff maintaining a base in the centre for meetings. Terms such as 'hot-desking' describe this situation in which employees drop in briefly, perhaps for a meeting with colleagues before they are off again, mobile phone in hand.

Figure 14.1 The Building Site.
The inhospitable, unwelcoming, even threatening nature of the building site is transmitted through the associated signage and generally alienating environs.

THE PLANNERS

As can be seen from earlier chapters, the planning profession is concerned with both urban and rural issues, and with all types of land uses, including retail, residential, commercial, industrial, open space and other amenities. Yet planning is not only concerned with the individual developments and sites, but with the whole built environment and with the traffic the different uses will generate. These days, as has been seen, planning is not limited to the 'built' environment, there is the whole new field of environmental planning, centred upon ecological issues, sustainability and pollution control. Likewise planners are not just concerned with the physical built environment, but with the social, economic and political factors that shape it, and thus with the needs and wants of its inhabitants.

Thus, physical land use planning is only a small component of the modern town planner's job, whereas once it was its *raison d'être* and reason for claiming professional status. Today there is much debate about what 'planning' really comprises. Is town planning a real profession, such as the law, architecture or civil engineering are often presumed to be, and does it need to be in order to operate? 'Planning' may be seen as a composite of subjects put together for various administrative and political reasons, which nonethe-

less exudes a certain 'mystique'. Nevertheless, regardless of the validity of its theoretical underpinnings (as discussed in Chapter 16), town planning remains a major bureaucratic function of local government, and an important component of the professional activities of the private sector property development world.

The main professional body to which most town planners belong is the Royal Town Planning Institute (RTPI). As can be seen from Table 14.1, the RTPI is a small but significant organization. All town planners (as can be seen from the last column) comprise only 6 per cent of the total membership of the built environment professions, because there are so many more engineers and surveyors. Yet, the power of the planners is disproportionate to their numbers (Greed, 1994a: 21; Greed, 1999b), because of their regulatory powers and managerial role over the built environment, through the auspices of the local government system.

The surrounding influence of the other built environment professions and the wider construction industry, of which town planning is officially one small part (CISC, 1994) cannot be underestimated. The influence of construction professionals goes way beyond individual building projects, they are among the 'great and the good' being called on to shape the built environment, at macro and micro levels, in a variety of capacities, posts and committees. For example, civil engineers may be heads of town

Table 14.1 **Membership of the Construction Professions, 1996**

Body	Student members			Full members			Total membership			% of whole sector[§]
	Total	Female	%	Total	Female	%	Total	Female	%	
Royal Town Planning Institute[†]	2196	957	43	13698	3025	22	17337	3972	23	6
Royal Institution of Chartered Surveyors	8193[†]	1267	15.5	71865	4886	7	92772	8062	8.7	35
Institution of Structural Engineers	4358	586	13.4	10114	137	1.3	21636	951	4.4	5
Institution of Civil Engineers	8353	978	11.7	42658	767	1.8	79480	3425	4.3	26
Chartered Institute of Building	9859	620	6.2	10244	94	0.9	33143	903	2.7	5
Architects and Surveyors Institute	–	–	–	–	–	–	5046	130	2.5	2
Royal Institution of British Architects	3500	*	31	22670	1819	8	32000	*	12	11
Association of Building Engineers	327	34	10.4	2292	39	1.7	4577	104	2.3	2
Chartered Institute of Building Services Engineers	2196	116	5.28	6275	66	1.05	15264	319	2	3
Chartered Institute of Housing	4190	2654	63	8258	3465	41	13490	6375	47	4
Architects Registration Board, ARCUK	–	–	–	–	(UK only)	25153	2892	11.5	ARCUK	
British Institute of Architectural Technology (total membership only)							5495	182	3.3	2

*RIBA figures are approximate owing to new format of presentation of figures on education statistics and membership. [†]Changes in total compared with previous figures may be accounted for by revisions in body's categories etc., but check the overall proportions. In some cases intermediate, honorary, graduate and licentiate categories make up the remainders of the totals. [†]Figures for RTPI as at end of 1996. [§]E.g. planners comprise 6% of all construction professionals.

Of 1.3 million in construction, 15% are professional; of these 6% are women: 0.9% of total membership. Approx. total for all: full members 195,000 (12000 females, 6%)

planning departments, transportation planners and planning inspectors (Greed, 1999b).

The RTPI was established in 1914 as a learned association (Ashworth, 1968; Millerson, 1964) of architects, surveyors, public health officers and civil engineers who were concerned with town planning issues, but gradually town planning evolved as a separate profession, as will be explained in later chapters.

These days, there are two main methods whereby people become town planners. Candidates may take a degree level course in town planning, or they may take a first degree in some other related subject, and follow this by a postgraduate course in town planning. In both cases they then have to satisfactorily complete a required period of professional experience in practice. Additionally, non-planning graduates who have been working in town planning for a number of years and have substantial related experience may be eligible for membership. All members are expected to undertake Continuing Professional Development (CPD).

Table 14.2 **Undergraduate Student Survey of Characteristics of First Year Entrants**

Factors		All Students			Professional Specialisms						
		All UK	Male	Female	Architect	Civil engineer	Building construction manager	Quantity surveyor	Building services engineer	Town planner	Building surveyor
All figures are %											
Gender											
1995/6	Male	82	–	–	75	86	93	87	75	68	85
1994/5	Male	84	–	–	75	87	91	87	92	65	94
1995/6	Female	18	–	–	25	14	7	13	25	32	15
1994/5	Female	16	–	–	25	13	9	13	8	35	6
Age											
1995/6	under 20	64	81	19	66	68	44	64	29	74	54
1994/5	under 20	75	82	18	81	81	70	67	60	87	47
1995/6	over 20	36	83	17	34	34	56	36	71	26	46
1994/5	over 20	25	87	13	19	19	30	33	40	13	53
Ethnicity											
1995/6	White	88	82	18	83	86	91	92	71	90	94
1994/5	White	90	85	15	88	90	90	94	86	88	91
1995/6	Other	12	79	21	17	14	9	8	29	10	6
1994/5	Other	10	79	21	12	10	10	6	13	12	9

Source: Kirk Walker 1997

Town planning is a relatively broad profession, and incorporates a wide range of people with different areas of expertise. Town planning practice covers a huge variety of different activities and specialisms, and planners tend to gravitate to the areas of practice which relate to their particular background and areas of expertise. There are a number of people working in town planning who have dual professional qualifications, such as in architecture, law, civil engineering, or surveying. One might find architects involved in those aspects of town planning which relate to conservation policy and design; lawyers involved in development control; and economists, statisticians, and sociologists involved in the wider policy making levels of the preparation of structure plan policies. Likewise a feature of town planning work is that a wide range of people with different types of expertise work together as a large team, both in respect of the production of the Development Plans within local government, and in the case of large-scale private sector projects.

This is rather different, relatively speaking, from the situation in surveying practice, where there is still more room for the sole practitioner, although in London many surveyors are members of very large firms which are subdivided into specialist offices and sections. As a general principle much of the work that goes on in the landed professions is strongly team orientated. Although most town planners are employed within central and local government over 30 per cent are today working in the private sector, acting as advisors to a range of public and private sector interests, ranging from property development companies to smaller local authorities who buy in expertise when needed, rather than keeping a large permanent staff.

In addition to the main professional body, the RTPI, there are other influential town planning organizations. One of the foremost is the Town and Country Planning Association (TCPA), which is not a professionally qualifying body, but a prestigious pressure group originally founded at the beginning of the twentieth century to promote the idea of Garden Cities and Ebenezer Howard, as discussed in Part II. There is a measure of overlap in that some 'planners' are also chartered surveyors who have qualified within the Planning and Development division of the Royal Institution of Chartered Surveyors (RICS).

THE SURVEYORS

The main professional body for surveying is the Royal Institution of Chartered Surveyors (RICS) whose roots goes back over many centuries (Thompson, 1968). The RICS is a much larger body (membership approximately 86,000 including students) than the RTPI. The RICS contains within it a range of specialist groups, including general surveyors, land agents, land surveyors, minerals surveyors, quantity surveyors, and building surveyors (Avis and Gibson, 1987). The Commercial and Residential division is the largest in which general practice surveyors, valuers, estate managers, and housing managers are located. Quantity surveyors make up nearly a third of the membership of the RICS and are therefore the second largest group.

Some surveyors specialize in Planning and Development matters and primarily carry out 'town planning' on behalf of developers and other private sector clients. Some chartered surveyors may also belong to the RTPI. Likewise there substantial numbers of people who hold joint membership of the RIBA and are architects (Nadin and Jones, 1990). There is definitely an overlap in terms of planning practice between the two professions, but many surveyor-planners are to be found working in the private sector.

However, it would be wrong to imagine, that because relatively few surveyors are specifically employed in town planning authorities, therefore they have little influence on the nature of the built environment. They are the main advisors of the private sector, and thus, in a sense, 'the enemy'. They are the people on the 'other side of the fence' whose development activities local government town planners are there to control. Such surveyors represent interests which can often conflict with the objectives of the planning system. The commercial and valuation emphasis throughout the world of surveying colours the world view of all surveyors and is distinctly different from that of the planners.

COMPARISONS BETWEEN PLANNERS AND SURVEYORS

Academic or Practical?

Over half of all town planning courses are postgraduate ones, whereas the vast majority of surveying courses are at the undergraduate level. There are a number of town planners, as mentioned above, who originally took a first degree in geography, economics, sociology, or law who then went to take a postgraduate conversion degree in town planning (for the range of courses available see the special edition of *Planning* on planning education produced every April by the RTPI). However, with modularization of courses within the large new faculties of the new universities, there may be more shared learning and such divisions may not become strongly evident until the final years of the courses taken.

So the emphasis in the RTPI is somewhat different, with town planning having a relatively more 'academic' emphasis than within the RICS which has always prided itself on its practicality, and common sense. One of the main reasons students give for choosing surveying is because (as would-be students often put it at interview) we don't want to be stuck in an office all day but want to get out and about. There has been continued growth and diversification of undergraduate and postgraduate education within the landed professions. People tend to choose their profession carefully in relation to future prospects and salaries, and at present it is noticeable that surveyors earn more than planners and have a higher, but more precarious status in the private sector.

Public or Private?

Whilst nearly 70 per cent of RTPI members are employed in the public sector, the situation is reversed regarding RICS members, with over 80 per cent of surveyors working in the private sector in private partnerships, or for large investment and development concerns. The majority of town planning surveyors will see their work as mainly advising their clients on how to beat the planning system. Many career and publicity leaflets on general practice surveying make much of the positive role of the surveyor set against that of bureaucracy and planners, and what 'he' can do for the hard-pressed developer. There are other quite marked differences between the two land use professions, each having their own professional 'culture' (Joseph, 1978; Greed, 1991). The RTPI has the image of being somewhat more sociological, political, interventionist and governmental in outlook; and the

Table 14.3 **Accepted Candidates in UCAS Subject Group: Architecture, Building and Planning**

Age at 30.9.96	Under 21		21 to end of 24		25 and over		Total	
Sex	Male	Female	Male	Female	Male	Female	Male	Female
Ethnicity:								
Unknown	179	30	81	14	95	23	355	67
White	2967	764	435	56	354	88	3756	908
Black	44	17	20	6	55	25	119	48
Asian	209	55	33	2	17	5	259	62
Other	20	11	4	3	12	3	36	17
Total	3419	877	573	81	533	144	4525	1102
Class:								
Unknown	254	57	105	24	145	44	504	125
Professional	530	170	56	6	33	15	619	191
Intermediate	1373	338	150	23	120	42	1643	403
Skilled non-manual	355	102	50	12	49	27	454	141
Skilled manual	624	140	152	9	141	10	917	159
Partly skilled	225	61	46	7	31	5	302	73
Unskilled	58	9	14	–	14	1	86	10
Total (same)	3419	877	573	81	533	144	4525	1102

Adapted from HESA figures, note class is based on father's occupation.

RICS is seen by many as more conservative, private sector orientated and commercial in outlook. Albeit there are exceptions on both sides.

There is a growing number of RTPI planners who work in private planning consultancies advising private developers or carrying out contract work for local planning authorities, who, therefore, have an influential input into the planning process and policy. Increasingly, as local government structures change, as a result of government pressure to make them less bureaucratic and more cost-effective and entrepreneurial, Compulsory Competitive Tendering (CCT) is being introduced, under which professional staff, such as planners, are hired for specific contracts, rather than being employed permanently. Such changes break down the public/private divisions which have so riven the built environment professions. Likewise, introduction of audits and a greater emphasis upon performance criteria have changed, if not speeded up, the work of the local authority planner. Local government is becoming more 'privatized', buzz words being 'client' rather than 'member of the public' and 'best value' rather than 'public service' (Audit Commission, 1999). There has been much criticism among minority groups of these changes. For example, the establishment of so-called representative 'stakeholder groups' have proved to be mainly male, middle-class and white in composition. Such groups are often composed of participants who are drawn from the 'wrong' level of society, mainly professional and managerial individuals who have little contact with the ordinary people and with minority groups in general.

Male or Female?

Approximately 30 per cent of students on planning courses are women, a considerable increase on the 10 per cent of 20 years ago. But there has also been a drop in the popularity of planning courses as a whole. As can been seen from Table 14.1, 23 per cent of all members of the RTPI are female, 22 per cent of full members are female, and 43 per cent are student members. As can be seen from the tables in this chapter most of the built environment professions are still predominantly white, middle-class and male (cf CIB, 1996; Kirk Walker, 1997)

Taking the land use and construction professions together (see Table 14.1) less than 6 per cent of those in professional practice are women. There is concern at the continuing under-representation of minority groups and interests in the development process (Rhys Jones *et al.*, 1996; Druker *et al.*, 1996). This under-representation undoubtedly contributes to the nature of professional decision-making, and creates an unsatisfactory end product. Arguably an individual professional's life experience will affect their judgement of priorities and appropriate policies when undertaking urban decision-making.

In contrast as stated earlier 52 per cent of the population in Britain is female (ONS, 1999). These factors may be irrelevant to urban policy making if women's needs are perceived to the same as those of the men, or if it is believed that the professional man is equally capable of planning for all groups in society. But as research and human experience have shown, women suffer disadvantage in a built environment that is planned by chiefly by men, primarily for other men and so changes need to be made (Stimpson, *et al.*, 1981: Little *et al.*, 1988; WGSG, 1984, 1997).

There are relatively few women in the more technological areas of surveying, but greater concentrations in general practice surveying (especially within the housing option). However, the number of women entering surveying is growing at a greater rate than the overall expansion of the profession. Even allowing for their small numbers in the past, disproportionately fewer women than men are reaching positions of seniority or full partnership level. Likewise, relatively few women town planners are reaching higher positions in local authorities, or senior partner level in planning consultancies. This is likely to be one of the main issues of contention for the future. Unless women reach the decision making levels of the professions they will not be able to shape the future structure of the profession or influence the nature of the built environment through their professional activities and decisions. Surveying practice is segmented (Greed, 1991) in that women are more likely still to be found in the public sector and less in the mainstream private sector. Similarly, due to a perceived lack of equal opportunities and employment flexibility in local government, more women town planning graduates are obtaining jobs in the private sector, and this seems to have been a continuing trend for more than 10 years (Morphet, 1993; RTPI, 1999).

While there is growth, many of the professional bodies are concerned about a future 'manpower' crisis, as there is going to be a substantial drop in the numbers of school leavers in the future, due to the falling birth rate over the last 20 years. Once the market starts declining redundancy notices are issued, often on the basis of last in, first out. However, some areas are still flourishing and there are continuing attempts to attract a wider range of entrants, including women, ethnic minority people, and bright working class people (not mutually exclusive groups). Not so long ago that many people from these groups felt they were being actively discouraged from entering the professions.

Black or White or Diverse?

The numbers of ethnic minority and black members are low in both professional bodies, although the RTPI has tried to promote a recruitment policy amongst black school leavers. Interestingly black women in particular have responded. Black students constitute around 5 per cent of students on planning courses overall. Some provincial colleges have none, but over half of students in some central London new universities are ethnic minority candidates (Baty, 1997). However, in the built environment and construction professions as a whole the level is nearer 9 per cent because of the larger numbers of male black students on more technical construction courses.

There is considerable concern about the need to recruit more ethnic minority planners (Ahmed, 1989). 'Ethnic issues' should not be seen as separate from so-called mainstream planning topics. For example, although there are perceived linkages between inner city planning and ethnic needs, local authorities in the Midlands have specifically developed policies on ethnic minority needs and recreational planning in the countryside, and London boroughs have investigated the likely linkages between urban conservation policy and the specific cultural housing design needs of ethnic groups.

It is significant that many observers are commenting that while more people are entering the professions these days they are not all ending up in the same quality of posts. There is a clear segmentation of the professions on the basis of gender and race, but also on the basis of class of origin of the entrants to a lesser extent (Crompton and Sanderson, 1990). The situation is far from a black/white dualism. These days there is a diversity and variety of types of people entering the built environment professions. An individual may experience shifting power relationships and differing levels of acceptance according the situation they are in, and with whom they are interacting. Differing mixtures of class, gender, race, age, background, and culture create complex power relationships. Asians generally outnumber Afro-Caribbeans in the built environment and construction professions. Some see a simplistic black/white division as a racist and exclusionary concept, leaving little space for recognition of the 'different' experience and heritage of Asian groups (Ismail, 1998). In London, in particular, there is a great diversity of ethnic minority groupings, cultures and lifestyles, which is only beginning to be reflected in student composition (Uguris, 2000).

Abled or Disabled?

There are very few disabled planners or surveyors, and attempts to get precise figures from the professional bodies in the course of the author's research have proved relatively fruitless. It is estimated that the disabled constitute 0.3 per cent of all built environment professionals. It should not be assumed that lack of disabled applicants is due to the nature of these professions, because much of the work is office based, and not all to do with 'going out and about' on site. Some would say that disabled people should be involved in the 'outside' survey and plan making work because they can more readily point out the barriers to mobility inherent in an urban layout or building design by undertaking an Access Audit. However, the reality is that, when 'disability' is discussed within the construction and built environment professions, it is usually in relation to 'access' and other 'design' issues rather than in respect of employment opportunities (Imrie, 1996).

Professional, Technical or Non-Aligned?

There are several other major professional bodies concerned with the environment such as the Royal Institute of British Architects (RIBA), Institution of Civil Engineers (ICE), Institution of Structural Engineers (ISE), Incorporated Society of Valuers and Auctioneers (ISVA), and the smaller professional bodies such as the Architecture and Surveying Institute (ASI). The Chartered Institute of Building (CIOB) in particular has experienced remarkable growth perhaps because of it emphasizes its role in 'construction management' rather than within 'building', which seems to be a dirty word nowadays. Much of the work of ISVA members is similar to that of the general practice surveyor, particularly in relation to valuation, auctioneering, and estate management which touches on the area of town planning from a developer's viewpoint. In 2000, ISVA and RICS merged to form one professional body.

The Chartered Institute of Housing (CIOH) is a relatively small body, but one with many women members (Brion and Tinker, 1980). It has some overlap in the nature of work with the RICS (Power, 1987; Smith, 1989; Leevers, 1986). In the past housing management was predominantly concerned with the management of local authority housing stock, but the profession has subsequently grown in numbers and prestige in response to the higher political profile given to the housing crisis in recent years. Nowadays local authorities, whilst still managing the bulk of housing, are not the builders, but the enablers, of new social residential development, the development role having passed to the housing associations.

There is a range of other specialist bodies concerned with aspects of property such as the National Association of Estate Agents (NAEA) with around 7,000 membership, of which 15 per cent are women, and the Institute of Revenues, Ratings and Valuation which has taken on a new lease of life since the controversy about the poll tax and the possible alternatives. Some solicitors (members of the Law Society) and barristers specialize in town planning law within private practice. Interestingly this branch of the law is attracting many women, who now make up over 50 per cent of new candidates. Lawyers employed by local authorities have an important role in the planning process, sorting out the finer points of planning law, and dealing with the details of enforcement, planning agreements and conditions of planning permission. In the wider development process itself, there are many other professionals involved, such as accountants, economists and financial analysts concerned with the viability of the development. Urban geographers, statisticians, economists and sociologists may be called upon to have an input to the development decision-making process.

There is a growing number of professional ecologists, environmentalists, and landscape architects who

Table 14.4 **Professional Membership Data, 1999**

The RTPI corporate membership total at the end of 1999 is 13,044 of which 3,105 are women and 9,939 are men, giving around 23% female representation. Female student membership is registered as 44% out of 1,870 student membership of whom 825 are female and 1,035 are male. The latter figure only includes those who have registered as student members of the RTPI not those in the universities where female representation on planning courses has dropped to around 20%. Total RTPI membership including students, corporate and others is 17,440.

In response to an RTPI survey of the corporate membership 336 classified themselves as Asian, 56 as Black African, and 25 as Black Caribbean. For students the figures were 70 Asian, 19 Black African and 2 Black Caribbean. These figures should be treated with caution for not everyone replied, ethnic origin and country of residence were not disaggregated in relation to international membership, and as stated not all students undertaking planning courses, and not all, but most, qualified planners chose to join the Institute.

The RIBA corporate membership total at the same date was 28,002 of which 2,586 are women and 25,416 are men. There are 4,771 student members of which 1,499 are women and 3,272 are men. The RIBA stated that they had no information on race or disability but did provide an age breakdown from which it was clear that nearly half the female corporate membership was under 40 with nearly 700 under 35, whereas male membership was more evenly spaced chronologically and around a quarter of the membership was under 40.

Figures for the other professional bodies have remained similar to those from the 1996 survey in spite of all the efforts to attract more women and ethnic minorities to the construction and built environment professions. The Chartered Institute of Housing continues to attract more ethnic minority candidates than other professions. Overall there has been a decline in both majority and minority students entering the construction and building fields. In contrast environmental studies courses continue to recruit well and geography courses are experiencing a growing popularity relative to courses which give professional exemptions.

At the time of writing research by the author is continuing on this topic and more detailed figures will be published when the data has all been collected and analysed in future publications. A full picture cannot be presented because of lack of response from some professional bodies, especially in respect of race and disability membership data.

offer expertise in the field of environmental assessment which is now a 'planning' requirement brought in by the European Commission. Another trend is for more people to offer their planning skills in an advocacy role on behalf of community groups to represent the demands of ordinary people, as professional community activists and enablers. However, significantly many of the environmental groups do not consider themselves to be 'professionals' nor are they seeking to become chartered bodies. This is because of a different subject ethos in which professionalism may be equated with old-fashioned, non-sustainable elitism. Construction, especially building roads and urban development on green field sites is seen as anti-environmental by some young people, who may as a consequence prefer to enrol on an environmental course, rather than to join what they may see as 'the enemy' by studying town planning, construction or surveying.

The above discussion has related chiefly to the professions, but this the tip of the iceberg – the elite few – as many other people are employed in the construction industry. There are vast numbers at technician and trades level in all aspects of the building industry. Many of these will have little contact with the big high-prestige schemes and will work in small building firms, which exist throughout the country and are prone to bankruptcy (Ball, 1988). Many local authorities formerly had their own Direct Labour Organization workforce (DLO). Nowadays local authorities are increasingly tendering out their work to the lowest bidder, creating more fluidity and business efficiency, but not necessarily more quality for the consumer (Wall and Clarke, 1996).

Besides professionally qualified practitioners, there are innumerable people working in the office and service sectors involved in all aspects of property, especially agency (including estate agency), investment, financial services. Many of these are not actually qualified within the main landed professions. There are large numbers of office workers mainly women, often carrying out fairly skilled quasi-professional work, especially in the realms of estate agency up and down the land. Anyone can become an estate agent, or for that matter a property developer, all one needs is money, or enough power to inspire confidence that others will take you seriously and invest in you. The creation of work-based, competence-related National Vocational Qualifications (NVQs) at Levels 3 and 4 (that is at the technical, support staff, and para-professional levels), for planning support staff may enhance these employees chances of progress.

THE PROFESSIONS AND THE EUROPEAN COMMUNITY

As explained in Chapters 2 and 9, there is now much closer links and open trade with Europe, in theory at least, giving access to a market of over 320 million people within the EU, larger even than the United States of America. Increasing EU harmonization of standards and procedures, to create a 'level playing field', will affect the building industry, especially in the area of 'public procurement' (public works contracts); building standards, construction products standards; and mutual recognition of professional qualifications and education. EC law increasingly affects all aspects of English law, including town planning and environmental law, because community law now takes precedence over national law in the member states.

The EU is likely to expand further. Since re-unification Germany offers great potential for the activities of property developers, and Berlin in particular has become the biggest building site in Europe. Such developments offer opportunities for British developers and construction companies, but the situation requires them to compete within in a larger pool alongside other European and international companies.

There now exist powerful trans-European property professional groups in which the British bodies claim a prominent position, for example FIABCI (a prominent European group representing the interests of property professionals). British bodies have to compete or harmonize with such bodies as the French, *La Confederation Nationale des Administrateurs de Biens* (biens meaning 'goods'). *Biens immobiliers* is the French for 'real property' in the sense of land and buildings (as in *agence immobilière* which is an estate agency; as against *biens mobiliers* which is 'personal property', such as chattels, anything which is 'mobile' that is not fixed to the ground, e.g. furniture, ornaments).

There are already links between British and other European planners, and there are many international planning organizations. But there are often considerable differences of opinion and culture, as to the ideal urban form, because of the greater emphasis on higher density cities and less suburban residential development on the European mainland. British planners were particularly concerned about the assumptions made by the European Commission in a consultative document entitled, *Green Paper on the Urban Environment* (CEC, 1990) which was based on the characteristics of a typical Continental European city where uses are normally much more concentrated than in Britain and the suburbs are often seen as low status 'cultural desert' areas. The EC has been criticized for assuming that it was possible to define an ideal city which was applicable right across Europe, regardless of national differences and climatic factors.

There is no exact equivalent to the British chartered town planner (or surveyor for that matter) in the different European countries. The professional cake is divided up in different ways, with architects, civil engineers, economists and geographers taking the role of 'the planner' in different situations (Williams, 1996 and 1999). More fundamentally there is something essentially 'English', even 'quaint', about being a 'professional' and belonging to a 'chartered' body, as against holding advanced higher degrees and demonstrating competence in a particular specialism, both of which are more frequently used as criteria of being accepted as a 'planner' in Europe (and North America for that matter). There is a great deal of mystique associated with the English idea of a professional elite (and the ideal of the professional gentleman) which does not fit well the realities of the modern, international competitive business world, nor with demands from a more educated population for greater involvement in the governmental decision making process in town planning (Knox, 1988). The very role of the planner is under question (Howe, 1980).

TASKS

Information Gathering

I. Gather careers information about the main construction and built environment professions.

II. Gather information about voluntary, community and minority groups in your vicinity which are concerned with town planning issues.

Conceptual and Discursive Tasks

III. Compare and contrast the roles of the town planner and the chartered surveyor, giving examples of their respective involvement in the development process.

IV. Critical mass theory, when applied to human organizations, has often been criticized for prioritizing quantitative, rather than qualitative, issues. Discuss in relation to one of the built environment professions.

Reflective Tasks

V. What are your impressions of the culture of the construction industry? Do you find it inviting or intimidating?

VI. How are eco-warriors presented in the media, in respect of individual characteristics and campaign issues?

FURTHER READING

There is a large range of publications on the nature of the different construction and built environment professions, some of which are written by the professional bodies themselves, often with a publicity or careers slant and can be obtained from the bodies in question.

A range of official reports on the need for change have been published in recent years such as Egan (1998), and Latham (CIB, 1996).

Academic studies of the professions include Millerson on the *Qualifying Associations* (1964), and Thompson on the history of the surveying profession (1968).

Texts on women in the professions include work on women in planning and surveying (Greed, 1991, 1994a; Booth *et al.*, 1996); and in engineering (Evetts, 1996; Carter and Kirkup, 1989); and architecture Silverstone and Ward, 1980. Generic management issues are discussed in a range of books including, Spencer and Podmore, 1997; Druker and White 1996; Langford *et al.*, 1994; Gale, 1994; Morris and Nott, 1991). See Acker, 1984 on women's participation in higher education. See Brion and Tinker, 1980 and Leevers, 1986 on women in housing. Texts on women and geography (a feeder subject to town planning and surveying), see Little (1994); McDowell (1983, 1987); McDowell and Peake (1990); McDowell and Sharp (1997); Rose (1993).

Sources on ethnic minorities and the construction and built environment professions include, De Graft-Johnson, 1999; SOBA, 1997; Harrison and Davies, 1995. There is little material on disabled built environment professionals as the disabled are generally seen as the recipients of professional decision-making rather than as prime movers themselves (Imrie, 1996; Imrie and Wells, 1993; Davies, 1999).

There is a vast range of material on community groups and organizations involved in planning. Again publicity material can be obtained from groups such as Planning Aid for London, and Friends of the Earth. The London Regeneration Network is an umbrella organization, with its own library and publications department which encompasses a vast range of organizations in London which are involved in urban community issues. More specific material on the mechanics of community involvement includes Kelly (1997) good practice guide on tenant involvement.

15

THE FUTURE

CHANGING THE AGENDA

CHANGING THE MAINSTREAM CULTURE

New Labour: New Opportunities?

Many of the policies and proposals discussed in Chapter 13 were never implemented (RTPI, 1999). This discursive chapter identifies new means and opportunities for generating policy change in the future in respect of the needs of minority groups. Potential top-down change agents are identified including global, European, UK governmental and local level agencies. Then the role of bottom-up change agents, including minority and community groups is discussed. For illustrative purposes Chapter 15 takes one example of an alternative approach to achieving urban change, from Continental Europe, namely 'time planning' as against 'spatial planning. This chapter incorporates examples from recent ESRC-funded qualitative research (Greed, 1999a and b), and with Chapter 16 contains more advanced conceptual and theoretical material.

Subcultural Perspectives

It is argued, from research, that in order to change the built environment, one first needs to change the subculture of the decision-makers who make the urban policy which shapes our towns and cities. That is the world-view, values, and perceptions of reality held within the hearts and minds of built environment professionals need to change. Professional decision-making is not socially-neutral but is influenced by an individual's perception of 'reality' as to how the world is seen, and how society is imagined to be (Greed, 1991: 5–6; Greed, 1999a).

It is helpful to see the built environment professional bodies as possessing their own subcultural values and world views. 'Subculture' is taken to mean the cultural traits, beliefs, and lifestyle peculiar to those, for example, in the planning tribe. One of the most important factors seems to be the need for a person to fit in to the subculture. It is argued that the values and attitudes held by its members have a major influence on their professional decision-making, and therefore ultimately influence the nature of 'what is built'. The need for the identification with the values of the subculture would seem to block out the entrance of both people and alternative ideas that are seen as 'different' or 'unsettling'.

The concept of 'closure' in the relation to the power of various subculture groups to control who is included in, or out, is a key factor in understanding the composition of the professions (as discussed by Parkin, 1979: 89–90; and developed by Weber, 1964: 141–152,236, and see Greed, 1994a: 25). Even if individuals do enter professional courses with alternative views, and believe they can change it by 'joining in' and biding their time until they are in a position to alter the *status quo*, they soon find that they are subjected to powerful professional socialization processes (Knox, 1988). Students, especially those from working class backgrounds, all girls schools, and/or ethnic minority origins, often experience considerable group pressure to 'believe' what they are told by authoritative lecturers and by fellow students. Disabled would-be students may never gain entrance in the first place.

Closure is worked out on a day-to-day basis at an interpersonal level out in practice, with some people being made to feel awkward, unwelcome and 'wrong' and others being welcomed into the subculture, and made to feel comfortable and part of the team, and thus encouraged to progress to senior posts and the decision-making levels within it, and are therefore in a position to shape the built environment. While women may encounter 'glass ceilings' (that is invisible barriers to promotion), black and disabled candidates may encounter 'glass walls' that prevent them entering their chosen profession in the first place.

Generating Change

A key question is, how can change be generated within professional subcultural groups and transmitted on to the built environment? This may involve, for example, changing the social composition of the planning profession, even more, so that they are more representative of society as a whole. It is vital to alter the process and personnel involved in the 'reproduction over space of social relations' (Massey, 1984: 16). In what often appears to be a fortress-like setting, in which outsiders and minority individuals seeking to bring change, are either 'socialized' to conform, or are marginalized or ejected; this is no easy task.

Conceptualizing Change: Critical Mass?

It is important to identify potential agents of change, and to 'map' pathways of change. Concepts which inform the investigation of change include (the ever popular but somewhat questionable) critical mass theory as to 'how many people are needed to change an organizational culture', (cf. Morley, 1994: 195, who refers to Bagilhole's work (1993), and see subsequent work by (Bagihole et al., 1996) on women in construction. Kanter (1977) suggests 15–20 per cent (minority composition) is needed to change the culture of an organization, whilst Gale (1994) suggests 35 per cent is necessary in the construction industry, and respondents have suggested the percentage should be much higher.

Ironically town planning has one of the highest percentages of women in any of the built environment chartered professional bodies (except for housing) (Chapter 14), however, commensurate change has been manifested, in spite of the constant efforts and writings of 'women and planning' groups. Originally, in physics, from which the theory is derived, critical mass was defined as an amount, not a percentage (like the minimum size snowball that holds together without melting), which would trigger a chain reaction. Only 20 lbs of Uranium 235 was needed to create critical mass in an atomic bomb weighing 9000 lbs which is 0.2 per cent of total matter (Larsen, 1958, pp. 35, 50, 55, and 73) – comparable to the percentage of minority individuals in some branches of construction or the number of women in some district planning offices. However, a planning colleague with a physics background, subsequently pointed out that it only takes one iota of contaminated material of the 'wrong sort' to stop the entire chain reaction and fusion process.

An increase in minority representation does not necessarily make any difference. 'More' does not necessarily mean 'better' (Greed, 1993). In other words a quantitative increase in the numbers of minority professionals does not necessarily mean that they will be in a position to alter the nature of the policies and culture of the professional body, that is to effect qualitative change. It has often been argued that in order to effect change, and to make social planning policy more reflective of society there is a need for the composition of the professional bodies, from which the decision-makers are drawn, to be more reflective and representative of society as a whole.

But, this does not necessarily follow. Much depends upon the personal perspective, ideological base (if any), self-interest, background and education of the minority individuals in question (Stark, 1997). In other words changing the culture is more important than changing the composition, and quality may be more important than quantity. A small well-organized group, or one or two totally dedicated charismatic individuals may prove more effective than hundreds of new minority individuals, who appear confused and unsure of their role at a personal level, having such low expectation and high tolerance levels that they may declare, I simply don't know what the problem is, and are thus easily socialized into the mainstream.

There is a range of theories which deal with such group dynamics, the role of individuals, and the

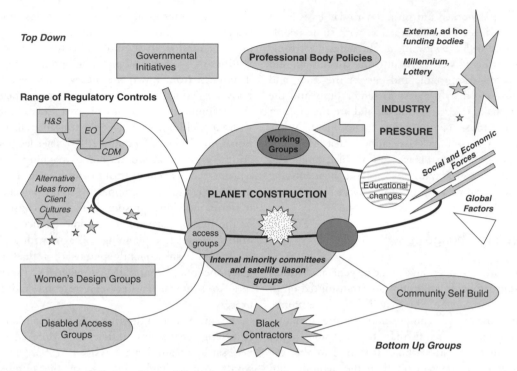

Figure 15.1 Diagram of Change Agents Impinging on Planet Construction.

significance of networks which ensure either social inclusion or exclusion or 'new' or 'different' individuals. Actor network theory is of particular interest, which is concerned with asking 'what are the networks by which social power is maintained, or the pathways through which social change might be brought about?' (Callon *et al.*, 1986; Murdock, 1997). Such research is also concerned with the role of 'prime movers' in detonating critical mass explosion (Kanter, 1983: 296). Also, not to be dismissed, is the extensive range of 'New Age' ideas and theories, which delve into more 'spiritual' realms as to how to create change, of which the Celestine series is a best selling example (Redfield, 1994).

Such work has proved popular among some women's groups seeking social change such as the Women's Communications Centre, who undertake a massive national opinion survey among women, published as *Values and Visions: What Women Want* (WCC, 1996). When all material, physical and statutory means have failed, it is necessary to 'ask the Universe', in other words to pray to God for change.

A resilient and influential minority of women exist within the construction and built environment professions who *are* likely to hold alternative viewpoints. This group is likely to increase as the present young cohorts of women professionals grow older and become more 'cynical', who might contribute to the build-up of critical mass. But, one still hesitates to use the phrase 'critical mass', although it is argued that there is some truth in the concept that once a certain proportion of women is achieved, the culture will shift – not necessarily for the better, but perhaps in another unexpected way. In parallel with the situation in physics, it is easier to create an uncontrolled, rather than controlled chain reaction resulting from detonation, particularly when the setting is unstable (Larsen, 1958: 50). But, critical mass is one of the most frequently used terms in the industry when discussing equal opportunities. It fits well with the scientific and quantitative bent of the construction subculture (Larsen, 1958), but is highly optimistic and oversimplistic if used as a predictive social concept without considering qualitative, cultural forces too. Clearly much depends upon the role of outside change agents too, which can help change policy perspectives.

TOP DOWN CHANGE AGENTS

Change Agents: Generic or Gendered?

Two main types of change agent will be discussed in the next section, 'top down' and 'bottom up'. The first group 'top down' includes governmental, international, nationwide, professional body, and other official agents. Many of these are concerned with 'generic' change, for a variety of reasons, rather than with 'gender' or other social issues. But, nevertheless aspects of their work may, incidentally, benefit minorities. The second group, 'bottom up' includes a range of minority, grass roots, community, and single issue groups, most of whom are concerned with specific minority issues, including 'gendered' and ethnicity considerations.

Global Forces

At the international level a range of top-down change agents, such as UN, OECD, WHO and the EU itself, has been already been identified as influencing the structure and objectives of British town planning. Overarching global movements such as 'the Green movement' and more specifically 'planning for sustainability' have been very influential in challenging and reshaping British town planning. More diffuse, but undoubtedly powerful, cultural movements have also been at work. The growth of mass tourism and the fact that air travel has increased by 75 per cent in the last 10 years, has facilitated a more globalised culture (Davidson and Maitland, 1999). This has encouraged the rapid transmission of ideas relating to popular culture, heritage, leisure and public art, among competing tourist cities in different countries. This change is reflected in Britain in the renaming of the Department of National Heritage, as the Department of Culture, Media and Sport (DCMS) by the incoming Labour government in 1997. It has also introduced people to a range of different ways of living, and encouraged both the public and professionals to challenge the *status quo*, especially in respect of city facilities and design.

***Figure 15.2* Sport as a Major Cultural Planning Issue.** Currently there are plans to rebuild Wembley Stadium, removing the two white towers, and making it more than just a football stadium by adding athletics facilities. But, do all the community benefit from such investment, especially from Lottery funding for sporting facilities?

At an international level, gender issues are increasingly incorporated into planning for development within Third World countries. International programmes such as the Healthy Cities Project initiated by the World Health Organization cover both developed and developing countries, and in the latter conditions are vastly different from the situation in the UK. Significantly, women comprise the majority of the world's poor, homeless, refugees and slave labourers (Moser, 1993).

When seeking to improve the urban conditions of the poor it is unrealistic and counterproductive to separate out the built environment from the economic and social factors which shape it, and from the quality of the lives of the people who inhabit it, therefore the issues of health, sustainability and equality need to be dealt with together. With the increasing globalization of economies in the future it is likely that the insularity of British town planning will be challenged by such more inclusive approaches to policy making. This is particularly important as a response to the needs of large scale global population movement, including migration and population displacement, as a result of wars, natural disasters, political and religious persecution. Such factors result in new ethnic minority communities settling in British and other European cities, and new challenges for planning authorities.

***Figure 15.3* Global Sophistication and Diversity: Japan.**
A Japanese nightclub. These days national cultural boundaries are breaking down globally and popular art and shop-front graphics manifest a mixture and borrowing of styles.

European Initiatives

The EU's approach to town planning, has not only been more environmental in outlook, but also more orientated towards 'social planning' and related to concepts of 'equal treatment' and 'social justice'. European Union (EU) legislation and policy harmonization requirements may provide salvation (OECD, 1994). A European Charter for Women in the City has already been produced by DG V, Equal Opportunities Unit (Booth and Gilroy, 1999; Eurofem, 1998, 1999). The allocation of structural funds, for the various projects and policies, with the EU is increasingly subject since 1994 to funding conditionality in respect of Equal Opportunities considerations, especially 'gender proofing'. In other words the EU sets certain 'conditions' on the funding beneficiaries in respect of maintaining equal opportunities policy in tendering, procurement, recruitment and employment in respect of the programme in question. This is similar to the system operated by US government bodies under the name 'contract compliance'. For example, 'Objective I' projects under the EU structural funding programme, for regional infrastructure and employment, are now subject to this funding conditionality (Gilroy and Booth, 1999).

Likewise in some other countries a Social Impact Analysis (SIA) is undertaken parallel to Environmental Assessment, and economic analysis, to cover the three components of sustainability as has been undertaken for example in Sweden. The gender implications of development plan policies are considered, including those related to transport, infrastructural policy at both urban or supra-urban levels. Within other EU countries there is generally less focus on physical land use planning than is found in Britain, and those countries which have a national, and regional planning system can more readily incorporate social issues, and economic strategy into their plan making procedures. With increased EU harmonization and trans-national policy co-operation such approaches may impact upon the UK system too.

While 'women and planning' has ceased to be seen as topical in the UK by mainstream planners, gender issues remain important elsewhere. But gender issues still figure prominently within the EU. A pan-European network was established, entitled Eurofem, and a major international conference was held in Finland in 1998, entitled, 'Gender and Human Settlements: Local and Regional Sustainable Human Development from a Gender Perspective', at which representatives of 'women and planning' groups from a range of European countries spoke. For example a presentation was given by German delegates (Spitzner, 1998) who are part of the Frauen Umwelt Netz (FUN, 1998) (women and environment network), which is concerned with many of the same issues that preoccupy British women planners. Similar groups, are nowadays to be found across the globe as was manifest at the Habitat II conference in Istanbul (1996) at which the Turkish women's architects group ran a series of meetings, with representatives from other Mediterranean and Middle East women planners' groups contributing (Shariff, 1996; Nisancioglu and Greed (1996).

Such networks was previously established in Paris at a foundational conference held at the OECD in 1994, where significantly the Italians acted as key facilitators of change (Bianchini, 1998). Also many European women feel much more at ease with specifically European urban feminist ideas, than North American feminism. The latter was invaluable in the 1970s and 1980s in establishing foundational texts, networks, and theories (cf. Hayden, 1984 and others detailed above). But the differences between US and EU cities, class systems, national cultures, and gender structures often proved mutually incomprehensible. Nevertheless many of the 'women and planning' movements are multi-ethnic in membership, thus benefiting from cross-cultural perspectives on planning issues.

Central Government

Top down organizations such as the Lottery, Millennium Fund, Sports Council, and Arts Council exist outside and separate from the construction and built environment world. But they have higher powers to require higher accessibility and design standards in buildings than are found under 'normal' legislation in respect of 'what is built' and 'who ' is building it (Arts Council, 1996). Thus a new form of social town planning initiative has developed within the world of arts and media funding. Voluntary bodies, representing minority groups are likely to be among the beneficiaries of their grants, thus enabling them to produce exemplar schemes in terms of both design and employment practice. This creates fusion between top down and bottom up groups, which should, in theory, generate change.

Government initiatives such as the Foresight programme (Department of Trade and Industry) and Partners in Technology (Department of Transport, Regions and the Environment); working groups including CISC (1994), Latham (CIB, 1996) and Egan (1998); and a range of research projects have all highlighted the need for cultural change within the construction industry and related built environment professions. Reasons for change variously include 'the business case'; increased efficiency of industrial processes within the industry; health and safety considerations; greater competitiveness; recruitment crises; European harmonization; down-sizing; multi-tasking; greater flexibility; environmental, economic and social sustainability; improved human resource management; qualification rationalization; educational reform; urban renewal; urban regeneration, and the need for creating a climate of technological innovation, economic prosperity and progress.

Town planning, too, has got swept up in the demands for cost cutting, speedier planning, greater efficiency, constant audits, 'best value' service delivery, more privatization, CCT, and entrepreneurialism.

Within this climate non-profit making social considerations exist in an uneasy limbo. Many of the above initiatives adopt a generic approach, not 'disaggregating' the needs of different groups upon the basis of gender, race, age or other social differences. Thus minority initiatives, groups and key individuals remain 'invisible' to mainstream committees and outside of professional networks and terms of reference, when it comes to looking for new committee members, or seeking advice on equal opportunity policies.

Likewise higher education is having to show greater productivity, rationalization and efficiency, accompanied by a spate of modularization, standardization, semesterization, all within a strongly managerialist and arguably anti-academic ethos. In spite of all the activity and enthusiasm of minority groups, there is very little space left any more for subjects such as equal opportunities or urban sociology. According to recent research, students are lucky if they get one afternoon session in three years, even in ostensibly progressive, new universities. Feminist scholarship is not being 'woven' into the main literature of urban academia through citation, cross-referencing and recommended reading, to the extent one would have expected by now (Bodman, 1991). It seemed, from the author's research, that some senior men planners, both in education and practice, had never even heard of women's issues, or other minority demands, it was as if they were living in a separate world. But, I knew these issues were 'real' and that, in contrast, they had been taken on board by other majority and minority organizations, particularly outside the world of construction and the built environment. Clearly there is not an equal relationship between planners and planned, between community and professionals at any level.

Local Government

Human Resource Management

Local government still has a role to play, not only in planning policy, but also in terms of operating EO policy in employment practice, and also in providing training opportunities in construction and built environment related specialisms. There has been a decline in DLO (Direct Labour Organizations) which used to be likely helpful for women and other minorities providing them with support, training, and often the first opportunity for genuine employment in construction. Local Labour in Construction Initiatives, such as GLLiC (Greenwich) provide employment and information (LWMT, 1996), in association with major contractors and developments in the area, whilst providing liaison with training schemes and local small business initiatives. Getting people involved in construction may prove a route into getting them interested in town planning and wider urban policy. National Vocational Qualifications (NVQs) and General National Vocational Qualifications (GNVQs) at pre-degree level encompass a range of subject modules, and do not make the distinction between spatial and aspatial topics. They combine detailed construction modules, alongside more conceptual urban policy units. Such programmes are crucial in bringing the possibility of built environment education and qualification right into the community setting (Millward, 1998).

Planning Procedures

Planning for sustainability may provide space to plan for minority groups' needs too. Whilst, as stated, in the UK planners have prioritized the environmental dimension, in some other countries the social equality aspects are given greater emphasis. As stated, according to Brundtland (1987) and the subsequent Rio Declaration (Rio, 1992) sustainability comprises three components, social equality, economic self-sufficiency and environmental balance. Environment assessment, and the production of EU stipulated Environmental statements, in Britain has been applied strictly to deal primarily with physical, rather than social issues. In Scandinavia, for example, the environmental aspect is taken to have social and economic implications, including gender considerations (Skjerve, 1993, Eurofem, 1998).

Some London borough town planning departments make it a requirement of any major planning permission that under a 'Section 106 Agreement' certain equal opportunities measures and design features should be integrated in the development. As stated earlier, such measures have frequently been subject to legal challenge, as *ultra vires* that is 'outside the law'. In comparison a system of 'zoning bonusing' in some North American states operates in a similar manner. Provision under such agreements might

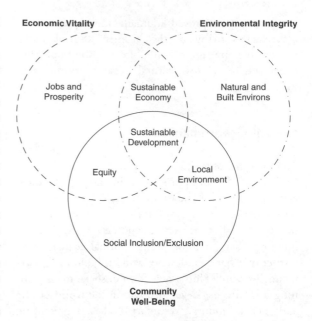

Figure 15.4 Circles of Sustainability.
The sustainability movement may yet provide the means to achieve social equality, economic fairness and environmental harmony to the advantage of all minorities (Brand, 1999).

include crèche and childcare provision (daycare) as part of the development; improved public facilities; improved access; and environmental improvements. Clearly the process of town planning is open to negotiation, because it is a highly political and financially-driven process being concerned with property, land and development rights. (Cullingworth and Nadin, 1996). It is unfortunate that, often, the only way to achieve high social planning goals is through such questionable dealing (Greed, 1994a).

BOTTOM UP CHANGE AGENTS

Satellite Organizations

Far from altering the culture of built environment professions, one result of increased access by women, ethnic minority individuals, disabled practitioners, and other outsiders has been the development of a series of new satellites circling 'Planet Construction' with their own subcultures and organizational structures (Figure 15.1).

Significant groups include the Centre for Accessible Environments (disability group); Planning Aid for London (PAL); London Planning Aid Service (LPAS); London Women and the Manual Trades (LWMT, 1996); London Regeneration Network (LRN); Society of Black Architects (SOBA); Age Concern (Gilroy, 1999); and Women's Design Service (WDS, 1997). These groups may be seen as potential prime movers for change, albeit, effectively 'outside' the mainstream (cf. Kanter, 1977, 1983: 296) but 'containing' minority construction professionals.

Many minority professionals who have entered the mainstream professions have not progressed as they might have wished, and may feel marginalized into low status areas of work. New satellite groupings have developed in response to a sense of being unwelcome and undervalued. Many of the people in such influential satellite groups are strongly socially motivated, but they are not all necessarily town planners. Rather they are likely to include other built environment professionals, such as engineers; pressure group representatives very often of the minority group themselves such as disabled; and/or community group residents.

Those actively involved are admittedly quite small in number but they may be seen as a force for change in that they form part of a powerful network of alternative groups, they are often highly productive in publication, research and campaigning. Furthermore, the organizations they run offer a model of alternative management structures, which are often based on a more co-operative, inclusive attitude towards employees at all levels, and a greater level of the communication with 'society' particularly when their 'client' is the community, or a disadvantaged or under-represented minority group. Whilst it may be argued these organizations are not commercial enterprises and therefore irrelevant as models for the construction industry, yet their ability to achieve a great deal with limited resources shows they have a respect for the 'cost factor' and for efficiency, economy, and flatter management structures, which might be emulated. One often finds among women's groups a complete lack of the social division between manual trades and professional levels found in the mainstream industry.

Pan-Professional Networks

Whilst the world of town planning had, arguably, become inured to the demands of the minority groups, a range of dynamic minority organizations has emerged within the other built environment professions. For example, a pan-professional Equal Opportunities Task Force has been developed to represent the needs of women and other minorities in construction. In parallel the construction industry gave more mainstream attention to under-representation of minorities (CIOB, 1995; CIB, 1996). Black and other ethnic minority professionals are now active across a range of construction specialisms, seeking to shift the balance to create a more inclusive environment, including the Society of Black Architects (SOBA). An individual professional may belong to more than one minority group in terms of gender, race, class, age and culture. Attempts are also being made to record and monitor construction industry statistics in such a way that this diversity is acknowledged (Kirk-Walker, 1997; SOBA, 1997). SOBA is seeking to encourage and mentor more young black architects and to develop networks, as so often black professionals are excluded when it comes to offers of jobs and contracts (Graft-Johnson, 1999).

There is often an emphasis in such groups upon passing the 'knowledge' down to the next generation, for example, through mentoring schemes (SOBA, 1997), and through work shadowing programmes for young women surveyors and construction managers. In those branches of the built environment professions where private practice predominates, black professionals and contractors have set up alternative business networks (cf. Grant, 1996; Harrison and Davies, 1995). Black built environment professionals have set up a range of network groups, to raise the 'visibility' of all black practices and individual practitioners, to counter further 'assimilation' or 'exclusion' (SOBA, 1997).

Inside the world of construction, inter-professional groups such as the Construction Careers Forum, minority pan-professional groups such as the Equal Opportunities Taskforce, and the sensitive efforts of 'exceptional' contractors are all contributing to change. Such groups can act as transmitters and pathways to channel beneficial external influences into the mainstream. Bodies and groups representing minority groups within the professions, but strongly linked to 'bottom up' groups within the community might act as conduits through which change might flow. But this cannot be done on the cheap without support and resources, and many minority groups are weary of being expected, single-handed, to change the industry with little support from the industry.

Community Groups

Community, voluntary and minority groups have a role in the planning process. In discussing the development process the role of public participation and community involvement was highlighted (in Chapter 3). Such groups may also act as change-agents, albeit in an adversarial capacity. Many planning decisions are criticized by the general public, and that minority groups in particular often find that their needs appear not to be taken into account in the planning and design processes. In this process some members of the general public act as quasi-professionals, as leaders, and spokespersons for change.

Community groups continue to battle the planners over traffic problems, parking, housing, local facilities, children's play areas, safety, crime, pedestrian rights, cyclists needs, and the problems of public transport. Some groups have become highly effective, and respected such as Friends of the Earth, whilst others have remained marginalized, such as ethnic minority community groups. Liaison between powerful community groups and minority practitioners with an alternative perspective can generate powerful forces for change.

Changing the Majority?

A key question to ask is, 'what is wrong with the built environment professions, and especially with planning?' rather than 'what is wrong with minority groups for not wanting to enter these professions?'. The unattractive aspects of the built environment professions which put women off, appear to put other minorities off too. Whilst the professions want 'more women and ethnic minorities' there seems to be little concern about the likely changes that increased minority representation would bring and demand (CIB, 1996).

Clearly 'more' minorities does not necessarily mean 'better' in respect of policy priorities, and human resource management, unless fundamental cultural and organizational change also occurs within the profession (Greed, 1988).

Some ethnic minority parents, particularly those originally from the Indian subcontinent, are unhappy about their children going into this field when it is considered they could do 'better' and enter law, accountancy or pharmacy instead. Other young people may prefer areas where there are existing role models and a substantial number of other minority students, such as for example electronics, media studies, and business studies. Others may feel committed to continue the family business. For example, of the 300,000 people of Bangladeshi origin in Britain, over 90 per cent own or work in 'Indian' restaurants and takeaways, and many will have had 'trouble with the planners'. Catering may be seen as either a low status occupation or a potentially high class entrepreneurial business, but at least it is familiar territory. In comparison planning has still got a dull local government municipal image which may well put people off who are used to a more entrepreneurial family culture.

As shown in Chapter 14, there are very few black town planners male or female and it has been acknowledged by the RTPI that this may affect the nature of town planning policy (RTPI, 1983 written in conjunction with CRE). It is a fundamental 'social aspects' question, as to whether white, male, middle class town planners possess sufficient professional neutrality and understanding to plan equally well for the needs of the rest of the population who are not like themselves; this being a particularly sensitive issue in inner city ethnic areas. In fact there has been much criticism suggesting that the town planners cannot do so. This first came out particularly strongly in the inquiry following the 'race riots' in Brixton, in South London in 1982, when Lord Scarman attributed much of the blame to the planners (Scarman, 1982). The area had become run down and subject to planning blight as a result of indecision and insensitivity on the part of the planners regarding the future development of the area. Planners are an easy target to blame and many would argue that other public bodies such as the education authority, police, social services also contributed to the situation.

Creating Fusion

Building up a 'critical mass' of minority groups and individuals within the industry is not enough on its own. There is a need for empowering linkages to be made between external minority 'bottom up' groups and 'top down' change agent bodies. Bringing these two groups of bodies together (to continue the nuclear physics analogy) will generate fusion and create a chain reaction which will change the culture construction. This fusion might occur inside or outside the structures of the built environment professions.

Creating actual, as against nominal, cultural change is difficult. New *ad hoc* 'social planning' initiatives, such as the Single Regeneration Budget programmes and Housing Association schemes, have created new possibilities for involvement of local people and professionals on specific building projects, with inevitable cultural clashes and re-education on both sides (WDS, current). A range of controversial 'top down' urban renewal schemes in inner London has created tremendous levels of community involvement and 'bottom up' response, potentially creating 'fusion'.

Such schemes include the King's Cross development site and the 'Guinness Site' (Gargoyle Wharf) in Wandsworth (both in London) where demands have been made for the use of local labour, designers and planning ideas. All this may be a major headache for those managing the development process but it is a sign of the desire of ordinary people to be more involved in built environment and construction matters, and as a result, some of them, or their children (or mothers), may want to enter the built environment professions as a career. Also such schemes provide a setting for planners and planned to become more aware of each others' culture and priorities, as part of an ongoing learning process.

Participation or Political Power?

Public consultation does not ensure that minorities will have a voice in the decision-making process. There is a strong gender dimension to the whole public participation and community involvement debate in planning, 'community' often being defined, by default, as 'really' meaning, women and children, ethnic minorities, and inner city and working class people. These are the very people in society who are unlikely to be in on the decision making process in the first place as members of that dominant middle class group from which planners derive.

Organizations such as Planning Aid provide individuals and communities with assistance 'against' the planners, and to put forward positive alternatives to planning proposals (Parkes, 1996). Some, however, have not given up faith in the existing system, and have sought to develop new forms of public participation, and involvement of the general public in the planning process, breaking down the 'them and us' syndrome. Traditionally the public has been invited to comment upon the proposals in a new development plan before their adoption and their views will be sought through public meetings, exhibitions and questionnaires. The process has been much criticized as it may only attract the more articulate. No real choice of policy may be on offer. Much depends on what questions are asked, and what issues are seen to be relevant to the planning process.

Some local authorities have pioneered more meaningful, long-term programmes of consistently working with minority groups in the community, in schools and with voluntary organizations, 'teaching' the participants about how the planning system works and discussing policy alternatives with them, until after several months they are in a better position to participate constructively in the planning process – in contrast to the 'hit and run' approach of one-off participation exercises.

Yet, the majority of the politicians, including members of parliament at central government level and councillors at the local government level, like the planners are men. Women's low representation in planning committees at the local council level must affect the nature of urban decision making. There are still relatively few women chief planning officers are female (Nadin and Jones, 1990). Many of the recent initiatives introduced by New Labour potentially give space for more integration of women's issues, and the inclusion of a wide range of other social planning issues (Greed, 1999b). But concern has been expressed, as stated earlier, that gender and race do not figure strongly on the agenda. Women and ethnic minorities are under-represented on the managing boards of the various *ad hoc* committees that have been set up to deal with urban issues, and which are such a feature of New Labour's approach to urban governance. For example, it would seem that neither gender nor race have fully been included in the ambit of the 'New Deal for Communities' programme (Darke and Brownill, 1999). Likewise the current 'Audit Culture' with its emphasis upon Best Value, quality assessments, and 'reality checks', barely leaves space for issues of equality (Thomas and Piccolo, 1999), although, ostensibly the purpose is to provide a better service to the citizen.

Some 'women and planning' groups are highly suspicious of the *ad hoc* Lottery approach to funding which is based upon competition, rather than comprehensive long term policy, and which may yet prove temporary. But, black groups may still be excluded even when other community groups are getting recognition, particularly when it comes to 'architectural competitions' for new schemes. Many are critical of the perceived racism of some housing associations who put black women professionals on their management committee, because it looks good, but never actually use black professionals in construction projects (Harrison and Davies, 1995).

Community-related groups such as Planning Aid for London and London Regeneration Network (LRN, 1997), *inter alia*, have sought to monitor quite 'who' is asked on to key committees, and, unsurprisingly, have found that many key *ad hoc* 'social

***Figure 15.6* High Volume Public Transport Provision.**
Japanese tram: global changes in transport patterns and personal mobility cultures are occurring. To be sustainable emphasis is put upon the growth of public transport rather than private car ownership.

planning' agencies, such as regional committees, urban regeneration boards, and housing steering groups have remained white and male in composition, in spite of the influx of so many new minority professionals, particularly in London. Many of the new urban regeneration programmes and major research studies barely mention gender, although they are nowadays more likely to mention ethnicity than class as a key policy factor.

Clearly a sustained and serious programme of social inclusion would, with time, turn the tide and transform the nature of the built environment. But whether the chief agent to achieve this process will be statutory town planning is another matter altogether. As explained in earlier chapters many 'planning' functions are undertaken by other government departments nowadays. New Labour has created a whole range of *ad hoc* committees to deal with different issues, separate from local planning departments. Indeed 'town planning' is seen by many as a rather old-fashioned concept, a temporary container for the promotion of urban policy in the post-war era which has now been superseded by a wider environmental planning and by a range of urban governance bodies. Also, as explained in the final chapter the organization, process and theoretical basis of modern planning has changed. In conclusion governments will still seek to deal with

***Figure 15.5* Islam and Tourism: Singapore.**
The growth of religion in many parts of the world may itself generate social, urban and cultural change and in turn create new townscapes and land-use patterns.

urban problems and issues in the future, but whether those undertaking this tasked will be called 'town planners' or even 'planners' is open to debate.

TIME PLANNING

Entirely different approaches to planning such as time planning might yield better cities and social change. The British planning system has been obsessed with utilizing spatial, land-use control as a means of ordering cities and dealing with urban problems. (*Planning*, Greed, 1997c), another form of planning which derived from Italy, namely 'time planning' is discussed, which is, arguably, more sensitive to cultural issues. Arguably, many the problems which confront modern cities are not primarily spatial in nature, but are generated by the way time is organized and divided up for different uses and activities, – that is they are temporal rather than purely physical.

Lack of temporal organization results in functional inefficiency. Socially, many people, especially parents with caring responsibilities, find it extremely difficult (temporally and spatially) to get their children to school and themselves to work in the morning, or to undertake simple tasks like going to the Post Office, or undertaking all the other 'little things' that are so undervalued in our society but are essential to existence, such as, variously, getting to the shoe-repairer, dry cleaner, library, vet, dentist and library. These problems particularly affect women because of their different roles. They also affect shift-workers, night-workers, and therefore especially ethnic minorities who are more likely to work in catering, social care and service sector industries.

Many of these problems could be ameliorated by the introduction of Time Planning, following the example of several European cities. This should NOT be confused with the currently trendy, and arguably male, concept of the '24 hour city' for leisure purposes (Montgomery, 1994). The full range of possibilities and perspectives are discussed in a special issue on 'Emplois du Temps' in *Les Annales de la Recherche Urbaine* (ARU, 1997).

Italian planners pioneered time planning (Belloni, 1994), Local government reforms, introduced in 1990 (under Article 36, 142/1990), gave elected city mayors the powers to formulate 'time plans' in association with business and school representatives, and to 'change hours' that is to rationalize the efficiency and convenience of the times of opening of shops, schools, places of work and public services. These time reforms have been the result of pressure from feminist politicians, sociologists and planners many of whom have links with the Democratic Party of the Left (Bianchini, 1998, 1999). There have also been 'time planning trials' in North European countries, especially Germany (Henckel, 1996). Women in Germany have pressed for many years for reform of shop opening hours which are some of the earliest closing in Europe. Also women planners in Germany have found that the Green Movement, (and sustainability initiatives in general) has been particularly supportive of both gender issues and time planning (Spitzner, 1998). Currently there are moves to integrate time planning principles into EU planning directives.

Many of the principles of time planning might be applied in Britain too. A Temporal Master Plan would go towards solving many of the problems of childcare, 'latchkey kids', stress, congestion and impossible schedules in our cities. The Office of National Statistics is undertaking a 'Time Use Survey', for the first time as part of a Eurostat EU wide time study, based on a national sample of participants filling in a 24 hour diary. Women in London more than 20 years ago advocated co-ordination of all office, factory, shop, public building, transportation and school hours within the GLC women's committee. The introduction the European Work Time Directive provisions from 1998 has made time a topical issue for discussion. Arguably the time is right, and the new Greater London Authority will consider the value of time planning as well as spatial planning.

Other future factors include particular the impact of telecommunications, the internet, and thus telecommuting (Graham and Marvin, 1996) is an area to keep an eye on for the future. Claims that telecommuting, that is working from home using a modem link, will render rush hour traffic jams and central area business districts redundant are arguably overstated. Whether the Internet, e-mail and related modem-based computer communication systems are really going to alter the nature of towns and cities is open to debate. At present, in Britain at least, downloading time is extremely slow and expensive. Ordinary people used to the immediacy of the television and telephone are not impressed by the expense, delays, and unreliability of using e-mail and the web. Working from home is not necessarily an ideal solution for women seeking to combine work and home responsibilities. It may degenerate into a modern version of home piece-working. The much vaunted 'flexibility' ascribed to such an arrangement is arguably all on the side of the employer rather than the employee.

At present a minority of people use such computer-based communication systems at home. Only around 5 per cent are regularly tele-commuting by modem it is estimated. But, technological advances and attempts to make systems more user-friendly are progressing by leaps and bounds. Parallels may be drawn with the growth of television ownership. Television broadcasts were first made available to the general public in 1936. At first ownership was limited to the rich or technically minded. Less than 1 million people owned sets immediately after the World War II, whereas today ownership is widespread. Future technological changes further alter women's and men's working patterns and way of life. But if these are to benefit women, there is a need for parallel cultural changes in attitudes both within society and the built environment professions.

TASKS

Information Gathering Tasks

I. Visit a town centre shopping centre at 11 am, 1 pm, 4.30 pm and in the evening. Who are the main shoppers, men or women? Can you give an approximate percentage of each? Do the same for an out of town hypermarket.

II. Check the current activities of the organizations mentioned above under 'Further Reading'.

Conceptual and Discursive Task

III. To what extent do global trends and international policy influences affect British Town Planning? Discuss, illustrating your answer with examples where relevant.

Reflective Task

III. What are the main social issues of relevance that you personally consider planners need to take on board? These may include ones which have not be mentioned, for example the needs of young people, housing problems, student loans and professional education.

IV. What do you see as the future of 'planning'?

FURTHER READING

For material on the change in the construction industry and the related built environment professions Gale, Egan, Druker, Latham, Bagihole. Also check the publications and activities of the many minority organizations mentioned including SOBA, LRN, WDS, LWMT, WCED.

Material on the global situation, in terms of population movement, sustainability policies and other international trends may be obtained from organizations such as OECD, United Nations, UNESCO, WHO, Oxfam, and other governmental and non-governmental organizations.

For material on time planning see Bianchini, Belloni, Eurofem, Henckel, and ARU.

16

PLANNING THEORY
IN RETROSPECT

THEORETICAL PERSPECTIVES

The Importance of Studying Theory

The purpose of Chapter 16 is to identify the theoretical perspectives that have shaped the scope and nature of planning. The first half of the chapter discusses theory and introduces the reader to the related field of research. The shifting paradigms within underlying academic theory are investigated. In the second half of the chapter the story of planning is re-run from the Industrial Revolution to the present day, in order to reflect upon theoretical perspectives which informed planning in each main epoch. This section provides a concluding summary of the story of planning up to the present day. Inevitably the final parts of this chapter contain discursive commentary and personal analysis on the present day situation. However, such is the nature of planning it is always controversial and generates a range of responses. Studying theory increases awareness of the factors that have shaped the social construction of town planning, thus facilitating a more informed and balanced approach towards understanding and evaluating the various manifestations of policy and practice. Therefore readers are encouraged to interact with the text and develop their own conclusions on the story of planning. The concluding section returns the reader to a consideration of substantive policy issues as the planning problems of our towns and cities are yet to be solved.

The Scope of Planning Theory and Related Research

Planning theory is an elastic term which may be used to describe a variety of intellectual activities. At its broadest studying 'planning theory' involves thinking about some very general questions about the nature of town and country planning, such as 'what is town planning?', 'what are the skills that are needed to practice town planning?', 'what should town planning be trying to achieve?' and 'what effect has town planning had on cities and society?' (Taylor, 1998). More specifically, 'theory' from the Greek, 'thereo' 'I see', may be defined as the way in which 'planning' is seen, and understood. Dictionary definitions of 'theory' include, 'the systematic organization of knowledge in a particular subject'; 'a system of principles, assumptions and rules of procedure devised to analyse, predict, and explain a set of phenomena'; 'abstract principles and speculation'; and 'a set of ideas or beliefs which form the basis of action'. Many dictionaries make the distinction between 'conceptual theory' being based upon 'abstract conceptualization and conjecture' as against 'empirical theory' which is based upon 'gathering data through experimentation, observation and applying scientific methods'.

In the case of a 'practical' subject such as town planning, it might be assumed that 'theory' is more likely to be based upon empirical study and tied into planning practice. On the contrary, much of the theory produced is conceptual, rather than empirical in nature. Yet because planning is a policy-based subject in practice, guidance arising from planning research may be strongly 'normative' too, that is it prescribes what planning 'ought to be' doing. Thus planning theory contains empirical, conceptual and normative aspects.

In a subject area where there is still an emphasis upon technical expertise, 'standards' and 'law', there is a need for planners to develop an appreciation of the process of the creation of theory, and the role of academic research in this process, in order to be able to judge and weigh the significance of new theory, and validity of the research upon which it is based. It is important, therefore, to understand the epistemology of planning, that is 'the nature and origin of knowledge'. Undertaking an undergraduate dissertation is a valuable step in this process (Bell, 1996; Bell and Newly, 1980).

Much practice-related research, particularly statistical research related to the preparation of surveys and forecasts in the plan-making process, is 'quantitative', that is concerned with investigating 'how many' 'what' and 'where'. In contrast 'qualitative' research is concerned not only with 'what' but 'why' and 'who in particular', that is with understanding, and 'making sense of' the social forces which shape reality (Silverman, 1985; Miles and Huberman, 1996). Modern planning theory and research draws upon both quantitative and qualitative sources. But, there has been much questioning of the objectivity of policy decisions which were based upon quantitative research that has ignored the needs of minority groups. Such incomplete data provided a shaky foundation for planning policy making (as discussed in Chapter 11). It is important when reading about theories of society and cities to consider who and what is included in and out of the terms of reference.

Professional decision-making, and academic theory-making, are not socially-neutral processes. They are influenced by how the participants in these processes 'see' the world and how they imagine society and the city ought to be. This issue has been developed in detail in earlier work on the surveying and planning professions (Greed, 1991: 5–6; Greed, 1994b; Greed, 1999a). These studies are examples of qualitative research, which investigated the subcultural values of built environment professionals, and thus their perceptions of reality. Primarily qualitative methods were used, including ethnography as a means of getting below the surface. Ethnography is based on observing the culture of the various construction

'tribes', and seeking to understand their perception of 'reality', not least how they see 'others' who are unlike themselves (Hammersley and Atkinson, 1999).

As can be seen, planning research covers a wide range of different types of activities and uses a range of methodologies. Planners, and indeed planning theorists, are not unitary groups, but include a great diversity of individuals and 'schools of thought'. But there is not necessarily one dominant form of planning current at any one time, there may be many 'plannings' co-existing, each with their own heroes, theories, ways of doing things and social allegiances. Thus, for example, in the 1970s, neo-Marxist planning theorists, traditional urban design planners, pro-market planners and community advocacy planners could all be accommodated under the umbrella of 'planning'.

Yet, there always appear to be certain groups of local authority planners who seem to be completely oblivious to all this intellectual turmoil all around them. They carry on 'planning' and operating the development control system as they think best, unaware of the fact that their actions and decisions might be seen by some academic researchers as manifestations of a particular theoretical approach to planning. There is often a gulf between academic planners who attend planning theory conferences and read the related literature (Sheffield, 1999) and those who operate the planning system at the local government level. Nevertheless, nowadays, all those who wish to become planners must study at least some planning theory, and it is hoped that more reflective and reflexive practitioner is emerging who is more aware and conscious of the implications of professional policies upon society (Schon, 1995; Hillier, 1999).

Textbox 16.1   Key Dualisms in Planning Theory

Empirical/Conceptual
Empirical/Normative
Causal/Normative
Substantive/Procedural
Definitional/Critical
Quantitative/Qualitative
Spatial/Aspatial
Theories *in* (for) Planning/Theories *of* Planning

Definitions of Planning Theory

Planning theory may be construed to refer to the theories, political ideologies and philosophies which have sought to define the function, role and nature of planning and planners within society and the economy. Secondly 'planning theory' may more broadly be construed to include all the theories which have shaped planning policy (Fainstein, 1999). Planning theory has been influenced by concepts from a wide range of academic subject realms. The planning discourse may be seen as a hall of mirrors reflecting back a range of theories coming from outside the subculture (cf. Greed, 1996b, Chapter 1; and Hobbs, 1996) including geography, economics, sociology, philosophy and science. Such theories have both increased planners' understanding of the urban phenomenon but have also often been highly critical of planning policy. Those theories that have arisen from ideological movements and minority groups, such as environmentalism, or feminism have been particularly critical in their condemnation of planning and planners.

Before proceeding, a distinction must be made between 'theories *for* planning', also described as 'theories *in* planning' which have been developed by planners in order to facilitate 'better' planning, and secondly 'theories *of* planning' which have been developed by non-planners from a more critical and analytical perspective as described above (Faludi, 1973).

A further division must be made between those theories which are concerned with substantive planning policy issues, that is with the substance and content of planning; and procedural theories which is concerned with the way that planning is carried out (Thornley, 1991; Brindley *et al.*, 1996). Procedural planning is concerned with the process of planning, with the changing organizational structures which are used to deliver planning, and the skills required to operate the planning system, that is to be a planner.

The theory of planning is concerned with the nature and role of planning that is with the question 'what is town planning?', that is *definitional* or *explanatory* theory. This is frequently followed by the more critical question 'what is wrong with town planning?', that is *critical* theory. This leads to the question of 'what should be the aims of town planning?' that is planning theory also embraces the issue of 'how

to plan' and 'how to plan "better"', that is *normative* theory which is concerned with how things ought to be. In contrast *causal* theory is concerned with explaining 'why' planning is as it is now.

KEY THEORETICAL QUESTIONS

What is Planning?

This question is both definitional and substantive. Most of the categories of types of planning identified by commentators fall either into the spatial or aspatial category (Foley, 1964), as explained in Chapter 1. Spatial matters are those concerned with physical land use and development. Aspatial matters are those social, economic, managerial and political forces and decisions which generate the need for development in the first place and which shape 'what is built'. Much of post-war planning has been dealing with the spatial 'end product' that is with the built environment, rather than with more radical policy concerned with shaping the forces that determine the nature of the built environment in the first place (Massey, 1984).

Healey identifies three main types of planning (Healey, 1997: Chapter 1, page 11). These are physical development planning, economic planning, and thirdly urban governance. Thus she identifies one spatial and two aspatial types of planning. Arguably, her first two categories are defined by the substantive nature of the planning undertaken and her third category is defined in relation to procedural approaches to planning. Much of British planning has been and remains spatial in character.

Second, Healey identifies state-led economic planning. Although aspatial in its objectives, for example 'to reduce unemployment' this form too, has generally had a spatial emphasis. Policy has been developed with reference to the perceived needs of different areas, especially in respect of 'depressed regions' and 'the inner city'. Economic planning has generally been concerned with state intervention within a mixed economy situation, and has been primarily favoured by Labour governments.

Third, Healey argues, planning has been construed as a management tool, as a form of urban governance, that is as an aspatial process. In this procedural perspective on planning, the substantive, policy

	ASPATIAL	SPATIAL
19th century to Pre-WWII	Utopian ideals, model towns, Garden cities, and suburbs communitarianism.	Sewers and drains, Town planning schemes, council housing estates, Municipal surveying and building.
	Regional economic planning of depressed industrial areas. State planning in Soviet Europe.	European Grand Manner style, squares, boulevards, urban design Planning as 'Big Architecture'.
Post-war Reconstruction Planning 1945–1960	Creation of Welfare State, introducing the 'planning' of health, housing, education, the economy, and land. Manifested in Regional Economic planning, Nationalisation of land values, Community planning and control in the New Towns.	Physical land use planning, zoning. Master plans especially Development Plans. 'Solving' housing problem and urban social problems by building new towns, slum clearance, design of neighbourhoods, emphasis on environmental determinism.
1960s	Move towards strategic aspatial planning, systems view, planning concerned with rational scientific Processes and managment. Use of new computers and models.	Continuation of development plan and development control systems in local authorities. Central area redevelopment, new housing, urban motorway construction.
1970s	Planner as neo-Marxist, élite controller, growth of planning schools and academic theorists But growth of theories of planning for gender, disability, community and ethnicity.	Continuation of statutory planning as above. Last throws of regional area planning under Old Labour. Inner city initiatives, continuation of road programme.
1980s	New Right, enterprise planning, entrepreneurialism, market theory, European Union policy, economic globalization.	Ecological movement, global environmentalism. Practical physical outworkings affecting planning, LA21, ESS, EIA.
1990s	New Labour, continuation of much of above, but emphasis upon collaborative, communicative theory, diversity and culture	Renaissance of urban design but with greater user emphasis, Disability access design, traffic calming, anti-transport planning.

N.B. The boxes show broadly the aspatial manifestations on the left and the spatial on the right. But some aspects overlap or do not fit. There is often a gulf between what planning theory said planners should be doing and the form that planning took. The sequence of boxes is chronological, with time frame broadly indicated alongside.

Figure 16.1 **Planning: Spatial or Aspatial?**

content is secondary. Planning is a management tool aimed at increasing efficiency, equally applicable to large private sector organizations and to government agencies and public administration departments Healey (1997) stresses that importance should be given to policy analysis and to the process of planning, in achieving effectiveness and efficiency, for example, within the context of goals set by public administration bodies.

Rydin provides a similar taxonomy and adds that environmental 'green' planning has become another major category of British town planning in recent years (Rydin, 1998). It is argued this has been 'tamed' and incorporated within the spatial tradition of British planning, in spite of the fact that internationally sustainability is concerned with environmental, social and economic criteria. One might argue that social town planning is also a specific type of planning

(Greed, 1999b). Urban design may be seen to be another distinct type of planning. Both urban design and social town planning combine spatial and aspatial components. Their supporters, especially those concerned with women's rights, disability issues, and anti-racist measures, have stressed the need for practical, spatial outworkings of policy implementation rather than majoring on theoretical abstractions associated with earlier more esoteric incarnations of social town planning The situation is complex. There are many 'plannings' combining a variety of procedural and substantive components. The author has previously stated that planning can be defined as 'anything you want it to be' (Greed, 1994b), in order to draw attention to the diversity and chameleon-like changeability of planners uncovered during research on the last 200 years of town planning.

What is the Relationship between Planning and Politics?

Before revisiting the story of planning it is important to establish the limits to the role and power of the planner and planning. A distinction must be made between what a planner actually is and can do within the British system, and what a planner might 'be' and 'should do' as portrayed within planning theory. Thus definitional realities and normative aspirations must be distinguished. Whilst, the political system gives the planners a measure of power to put planning theory into practice through policy-making, the ultimate power resides with the politicians, for planning is a political process as stated in Chapter 1.

To recap planning is political for three main reasons. First, in summary, planning is political because it is concerned with controlling property and land, and therefore with money and power. Therefore, it is inevitably a highly political activity, inextricably linked with the prevailing economic system, and with the allocation of scarce resources (Simmie, 1974). Second, it is political as it has become a component of the agenda of national party politics and political ideology (Montgomery and Thornley, 1990; Tewdwr-Jones, 1996). Third, the planning process is extremely political at the local area plan level, where community politics and grass roots activity thrives, and where individual personalities, especially councillors, exert influ-

ence over planning decisions. Planners operate the statutory framework as an arm of the bureaucracy of government and therefore it is inevitably political.

In comparison Rydin gives the following three reasons for viewing planning as political (Rydin, 1998, p. 6). First, it is concerned with the allocation of scarce resources, especially land and the right to develop, and thus it can alter land values, and the cost of development. She comments that the recent introduction of environmental legislation that requires the polluter to pay for cleaning up contamination has in itself repoliticized planning, at a time when New Right, and subsequently New Labour, attitudes towards traditional planning control have become more lenient. Second, she argues that it is political because it involves struggle and negotiation between conflicting interest groups, such as developers, environmentalists and local communities. Third, she argues planning is political because it is shaped by ideology. The operation of the planning system is influenced by the perspectives of the government in power, and by power politics at the local government level. Planning is a public sector activity seeking to regulate and control the activities of businesses, households and citizens.

As to political context it may broadly be stated that planning has received more support under Labour governments than under Conservative governments but with the proviso that different types and topics within the planning agenda have been favoured by successive administrations for a variety of reasons. At any one time wider political influences and movements are at work within society and academia, shaping planning theory, which do not necessarily correspond in perspective to the political party which won the last general election, particularly at the local level.

There are new political movements that are not necessarily contained within traditional party politics, but which are reshaping planning. Green politics, and the related environmental movement, challenges both capitalist and socialist politics. They are both based upon non-sustainable attitudes to the earth's resources, both being obsessed with production and consumption. Likewise feminist theorists and activists have questioned the patriarchal nature of all mainstream party politics. The situation is confused by the use of jargon and shorthand terms in the media to describe different factions, such as Old Labour, New Labour, New Left, New Right, Third Way, *inter alia*. These labels by no means encompass the diversity, contradictions, unexpected allegiances, and individual alliances that are likely to manifest themselves in response to a major planning conflict at local level. Planning theory purports to increase understanding of these very processes. Theory, like planning, is continually changing. Each new decade brings forth paradigmatic changes that reshape understanding of what theory is meant to be, and discredit those theories that went before. Before recounting the story of planning, key theoretical paradigms will be presented.

Paradigms and Paradigm Shifts

In each generation, it would seem that theory and philosophy undergo a 'paradigm shift' that is a major shift in theoretical perspectives, both across academia as a whole, and within the various subject areas such as town planning. In the field of town planning, there has been a series of paradigm shifts. Taylor highlights two shifts in particular, namely, from planning being a design discipline to a science in the 1960s, and from the planner being a technical expert and scientist to becoming a 'communicator' and negotiator in the 1980s (Taylor, 1998). Innes (1995) gives a seminal account identifying current paradigm shifts in planning.

A paradigm may be described as the prevailing, dominant set of theories and ideas that inform a subject area, and the term was originally derived from science (Kuhn, 1962). A paradigm shift describes the situation when existing paradigms are replaced by a completely new way of seeing things, that is when a seachange occurs (Taylor, 1998: chapter 9). Higher level shifts which are reshaping society and grand philosophical theory, include moves towards environmentalism, feminism and new ageism (Taylor, 1998; Guba, 1990; Guba and Lincoln, 1992; Hammersley, 1995), all of which are impacting upon the scope and nature of planning.

The term 'paradigm shift' should be used sparingly, so as not to devalue it. Not every change of fashion or new trend experienced within the town planning world is necessarily a paradigm shift. This is particularly so when the phenomenon in question does not replace the status quo, and when it is absorbed, and possibly marginalized, as an additional consideration rather than as dominant factor. As stated, planning is a very broad church that can accommodate many different 'plannings', all of which may be very important to their devotees, but few of which will lead to revolutionary change.

Western intellectual thought has itself undergone several paradigm shifts and these changes have been mirrored within the world of planning. Guba and Lincoln (1992) identify four main paradigms which have shaped the nature of the social sciences and indeed academia as a whole, these they define as Positivism, Post-positivism, Critical Theory and Constructivism. They also identify the main characteristics of each in terms of ontology, epistemology and methodology. To clarify, ontology refers to the researcher's conception of reality, that is his world view, that is, what does the researcher assume to be 'the real world?'. Epistemology is the study of the theory of knowledge, and refers to the ways in which the knowledge is gained, interpreted and organized. Methodology refers to the research process by which the research is undertaken. Elaborating on Guba and Lincoln, the four paradigms will now be described.

Positivism

Positivism ruled virtually from the Enlightenment to the late 1950s as the predominant paradigm. It emanated from the natural sciences and was subsequently adopted in the developing social sciences field in the nineteenth century. Ontologically the researcher acknowledged but 'one reality', which was essentially 'scientific' and presumed to be the right one. Epistemologically the positivist's research output consisted of 'findings' that 'proved' a particular hypothesis to be true or false. Or they provided the answer to a finite question or problem that had to be solved. Methodologically positivism was based upon the scientific method, using quantification, observation and experimentation. Emphasis was put upon 'hard facts', and upon maintaining objectivity and detachment in the research process. In the social sciences the researcher did research 'upon' the researched and maintained his distance from his 'subjects'. Positivism in Britain flourished along with Imperialism, national self-confidence and technological dominance, broadly across the period 1850–1950, when access to university, and thus to chances of becoming a theorist were limited, with few exceptions, to elite male academics.

Guba and Lincoln draw attention to the manipulative and deceitful nature of positivism. Any 'realities', 'facts', or so-called 'minority viewpoints' which did not tie in with the researcher's world-view were likely to be ignored or excluded as 'irrelevant' or 'unscientific'. In the social sciences the era of positivism co-incides with that of Grand Theory, of macro-level conceptualizations of society. All-embracing Victorian and Edwardian theories of society in which great emphasis was put on the importance of male social-class as the main determinant of the structure of society, as were underlying economic factors the main determinants of social change, these are both positivist in mentality and methodology.

Post-positivism

Post-positivism also assumes that 'reality' exists. But its adherents acknowledge that the researcher's comprehension of it is likely to be incomplete, because of the complexity of many natural and social phenomena, and imperfect knowledge. There is space for admitting the researcher does not known the answer, for acknowledgement of difference and inconclusiveness. Epistemologically post-positivists acknowledge that plain right/wrong answers to research questions are an over-simplification, but that, at least, a 'regulatory ideal' can be established by doing research. Thus experimentation and observation were intended to produce 'replicated findings' that suggest that a particular hypothesis is probably, generally true. Post positivists favour many of the traditional approaches used by positivists but intellectually they retain a more critical, even cynical perspective.

These days in the natural sciences, such a stance allows for acknowledgement of concepts such as relativity, fuzzy-logic, and other less-than-absolute theoretical perspectives. In the social sciences post-positivism allows for a more pluralistic perspective, and for a greater diversity of methodological approaches, both quantitative and qualitative. Thus the social researcher aims at 'empirical illumination of theoretical concepts' rather than 'proving hypotheses' as Cooke (1987) commented in respect of urban geographical research (Greed, 1991, Chapter 1). Such is the nature of macro sociological theory that is concerned with

causation that it may be unprovable, as Acker (1984: 36) points out with respect to the sociology of professional education. Much of today's research in the social sciences may be seen broadly to be 'post-positivist' and much of it falls beyond into the critical and constructivist categories. We live in a post-modernist, post-structuralist, and post-modernist academic world, in which difference, relativism, diversity, and uncertainty are key factors in the academic discourse as indicated in earlier chapters. Indeed to call someone a positivist is generally seen as a term of abuse. But much of the quantitative data gathering and 'number-crunching' undertaken in local planning authorities for the purposes of preparing reports of survey and analysis work in relation to the development plan process remains positivist, quantitative and traditional in approach.

Critical Theory

'Critical Theory' is a term used to refer to a range of subsequent theoretical perspectives, and 'isms' in the social sciences, all of which are post-positivist. This allows for an acknowledgement of the importance of a range of social, political, economic and cultural factors – including class, gender and race – in shaping 'reality'. It is acknowledged that a variety of 'realities' exist depending upon the perspective and position of the inquirer. Much critical theory questions received perceptions of 'reality' and the power relations within society which maintain such images. Marxist, feminist, and anti-racist perspectives *inter alia* are all critical theoretical perspectives, radical in their analysis of society and often demanding political action from their adherents. However, none of these 'isms' are unitary groups, they all contain a diversity of perspectives, some of which manifest symptoms of other paradigmatic perspectives. For example, feminist and socialist theorists have been criticized for 'essentialism' and 'positivism' in identifying macro-level structural factors such as 'patriarchy' or 'capitalism', respectively, as absolute determinants of 'oppression'.

Constructivism

Constructivism may be seen as the next stage along the hard/soft, positivist/post-positivist spectrum. It allows for the existence of multiple-realities and conceptualizations of society. There is space for the acknowledgement of the influence of micro-level

TRENDS	COMMENTARY
POSITIVISM	
Nineteenth-century surveys of urban conditions. Scientific approach to public health, disease, overcrowding.	In retrospect much of this may be seen as classists, and eugenic in approach. But also valuable urban infrastructure created.
Early urban sociological studies also based on the scientific methods. Comte and neutral, academic approach.	Utopian visionary ideals, of model communities also existed as basis of planning. Social policy as against sociology.
First half of twentieth century, growth of discipline of planning, 'survey, analysis, and plan', elitist scientific and spatial approach, impersonal methodology.	Planning was ideologically and politically laden, albeit planners may have been unaware of this being 'practical types'.
1960s systems planning is even more positivist and scientific in approach inspired by the Space Programme.	Planners out of step with rest of academia which is moving towards post-positivism by the late 1950s.
POST-POSITIVISM	
Within urban sociology in the 1960s move towards post-positivism.	Other types of urban sociology emerging more ethnographic, interactive, qualitative and sensitive.
Structure plans more flexible, setting objectives rather than absolute policies, realisation of uncertainty in predicting the future. More incremental approach.	Planning recognized as a political and imperfect process, in which there is no one right answer for everyone.
CRITICAL THEORY	
By 1970s urban conflict theory, and subsequently neo-Marxism theory took over, deterministic and objective in application, little space for alternatives.	Other critical theories impinging on planning, including feminism, anti-racism, social model of disability and environmentalism.
CONSTRUCTIVE THEORY	
Post-modernism, post-structuralist, emphasis upon small scale differences, culture, accepting multiplicity of views, Planning for diversity, communicative, collaborative, institutionalist approach to doing planning.	Much more yet to come, only at the start of all this. Need for change in the approach to survey, towards a more qualitative, reflexive approach, in the plan-making process, but this will increase the complexity of doing planning in the next Millennium.

Figure 16.2 Diagram of Paradigm Shifts in Planning Theory.

localized, individual, and subcultural factors in the shaping of realities, as well macro-level factors. Shifting changing realities and differing power-relations according to the situation are allowed for. Epistemologically emphasis is put upon interactive, subjective and transactional developments. The values and life-experiences of the researcher and researched, are not excluded from the research process but openly acknowledged and capitalized upon. Theories such as symbolic interactionism which is concerned with the details of human relationships and group formation fall into this category. However it may be argued that symbolic interactionism can be built into a macro-theory of society too (Blumer, 1965). Human inter-actions are seen as forming the building blocks of the edifice of society (Greed, 1991, chapter 2).

Greater emphasis is put upon interaction between and among researcher and researched, with acknowledgement that both are part of society themselves. Politically this potentially encourages the empowerment and valuing of the individual citizen. The researcher, may, as a spin-off of the research process, facilitate consciousness-raising and politicization among the researched. As will be explained, this movement parallels the trend towards collaborative, communicative approaches within the urban planning process and towards greater involvement of local people in the urban design process.

In fact a research project may incorporate aspects of all four approaches, and it is difficult, and arguably fruitless, to label research precisely. In seeking to 'place' a piece of research it may be more helpful to place it somewhere along the spectrum between positivist and constructivist, rather than trying to make a piece of research fit into only one compartment. Whilst the model of four key paradigms is helpful to a degree, if one seeks to categorize planning theories into just four paradigms it will be found that some theories fit easily into several paradigms at once, or are composed of a mixture of paradigmatic factors, and some scarcely fit at all. But, presenting such a schema is intended to help the reader become aware of underlying theoretical debates and trends. Thus in studying the following account of the evolution of planning theory in true post-positivist style the reader should be informed by the discussion of the four categories identified above, but not feel bound by it.

The reader may find it helpful to consider what main academic realm planning theory was drawing upon each decade. Planning theory has drawn strongly upon the following fields: design, geography, science, management, sociology, politics, environmentalism *inter alia*. To state a truism fashion tends to go in cycles and trends always come back into fashion if one waits long enough. Design, for example, is now coming back into fashion, and environmentalism is beginning to lose its appeal, perhaps to be replaced by a new more sociological form of planning based upon 'Third Way' communitarianism.

THE STORY OF PLANNING REVISITED

The story of planning will now be revisited in order to highlight theoretical underpinnings and the main paradigm shifts which have occurred using Guba and Lincoln's taxonomy. This section also provides a summary overview to the whole story of planning for revision purposes. In seeking to develop an understanding of 'theories in planning' and 'theories of planning' readers are advised to bear in mind the following questions, which are broadly covered in the text:

Textbox 16.2 Key Questions in Studying Planning Theory

What form did planning take at each stage of development, e.g. economic, physical social etc?

Who were the planners and what skills they were seen to need, e.g. architects, sociologists.

What theories and ideas informed planning? e.g. Marxism, market economics, sustainability?

Wat was the planners' view of 'reality', or ontology, at the time in question?

What function did planning perform? e.g. facilitating development, protecting the environment.

How was planning done? What organizational and procedural structures were required?

What were the implications for 'the real world' in terms of planning practice and policy?

Who were seen as the stakeholders and receivers, that is the 'planned'?

In summary planning theory is concerned with:

  Scope and nature of planning.
  Type of planners.
  Nature of planning theory.
  Nature of the planning process.
  Political context.
  View of reality.
  Nature of the societal context.
  Wider economic, social and cultural trends.

The Nineteenth and Early Twentieth Century

The Industrial Revolution, and the accompanying urbanization and population growth in the nineteenth century precipitated the development of modern town planning and related state intervention and organizational structures. Embryonic town planning was closely linked to the public health and housing reform movements. Ideologically and politically the early town planning initiators was motivated by a range of liberal and reformist principles. The Liberal reforming governments headed by Gladstone in the second half of the century, introduced a foundational range of housing, planning and public health acts. The local government reform movement was strongly linked to concepts of citizenship and civic pride, epitomized, for example, in Manchester, and other major civic centres, in 'gas and water socialism'.

The late nineteenth century and early twentieth century may be characterized as an era when spatial planning predominated, and planning was conceptualized as urban design, or simply as 'Big Architecture' (Greed and Roberts, 1998). Emergent planning theory, such as it was, may be characterized as being positivist in character, and planning itself appeared relatively crude and simplistic in its understanding of complex urban forces. Theoretically, the early movement can be seen as being focused around the powers of environmental determinism, that is 'salvation by bricks'.

But many of the utopian planning projects, treatises and ideals were more holistic and aspatial in approach, dealing with social, economic and environmental issues too. Non-governmental, and more 'radical' strains of planning developed too, expressing their aspirations in 'imagineering' ideal urban communities. For example, Howard sought to create sustainable settlements in which social, economic, environmental and aesthetic factors were integrated. Subsequent development of speculative garden suburbs and state New Towns were travesties of Howard's original concepts, by putting an over-emphasis upon physical layout and architectural considerations.

Architects, engineers and surveyors manned the new local authority planning departments. Planning was seen as both a design discipline and as a compo-

nent of the public health movement, which itself had a positivist scientific approach to problem solving. There was limited space for a consideration of social planning factors within the new local government-based regulatory system which was obsessed with producing planning schemes, based on physical land use zoning. In the aligned area of housing policy there remained a greater social awareness, albeit often tinged with paternalism towards the 'working classes', and also this was one of the few professional areas where there were a significant number of women involved (Greed, 1999a).

At the dawn of the twentieth century a more sophisticated theoretical perspective, albeit still positivist, was being developed by geographers, sociologists and earth scientists who were taking an interest in the urban situation. Early contributors to the theory of 'how to plan' included Geddes, who promoted a 'scientific' approach to the planning process, based on the principles, 'survey, analysis, plan'. Also a range of theorists, writers and researchers developed theories of urban geography (Van Thunen); urban history (Mumford) and sociology (Rowntree). Although emphasis was put upon use of scientific, and unbiased methods, it is of note that many such theories were heavily laden with racial, sexist and classist ideology (Rydin, 1998: 17; Matless, 1992; Greed, 1994a). In contrast ideal community design based upon utopian socialist principles often manifested links with first wave feminism. As detailed elsewhere much of this foundational work was conveniently lost and forgotten as the century progressed (Hayden, 1976).

After the First World War a separate town planning profession gradually developed. With the establishment of the RTPI in 1914 it was possible to be a town planner without also being an architect or a surveyor. The Housing and Town Planning Acts of 1909 and 1919, introduced again by Liberal governments, established a rudimentary development plan system. The first Labour government came into power in 1924 but did not concentrate upon town planning issues. Subsequent Acts in the 1930s increased the influence of the planners. But it was not until the Town and Country Planning Act 1947 that physical land use planning enabled national blanket coverage of development plans and development control. In the inter-war years physical town planners were mainly concerned with designing new council housing estates or were working for the private sector building suburbia, with nearly 3 million houses being built between the wars. But planning controls were limited and ineffective, and concerns were expressed about the loss of the countryside to urban sprawl.

Whilst physical land use planning remained in the doldrums, in contrast, economic planning gained momentum. Emphasis was being put upon regional planning as a means of ameliorating high levels of unemployment in depressed areas. Labour governments took charge between 1929–35, and introduced rudimentary regional planning legislation. Culturally employment problems were primarily perceived as consisting of unemployment among male workers in primary and secondary industries, where the main trades union support for the Labour party was to be found. Whilst at the time the Labour party might have seemed 'new' and 'radical' at the time, in fact by today's standards the agenda was essentially 'Old Labour', non-sustainable and low on gender awareness, and primarily concerned with production, industry, and male employment.

Post-war Reconstruction Planning

A Labour government came to power in 1945, after the Second World War, which from today's perspective might be classified as 'Old Labour', although its agenda was entirely new at the time. A series of comprehensive town planning acts were introduced after the Second World War in the late 1940s. The 1947 Act established the modern development plan and control system which was focused upon the objective of controlling land uses, by means of zoning and other physical planning measures. Planning, like rationing, was seen as a logical process, simply concerned with the allocation of resources, in this case land uses, in a no-nonsense military manner. There was little space for doubt, for users' viewpoints, or for the fact that there might be a plurality of conflicting needs within society.

Planners were both state bureaucrats and urban managers, albeit with a strongly spatial (physical), rather than aspatial (socio-economic) brief. 'The new Britain must be planned', was the slogan of the day (*Picture Post* Editorial, Lake, 1941). However, planners did not have to 'do everything' as planning was just one part of the whole panoply of the new Welfare State, in which other government agencies and departments also 'planned' for the nation's health, employment, education and welfare. Although the Labour government of the time was no doubt seen as radical compared with previous administrations in many respects its members were highly traditional and conservative (with a small 'c').

(cf. Table of British Prime Ministers and Governments, see Table 9.1.)

The Welfare State was established to cater for the needs of the 'family' in which the man was seen as the breadwinner and the woman was seen as dependent wife and mother. For women it was 'only half way to Paradise'. The new Welfare State rendered them dependent upon the male breadwinner with limited benefits in their own right (Wilson, 1980). However, the demand for female labour was growing as the post-war economy developed. In particular the service sector grew with a greater demand for female office workers. But it was to be many years before town planners were to acknowledge women's employment as a consideration in developing either regional planning policy or development plan land use policy objectives.

In retrospect, the planning system that was established in the post-war reconstruction period appears a disjointed mixture of components, fired by conflicting ideologies, within a tangle of diverse theoretical perspectives and paradigms. Nationalization of development rights, through a complex system of betterment levies, and an enthusiasm for economic planning measures reflect an apparent longing for a form of state socialism, as was current in Soviet Block countries at that time. Paradoxically, the development plan system with its emphasis upon control, required a private sector to control, and its establishment was reflective of a typically British compromise, the maintenance of a mixed economy, shored up by welfare economics and a Welfare State. As Rydin notes it was assumed that the economy could be directed externally, and that a range of regional economic planning policies could redirect investment without any more structural measures being required.

Planners underestimated the economic forces involved and held an oversimplified view of the relationship between 'aspatial' (economic, political, social) forces and the spatial (physical) land uses and developments they generated. Likewise the National Parks and Access to the Countryside Act 1949 evidenced the combination of a patrician concern for preserving the countryside, and an unquestioning support for farming interests, with a leveller's concern for rights to roam, and an embryonic concern with environmental conservation. Many strands, and potentially conflicting elements comprised the span of post-war planning legislation.

Subsequently in 1951 a Conservative government was returned which retained power until 1964. This administration lifted many of the controls on private sector investment and development, but which nevertheless maintained a commitment to many of the principles of the Welfare state. Great emphasis continued to be placed upon the housing programme, with new towns, expanded towns and council estates being built in profusion, within the late 1940s and 1950s. All this development was 'for' the working classes, whilst at the same time there was little evidence of any planners actually listening to objections of the people when their houses were condemned as 'unfit for human habitation'. Planners were increasingly, by default, taking on the role of social engineer (Carey and Mapes, 1972). In retrospect it is astounding how much power local planning and housing departments had in the post-war years, to demolish entire tracts of historic cities and to place thousands of people in distant housing estates, and in the 1960s into tower blocks.

There was growing criticism of the activities of the planners, both from the community and from academics. In the post-war New Towns of the late 1940s, some planners sought to influence people's behaviour by means of the way they designed the environment. They sought to put people at high densities in neighbourhoods to engender a 'sense of community'. This was a manifestation of environmental determinism which was one of the dominant, although unstated planning ideologies of the time (Chapter 13). Traces of both post-positivism and critical theory perspectives *of* planning may be seen in planning literature of the later 1950s and 1960s as sociologists investigated the experiences of new town and inner city populations (Broady, 1968).

The role of the town planner was seen as being similar to that of the referee, or umpire, who set out 'the pitch', resolved conflict between opposing teams and enforced the basic ground rules, and framework for 'fair play', within which the 'game' of property development was carried out. With the wisdom of hindsight, this appears a strangely apolitical and sanitized view of the planner's role. The planner's brief was to ensure that towns and cities developed logically and conveniently with an emphasis being put on zoning. This provided a framework for the design of the road network and the provision of other infrastructural services, and gave the market confidence in the future security of the area.

Planning control ensured that space was available for the non-profit making and more social uses which were essential to the urban population but which were not attractive investments for the private sector itself, such as recreational space and facilities, schools, health and community buildings, and sewers and drains, all of which were provided by other local government departments and statutory undertakers. In those days there was more money available from the state for the provision of infrastructural services, and many of the public utilities had been nationalized in the immediate post-war period. These days, looking back across the wake of privatization, and the widespread cutbacks of the 1980s and 1990s, it is astonishing how many 'social goods' were provided 'free' in the 1960s without the need for planners to enter into protracted planning gain negotiation and to adopt a more entrepreneurial role as is the case today.

The planner was seen as generic decision-maker, exercising procedural control over a whole range of human activities through the insensitive instruments of land use zoning, demolition, and redevelopment policy. The planner was a generalist, who apparently could plan anything, and was to be credited with great knowledge or ignorance about a great range of human activities. Planning was seen as a relatively straightforward procedure (Rydin, 1998: 37). The presumed objectives of planning were so 'obvious' that they did not merit special attention or justification in the new development plans and instead emphasis was put upon implementational policies. The emphasis was upon producing the 'Master Plan' a highly prescriptive and absolute document covering planning for the area in question for the next 5 years or more. The masterplan approach to planning contrasts with what the more incremental approach which was to become popular in later years (Taylor, 1998). An incremental approach to planning is based upon a more gradual evaluation of all parameters and an acceptance of continuous change within what is being planned, so that policy adapts to change. Broad goals and objectives are set, but a variety of ways of achieving them is accepted as the only realistic way to achieve policy implementation.

The post-war planner was likely to be equipped to do all this with only a diploma in surveying or a highways engineering qualification, and probably no social sciences background whatsoever. But the power and role of the planner was increasingly being questioned (Simmie, 1974; Goldsmith, 1980; Montgomery and Thornley, 1990). Planning was based upon a 'top down' rather than 'bottom up' approach.

In concluding this section there is a need to consider the question of whether immediate post-war planning primarily physical or social? The town and country planning system was grounded within a strongly spatial setting, its roots drawing on earlier urban design, and geographical traditions in planning. Planning theory such as it was, seemed very spatial compared with what was to come in the 1960s. But, by default, planning policy and practice were aspatial too as so many of the policies had immense, and often unexpected, social, economic and political results. Town planning was but one branch of governmental planning at the time, set within the crown of Welfare State policy alongside state planning of educational, health, industry and housing, all of which were both spatial and aspatial in agenda. This is a question that cannot easily be answered.

Systems or Society?

In the 1960s a paradigm shift occurred within planning, as planners moved from being urban designers obsessed with physical land use planning, to becoming 'scientists', technical experts, and managers of both spatial and aspatial urban systems. A range of new ostensibly scientific theories of the city as a 'system', mainly from North America, began to shape planning theory in Britain (McLoughlin, 1969; Eversley, 1973; Faludi, 1973). Emphasis was put upon seeing 'planning' as a rational, scientific process with its roots in Western Enlightenment thinking (Davidoff and Reiner, 1962; Faludi, 1973; Hall and Gieben, 1992). That is 'planning' was seen as the application of scien-

tific method to decision-making, rather than primarily being concerned with designing towns and cities. Planning theory, therefore, was concerned with procedure, rather than with substantive policy issues. Systems theory was a theory *for* or *in* planning, but it was to generate many critical theories *of* planning, outside and often against planning.

From 1964–70, a Labour government took charge under Harold Wilson who believed in 'planning' as a key tool of government, and guidance of the economy, and who put much emphasis upon progress being fired by the 'white heat of technology'. Again this government may be portrayed as 'Old Labour' but one which welcomed scientific advance and which was likely to be supported by those middle class workers employed in the burgeoning public sector state apparatus.

An expansion of higher education in the 1960s enabled the creation of more full-time planning degrees, and thus planning took on a more academic persona than previously (Schuster, 1950). Planners needed to find a theory that would enhance and legitimate their role as technical experts and academic thinkers, in the wake of continuing criticism of their role as urban designers. Systems theory met this requirement. The city was seen as a system which the

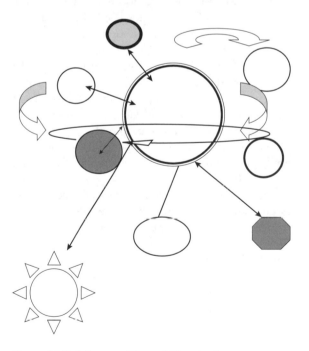

***Figure 16.3* A Systems View of Planning?**

planners could direct and control, and to do this the planners were aided by computers. Their right to plan could now be based upon the accumulation of statistical and scientific data about the city. Planning methodology became obsessed with information gathering, monitoring, forecasting and evaluation techniques. The planner was seen as the 'helmsman' guiding the city into the future, and he needed all this information to steer a straight course (McLoughlin, 1969). In retrospect, this role foreshadows that of the later trend towards seeing the planner as urban manager, but with much greater presumed power and confidence. In an era in which scientists sent the first man to the moon, who could question the planner in his new role as scientist and cybernetic systems analyst?

Proponents of systems planning in the 1960s sought to project a modern scientific image. But systems theory may, paradoxically, be seen as positivist, and thus not reflective of changing academic paradigms of the time. Many other academic fields were moving from the positivist to the post-positivist, whilst planning was moving from a pre-Enlightenment system, based on 'intuition' and 'instinct' to embracing a 'modern' scientific approach. Indeed planning seemed curiously disconnected from, and unconcerned with the cultural, political, social and economic forces that were reshaping urban society. It always seemed one step behind intellectual change. Systems planners seemed strangely dismissive of the realities of the economy and the related market context of property development and land use. Yet it had a huge influence, and subsequent revisions to development plan making procedures, reflected systems theory, particularly the guidance over the production of Structure Plans in the late 1960s and early 1970s.

The systems planning was markedly 'peopleless', as discussed in Chapter 9. It was also purposely 'valueless', because the scientific, objective method of decision-making that planning had to be pure and unpolluted by subjectivity and opinion. But, there was increasing dissatisfaction with the effects of planning policy, particularly among minority groups whose needs barely registered in the computer data of these new urban systems analysts. Indeed, it was argued by such groups that planning was not neutral, or objective, but that the unacknowledged personal views, life experiences and subcultural values of the new planners inevitably shaped and biased their decision-making processes. Planning for a scientifically constructed 'average' resulted in planning successfully for no-one, and excluded the needs of many from the decision-making agenda.

The apolitical, and non-political, nature of scientific decision-making was being questioned. As described in Chapter 13, a range of urban sociologists and other academics were highly critical of planning policy and the planners, thus developing their own theories *of* planning (Simmie, 1974). Planners were seen as powerful urban gatekeepers ensuring unequal distribution of urban resources, and increasingly a conflict-laden interpretation of the situation was adopted. Scientific objectivity was not seen to be practised by planning authorities, and by their planning committees, in areas where the property boom of the 1960s was in full swing. Where the financial stakes were high, in some instances, subsequently, bribery and corruption came to light.

Increasingly grass roots community groups mobilized in relation to the effects of planning on their area. With the rise of the second wave of feminism in the 1960s, the civil rights movement, and the drive for equal opportunities, specific critiques of the planning system were emanating from the different minority groups. As discussed in Chapter 13 a new wave of urban sociological literature, urban feminist literature, and ethnic minority studies was bubbling forth, some of which was co-opted by planning academics as a component in courses at planning schools. But it would seem that few out in practice heeded the criticisms inherent in this literature. Thus a range of critical theory perspectives and related minority movements were highly influential within wider academia and society were challenging the planners' authority.

The planners had achieved an enhanced professional status and had given themselves delusions of grandeur, as all-controlling technocrat. In reality, the activities of local authority planning departments led to increasing contempt for planners among the general public. The application of systems theory to planning soon became discredited. Planners simply did not have the knowledge, expertise or computer power to control the urban system. Subsequently theorists argued for less extreme versions of systems theory, which incorporated an acknowledgement of the complexity of urban decision-making. Theorists, for example, went back to the work of Lindblom (1959) who argued for the science of 'muddling through', that is for a more incremental, less absolutist approach to decision-making, whilst Etzioni (1967) built upon this and proposed what he called 'mixed-scanning'. He sought to mix the best of grand systems theory with the realities of *ad hoc* decision-making within complex, politically-charged local government situations, in which planners have limited problem-solving capabilities and powers, within uncertain, changing contexts. It is generally acknowledged these days that the great value of a systems view of the city was to give a macro-level overview, but this has to be balanced by an appreciation of the complex diversity, uncertainty and complexity inherent at the detailed level of 'doing planning'.

Marxists or Managers?

By the early 1970s, a range of factors, including a property recession fuelled by increased oil-prices, and the return of a Conservative government under Edward Heath, between 1970–74, led to a diminution and reassessment of the role of planners. High level planning, of either city or economy, had not proved its worth, and had not replaced either local democracy or the market. Labour was returned under Harold Wilson from 1974–76, and following him, James Callaghan took over from 1976–79, running arguably a less confident and more middle of the way administration. Relatively speaking greater emphasis was being put upon incrementalism as against long-term planning, and indeed a more subdued managerialist ethos began to pervade local authority planning departments.

A variety of other types of planning and planning theory were evolving, and soon systems planning was long-forgotten, although significantly computers were to become a valuable tool, nowadays used in virtually every planning department in Britain. There was gradual move towards a more subdued, middle of the way version of planning, in which the emphasis was put upon planners as reconstructed managers within the local government system. Within the less pro-planning political climate of the 1970s, planners recreated themselves as negotiators, networkers and

co-ordinators, rather than as controllers and 'gods'. Local government reorganization in 1974 provided the opportunity for planners to take a new role within the corporate affairs of the local authority, but this role was not sustained in all cases as a result of subsequent political, financial and organizational changes in local government. Planning gain and bargaining became the main way to 'tax' the developers, as the vestiges of development land tax had been repealed by the 1974, when the White Paper titled 'Land' was issued as a last forlorn attempt at tackling the land value issue and the question of development gains tax.

While local authority planners were taking on the persona of managers, or were returning to their original training as architects and designers, planning theorists in academia were presenting themselves as Marxists. As stated, many 'plannings' can exist at the same time. Each new generation of 'angry young men' goes through a phase of adopting a radically different approach from its elders to gain dominance. Subsequently, this group is likely to tone down its radicalism and become the old guard from which yet another generation needs to wrest power. More radical critiques of planning were emerging by the 1970s as a result of the popularity of neo-Marxism within certain academic circles. Planners were seen to be lackeys of the bourgeoisie, functionaries of the state, 'oiling the wheels of capitalism'. Ironically those on the Right saw planners as obstructing private development and capitalism itself. Many books, conferences, research projects, academic careers, and complex theoretical studies were manufactured in the name of neo-Marxism.

Neo-Marxism, significantly, had little time for the spatial/physical dimension of planning, and in this respect, shared the aspatial, indeed often anti-spatial, perspective of some systems planners, and careerist manager-planners at the time. Also, as discussed elsewhere it sat uneasily both with feminist and environmentalist perspectives. Both of these movements were critical in theoretical perspective, but they retained a strong 'spatial' component, and both of which questioned the obsession for production, progress and industrialization, found in both Marxism and marketism. It is noticeable that whilst planners always appear good at picking up the latest fashionable academic trend (Hobbs, 1996), once having got one that suits them they appear so obsessed with it that they

miss out on subsequent trends, and also seem incapable of coping with more than one trend at a time.

Whilst the neo-Marxists, in many respects may be
described as part of the 'Hard Left', a new softer 'New
Left' was also developing concerned with community
issues, women's rights, the inner city, equal opportunities, and ethnic minority issues. Rather than 'class'
being seen as the sole determinant of oppression a
plurality of factors could now be taken into account,
including gender, ethnicity, sexuality, age, disability,
religion and cultural difference. Differing levels of
power were seen to determine a group's likely influence upon policy and society, thus a neo-Weberian
perspective was back in fashion (Weber, 1964). Much
of the pioneer work to bring these perspectives into
the world of town planning was carried out by
minority planners, supported by more progressive
metropolitan authorities, and in particular by the
example of the GLC in London. Thus planning
became a form of community participation, in which
the planners acted as enablers and advocates (Rydin,
1998: 69). A new plurality was coming into being,
which no doubt seemed quite bewildering to traditional planners on the right and left. The danger of a
participatory approach planning is that it can appear
enlightened and inclusionary and yet prove merely to
be a control mechanism having been used to control
not empower minorities (Arnstein, 1969).

The whole planning agenda was changing. New
ideas and policy perspectives were adopted from the
international and European realms. 1970 was European Conservation Year, and the Environment Action
programme began in the following year. There was an
increasing concern for urban and rural conservation,
and in parallel the development of the environmental
movement, which it is difficult to 'place' within the
context of either systems theory or neo-Marxism. It
must be appreciated that planners and planning
theorists are not necessarily the same people. Local
planning authorities were seen to be suffering from
'cultural lag' that is they were not up to speed in
terms of changes in planning theories, and the use
of computers and other new technology. Perhaps
this was for the good as valuable earlier incarnations
of 'planning' remained hidden away in the recesses of
planning offices, ready to spring back into life once
the paradigm shifted again. Urban design had never
gone away, and was still a component of local

authority planning. The production of the *Essex Design
Guide* in 1974 brought this aspect of planning back
into the fore – for some planners at least. Likewise,
the urban conservation movement continued apace.
These more aesthetic dimensions of planning may be
seen as relatively apolitical and espousing traditional
conservative values of a bygone England, receiving
royal support (Prince of Wales, 1989).

Entrepreneurial, Environmental or Equality Agendas

The Conservative government gained power under
Mrs Thatcher in 1979, and it would seem that
planning was doomed, as described in Chapter 10.
The 'New Right' government arguably lacked the
paternalistic custodial attitude towards the people and
the land that had been found to a degree in previous
more gentlemanly 'Old Right' conservative governments. The New Right appeared much brasher, more
businesslike and commercial in demeanour, and was
inspired by New Right American economic theory
(Friedman, 1991). Social awareness was not a feature
of this group, and Mrs Thatcher herself is rumoured
to have declared, '*there's no such thing as society*'.
Instead emphasis was put upon the individual who
apparently could shape his or her own destiny by hard
work, enterprise and initiative, regardless of the social
structures and economic forces which tend to keep
people down. Those planners who had pioneered a
greater emphasis upon the social aspects of planning,
and who had brought equal opportunities issues into
the foreground, were to find that 'equality' was now
redefined as 'anyone can succeed in business'. But not
everyone started from the same advantageous position
in the first place.

Since the emphasis was upon individual freedom,
planning had little place in this scenario. Planners,
to survive, became much more entrepreneurial in attitude, and a greater number entered the private sector.
Planning was initially viewed by the Thatcherites as a
brake on development, which could be dispensed
with entirely. Michael Heseltine her Secretary of State
at the DoE, spoke of 'jobs being locked up in filing
cabinets' presumably in dusty planning departments
where time stood still. With time the traditional role
of the planner as arbitrator and daysman came to be

recognized as of value, if only to help 'oil the wheels of capitalism'.

Paradoxically, the authoritarian element in the Conservative approach to government resulted in, arguably, even greater state control, or at least greater centralization of governmental powers, away from the grips of wayward New Left local authorities. In spite of publicly denouncing planning, a whole range of new urban policy measures were introduced in the Thatcher years, which *were* 'planning' in all but name. Planners recreated themselves reprising their role as urban managers, and as urban renewal experts, putting greater emphasis upon the process rather than upon the policy aspect of planning. 'Planning' had become a dirty word and few would confess to being a planner in polite society.

Meanwhile on the Left, much of the old radical and neo-Marxian theory no longer seemed appropriate in the context of the new political climate. Indeed the emphasis upon male working class workers which was so endemic within British socialism, and the related Trade Union movement was challenged by excluded minorities, and by changes in technology. The New Left had a strong community basis for its power, and seemed generally to be more in contact with 'real people', particularly within inner city areas. The socially-concerned planner might act as 'advocate' as in the case of 'Planning Aid for London' or as champion of equal rights as in implied by the publications of the Greater London Council (GLC), planning department (GLC, 1984).

Likewise the growing Green movement, relatively speaking, drew its support from a cross-class base and from shared opposition to anti-environmental policies, not least unfettered road and house building. The environmental movement embodied especially the concerns of the younger generation. Gradually environmentalism and demands for sustainability transformed the planning agenda, and its paradigm shifted from being 'red' (socialist) to 'green' (environmental). The greening of planning was seen by some as its depoliticization. But as stated earlier, and as Rydin argues, the principle of 'let the polluter pay' repoliticized the agenda. Once big business realized that the new movement had legislative and fiscal power, much of which emanated from the European Union, corporate interests sought to absorb rather than ignore the green movement.

Meanwhile ordinary people were experiencing an increasingly hostile attitude towards the motor car from the planners. The adage 'predict and provide' was replaced by measures such as traffic calming and restraint, which increasing politicized green issues among the general public. Arguably many so-called green measures were seen by the public as simply new means of increasing taxation and state control, which had very little relationship to their own attempts to live ordinary lives on limited incomes. One must question the sustainability of policies which are based upon negative controls with very little consultation and without proactive alternatives being offered. Many people who would sincerely like to use their cars less for example find there is simply no alternative because of the demise of public transport and the decentralization of main land uses and employment centres. It is argued that the transport planners, scarcely renown for their social awareness, have proved to be the unexpected and forgotten rogue card in the pack. They are part of the planning system, but in many ways separate from it. Their socially dubious policies can be legitimated because they are apparently contributing to 'sustainability'. For the future more research and development of theory is needed on their role and power in shaping cities.

Collaborative Community-based Planning

Many imagined that New Labour, which came to power in 1997, would re-establish the power of town planning and adopt a more socially and environmentally aware programme of urban policy. At first little happened except for the creation of the DETR (combining the old DoE and DoT) and the publication of a series of consultative documents on the importance of urban renewal, socially inclusive policies, joined up thinking and community development. It was time for planners to recreate themselves again. A new power base and agenda were needed. So, planners began to take on the role of champions and advocates of the community, minorities, and inner city residents, that is the very groups which had been so critical of planning policy in the past. Many of the minority and community groups described in earlier chapters had been empowered by their experiences, and have been setting the agenda for change within

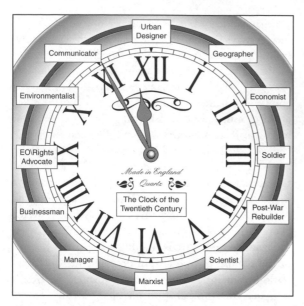

Figure 16.4 **The Changing Persona of the Planner Across the Century.** I = 1900. XII = 2000.

society and for the built environment professions from the bottom-up. The planner's image was now cast as enablers and regenerators rather than as bureaucrats.

A whole new set of planning theories, methodologies, organizational structures and ways of doing planning have been developing in the 1990s to justify this shift towards what is termed a collaborative, communicative approach to planning. In parallel an Institutionalist approach to planning has developed. In other words greater attention is given to working with and through social and community networks, agencies and social *institutions* to facilitate policy change (Healey, 1997: 5). This re-orientation reflects a wider paradigmatic shift within academia towards the importance of the micro level of society, that is towards the individual, the local community and social interaction; and away from the heavy, macro-level structural theories of society of the past.

According to Healey an institutionalist approach is concerned with changing social relations through which daily life and business organization are conducted, and the way in which the social and the biosphere interweave (Healey, 1997 chapter 2). Thus it enables the inclusion of a range of current topical movements and groups within the planning process, including the environmental movement and com-

munity groups. It thus provides a depoliticized 'Third Way' between the rocks of the Left and the Right. It enables a communicative approach to the design of governance systems and practices, focusing on ways of developing collaborative and consensus-building practices. The Institutionalist approach also allows for diversity and the participation of a range of stakeholders in the planning process. The emphasis is upon participatory democracy within a pluralistic society.

Healey, one of the main advocates of the institutionalist approach, argues for a more sensitive 'collaborative' and 'communicative' approach towards policy making in town planning (Healey, 1997). The approach to planning is based upon negotiation, networking, and liaison with community groups, rather than upon autocratic direction and coercion. As can be seen collaborative planning takes aspects of methods and practices used previously in the women and planning movement and by planning advocacy groups such as Planning Aid for London. Both institutionalist and collaborative planning theory may be seen as procedural planning theories.

But there are considerable problems with collaborative planning approaches. Minority groups have expressed concern that the stakeholders are not necessarily disaggregated in such a way that would allow space for the consideration of the differing needs within the community on the basis of class, race, gender and age. Concern is expressed that many planners are ill-equipped to operate a more communicative egalitarian planning system, when they have clearly not all taken on board the basic principles of equal opportunities and lack social awareness or understanding of the needs of the planned. There is also the major problem of differential levels of power between planners and planned. Although the theories are now becoming widespread within academic planning circles at local government level there is little training or preparation for planners to take on this new softer role. Indeed in many a local planning authority planning practice has changed little, although now a new script can be recited to legitimate planning decisions which are not necessarily in the interests of the planned.

Real collaborative planning requires accountability because 'the planned' are now to be seen as citizens, customers, clients, and stakeholders, rather than as the masses who has to be planned 'for'. Statutory planning is seen as a service, and one that must be shown to be efficient, economical and rapid. Therefore in this vein a series of initiatives have been introduced to speed up and improve the planning service, such as Audits and Best Value initiatives. Policy statements such as the Citizens Charter have sought to provide guidance on this more accountable form of government service. But theory and practice are not necessarily in harmony, according to feedback from minority groups.

The surrounding intellectual climate has also undergone change (Amin and Thrift, 1995). Gone are the grand, total, determinist theories of the past, such as Marxism. A paradigm shift has occurred towards a more relativistic, fragmented, pluralistic, uncertain set of theories. A post-structuralist, post-modernist, and post-Fordist climate has developed (for Fordism see chapter 10). This has introduced space for diversity, difference and plurality. Thus an institutionalist, collaborative approach fits well within this intellectual context.

The theory of Institutionalism may be classified as a branch of constructivist theory, drawing on traditional theories such as symbolic interactionism and upon the work of modern philosophers. The academic origins of the new institutionalist approach to planning are to be found in the work of two men in particular, namely Giddens and Habermas, who themselves were agents of this seachange. Gidden's work on structuration theory stresses the importance of the interaction between structure and agent, that is potentially between society and the individual, creating a two-way process. This transformed the traditionally deterministic stance of the Left, and has given value to the actions of individuals. In other words Gidden's work moves the debate on from 'one way' top-down determinism, towards a post-structuralist perspective in which both 'top down' and 'bottom up' forces are acknowledged as shapers of society (Giddens, 1989).

More recently Giddens has become the guru of Blairism. Giddens has given academic support to Blair's 'Third Way' approach to government, which is based upon a more interactive model of society and social empowerment, which is both post-Marxist and post-capitalist in perspective. Habermas has also had a major input to these new theoretical perspectives (Habermas, 1979, 1987). His work is concerned with how this process might be furthered, by extending participatory democracy as a means of enabling citizens to engage in debate and to open up the public

Figure 16.5 Life Continues: Pigeons.
Pigeons inhabit the city whatever theory is fashionable and ordinary people go about their daily round as users of the built environment.

arena of decision-making in a more inclusionary manner.

In the world of planning a new range of more inclusionary and sensitive mechanisms of governance has developed. Emphasis is put upon developing 'webs' of communication (Healey, 1997: 58–9). Such are the barriers between planners and planned that as Hillier states, the two groups tend to talk past each other even when they wish to communicate (Hillier, 1999). Yet planners are now portrayed as communicators, networkers, and facilitators, and the necessary skills to be a planner are those of communication and negotiation. They are also, conflictingly, required to be assessors, auditors and financial managers, in an audit culture in which everyone is now checking on everyone else. Needless to say, many minority group individuals would argue that traditional planners are in no position to take on this more interactive, communicative role, having previously proved themselves incapable of communicating with ordinary people.

CONCLUSION

As can be seen from the story of planning, town planning has undergone many changes and taken on many different guises over the last 200 years, planners have recreated themselves several times over. Planners have manifested themselves as technical experts, urban designers, umpires, economic planners, property

***Figure 16.6* The Author Reflects upon the Continuing City.**
'Making the familiar strange' The author standing back and observing the urban environment whilst attending a conference in Japan.

developers, environmental police, social engineers, corporate managers, facilitators, advocates and entrepreneurs. Planners have operated, and survived under a range of governments, and espoused a variety of political ideologies and theoretical stances, ranging across the full spectrum from Old Left to New Left, Old Right to New Right, under Red, Blue and Green ideologies and at various governmental levels. Indeed the different types of planners may not even be able to communicate with each other, they are such different beings, with distinct objectives and subcultural values.

Yet, arguably, the problems which planners have sought to address have become worse not better in spite of all the theory-making, policy-analysis and shifts in paradigms. The problems of traffic, environment, social deprivation and the ugliness and impractical design of the built environment have not been solved. Many of the problems have been rendered worse as a result of planning intervention. However, many planners have made successful and profitable careers out of

this situation, while the needs of the planned have remained unmet and often unrecognized.

There is a need to return to issues of substantive policy content. It is argued again that that there is a need to create the city of 'everyday life', a functional, human-scale, multi-centred city, a 'city of short distances' with an emphasis upon fuller provision of public transport. This would not be a new settlement on a green field site. Rather this scenario is intended to provide the principles for the restructuring of the existing built environment. Its implementation would involve a gradual move towards a greater mixture of land uses, an element of dezoning, combined with a return to a multi-nucleated (many centred) urban cell structure at district, local and neighbourhood level. This would provide a more even and available distribution of retail, employment, education and leisure facilities throughout the city, and in turn generate less car journeys. Such an arrangement would create a more sustainable city environmentally where there was less need to travel to work by either car or public transport. It would provide greater accessibility for the disabled and a less dangerous environment in respect of both traffic accidents and personal safety.

It is a superficial strategy to try to 'solve' the traffic problem by building yet more roads and car parks, without considering why the cars are travelling in the first place. If everyone is heading for the central area offices from the suburbs, the way to solve, at least, some of the parking problem might be to decentralize certain types of office development into the suburbs, or encourage inner city, middle class housing development. Nowadays finding solutions to such problems as urban congestion has become more pressing because of overarching environmental concerns, the requirements of European Union directives, and international policy guidance to make cities sustainable (Fudge, 1999; DETR, 1999e).

The subdivision of cities into smaller, viable, local areas within this multi-nucleated city structure, would, perhaps, engender greater local democracy and accountability and therefore perhaps greater social equality and less unemployment. Such a city form would make life easier for women and other carers who at present have to juggle and organize their daily round within spatially decentralized and disparate city form, as they seek to combine work and home, and they have to travel themselves and their dependants between school, home, shops, work, leisure, recreation and other social facilities. It would also provide a facilitating framework to enable men to contribute more to essential care-related and home-making work within the home, as well as pursuing careers and leisure activities outside the home.

Such an urban model combined with good management, sustainable waste disposal and recycling, and efficient maintenance would create cities that were both functional and beautiful, that is they would be live-in-able.

TASKS

Information Gathering Tasks

I. Take any one decade and list the following characteristics of planning at that time as to:

- the scope and nature of planning, how did 'planning' manifest itself?
- the type of planners, who were the planners?
- the nature of planning theory, what paradigm reigned?
- the nature of the planning process, organizational and procedural structures?
- the political and economic context, relationship with national and local politics
- social forces and cultural trends, role of minorities and 'isms', compared with majority national trends?

Conceptual Tasks

II. Was post-war planning just spatial or aspatial too? (1945–1960).

III. Write an essay of 2000 words on the following, 'Define and discuss the scope and nature of British town planning in relation to any one decade in the second half of the twentieth century'.

IV. Write two pages of summary notes as a basis for discussing the following question 'The planning process has been identified as being inevitably political and never neutral. Do you agree with this? Discuss giving reasons for your views'.

Reflective Tasks

V. To what extent do you consider a collaborative approach planning to be a valid tool in policy making and implementation?

VI. What do you consider to be the next new fashion in planning that is emerging?

FURTHER READING

For a history of planning theory since 1945 readers should consult Taylor (1998, 1999). For details of more recent initiatives, such as collaborative and communicative approaches to the planning process see Healey, 1997. Texts that give a political analysis of planning, combined with a theoretical perspective include Tewdwr-Jones, 1996: Rydin, 1998; Brindley *et al.*, 1996. Healey has written extensively on planning and planning theory, in particular consult Healey, 1997. Advanced readers may also consult work by Faludi, and Feinstein. The wider political and economic context of planning is covered by Thornley, Rydin, and Oatley.

For discussion and debates on the nature of social theory and changing paradigms read Hammersley (1995 and 1999). The concept of paradigm is defined in Kuhn, 1962. Advanced readers may tackle work by Giddens and Habermas. For more feminist perspectives on research methodology see Stanley and Roberts, H.; and Greed, 1991, 1994a.

Check the newspapers and television for discussions of 'Third Way' politics and Blairism, For example, see short article 'Giddens defends third-way politics' by A. Thomson in *Times Higher*, 29.10.1998, page 5.

BIBLIOGRAPHY

Abercrombie, P. (1945) *Greater London Development Plan*, London: HMSO.*

Acker, S., (1984) 'Women in higher education: what is the problem?' in Acker, S., and Warren Piper, D., (eds) (1984) *Is Higher Education Fair to Women?*, Slough: NFER–Nelson.

Acker, S. (1995) *General Education: Sociological Reflections on Women, Teaching and Feminism*, London: British Journal Sociology of Education.

Adams, E., and Ingham, S. (1998) *Changing Places: Children's Participation in Environmental Planning*, London: Children's Society.

Adler, D. (1999) *New Metric Handbook: Planning and Design Data*, London: Architectural Press, Butterworth.

Age Concern (1993) *Housing for All*, London: Age Concern England.

Ahmed, Y. (1989) 'Planning and Racial Equality', *The Planner*, vol. 75, no. 32: 18–20, (1.12.89) London: Royal Town Planning Institute.

Aldous, T. (1972) *Battle for The Environment*, Glasgow: Collins.

Aldridge, M. (1979) *The British New Towns*, London: Routledge & Kegan Paul.

Allinson, J. (1998) 'GIS in Practice', *Planning*, May edition; 'Electronic Revolution: A Special Report', September 1998; 'Managing IT in a pressured environment', September 1998.

Ambrose, P. and Colenutt, B. (1979) *The Property Machine*, Harmondsworth: Penguin.

Ambrose, P. (1986) *Whatever Happened to Planning?*, London: Methuen.

Amin, A. and Thrift, N. (eds) (1995) *Globalisation, Institutions and Regional Development in Europe*, Oxford: Oxford University Press.

Arnstein, S. (1969) 'A ladder of citizen participation', *Journal of the American Institute of Planners*, 35: 216–24.

Arts Council (1996) *Equal Opportunities: Additional Guide*, London: National Lottery.

ARU (Les Annales de la Recherche Urbaine) (1997) *Emplois du Temps* , Special Issue on 'Time Planning', December,

1977, no. 77, Paris: Plan Urbain, Ministère de L'équipement du Logement, des Transports et du Tourisme.

Arvill, R. (1969) *Man and Environment: Crisis and The Strategy of Choice*, Harmondsworth: Penguin.

Ashworth, W. (1968) *The Genesis of Modern British Town Planning*, London: Routledge & Kegan Paul.

Atkins, S. and Hoggitt, B. (1984) *Women and The Law*, Oxford: Blackwell.

Atkinson, R. and Moon, G. (1993) *Urban Policy in Britain: The City, the State and the Market*, London: Macmillan.

Attfield, J. (1989) 'Inside Pram Town, A Case Study of Harlow House Interiors, 1951–61', in Attfield, J. and Kirkham, P. (eds) *A View From The Interior: Feminism, Women, And Design*, London: Women's Press.

Audit Commission (1999) *From Principles to Practice*, London: The Audit Commission.

Avis, M. and Gibson, V. (1987) *The Management of General Practice Surveying Firms*, University of Reading: Faculty of Urban and Regional Studies.

Bacon, E. (1978) *Design of Cities*, London: Thames & Hudson.

Bagilhole, B. (1993) 'How to keep a good woman down: an investigation of institutional factors in the process of discrimination against women', *British Journal of Sociology*, 14(3), pp. 262–74.

Bagihole, B., Dainty, A., Neale, R. (1995) 'Innovative personnel practices for improving women's careers in construction companies: methodology and discussion of preliminary findings', *Proceedings of the 11th Annual Arcom Conference*, York, 1995, pp. 686–95. Association of Researchers in Construction Management.

Bailey, J. (1975) *Social Theory for Planning*, London: Routledge & Kegan Paul.

Balchin, P. and Bull, G. (1987) *Regional and Urban Economics*, London: Harper & Row.

Ball, M. (1988) *Rebuilding Construction: Economic Change in The British Construction Industry*, London: Routledge.

Ball, S. and Bell, S. (1999 [1995]) *Environmental Law*, 4th edition, London: Blackstone.

*Note since 1998 HMSO has been re-named The Stationery Office (TSO)

Barlow Report (1940) *Report of The Royal Commission on The Distribution of The Industrial Population*, London: HMSO, Cmd. 6153.

Barton, H. (1998) 'Design for Movement' in Greed, C. and Roberts, M. (eds) (1998) *Introducing Urban Design: Interventions and Responses,* Harlow: Longmans, Chapter 8, pp. 133–52.

Barton, H. and Bruder, N. (1995) *Local Environmental Auditing*, London: Earthscan.

Barton, H. (1996) 'Planning for sustainable development' in Greed, C. (1996) (ed.) *Investigating Town Planning*, Harlow: Longmans.

Barton, H., Davis, G. and Guise, R. (1995) *Sustainable Settlements: a guide for planners, designers and developers,* (Bristol: University of The West of England and Luton: LGMB.

Bassett, K., and Short, J., (1980) *Housing and Residential Structure: Alternative Approaches*, London: Routledge.

Baty, P. (1997) 'Is the Square Mile colour blind?', *Times Higher Education Supplement*, 7 November 1997, p. 6

Bell, C. and Newby, H. (1978) *Community Studies*, London: George, Allen & Unwin.

Bell, J. (1996) *Doing your Research Project: A Guide for First-time Researchers in Education and the Social Sciences'*, Milton Keynes: Open University Press.

Bell, C. and Bell, R. (1972) *City Fathers: The Early History of Town Planning in Britain*, Harmondsworth: Penguin.

Bell, F. (1911) *At The Works*, London: Thomas Nelson.

Bell, C. and Newby, H. (1980) *Doing Sociological Research*, London: George, Allen & Unwin.

Belloni, C. (1994) 'A woman-friendly city: politics concerning the organisation of time in Italian cities', International Conference on *Women in The City: Housing Services and Urban Environment*, Paris: Organisation for Economic Cooperation and Development.

Benevelo, L. (1976) *The Origins of Modern Town Planning*, London: Routledge & Kegan Paul.

Bentley, I., Alcock, A., Murrain, P., McGlynn, S. and Smith, S. (1985 [1996]) *Responsive Environments: A Manual for Designers*, London: Architectural Press in association with Oxford Brookes University, Oxford.

Betjeman, J. (1974) *A Pictorial History of English Architecture*, Harmondsworth: Penguin.

Bianchini, F. (1998) 'The twenty-four hour city', in *Demos*, Quarterly, Issue 5.

Bianchini, F. and Greed, C. (1999) ' Cultural planning and time planning' in C. Greed (ed.) *Social Town Planning*, London, Routledge.

Bilton, T., Bonnett, K., Jones, P., Skinner, D., Stanworth, M. and Webster, A. (1997) *Introductory Sociology*, London: Macmillan.

Birmingham University (1987) *The Empire Strikes Back*, Centre for Continuing Cultural Studies.

Blackwell, J.V. (1998) *Planning Law and Practice*, London: Cavendish.

Blackwell, J.V. (1998) *Planning Law and Practice*, London: Cavendish.

Blowers A. (ed.) (1993) *Planning for a Sustainable Environment: A Report by The Town & County Planning Association* London: Earthscan with TCPA.

Blumer, H., (1965) 'Sociological implications of the thought of George Herbert Mead', in Cosin, B., Dale, I., Esland, G., MacKinnon, D. and Swift, D., (1977) *School and Society, A Sociological Reader*, London: Routledge and Kegan Paul.

Boardman, P. (1978) *The World of Patrick Geddes*, London: Routledge & Kegan Paul.

Bodman, A. (1991) 'Weavers of influence: The structure of contemporary geographic research', *Transactions of The Institute of British Geographers*, vol. 16, no. 1: 21–37.

Bolsterli, M. (1977) *The Early Community At Bedford Park: The Pursuit of Corporate Happiness in The First Garden Suburb*, London: Routledge, Kegan Paul.

Booth, C. (1996) 'Breaking down barriers' chapter 13, pp. 167–82, in Booth, C., Darke J. and Yeandle, S. (eds) (1996) *Changing Places: Women's Lives in The City*, London: Paul Chapman.

Booth, W. (1890) *In Darkest England and The Way Out*, London: Salvation Army.

Booth, C., Darke J. and Yeandle S. (eds) (1996) *Changing Places: Women's Lives in The City*, London: Paul Chapman Publishing.

Booth, C. (1999) 'Approaches to meeting women's needs' *Gender Equality and the Role of Planning: Realising the Goal* National Symposium, 1.7.99, Report of Proceedings, London: Royal Town Planning Institute.

Booth, C. (1968 [1903], Published in Series 1889–1906) *Life and Labour of The People of London*, Chicago: University of Chicago Press.

Booth, C., and Gilroy, R. (1999) 'The role of a toolkit in mobilising women in local and regional development', paper presented at the *Future Planning: Planning's Future* Sheffield: Planning Theory Conference, March 1999.

Bor, W. (1972) *The Making of Cities*, London: Leonard Hill.

Bottomore, T. (1973) *Elites and Society*, Harmondsworth: Penguin.

Bowlby, S. (1989) 'Gender issues and retail geography', in Whatmore, S. and Little, Jo. (eds) (1989) *Geography and Gender*, London: Association for Curriculum Development in Geography.

Boyd, N. (1982) *Josephine Butler, Octavia Hill, Florence Nightingale: Three Victorian Women Who Changed The World*, London: Macmillan.

Braidotti, R. (ed.) (1994) *Women, the Environment and Sustainable Development: Towards a Theoretical Synthesis*, London: Zed Books.

Brand, J. (1996) 'Sustainable development: the international, national and local context for women' in *Built Environment*, vol. 22, no. 1, pp. 58–71.

Brand, J. (1999) 'Planning for health, sustainability and equity in Scotland' in Greed, C. (1999) (ed.) *Social Town Planning*, London: Routledge.

Briggs, A. (1968) *Victorian Cities*, Harmondsworth: Penguin.

Brindley, T., Rydin, Y. and Stoker, G. (1996) *Remaking Planning: The Politics of Urban Change*, London: Routledge.

Brion, M. and Tinker, A. (1980) *Women in Housing: Access and Influence*, London: Housing Centre Trust.

Broady, M. (1968) *Planning for People*, London: NCSS/ Bedford Square Press.

Brown, C. (1979) *Understanding Society: An Introduction to Sociological Theory*, London: John Murray.

Bruntland Report (1987) *Our Common Future*, World Commission on Environment and Development, Oxford: Oxford University Press.

Bruton, M. (1975) *Introduction to Transportation Planning*, London: Hutchinson.

BSI (1995) *Sanitary Installations Part I: Code of Practice for Scale of Provision, Selection and Installation of Sanitary Appliances*, London: British Standards Institute (HMSO).

BTA (British Toilet Association) (1999) *Better Public Toilets* Winchester: BTA

Buchanan, C. (1972) *The State of Britain*, London: Faber.

Buchanan, C. (1963) *Traffic in Towns*, Harmondsworth: Penguin.

Built Environment (1984) Special Issue on 'Women and The Built Environment', *Built Environment*, vol. 10, no. 1.

Built Environment (1996) Special Issue on 'Women and The Built Environment', *Built Environment*, vol. 22, no. 1.

Bulmer, M. (1984) *The Chicago School of Sociology*, London: University of Chicago Press.

Burke, G. (1977) *Towns in the Making*, London: Edward Arnold.

Burke, G. and Taylor, T. (1990) *Town Planning and the Surveyor*, Reading: College of Estate Management.

Burke, G. (1976) *Townscapes*, Harmondsworth: Penguin.

Cadman, D. and Topping, R (1995) *Property Development*, London: Spons.

CAE (Centre for Accessible Environments) (1998) *Keeping up with the Past – making historic buildings accessible to everyone* (Video), London: Centre for Accessible Environments.

Callon, M., Law, J. and Rip, A. (1986) *Mapping The Dynamics of Science and Technology*, London: Macmillan.

Campbell, B. (1985) *Wigan Pier Revisited: Poverty and Politics in the Eighties*, London: Virago.

Carey, L. and Mapes, R. (1972) *The Sociology of Planning: A Study of Social Activity on New Housing Estates*, London: Batsford.

Carson, R. (1962) *Silent Spring*, Harmondsworth: Penguin.

Carter, R. and Kirkup, G. (1989) *Women in Engineering*, London: Macmillan.

Castells, M. (1977) *The Urban Question*, London: Arnold.

CEC (1990) *Green Paper on the Urban Environment*, Fourth Environmental Action Programme 1987–1992 COM(90) 218 CEC (Commission of the European Communities), Brussels.

CEC (1991) *Europe 2000: Outlook for the development of the Community's territory*, Directorate-General for Regional Policy and Cohesion, Brussels. COM(91) 452 CEC, Brussels

CEC (1992) *Towards Sustainability: Fifth Environmental Action Programme* Brussels.

Chadwick, E. (1842) *Report on the Sanitary Condition of the Labouring Population of Great Britain*, London.

Chapin, F. (1965; and 1979 edition with J. Kaiser) *Urban Land Use Planning*, Illinois: University of Illinois Press, pages 12–25.

Cherry, G. (ed.) (1981) *Pioneers in British Town Planning*, London: Architectural Press.

Cherry, G. (1988) *Cities and Plans*, London: Edward Arnold.

Chinoy, E. (1967) *Society: An Introduction to Sociology*, New York: Random House.

Chapman, D. (ed.) (1996) *Neighbourhoods and Plans in the Built Environment* London: Spons.

CIB (1996) 'Tomorrow's Team: Women and Men in Construction', Report of Working Group 8 of Latham Committee, *Constructing The Team*, London: Department of The Environment, and Construction Industry Board (CIB).

CIOB (1995) *Balancing The Building Team: Gender issues in the building professions*. Institute of Employment Studies, Report no 284, Chartered Institute of Building.

CISC (Construction Industry Standing Conference) (1994) *CISC Standards 1994: Occupational Standards for Professional, Managerial, and Technical Occupations in Planning, Construction, Property and Related Engineering Services*, London: CISC, The Building Centre, 26 Store Street, London, WCIE 7BT.

CITB (1997) *The Construction Industry: Key Labour Market Statistics*, Construction Industry Training Board, King's Lynn.

Cockburn, C. (1977) *The Local State: Management of People and Cities*, London: Pluto.

Coleman, A. (1985) *Utopia on Trial*, London: Martin Shipman.

Collar, N. (1999) *Planning: The Scottish System* Edinburgh: Green.

Cooke, P., (1987) 'Clinical inference and geographical theory', *Antipode: a Radical Journal of Geography*, vol. 19, no. 1: 69–78, April.

Corbusier, Le (1971, was 1929) *The City of Tomorrow*, London: Architectural Press.

Countryside Commission (1990) *Planning for A Greener Countryside*, Manchester: Countryside Commission Publications.

CRE (1995) *Building Equality: Report of a formal investigation into The Construction Industry Training Board*, London: Commission for Racial Equality.

CRE (Commission for Racial Equality) (1989) *A Guide for Estate Agents and Vendors*, London: CRE.

Crompton, R. and Sanderson, K. (1990) *Gendered Jobs and Social Change*, London: Unwin Hyman.

Crookston, M (1999) 'The Urban Renaissance and the "New Agenda" in Planning', *Planning Law Conference,* London: Law Society, 26.11.99.

Crouch, S., Fleming, R. and Shaftoe, H. (1999) *Design for Secure Residential Environments,* Harlow: Pearson Education (Longmans).

Cullen, G. (1971) *Concise Townscape,* London: Architectural Press.

Cullingworth, J.B. (1997) *Planning in the USA,* New York: Routledge.

Cullingworth, J.B and Nadin, V. (1997 [1994]) *Town and Country Planning in Britain,* London: Routledge.

Dahrendorf, R. (1980) *Life Chances: Approaches to Social and Political Theory,* London: Weidenfeld and Nicolson.

Darke, J. and Brownill, S. (1999) 'A new deal for inclusivity: Race, Gender and Recent Regeneration Initiatives' Paper presented at the *Future Planning: Planning's Future,* Sheffield: Planning Theory Conference, March 1999.

Darley, G. (1990) *Octavia Hill,* London: Constable.

Darley, G. (1978) *Villages of Vision,* London: Granada.

Davidoff, P. and Reiner, T., (1962) 'A choice theory of planning' in *Journal of the American Institute of Planners* Vol 28, May (reprinted in Faludi, 1973, pp. 277–96).

Davidson, R. and Maitland, R. (1999) 'Planning for tourism in towns and cities' in C. Greed (1999) (ed.) *Social Town Planning,* London: Routledge.

Davies, L. (1992) *Planning in Europe,* London: RTPI.

Davies, L. (1998) 'The ESDP and the UK' in *Town and Country Planning,* March 1998: 64–5, vol. 67, no. 2.

Davies, L. (1999) 'Planning for disability: barrier-free living' in Greed, C. (ed.) *Social Town Planning,* London: Routledge.

De Graft-Johnson, A. (1999) Gender and Race' in Greed, C. (ed.) *Social Town Planning* London: Routledge.

Deem, R. (1986) *All Work and No Play?: The Sociology of Women and Leisure Reconsidered,* Milton Keynes: Open University Press.

Delamont, S. (1985) 'Fighting familiarity', *Strategies of Qualitative Research in Education,* Warwock: ESRC Summer School.

Denington Report (1966) *Our Older Homes: A Call to Action,* London: HMSO.

Denyer-Green, B. (1987) *Development and Planning Law,* London: Estates Gazette.

Department of Transport (DoT) (1990) *Roads in Urban Areas,* HMSO: London.

Department of Health (1998) *Our Healthier Nation: A Contract for Health* London: HMSO.

DETR (annual) *Housing and Construction Statistics,* London: HMSO (produced quarterly and annually), London: Department of Environment, Transport and the Regions.

DETR (1997) *General Policy and Principles, Planning Policy Guidance Note no.1* (PPG 1), London: HMSO.

DETR (1998a) *Development Plans an Regional Guidance: Planning Policy Guidance Note 12* (PPG 12) London: HMSO.

DETR (1998b) *The Future of Regional Planning Guidance: Consultation Paper* London: HMSO

DETR (1998c) *Modernising Planning* A Policy Statement by the Minister for the DETR, London: HMSO.

DETR (1998d) *A Householder's Planning Guide for The Installation of Satellite Television Dishes,* London: HMSO.

DETR (1998e) *Transport the Way Ahead,* Consultation Paper, London: DETR.

DETR (1998f) *A New Deal for Transport: Better for Everyone,* London: HMSO.

DETR (1998g) *Opportunities for Change: Consultation Paper on a Revised UK Strategy for Sustainable Development,* London: HMSO.

DETR (1998h) *Places, Streets and Movement: a companion guide to Design Bulletin 32 (Residential Roads and Footpaths Design),* London: DETR.

DETR (1999a) *Outdoor Advertisement Control,* Consultation Paper, London: DETR.

DETR (1999b) *Leylandii and other High Hedges* – Briefing note, London: DETR.

DETR (1999c) *Housing,* Planning Policy Guidance Note no. 3 (PPPG 3), London: DETR.

DETR (1999d) *Residential Roads and Footpaths Design,* Design Bulletin 32 (second edition) London: DETR

DETR (1999e) *Modernising Planning: a Progress Report,* London: DETR, Statement by R. Caborn.

DETR (1999f) *Design in The Planning System: a companion guide to planning, Policy Note 1: General Policy and Principles,* London: TSO (The Stationary Office).

DETR (2000) *By Design: Urban design in the planning system, towards better practice,* London: TSO.

Devereaux, M. (1999a) *The UK System of Government and Planning,* Bristol: University of the West of England, Module Guide.

Devereaux, M. (1999b) *Administration of the French Planning System,* Bristol: University of the West of England, Module Guide.

Devereaux, M. (forthcoming) *The UK System of Government and Planning,* Bristol: University of the West of England, Occasional Paper.

Dixon, R. and Muthesius, S. (1978) *Victorian Architecture,* London: Thames & Hudson.

DoE/SS/LGMB (1993) *Guide to The Eco Management and Audit Scheme for UK Local Government,* London: HMSO, Command no. 2426.

DoE/DoT (1993) *Reducing Transport Emissions Through Planning,* London: HMSO.

DoE (1971) *Sunlight and Daylight: Planning Criteria and Design of Buildings,* London: HMSO.

DoE (1972a) *How Do You Want to Live?: A Report on Human Habitat,* London: HMSO.

DoE (1972b) *Development Plan Manual,* London: HMSO.

DoE (1990a) *This Common Inheritance: Britain's Environmental Strategy,* London: HMSO London, Command no. 1200.

DoE (1990b) *Roads in Urban Areas,* London: HMSO.

DoE (1992a) *Development Plans: Good Practice Guide,* London: HMSO.

DoE (1992b) *Planning Policy Guidance Note 12: Development Plans and Regional Planning Guidance*, London: HMSO.

DoE (1992c) *Land Use Planning Policy and Climate Change*, London: HMSO.

DoE (1993a) *Good Practice Guide on The Environmental Appraisal of Development Plans*, London: HMSO.

DoE (1993b) *Schemes at Medium and High Density*, Design Bulletin, London: HMSO

DoE (1994a) *Sustainable Development: The UK Strategy*, London: HMSO, Department of the Environment.

DoE (1994b) *Climate Change: The UK Programme*, London: HMSO Command no. 2427.

DoE (1994c) *Bioversity: The UK Action Plan*, London: HMSO Command no. 2428.

DoE (1995) *Projections of Households in England to 2016*, London: HMSO, Cmnd 3471.

DoE (1996a) *Development Plans: Code of Practice*, London: HMSO.

DoE (1996b) *Household Growth: Where Shall We Live?* London: DoE.

Donnision, D. and Ungerson, C. (1982) *Housing Policy*, Harmondsworth: Penguin.

Donnison, D. and Eversley, D. (1974) *London: Urban Patterns, Problems and Policies*, London: Heinemann.

Dower Report (1945) *National Parks in England and Wales*, London: HMSO.

Dresser, M. (1978) 'Review Essay' of Davidoff, L. *et al.* (1976) 'Landscape with Figures: Home and Community in English Society' in *International Journal of Urban and Regional Research*, vol. 2, no. 3, Special Issue on 'Women and The City'.

Druker, J., White, G., Hegewisch, A. and Mayne, L. (1996) 'Between hard and soft HRM: human resource management in The construction industry', *Construction Management and Economics*, vol. 14, pp. 405–16.

Druker J. and White, G. (1996) *Managing People in Construction*, London: Institute of Personnel and Development.

Dudley Report (1944) *Design of Dwellings*, London: HMSO, Central Housing Advisory Committee of The Ministry of Health.

Dunleavy, P. (1980) *Urban Political Analysis*, London: Macmillan.

Durkheim, E. (1970) *Suicide: A Study in Sociology*, London: Routledge & Kegan Paul.

Dyos, H. (ed.) (1976) *The Study of Urban Form*, London: Edward Arnold.

Edwards, T (1921) *Good and Bad Manners in Architecture* London: Dent.

Egan Report (1998) *Rethinking Construction: The Report of the Construction Task Force* London: HMSO. The Egan Report, Construction Industry Council.

Ekistics (1985) 'Woman and Space in Human Settlements', *Ekistics: Special Edition* vol. 52, no. 310 January.

Elkin T. and McLaren D. (1991) *Reviving The City: Towards Sustainable Urban Development*, London: Friends of The Earth and Policy Studies Institute.

Elson, M. (1986) *Green Belts*, London: Heinemann.

English Nature (1994) *Sustainability in Practice, Issue 1: Planning for Environmental Sustainability*, Peterborough: English Nature.

ESDP (1999) *European Spatial Development Perspective Towards Balanced and Sustainable Development of the Territory of the European Union*, Brussels, European Commission.

Esher, L. (1983) *A Broken Wave: The Rebuilding of England 1940–80*, Harmondsworth: Penguin.

Essex (1973) *A Design Guide for Residential Areas*, Essex: Essex County Council.

Essex (1997) *The Essex Design Guide for Residential and Mixed Uses*, Essex: Essex Planning Officers Association.

Etzioni, A. (1967) 'Mixed scanning: a third approach to decision-making' *Public Administration Review*, December (reprinted in Faludi, 1973, pp. 217–29).

Eurofem (1998) *Gender and Human Settlements Conference on Local and Regional Sustainable Human Development from a Gender Perspective*, Conference Proceedings of the Eurofem Network (European Women in Planning), Hämeenlina, Finland.

Eurofem (1999) *The Toolkit: Mobilising Women into Local and Regional Development*, revised version, Helsinki: Helsinki University of Technology.

Eversley, D. (1973) *The Planner in Society*, London: Faber.

Evetts, J. (1996) *Gender and Career in Science and Engineering*, London: Taylor and Francis, London.

Fainstein, S. (1999) 'The Future of Planning Theory: Keynote Address' Paper presented at the *Future Planning: Planning's Future*, Sheffield: Planning Theory Conference, 1999.

Faludi, Susan (1992) *Backlash: the undeclared war against women* London: Chatto & Windus

Faludi, A. (1973) *A Reader in Planning Theory*, Oxford: Pergamon.

Fearns, D. (1993) *Access Audits: a guide and checklists for appraising the accessibility of buildings for disabled users*, London: Centre for Accessible Environments.

Fitch, R. and Knobel, L. (1990) *Fitch on Retail Design*, Oxford: Phaidon.

Foley, D. (1964) 'An Approach to Urban Metropolitan Structure' in Webber, Melvin, Dyckman, John, Foley, Donald, Guttenberg, Albert, Wheaton, William and Wurster, Catherine, Bower (1964) *Explorations Into Urban Structure*, Philadelphia: University of Pennsylvania Press.

Fortlage, C. (1990) *Environmental Assessment: A Practical Guide*, Aldershot: Gower.

Foulsham, J. (1990) 'Women's Needs and Planning: A Critical Evaluation of Recent Local Authority Practice', in Montgomery, J. and Thornley, A. (ed.) (1990) *Radical Planning Initiatives*, Aldershot: Gower.

Frankenberg, R. (1970) *Communities in Britain*, Harmondsworth: Penguin.

Friedan, B. (1982 [1963]) *The Feminine Mystique*, Harmondsworth: Penguin.

Friedman, M. (1991) *Monetarist Economics*, London: Blackwells

Fudge, C. (1999) 'Urban Planning in Europe for Health and Sustainability' in Greed, C. (1999) *Social Town Planning*, London: Routledge.

FUN (Frauen Umwelt Netz) (1998) *European Seminar of Experts on Gender, Environment and Labour*, Frankfurt, December 1999, Conference Report.

Fyson, T. (1999) 'New planning powers to transform London?' *Planning*, pp. 4–7 of supplement 'A fresh start for London' June 1999, London: RTPI.

Gale, A. (1994) 'Women in Construction' in Langford, D., Hancock, M.R., Fellows, R. and Gale, A. *Human Resources in The Management of Construction*, Longmans, Chapter 9, pp. 161–87.

Gans, H. (1967) *The Levittowners*, London: Allen Lane.

Gardiner, A. (1923) *The Life of George Cadbury*, London: Cassell.

Gaze, J. (1988) *Figures in A Landscape: A History of The National Trust*, London: Barry and Jenkins and The National Trust.

Geddes, P. (1968 [1915]) *Cities in Evolution: An Introduction to The Town Planning Movement and to The Study of Civics*, London: Ernest Benn.

Giddens, A. (1989) *Sociology*, London: Polity.

Gilman, C. Perkins (1915, 1979) *Herland*, London: Women's Press.

Gilroy, R. (1999) 'Planning to grow old' in Greed, C. (1999) (ed.) *Social Town Planning*, London: Routledge.

Glasson J. (1994) *Introduction to Environmental Impact Assessment*, London: University College London.

GLC (Greater London Council) (1983) *On The Move*, London: GLC, Now available from Greater London Authority (GLA).

GLC (1984) 'Planning for Equality: Women in London' Chapter VI, of *Greater London Development Plan*, Draft Plan, London: GLC,

GLC (1986) *Changing Places*, Report, London: GLC.

Goldsmith, M. (1972) 'Blueprint for Survival'. *Ecologist Magazine*. January, Reprinted Harmondsworth: Penguin.

Goldsmith, M. (1980) *Politics, Planning and The City*, London: Routledge & Kegan Paul.

Graft-Johnson, A. (1999) 'Gender and Race' in Greed, C (1999) (ed.) *Social Town Planning*, London: Routledge.

Graham, S. and Marvin, S. (1996) *Telecommunications and the City: Electronic Spaces, Urban Places*, London: Routledge.

Grant, M. (1982) *Urban Planning Law*, London: Sweet and Maxwell.

Grant, M. (1990) *Urban Planning Law*, London: Sweet and Maxwell.

Grant, B. (1996) *Building E=Quality: Minority Ethnic Construction Professionals and Urban Regeneration*, London, House of Commons.

Grant, M. (1998) *A Source Book of Environmental Law*, London: Sweet and Maxwell.

Grant, M. (1999) (ed.) *Encyclopaedia of Planning Law*, London: Butterworths.

Greed, C. (1988) 'Is more better?: with reference to the position of women chartered surveyors in Britain', *Women's Studies International Forum*, vol. 11, no. 3: 187–97.

Greed, C. (1991) *Surveying Sisters: Women in a Traditional Male Profession*, London: Routledge.

Greed, C. (1992) 'The Reproduction of Gender Relations Over Space: A Model Applied to The Case of Chartered Surveyors', *Antipode*, 24, 1, pp. 16–28.

Greed, C. (1993) 'Is more better?: Mark II – with reference to women town planners in Britain', *Women's Studies International Forum*, vol. 16, no. 3, pp. 255–70.

Greed, C. (1994a) *Women and Planning: Creating Gendered Realities*, London: Routledge.

Greed, C. (1994b) 'The place of ethnography in planning: or is it 'real research'?', *Planning Practice and Research*, vol. 9, no. 2, pp. 119–27.

Greed, C. (1996a) *Implementing Town Planning*, Harlow: Longmans.

Greed, C (1996b) *Investigating Town Planning*, Harlow: Longmans.

Greed, C. (1997a) 'Cultural Change in Construction', *Arcom Conference Proceedings*, Cambridge, 15–17.9.97, Association of Researchers in Construction Management.

Greed, C. (1997b) *The Changing Composition and Culture of Construction*, End Report based on ESRC research on 'Social Integration and Exclusion in Professional Subcultures in Construction.

Greed, C. (1997c) 14.3.97 'Bad Timing Means No Summer in The Cities', *Planning*, Issue 1209, pp. 18–19.

Greed, C. (1999a) *The Changing Composition and Culture of the Construction Industry* Bristol: UWE, Faculty of The Built Environment, Occasional Paper.

Greed, C. (1999b) (ed.) *Social Town Planning*, London: Routledge.

Greed, C. and Roberts, M. (1998) *Introducing Urban Design: Interventions and Responses*, Harlow: Longmans.

Greed, C. (2000a) 'Can man plan? Can woman plan better?' *Non-Plan: Essays on Freedom, Participation, and Change in Modern Architecture and Urbanism*, London: Architectural Press, pp. 184–97.

Greed, C. (2000b) 'Urbanisation' entry in *Fontana Dictionary of Modern Thought*, London: Fontana.

Griffin, S. (1978) *Woman and Nature: The Roaring Inside Her*, London: The Woman's Press.

Grover, R. (ed.) (1989) *Land and Property Development: New Directions*, London: Spon.

Guba, E. (1990) *The Paradigm Dialog* Newbury Park, California: Sage Publications.

Guba, E. and Lincoln, Y. (1992) 'Competing paradigms in qualitative research', in Denzin, N. and Lincoln, Y. (eds) *Handbook of Qualitative Research*, Newbury Park, California: Sage Publications.

Habermas, J. (1979) *Communication and the Evolution of Society*, London: Heinemann.

Habermas, J. (1987) *The Philosophical Discourse of Modernity*, Cambridge: Polity Press.

Hall, S. and Jacques, M. (1989) *New Times: The Changing Face of Politics in The 1990s*, London: Lawrence and Wishart.

Hall, P. (1977) *Containment of Urban England*, London: Allen and Unwin.

Hall, P. (1980) *Great Planning Disasters*, London: Weidenfeld and Nicolson.

Hall, P. (1992 [1989]) *Urban and Regional Planning*, London: Unwin Hyman.

Hall, P. and Ward, W. (1999) *Sociable Cities: the Legacy of Ebenezer Howard*, London: Town and Country Planning Association & Wiley.

Hall, S. and Gieben, B. (1992) *Formations of Modernity*, Milton Keynes: Open University

Hambleton, R. and Sweeting, D. (1999) 'Delivering a new strategic vision for the capital', *Planning* Issue 1347, 3.12.99, pp. 16–17.

Hammersley, M. (1995) *The Politics of Social Research*, London: Sage.

Hammersley, M. and Atkinson, P. (1995) *Ethnography: Principles in Practice*, London: Tavistock.

Hammersley, M. (1999) *Taking Sides in Social Research*, London: Sage.

Hamnett, C., McDowell, L. and Sarre, P (eds) (1989) *Restructuring Britain: The Changing Social Structure*, London: Sage with The Open University.

Haralambos, M. (1995) *Sociology: Themes and Perspectives*, London: Unwin Hyman.

Harrison, M. and Davies, J. (1995) *Constructing Equality: Housing Associations and Minority Ethnic Contractors*, London: Joseph Rowntree Trust.

Hartman, H. (1981) 'The Unhappy Marriage of Marxism and Feminism', in Sargent, L. (ed.) (1981) *Women and Revolution*, London: Pluto Press.

Harvey, D. (1975) *Social Justice and the City*, London: Arnold.

Hass-Klau, C., Nold, I., Böcker, G., Crampton, G. (1992) *Civilised Streets: A Guide to Traffic Calming*, Brighton: Environmental and Transport Planning Department, Brighton City Council.

Hatje, G. (1965) *Encyclopaedia of Modern Architecture*, London: Thames and Hudson.

Hatt, P. and Reiss, A. (1963) *Cities in Society*, New York: Free Press.

Hayden, D. (1976) *Seven American Utopias: The Architecture of Communitarian Socialism, 1790–1975*, London: MIT Press.

Hayden, D. (1981) *The Grand Domestic Revolution: Feminist Designs for Homes, Neighbourhoods and Cities*, Cambridge, Massachusetts: MIT Press.

Hayden, D. (1984) *Redesigning the American Dream*, London: Norton.

Healey, P. (1997) *Collaborative Planning: Shaping Places in Fragmented Societies*, London: Macmillan.

Healey, P., Mcnamara, P., Elson, M. and Doak A. (1988) *Land Use Planning and the Mediation of Urban Change: The British Planning System in Practice*, Cambridge: Cambridge University Press.

Heap, D. (1996 [1991]) *Outline of Planning Law*, London: Sweet & Maxwell.

Henckel, D. (1996) 'Time in the City: Politicalisation of Time in German Society' Deutches Institut für Urbanistik, Berlin, working paper presented at *Politiche del Tempo in una Prospettiva Europea: Conferenza Internazionale*, Eurofem Conference, Aosta, Turin, September 1996.

Herrington, J. (1984) *The Outer City*, London: Harper and Row.

Hill, W. (1956) *Octavia Hill: Pioneer of The National Trust and Housing Reformer*, London: Hutchinson.

Hill, L. (1999) (ed.) *Municipal Year Book and Public Services Directory*, London: Newman Books.

Hillier, J. (1999) 'Culture, community and communication in the planning process' in Greed, C. (ed.) *Social Town Planning* London: Routledge.

Hobbs, P. (1996) 'The market economic context of town planning' in Greed, C. (1996) (ed.) *Investigating Town Planning*, Harlow: Longmans.

Hobhouse Report (1947) *Report of The National Parks Committee* (England and Wales), London: HMSO.

Hoggett, B. and Pearl, D. (1983) *The Family, Law and Society*, London: Butterworths.

Hoskins, J. (1990) *Making of The English Landscape*, Harmondsworth: Penguin.

House of Lords (1995) *Report from the Select Committee on Sustainable Development*, vol. 1, London: HMSO.

Howard, E. (1974 [1898]) *Garden Cities of Tomorrow*, reprinted 1974, London: Faber.

Howe, E. (1980) 'Role Choices of Urban Planners', *Journal of The American Planning Association*, pp. 398–401, October.

Hudson, M. (1978) *The Bicycle Planning Book*, Friends of the Earth, London: Open Books.

Hurd, G. (ed.) (1990) *Human Societies: Introduction to Sociology*, London: Routledge & Kegan Paul.

Hutchinson, M. (1989) *The Prince of Wales: Right Or Wrong?*, London: Faber and Faber.

IJURR (International Journal of Urban and Regional Research) (1978) *Women and The City*, Special Issue, vol. 2, no. 3, London: Basil Blackwell.

Imrie, R. (1996) *Disability and the City: International Perspectives*, London: Paul Chapman.

Innes, J. (1995) 'Planning theory's emerging paradigm: communicative action and interactive practice', *Journal of Planning Education and Research*, vol. 14, no. 3, pp. 183–9.

Ismail, A. (1998) An investigation of the low representation of black and ethnic minority professionals in contracting, UWE, Special research project.

Jackson, A. (1992) *Semi-detached London: Suburban Development, Life and Transport*, Oxford: Wild Swan Publications.

Jacobs, J. (1970) *The Economy of Cities*, Harmondsworth: Penguin.

JFCCI (Joint Forecasting Committee for the Construction Industries) (1999) *Construction Forecasts*, London: National Economic Development Office.

Johnson, W.C. (1997) *Urban Politics and Planning*, Chicago: American Planning Association.

Johnston, B. (1999) 'The province plans for the year 2025', in *Planning*, 26.3.99, pp. 16–17, issue 1311.

Joseph, M. (1988) *Sociology for Everyone*, Cambridge: Polity Press.

Joseph, M. (1978) 'Professional values: a case study of professional students in a Polytechnic', *Research in Education*, 19: 49–65.

Kanter, R. (1972) *Commitment and Community: Communities and Utopias in Sociological Literature*, Cambridge, Massachusetts: Harvard University Press.

Kanter, R. (1977) *Men and Women of The Corporation*, New York: Basic Books.

Kanter, R. (1983) *The Change Masters: Corporate Entrepreneurs at Work*, Counterpoint, London: Unwin. Page 296, prime movers.

Keating, M. (1993) *The Earth Summit Agenda for Change: a plain language version of Agenda 21 and the other Rio Agreements Centre for our Common Future*, Geneva

Keeble, L. (1969) *Principles and Practice of Town and Country Planning*, London: Estates Gazette.

Keeble, L. (1983) *Town Planning Made Plain*, London: Longman.

Keller, S. (1981) *Building for Women*, Massachusetts: Lexington Books.

Kelly, M. (1997) *The Good Practice Manual on Tenant Participation*, WDS (Women's Design Service) in association with DOE Special Grant Programme.

Kirk, G. (1980) *Urban Planning in a Capitalist Society*, London: Croom Helm.

Kirk-Walker, S. (1997) *Undergraduate Student Survey: A Report of The Survey of First Year Students in Construction Industry Degree Courses*, York: Institute of Advanced Architectural Studies, York (Commissioned by Citb).

Knox, P. (1988) *The Design Professions and the Built Environment*, London: Croom Helm.

Kuhn, T. (1962) *The Structure of Scientific Revolutions*, Chicago: University of Chicago Press.

Lake, B. (1941, reprinted 1974) 'A Plan for Britain', special issue of *Picture Post*, vol. 10, no. 1, 4.1.41 (Special Issue No 7, 1974), London: Peter Way Ltd.

Lambert, C. and Weir, C. (1975) *Cities in Britain*, London: Collins.

Lane, P. and Peto, M. (1996) *Guide to the Environment Act 1995*, London: Blackstone.

Langford, D., Hancock, M., Fellows, R. and Gale, A. (1994) *Human Resources in The Management of Construction*, Harlow: Longman.

Lappé, F., Collins, J. and Rosset, P., (1998) *World Hunger: 12 Myths*, London: Earthscan.

Larsen, Egon (1958) *Atomic Energy: The Layman's Guide to The Nuclear Age*, London: Pan.

Latham (1996) See under CIB (1996).

Lavender, S. (1990) *Economics for Builders and Surveyors*, London: Longman.

Law Society (1988) *Equal in The Law: Report of The Working Party on Women's Careers*, London: The Law Society.

Lawless, P. (1989) *Britain's Inner Cities*, London: Paul Chapman Publishing.

Le Corbusier (1971 [1929]) *The City of Tomorrow*, London: Architectural Press.

Leevers, K. (1986) *Women at Work in Housing*, London: Hera.

Legrand, J. (1988) *Chronicle of The Twentieth Century*, London: Chronicle.

Lewis, J. (1984) *Women in England 1870–1950*, Sussex: Wheatsheaf.

LGMB (Local Government Management Board) (1993) *Framework for local Sustainability: a Response by The UK*, Luton: LGMB.

LGMB (1995) *Sustainability Indicators*, Luton: LGMB.

Lichfield, N. (1975) *Evaluation in the Planning Process*, London: Pergamon.

Lindblom, C., (1959) 'The science of muddling through', *Public Administration Review*, Spring (reprinted in Faludi, 1973, pp. 151–69).

Little, J., Peake, L. and Richardson, P. (1988) *Women and Cities, Gender and The Urban Environment*, London: Macmillan.

Little, J. (1994) *Gender, Planning and the Policy Process*, Oxford: Elsevier Press.

Littlefair, P. (1991) *Site Layout Planning for Daylight and Sunlight: A Guide to Good Practice*, Watford, London: Building Research Establishment.

London Research Centre (LRC) (1993) *London Energy Study: Energy Use and The Environment*, London: LRC.

LPAS (London Planning Aid Service) (1986) *Planning for Women: An Evaluation of Local Plan Consultation by Three London Boroughs*, Research Report no. 2, London: TCPA.

LRN (1997) *Still Knocking at The Door*, Report of The Women and Regeneration Seminar, held May 1997, London Regeneration Network with London Voluntary Service Council).

LRN (1999) *Newsletter*, Monthly Newsletter, London Regeneration Network, 356, Holloway Road, London N7 6PA. Tel: 0171 700 8119.

Ludlow, D. (1996) 'Urban planning in a pan-European context' in Greed, C. (1996) (ed.) *Investigating Town Planning*, Harlow: Longman.

LWMT (1996) *Building Careers: Training Routes for Women*, London: London Women and Manual Trades.

Lynch, K. (1960 [1988]) *The Image of the City*, Cambridge: Massachusetts and London: MIT.

Macey, J. and Baker, C. (1983) *Housing Management*, London: Estates Gazette.

Maguire, D., Goodchild, M. and Rhind, D. (1992) *Geographical Information Systems: Principles and Applications*, London: Longmans.

Malthus, T. (1973 [1798]) *Essay on The Principles of Population*, London: Everyman Dent.

Manley, S. (1999) 'Creating accessible environments' and 'Appendix 2: Disability' in Greed, C. and Roberts, M. (1998) *Introducing Urban Design*, Harlow: Longman.

Markusen, A. (1981) 'City Spatial Structure, Women's Household Work and National Urban Policy' in Stimpson, C., Dixler, E., Nelson, M. and Yatrakis, K. (eds) (1981) *Women and The American City*, London: University of Chicago Press.

Marriott, O. (1989) *The Property Boom*, London: Abingdon.

Massey, D. (1984) *Spatial Divisions of Labour: Social Structures and the Geography of Production*, London: Macmillan.

Massey, D., Quintas, P. and Wield, D. (1992) *High Tech Fantasies: Science Parks in Society, Science and Space*, London: Routledge.

Massingham, B. (1984) *Miss Jekyll: Portrait of A Great Gardener*, Newton Abbott: David and Charles.

Matless, D. (1992) 'Regional surveys and local knowledges: the geographical imagination of Britain, 1918–39' in *Transactions*, vol. 17, no. 4: 464–80, London: Institute of British Geographers.

Matrix (1984) *Making Space, Women and the Man Made Environment*, London: Pluto.

Mawhinney, B. (1995) *Transport: The Way Ahead*, London: Department of Transport.

McLoughlin, J. (1969) *Urban and Regional Planning: A System's View*, London: Faber.

McDowell, L. (1983) 'Towards an understanding of the gender division of urban space', *Environment and Planning D: Society and Space*, vol. 1: 59–72.

McDowell, L. (1997) (ed.) *Undoing Place? A Geographical Reader*', London: Arnold.

McDowell, L. and Peake, L. (1990) 'Women in British Geography revisited: or the same old story', *Journal of Geography in Higher Education*, vol. 14, no. 1, 1990: 19–31.

McDowell, L. and Sharp, J. (1997) *Space, Gender, Knowledge: Feminist Readings*, London: Arnold.

McLaren, D., (1998) *Tomorrow's World: Britain's Share in a Sustainable Future* London: Earthscan with Friends of the Earth.

McLellan, D. (1973) *Karl Marx: His Life and Thought*, London: Macmillan.

Meadows D.H., Meadows D.L. and Randers, J. (1992) *Beyond The Limits: Global Collapse or a Sustainable Future*, London: Earthscan.

Meadows D.H. (1972) *The Limits to Growth*, London: Earth Island.

Merrett, S. (1979) *Owner Occupation in Britain*, London: Routledge & Kegan Paul.

Mies, M. and Shiva, V. (1993) *Ecofeminism*, London: Zed Books.

Miles, M. and Huberman, M. (1996) *Qualitative Data Analysis*, London: Sage.

Millerson, G. (1964) *The Qualifying Associations*, London: Routledge & Kegan Paul.

Mills, C. Wright (1959) *The Power Elite*, Oxford: Oxford University Press.

Millward, D. (ed.) (1998) *Construction and the Built Environment GNVQ Advanced*, Harlow: Pearson.

Mirza, H. Safia (ed.) (1997) *Black British Feminism*, London: Routledge.

Mishan, E.J. (1973) *Cost Benefit Analysis*, London: George Allen and Unwin.

Montgomery, J. and Thornley, A. (eds) (1990) *Radical Planning Initiatives*, Aldershot: Gower.

Montgomery, J. (1994) 'The evening economy of cities', *Town and Country Planning*, vol. 63, no. 11: 302–7.

Moore, V. (1999) *A Practical Approach to Planning Law*, London: Blackstone.

Moore, R. (1977) 'Becoming a sociologist in Sparkbrook', in Bell, C. and Newby, H. (eds) *Doing Sociological Research*, London: George Unwin.

Morgan, E. (1974) *The Descent of Woman*, London: Corgi.

Morgan, D. and Nott, S. (1995 [1988]) *Development Control: Policy Into Practice*, London: Butterworths.

Morley, L. (1994) 'Glass Ceiling or Iron Cage: Women in UK Academia', in *Gender, Work and Organisation*, vol. 1, no. 4: 194–204, October.

Morphet, J. (1993) 'Women and Planning', *The Planner, Town and Country Planning*, School Proceedings supplement, 23.2.90, vol. 76, no. 7: 58.

Morphet, J. (1997) 'Enter the EDSP: plan sans fanfare' in *Town and Country Planning* (October edition), pp. 265–67.

Morris, A.E.J. (1972) *History of Urban Form: Prehistory to The Renaissance*, London: George Godwin.

Morris, E. (1986) 'An Overview of Planning for Women From 1945–1975', in Chalmers, M. (ed.) (1986) *New Communities: Did They Get it Right?*, Report of a Conference of the Women and Planning Standing Committee of the Scottish Branch of The Royal Town Planning Institute, County Buildings, Linlithgow, London: RTPI.

Morris, E. (1997) *British Town Planning and Urban Design: Principles and Policies*, Harlow: Longman.

Morris, T. (1958) *The Criminal Area*, London: Routledge & Kegan Paul.

Morris, A. and Nott, S. (1991) *Working Women and The Law: Equality and Discrimination in Theory and Practice*, London: Routledge.

Moser, C. (1993) *Gender Planning and Development: Theory, Practice and Training*, London: Routledge.

Mumford, L. (1930) *The City*, Chicago: American Institute of Planners, in association with RKO, Hollywood [film].

Mumford, L. (1965) *The City in History*, Harmondsworth: Penguin.

Munro, B. (1979) *English Houses*, London: Estates Gazette.

Murdock, J. (1997) 'Inhuman/nonhuman/human: actor network theory and the prospects of nondualistic and symmetrical perspective on nature and society', *Planning and Environment D* vol. 15, no. 6, pp. 731–56.

Nadin, V. and Jones, S. (1990) 'A Profile of The Profession', *The Planner*, 26.1.90, vol. 76, no. 3: 13–24, London: Royal Town Planning Institute.

New Internationalist (1999) 'Green Cities: Survival Guide for the Urban Future' Special Edition of *The New Internationalist*, June 1999, no. 313 (see also May 1996 edition on cities and cars), Oxford: New Internationalist Publications.

Newby, H. (1982) *Green and Pleasant Land*, Harmondsworth: Penguin.

Newman, O. (1973) *Defensible Space: People and Design in the Violent City*, London: Architectural Press.

Nisancioglu, S. Takmaz and Greed, C. (1996) 'Bringing Down The Barriers', *Living in The Future: 24 Sustainable Development Ideas From The UK*, London: UK National Council for Habitat II Conference Istanbul, pp. 16–17.

Norton-Taylor, R. (1982) *Whose Land is it Anyway?*, Wellingborough: Turnstone.

Oatley, N. (1996) 'Regenerating cities and modes of regulation' in Greed, C. (1996) (ed.) *Investigating Town Planning*, Harlow: Longman.

Oatley, N. (1998) (ed.) *Cities, Economic Competition and Urban Planning*, London: Chapman Hall.

OECD (1994) *Women and The City: Housing, Services and The Urban Environment*, Organisation for Economic Co-operation and Development.

Oliver, P. (ed.) (1997) *Encyclopaedia of Vernacular Architecture of the World*, Cambridge: Cambridge University Press.

Oliver, M. (1990) *The Politics of Disablement*, London: Macmillan.

ONS (1998) *The ESRC Review of Government Social Classifications*, London: Office of National Statistics in association with ESRC.

ONS (1999) *Social Trends*, London: Office of National Statistics.

ONS (annual) *Social Trends*, London: Office of National Statistics.

ONS/ESRC (1998) *The ESRC Review of Government Social Classifications*, London: Office of National Statistics in association with the Economic and Social Research Council.

ONS (Office of National Statistics) (1998) *Making Gender Count: Report of the Gender and Statistics Conference 1998*, London: Gender Statistics Users Group, ONS.

OPCS (Office of Population Censuses and Surveys) see ONS (Office of National Statistics).

Pahl, R. (1977) 'Managers, Technical Experts and The State', in Harloe, M. (ed.) (1977) *Captive Cities*, London: Wiley.

Pahl, R. (1965) *Urbs in Rure*, London: Weidenfeld and Nicolson.

Palfreyman, T. and Thorpe, S. (1993) *Designing for Accessibility: An Introductory Guide*, London: Centre for Accessible Environments (CAE). Address: CAE, Nutmeg House, 60 Gainsford Street, London SE1 2NY. Tel: 0171 357 8182.

Palmer, K. (1997) 'Why I'm mad about minerals', *Planning*, 14.11.97, p. 12.

Pardo, V. (1965) *Le Corbusier*, London: Thames and Hudson.

Parkes, M. (1996) *Good Practice Guide for Community Planning and Development*, London: London Planning Advisory Committee (LPAC).

Parker Morris Report (1961) *Homes for Today and Tomorrow*, London: Central Housing Advisory Committee.

Parkin, S. (1994) *The Life and Death of Petra Kelly*, London: Pandora.

Parkin, F. (1979) *Marxism and Class Theory: A Bourgeois Critique*, London: Tavistock.

Pearson, L. (1988) *The Architectural and Social History of Co-operative Living*, London: Macmillan.

Penoyre, J. and Ryan, M. (1990) *The Observer's Book of Architecture*, Doubleday.

Pevsner, N. (1970) *Pioneers of Modern Design*, Harmondsworth: Penguin, and see Pevner's *Pocket Guides to England*.

Pickvance, C. (ed.) (1977) *Urban Sociology*, London: Tavistock.

Pinch, S. (1985) *Cities and Services: The Geography of Collective Consumption*, London: Routledge & Kegan Paul.

Pitman (annual) The *Housing and Planning Year Book*, London: Pitman Publications.

Power, A. (1987) *Property Before People: The Management of Twentieth-century Council Housing*, London: Allen and Unwin.

Prince of Wales (1989) *A Vision of Britain*, London: Doubleday.

Prizeman, J. (1975) *Your House, The Outside View*, London: Blue Circle Cement and Hutchinson.

Punter, J. (1990) *Design Control in Bristol: 1940–1990*, Bristol: Redcliffe Press.

Ratcliffe, J. and Stubbs, M. (1996) *Urban Planning and Real Estate Development*, London: UCL Press.

Ravetz, A. (1986) *The Government of Space*, London: Faber and Faber.

Ravetz, A. (1980) *Remaking Cities*, London: Croom Helm.

Reade, E. (1987) *British Town and Country Planning*, Milton Keynes: Open University Press.

Redfield, J. (1994) *The Celestine Prophecy*, London: Bantam.

Rees, G. and Lambert, J. (1985) *Cities in Crisis*, London: Arnold.

Reeves, D. (1996) (ed.) 'Women and The Environment', Special Issue, *Built Environment*, vol. 22, no. 1.

Reith Report (1946) *New Towns Committee: Final Report*, London: HMSO.

Rex, J. and Moore, R. (1967) *Race, Community and Conflict*, London: Institute of Race Relations.

Rhys Jones, S., Dainty, A., Neale, R. and Bagilhole, B. (1996) *Building on fair footings: improving equal opportunities in the construction industry for women*, Glasgow: CIB.

Richardson, B. (1876) *Hygenia, A City of Health*, London.

RICS (1989) *What Use is a Chartered Surveyor in Planning and Development?*, London: Royal Institution of Chartered Surveyors, London.

Rio (1992) *Rio Declaration: United Nations Conference on the Environment at Rio De Janiero*, New York: United Nations.

Roberts, M. (1991) *Living in A Man-Made World: Gender Assumptions in Modern Housing Design*, London: Routledge.

Roberts, M. and Greed, C. (2000) (eds) *Approaching Urban Design*, Pearson: Harlow.

Roberts, H. (1985) *Doing Feminist Research*, London: Routledge.

Roberts, M. (1974) *Town Planning Techniques*, London: Hutchinson.

Rogers, Lord R. (1999) *Towards an Urban Renaissance: The Urban Taskforce*, London: Routledge, Final Report, in association with DETR.

Rose, Gillian (1993) *Feminism and Geography: The limits of geographical knowledge*, Cambridge: Polity Press.

Rothschild, J. (ed.) (1999) *Design and Feminism: Re-visioning Spaces, Places and Everyday Things*, Rutgers University Press, New Brunswick, New Jersey and London.

Rowntree, B. (1901) *Poverty: A Study of Town Life*, London: Dent.

Rowntree (1992) *Lifetime Homes*, York: Joseph Rowntree Foundation.

Royal Commission on Environmental Pollution (1994) *Report of the Commission*, London: HMSO, Local Government Management Board.

RPG (Regional Planning Guidance) (1989) *Strategic Guidance for Tyne and Wear*, London: HMSO, Department of the Environment. RPG 1.

RTPI (Royal Town Planning Institute) (1983) *Planning for A Multi-Racial Britain*, London: Commission of Racial Equality.

RTPI (1986) 'Planning History' *The Royal Town Planning Institute Distance Learning Course*, Bristol: University of West of England and Leeds: Leeds Metropolitan University.

RTPI (1987) *Report and Recommendations of the Working Party on Women and Planning*, London: RTPI

RTPI (1988) *Managing Equality: The Role of Senior Planners*, Conference 28.10.88, London: Royal Town Planning Institute.

RTPI (1991) *Traffic Growth and Planning Policy*, London: RTPI.

RTPI (1995) *Planning for Women*, Planning Advisory Note, London: Royal Town Planning Institute.

RTPI (1999) *Gender Equality and the Role of Planning: Realising the Goal*, National Symposium, 1.7.99, Report of Proceedings, London: RTPI (paper by C. Booth).

Rubenstein, D. (1974) *Victorian Homes*, London: David & Charles.

Ryder, J. and Silver, H. (1990) *Modern English Society*, London: Methuen.

Rydin, Y. (1998) *Urban and Environmental Planning in the UK*, London: Macmillan.

Saunders, P. (1979) *Urban Politics: A Sociological Interpretation*, Harmondsworth: Penguin.

Saunders, P. (1985) 'Space, The City and Urban Sociology', in Gregory, D. and Urry, J. (1985) *Social Relations and Spatial Structures*, London: Macmillan.

SBP (Polytechnic of The South Bank) (1987) *Women and Their Built Environment*, London: Polytechnic of The South Bank, Faculty of The Built Environment, Conference Report (now South Bank University).

Scarman, Lord (1982) *The Scarman Report: The Brixton Disorders, 10–12 April 1981*, Harmondsworth: Penguin.

Scarrett, D. (1983) *Property Management*, London: Spon.

Schon, D. (1995) *The Reflective Practitioner*, Aldershot: Ashgate.

Schuster Committee (1950) *Report on the Qualifications of Planners*, Cmd. 8059, London: HMSO.

Scott Report (1942) *Report of The Committee on Land Utilisation in Rural Areas*, London: HMSO.

Scottish Office (1998) *Land Use Planning under a Scottish Parliament*, Edinburgh: Scottish Office

Seeley, I. (1997) *Quantity Surveying Practice*, London: Macmillan.

Senior, D. (1996) 'Minerals and the Environment' in Greed, C. (1996) (ed.) *Investigating Town Planning*, Chapter 8, pp. 135–53.

SERPLAN (South East Regional Planning Council) (1988) *Housing, Land Supply and Structure Plan Provision in The South East*, SERPLAN, no. 1070. Secretariat, 50–64, Broadway, London, SWIH ODB.

Service, A. (1977) *Edwardian Architecture*, London: Thames and Hudson.

Sewel, Lord (1997) 'Central and Local Government in Accord', Speech to the *Sustaining Change: Local Agenda 21 in Scotland Conference*, The City of Edinburgh Council City Chambers, Edinburgh, 21 November 1997.

Shariff, Y. (1996) 'Cities of the Future', *Architects Journal*, 4.7.96, p. 24.

Sheffield (1999) *Future Planning: Planning's Future*, Sheffield University: Planning Theory Conference, March 1999.

Shoard, M. (1987) *This Land is Our Land: The Struggle for Britain's Countryside*, London: Paladin.

Shoard, M. (1980) *The Theft of The Countryside*, London: Temple Smith.

Shoard, M. (1999) *A Right to Roam*, London: Blackwell.

Sibley, D. (1995) *Geographies of Exclusion*, London: Routledge.

Silverman, D. (1985) *Qualitative Methodology and Sociology*, Aldershot: Gower.

Silverstone, R. and Ward, A. (eds) (1980) *Careers of Professional Women*, London: Croom Helm.

Simmie, J. (1981) *Power Property and Corporatism*, London: Macmillan.

Simmie, J. (1974) *Citizens in Conflict: The Sociology of Town Planning*, London: Hutchinson.

Simonen L. (1995) *Agenda 21 Briefing Sheets*, Available, and updates, from Lin Simonen, The Create Centre, Smeaton Road, Bristol BS1 6XN.

Sjoberg, G. (1965) *Pre-industrial City: Past and Present*, New York: Free Press.

Skeffington (1969) *People and Planning*, London: HMSO.

Skjerve, R. (ed.) (1993) *Manual for Alternative Municipal Planning*, Oslo: Ministry of The Environment.

Smith, M. (1989) *Guide to Housing*, London: Housing Centre Trust.

Smith, N. and Williams, P. (1986) *Gentrification of the City*, London: Allen & Unwin.

Smith, S. (1989) *The Politics of Race and Residence*, Oxford: Polity.

SOBA (1997) 'Mentoring: to Tame Or to Free?', *Symposium Notes, Meeting of Society of Black Architects*, 27.11.97, Prince of Wales's Institute of Architecture, London.

Speer, R. and Dade, M. (1994) *How to Stop and Influence Planning Permission*, London: Dent.

Spencer, A. and Podmore, D. (1987) *In A Man's World: Essays on Women in Male-dominated Professions*, London: Tavistock.

Spitzner, M. (1998) 'Travel distances between home, work and community facilities', Paper presented at *Eurofem, Gender and Human Settlements Conference on Local and Regional Sustainable Human Development from a Gender Perspective*, Hämeenlina, Finland.

Stacey, M. (1960) *Tradition and Change: A Study of Banbury*, Oxford: Oxford University Press.

Stanley, L. (ed.) (1990) *Feminist Praxis: Research, theory, epistemology in Feminist Sociology*, London: Routledge.

Stapleton, T. (1986) *Estate Management Practice*, London: Estates Gazette.

Stark, A. (1997) 'Combating the backlash: how Swedish women won the war' pp. 224–44, in Oakley, A. and Mitchell, J. (eds) (1997) *Who's Afraid of Feminism?: Seeing Through the Backlash*, London: Hamish Hamilton.

Stimpson, C., Dixler, E., Nelson, M. and Yatrakis, K. (eds) (1981) *Women and the American City*, Chicago: University of Chicago Press.

Stoker, G. and Young, S. (1993) *Cities in the 1990s: Local Choice for a Balanced Strategy*, Harlow: Longman.

Strauss, A. (ed.) (1968) *The American City*, London: Allen Lane.

Summerson, J. (1986) *Georgian London*, Harmondsworth: London.

Sutcliffe, A. (1974) *Multi-storey Living: The British Working Class Experience*, London: Croom Helm.

Swain, J., Finkelstein, V., French, S. and Oliver, M. (eds) (1993) *Disabling Barriers – Enabling Environments*. Sage Publications, London, in association with the Open University.

Swenarton, M. (1981) *Homes Fit for Heroes*, London: Heinemann.

Taylor, J. (1990) 'Planning for Women in Unitary Development Plans: An Analysis of The Factors Which Generate "Planning for Women" and The Form this Planning Takes', Sheffield University: Town and Regional Planning Department, September, 1990, unpublished MA Thesis.

Taylor, N. (1999) 'Town planning "social" not just "physical"' in Greed, C. (ed.) (1999) *Social Town Planning*, London: Routledge.

Taylor, N. (1998) *Urban Planning Theory Since 1945*, London: Sage.

Taylor, N. (1973) *The Village in The City*, London: Maurice Temple Smith.

Taylor, B. (1988) 'Organising for Change Within Local Authorities: How to Turn Ideas Into Action to Benefit Women', Paper given at Conference *Women and Planning: Where Next?*, London: Polytechnic of Central London: Short Course Report, 16.3.88.

TCP (1999) 'Land use planning under a Scottish parliament', *Town and Country Planning*, vol. 68, no. 6, June, p. 214, unattributed article.

TCPA (Town and Country Planning Association) (1987) 'A Place for Women in Planning', *Town and Country Planning*, vol. 56, no. 10, special issue, London: Town and Country Planning Association.

Telling, J. and Duxbury, R. (1993) *Planning Law and Procedure*, London: Butterworth.

Tetlow, J. and Goss, A. (1968) *Homes, Towns and Traffic*, London: Faber.

Tewdwr Jones, M. (1996) *British Planning Policy in Transition: Planning in the 1990s*, London: University College London Press.

Theniral, R. (1992) *Strategic Environmental Assessment* London: Earthscan.

Thomas, H. (1980) 'The education of British town planners 1965–75' *Planning and Administration*, vol. 7, no. 2, pp. 67–78.

Thomas, H. (1999) 'Social town planning and the planning profession' in Greed, C. (1999) *Social Town Planning*, London: Routledge.

Thomas, H. and Lo Piccolo, F. (1999) 'Best value, planning and race equality', Paper presented at the *Future Planning: Planning's Future: Planning Theory Conference*, March 1999. Sheffield: University of Sheffield, Department of Planning.

Thompson, F.M.L. (1968) *Chartered Surveyors, The Growth of A Profession*, London: Routledge & Kegan Paul.

Thornley, A. (1991) *Urban Planning under Thatcherism: the Challenge of the Market*, London: Routledge.

Tönnies, F. (1955) *Community and Association*, London: Routledge & Kegan Paul.

Torre, S. (ed.) (1977) *Women in American Architecture: A Historic and Contemporary Perspective*, New York: Whitney Library of Design.

Tudor Walters Report (1918) *Report of the Committee on Questions of Building Construction in Connection with The Provision of Dwellings for The Working Classes*, London: HMSO.

Turner, T. (1996) *City as Landscape: A Post Post-Modern [sic] View of Design and Planning*, London: Spon.

Uguris, Tijen (2000 forthcoming) Ethnic and Gender Divisions in Tenant Participation in Public Housing, unpublished PhD under preparation, Woolwich: University of Greenwich.

UK Round Table on Sustainable Development (1996) *Defining A Sustainable Transport Sector*, London: HMSO.

UNCED (United Nations Conference on Environment and Development), (1992) *Earth Summit – Press summary of Agenda 21*, Rio de Janeiro: UNCED.

Unwin, G. (1912) *Nothing Gained by Overcrowding*, London: Dent.

Uthwatt Report (1942) *Report of The Expert Committee on Compensation and Betterment*, London: HMSO.

Walker, G. (1996) 'Retailing development: in or out of town?' in Greed, C. *Investigating Town Planning*, Harlow: Longman.

Wall, C. and Clarke, L. (1996) *Staying Power: Women in Direct Labour Building Teams*, London: London Women and The Manual Trades.

Ward, S. (1994) *Planning and Urban Change*, London: Sage.

Warren, K. (ed.) (1997) *Ecofeminism: Women, Culture and Nature*, Indianapolis: Indiana University Press.

WCC (Women's Communication Centre) (1996) *Values and Visions: The 'What Women Want' Social Survey*, London: WCC.

WDS (Current) *Women's Design Service Broadsheet Design Series*, WDS (Womens Design Service), 52–54 Featherstone St., London EC1Y 8RT. Tel: 020 7490 5210.
1. Race and Gender in Architectural Education.
2. Planning London: Unitary Development Plans.
3. Challenging Women: City Challenge.
4. Antenatal Waiting Areas.
5. Participation in Development.
6. Training in Building Design and The Construction Industry: Routes for Women.
7. UDP Policies: Their Impact on Women's Lives (LWPF Report, January 1994).
8. Designing Out Crime (LWPF Report April 1994).
9. Public Places, Future Spaces: Older Women and The Built Environment.
10. Women As Planners: is More Better? (LWPF Report, July 1994).
11. Street Lighting and Women's Safety.
12. Are Town Centres Managing? (LWPF Report October 1994).
13. Sisterhood, Cities and Sustainability (LWPF Report January 1995).
14. Residential Neighbourhoods: A Place for Children (LWPF Report, April 1995).
15. Government Urban Funding: Winners and Losers (LWPF Report, July 1995).
16. Public Surveillance Systems.
17. Local Pride: The Role of Public and Community Art.
18. Development Advice Work: Dealing with Realities.
19. Public Surveillance Systems: Do People Benefit?
20. Breaking Down The Barriers for Women.
21. Women and Planning in Europe.
22. Building Careers: Training Routes for Women.
23. Local Agenda 21 Update.
24. Professional Partners in Regeneration.
25. Policy Planning and Development Control.

WDS (1990) *At Women's Convenience: A Handbook on the Design of Women's Toilets*, London: WDS.

WDS (1994) *Planning London: Unitary Development Plans*, London: WDS.

WDS (1998) 'Gender Issues within Planning Education', *Broadsheet 28, London Women and Planning Forum.* London: WDS.

WE (Women and Environments) (1999) *Women and Environments International Magazine*, Toronto: The WEED Foundation (Women, Environments, Education and Development Foundation).

Weber, M. (1964) (Intro.ed Parsons, Talcott) *The Theory of Social and Economic Organisation (Wirtschaft Und Gesellschaft)*, New York: Free Press.

Wekerle, G., Peterson, R. and Morley, D. (eds) (1980) *New Space for Women*, Boulder: Westview Press.

WGSG (1984) *Geography and Gender*, London: Hutchinson, Women and Geography Study Group, Institute of British Geographers, London.

WGSG (1997) *Feminist Geographies: Explorations in Diversity and Difference*, Harlow: Longmans, Women and Geography Study Group of Royal Geographical Society and Institute of British Geographers, London.

WHO (1997) (World Health Organisation), *City Planning for Health and Sustainable Development*, Copenhagen: WHO.

Whitelegg J. (1993) *Transport for a Sustainable Future: The Case for Europe*, London: Belhaven.

Whitelegg, Elizabeth, Arnot, Madeleine, Bartels, Else, Beechey, Veronica, Birke, Lynda, Himmelweit, S., Leonard, D., Ruehl, S. and Speakman, M. (eds) (1982) *The Changing Experience of Women*, Oxford: Basil Blackwell with Oxford: Open University.

Whyte, W. (1981) *Street Corner Society*, Chicago: University Press of Chicago.

Williams, R. (1996) *European Union Spatial Policy and Planning*, London: Paul Chapman.

Williams, R. (1999) 'European Union: Social Cohesion and Social Town Planning in Greed, C. (ed.) (1999) *Social Town Planning*, London: Routledge.

Wilson, D. (1970) *I Know it Was the Place's Fault*, London: Oliphants.

Wilson, E. (1980) *Only Half Way to Paradise*, London: Tavistock.

Wilson, Elizabeth (1991) *The Spinx in the City: Urban life, the control of disorder and women*, London: Virago.

World Commission on Environment and Development (WCED) (1987) *Our Common Future* (The Brundtland Report), Oxford: Oxford University Press.

Young, M. and Willmott, P. (1957) *Family and Kinship in East London*, Harmondsworth: Penguin.

Young, M. and Willmott, P. (1978) *The Symmetrical Family: Study of Work and Leisure in The London Region*, Harmondsworth: Penguin.

Young, M. and Willmott, P. (1957) *Family and Kinship in East London*, Harmondsworth: Penguin.

GOVERNMENT PUBLICATIONS

All these publications are regularly changed and updated. Therefore it is important to check for the most recent version.

POLICY GUIDANCE NOTES

Planning Policy Guidance (PPGs)

1. General Policy and Principles
2. Green belts
3. Housing
4. Industry, Commercial Development and Small Firms
5. Simplified Planning Zones (redrafted 1992)
6. Town Centres and Retail Development
7. Countryside and Rural Economy
8. Telecommunications
9. Nature Conservation
10. Waste
11. Regional guidance (to be replaced)
12. Development Plans and Regional Planning Guidance
13. Transport
14. Development on Unstable Land
15. Planning and the Historic Environment
16. Archaeology and Planning
17. Sport and Recreation
18. Enforcing Planning Control
19. Outdoor Advertisement Control
20. Coastal Planning
21. Tourism
22. Renewable Energy
23. Planning and Pollution Control
24. Planning and Noise
25. Development and Flood Risk

Readers should note there has been no further PPG after number 24, but all are being updated.

Regional Planning Guidance (RPGs)

In summary the RPGs' publication and revision status is as follows:

1. Tyne and Wear 1989 to be incorporated into a new Northern RPG
2. West Yorkshire 1989 (superseded by 12)
3. London, reissued 1996
3a. London – Strategic View – 1991
3b. Thames 1997
4. Greater Manchester 1989 (superseded by 13)
5. South Yorkshire 1989 (superseded by 12)
6. East Anglia 1991
7. Northern 1993
8. East Midlands 1994
9. South East 1994 (and previously SERPLAN, 1988)
9a. Thames Gateway 1995
10. South West 1994
11. West Midlands 1995
12. Yorkshire and Humberside 1996
13. North West 1996

(*Source*: DETR, 1999)

In 1998 the DETR produced a consultation paper titled, 'The Future of Regional Planning Guidance' which suggested the new Regional Development Agencies should take over the role of producing regional guidance.

Minerals Planning Guidance (MPGs)

These run from 1–15 covering a range of minerals topics. Although coal mining has declined the MPGs are still very important in areas where there is open cast mining.

Examples:

1989 MPG7 The Reclamation of Mineral Workings
1995 MPG14 Environment Act 1995: Review of Mineral Permissions

Development Control Policy Notes

There is only one of these that has not been replaced by PPGs, significantly,

16. Access for the Disabled 1985

Design Bulletins

In the 1960s and 1970s a series of design bulletins were produced under the Ministry of Housing and Local Government, and then under the Housing section of the Department of the Environment. These were discontinued and unobtainable. The last ones were issued in 1974 entitled, *Spaces in the Home: Part I – Bathrooms and W.Cs* and *Part II – kitchens and laundering spaces.*

Of particular relevance to planning in respect of the problems of high rise development, was *Schemes At Medium and High Densities*, produced in 1963 by the Department of the Environment

But in 1998 an updated version of Design Bulletin 32 was issued *Residential Roads and Footpaths Design* (second edition) (DETR, 199b), with a related guidance document, namely *Places, Streets and Movement: a companion guide to Design Bulletin 32* (DETR, 1998c). Readers should note that these publications may mark the beginning of a new phase of Design Bulletin production.

This was ushered in with *By Design*, a guide produced by DETR, 2000.

This guide has been published to promote higher standards in urban design and provide sound, practical advice to help implement the Government's commitment to good design, as set out in Planning Policy Guidelines Note I General Policy and Principles. It encourages those who influence and shape development decisions to think more deeply and sensitively about the living environments being created.

Practice Guides

Examples include:

Development Plans: A Guide Practice Guide, DoE 1992
Environmental Appraisal of Development Plans: A Good Practice Guide, DoE 1994
PPG1: A Guide to Better Practice, DoE 1995

Circulars (some of the main ones of interest)

The DoE and its successor the DETR have produced circulars on every aspect of policy for the natural and built environment. The following list focuses on key planning-related circulars.

42/55	Green Belts
50/57	Green Belts
56/71	Historic Towns and Roads
82/73	Bus Operation in Residential and Industrial Areas
24/75	Housing Need and Action
36/78	Trees and Forestry
22/80	Development Control: Policy and Practice
38/81	Planning and Enforcement Appeals
10/82	Disabled Persons Act
22/83	Planning Gain (replaced by 16/91)
14/84	Green Belts
15/84	Land for Housing (cancelled by PPG3)
22/84	Memorandum on Structure Plans and Local Plans (Cancelled by PPG12)
1/85	The use of conditions in planning permissions
14/85	Development and Employment
30/85	Transitional Matters (cancelled by PPG12)
2/86	Development by Small Businesses
8/87	Historic Buildings and Conservation Areas [replaced by PPG15]
11/87	Town and Country Planning (Appeals) Regulations
12/87	Redundant Hospital Sites in Green Belts
13/87	Changes of Use of Buildings and Other Land
16/87	Development involving agricultural land (cancelled by PPG7)
3/88	Unitary Development Plans
10/88	Inquiries and Appeals Procedures Rules
12/89	Green Belts
15/88	Assessment of Environmental Effects Regulations
12/89	Green Belts
9/90	Crime Prevention: The success of the partnership approach
7/91	Planning and Affordable Housing (cancelled by PPG3)
12/91	Redundant hospital sites in green belts
16/91	Planning and Compensation Act 1991: Planning Obligations
17/92	Planning and Compensation Act 1991: Immunity Rules
23/92	Motorway Service Areas
8/93	Awards of Costs Incurred in Planning and Other Proceedings
10/93	Local Government Act 1992 (concerning CCT)

5/94 Planning Out Crime
7/94 Environmental Assessment
5/94 Planning out crime
11/95 Use of Conditions in Planning Permissions
13/96 Planning and Affordable Housing
1/97 Planning Obligations
5/97 Energy Conservation
1997/2 Enforcing Planning Control
1998/2 Prevention of Dereliction
1998/6 Planning and Affordable Housing

Command Papers

This list features only a few which have been mentioned in this book.

1989 WP 569 Future of Development Plans
1966 WP 2928 Leisure in the Countryside
1990 WP 1200 This Common Inheritance
1992 WP (annual) This Common Inheritance, Annual Report
1993 WP 2426 Guide to The Eco Management and Audit Scheme for UK Local Government.
1994 WP 2426 Sustainable Development: The UK Strategy
1994 WP 2427 Climate Change: The UK Programme
1994 WP 2428 Biodiversity: The UK Action Plan
1995 WP 3471 Projections of Households in England to 2016
1996 WP 3234 Transport: The Way Forward
1996 WP 3188 This Common Inheritance 3188
1997 WP 3814 Building Partnerships for Prosperity
1998 WP 3897 A Mayor and Assembly for London
1998 WP 3950 A New Deal for Transport: Better for Everyone

Consultation Papers

It is significant that following the election of Labour in 1997 greater emphasis appears to be put upon a range of consultation documents, most of which have the logo 'Streamlining Planning' upon them (see under DETR in the bibliography). Consultation papers are also known as 'Green Papers'. Usually these are superseded by a White Paper that is a Command paper on the topic following the consultation and discussion phases.

Examples include:

1997 New Leadership for London
1998 Modernising Planning: A Policy Statement by The Minister for The Regions, Regeneration and Planning.

1998 The Future of Regional Planning Guidance: Consultation Paper
1998 Transport the Way Ahead
DETR (1999) Leylandii and other high hedges – Briefing note, DETR
DETR (1999) Outdoor Advertisement Control, Consultative Paper

N.B: prior to the creation of the DETR, Command Papers on transport were produced in conjunction with the Department of Transport, such as 3234 above.

MAIN ACTS OF PARLIAMENT RELEVANT TO TOWN PLANNING

1835 Municipal Corporations Act (gave powers to local authorities)
1847 Sanitary Act (connection of houses to sewers)
1848 Public Health Act (minimum of 8 foot ceilings)
1851 Common Lodging Houses Act
1851 Labouring Classes Lodging Houses Act
1868 Artisans and Labourers Dwellings Improvements Act
1875 Public Health Act (bye-law housing, against back to backs)
1875 Artisans Dwellings Act, slum clearance of streets
1879 Public Health Act
1890 Housing of the Working Classes Act (council houses)
1894 London Building Act, (London building regulations)
1906 Open Spaces Act
1909 Housing and Town Planning Act
1919 Sex Disqualification (Removal) Act
1919 Housing and Town Planning Act
1932 Town and Country Planning Act
1935 Restriction of Ribbon Development Act
1945 Distribution of Industry Act
1946 New Towns Act
1947 Town and Country Planning Act
1947 Agriculture Act
1949 National Parks and Access to the Countryside Act
1952 Town Development Act
1953 Historic Buildings and Ancient Monuments Act
1957 Housing Act, (slum clearance)
1960 Local Employment Act
1965 Transport Act
1967 Civic Amenities Act
1968 Countryside Act
1969 Housing Act (General Improvement Areas)

1970	Community Land Act
1970	Equal Pay Act
1971	Town and Country Planning Act
1972	Industry Act
1972	Local Government Act
1974	Clean Air Act
1974	Town and Country Amenities Act
1974	Housing Act (Housing Action Areas)
1975	Community Land Act
1976	Race Relations Act
1978	Inner Urban Areas Act
1980	Highway Acts
1980	Local Government, Planning and Land Act
1981	Minerals Act
1981	Disabled Persons Act
1982	Local Government (Miscellaneous Provisions) Act
1982	Derelict Land Act
1985	Housing Act
1986	Housing and Planning Act
1988	Housing Act
1988	Local Government Act
1989	Children Act
1989	Local Government and Housing Act
1989	Water Act
1990	Town and Country Planning Act
1990	Planning (Listed Buildings and Conservation Areas) Act
1990	Environmental Protection Act
1990	Planning (Hazardous Substances) Act
1991	Water Industry Act
1991	New Roads and Street Works Act
1991	Planning and Compensation Act
1992	Local Government Act
1992	Transport and Works Act
1993	Leasehold Reform, Housing and Urban Development Act (Part III creation of the Urban Regeneration Agency)
1993	Traffic Calming Act
1993	Housing and Urban Development Act
1994	Local Government (Wales) Act
1995	Disability Discrimination Act
1995	Noise Act
1995	Environment Act
1996	Housing Grants, Construction and Regeneration Act
1997	Road Traffic Act
1997	Road Traffic Reduction Act
1998	Housing Act
1998	Human Rights Act
1998	Regional Development Agencies Act

There are also a series of Regulations and Orders which enable the legislation to be implemented, such as the General Development Order, described in the chapter on development control. For example the full extent of the GDO is contained within two linked documents:

1995	Town and Country Planning (General Development Procedure) Order
1995	Town and Country Planning (General Permitted Development) Order

European planning controls

Article 119 of the Treaty of Rome 1957 established the principle of equal opportunities and the Equal Treatment Directive 76/207 codified this.

1987	Single European Act

EC Directive 85/337 (now updated 97/11) on Environmental Assessment 'The Assessment of the Effect of Certain Public and Private Projects on the Environment' is applied in Britain under the 'Assessment of Environmental Effects Regulation' No. 119, of the 1988 Town and Country Planning Regulations. All EU legislation has to be embodied in the local nation state legislations, in this case within UK planning legislation.

The EU produces a range of policy documents called EU 'Green Papers'. These have a similar status to UK White papers, for example see *Green Paper on the Urban Environment*, COM (1990) 218. But in the British Context a 'Green Paper' normally refers to a consultative document which precedes the issue of a White Paper that is a Command paper.

1977	WP 6485 Policy for Inner Cities
1985	WP 9517 Lifting the Burden

WALES

Technical Advice Notes (TANs)

1. Joint Housing Land Availability Studies
2. Planning and Affordable Housing
3. Simplified Planning Zones
4. Retailing and Town Centres
5. Nature Conservation and Planning
6. Development involving Agricultural Land
7. Outdoor Advertisement Control
8. Renewable Energy
9. Enforcement of Planning Control
10. Tree Preservation Orders
11. Noise
12. Design
13. Tourism
14. Coastal Planning
15. Development and Flood Risk
16. Sport and Recreation

NORTHERN IRELAND

Development Control Advice Notes

1. Amusement Parks
2. Multiple Occupancy
3. Bookmaking Offices
4. Hot Food Bars
5. Taxi Offices
6. Restaurants and Cafes
7. Public Houses
8. Small Unit Housing in Existing Residential Areas
9. Residential and Nursing Homes
10. Environmental Impact Assessment
11. Access for People with Disabilities
11a. Nature Conservation and Planning
12. Hazardous Substances
13. Crèches, Day Nurseries and Pre-school Playgroups
14. Telecommunications

Planning Policy Statements Include:

1. Northern Ireland Planning System
2. Planning and Nature Conservation
3. Planning and Roads Considerations
4. Industrial Development
5. Retailing and Town Centres

SCOTTISH PLANNING PUBLICATIONS

The Scottish Office produce several different series of planning guidance publications guidance publications. These include:

Scottish Office Environment Department Circulars
Planning Advice Notes
National Planning Guidance
National Planning Policy Guidelines (NPPGs)
Scottish Natural Heritage

Of these the NPPGs are listed for illustrative purposes, being among the most important.

Scottish National Policy Guidelines (NPPGs)

1. The Planning System
2. Business and Industry
3. Land for Housing
4. Land for Mineral Working
5. Archaeology and Planning

6. Renewable Energy
7. Planning and Flooding
8. Land for Waste Disposal
9. Roadside Facilities on Motorways
10. Retailing
12. Sport and Physical Recreation

Other Scottish Office planning publications cover a vast range of topics, such as sustainability, transport and rural development.

STATISTICAL DATA SOURCES

1. *Census of Population*, carried out every ten years since 1801, and based on 100% survey. Invaluable 'time series' for trend projection, OPCS/HMSO.
2. *Labour Force Survey*, Carried out bi-annually since 1975, proving useful data on employment trends in conjunction with other data. HMSO.
3. *The General Household Survey*, continuous ongoing social survey, HMSO.
4. *Social Trends* Produced by Office of National Statistics (ONS).
5. *Regional Trends* (ONS).
6. *Housing and Construction Statistics*, produced annually, and quarterly version (DETR).
7. *Local Housing Statistics* – Quarterly, gives local statistics on house building (DETR).
8. *Household Projections 1989–2011*, gives estimates for counties, districts and boroughs with trend projection. DETR.
9. *Digest of Environmental Protection and Water Statistics* – Annual DETR.
10. *Land Use Change in England*, statistics on changes in land use based on Ordnance Survey data.
11. *Development Control Statistics* DETR.
12. *Private House Building Statistics*, produced by NHBC, Quarterly.
13. *Building Society House Price Data*, available from Halifax, Nationwide.

WEB SITES

Agenda 21
http:// www.agenda21.se

European Union
http://www.europa.eu.int
http://www.inforegio.cec.eu.int

European Environmental Agency
http://www.eea.dk/

For ESDP details, publications and maps see http://www.inforegio.org

DETR

http:// www.open.gov.uk

http://www.planning.detr.gov.uk/consult/ (for consultation papers)

http:/www.highways.gov.uk (Highways Agency within the DETR)

The Local Government Association

http://www.lga.gov.uk

RTPI

http://rtpi.co.uk

UK Government index including DETR and Scottish Office

http://www.open.gov.uk/detr

Urban design issues

http://www.towns.org.uk

ONS statistical data may be downloaded from the Web page http://www.statistic.gov.uk.

The Stationary Office www.tso-online.c.uk

DISABILITY

Many aspects of disability are controlled more by the Building Regulations than through planning control. The Building Regulations put into operation the requirements of the linked British Standards Documents. In 1987 Part M of the Building Regulations based upon BS5810 was first introduced, and in 1999 Part M was revised, notably introducing requirements for a level threshold (rather than steps) to be provided on new residential development, a ground floor toilet, and other access reforms. Details are contained in Package PB191CP (TSO).

Regulations related to Disability

BS5810 Access for Disabled People.

Other British Standards affecting access include:

BS6465 Sanitary Installations (revised version 1995)
BS5776 Powered Stairlifts
BS5588 Means of Escape from Buildings
BS6460 Lifting Platforms

Legislation affecting disability access includes:

1970	Chronically Sick and Disabled Persons Act
1981	Disabled Persons Act
1986	Local Government (Access to Information) Act (affects access to public meetings)
1995	Disability Discrimination Act

Other Useful Disability Standards

Access for Disabled People: Access Committee for England
Centre for Accessible Environments
Adler, 1999 with CD ROM of design standards.
Development Control Policy Note 16: Access for the Disabled 1985 (DoE)
RTPI PAN 3 (Planning Advice Note) Access for Disabled People, 1988

Other Sources of Planning Information

The *Housing and Planning Year Book*, *Municipal Yearbook* and *Public Services Yearbook* provide information on central and local government planning departments, progress of plans, names of chief officers, and details of main policy changes and publications for each year. They also include maps of local government boundary changes.

ACRONYMS

GNP	Gross National Product
ACE	Access Committee of England
AEE	Assessment of Environmental Effects
AONB	Area of Outstanding Natural Beauty
ARB	Architects Registration Board
ARCOM	Association of Researchers in Construction Management
ARU	Les Annales de la Recherche Urbaine (Journal of Urban Research) (France)
ASI	Architecture and Surveying Institute
BR	Building Regulations
BS	British Standards
BSE	'Mad cow disease' Bovine Spongiform Encephalopathy
BSI	British Standards Institution
CAD	Computer Aided Design
CADW	Translation: Welsh Built Heritage Agency
CAE	Centre for Accessible Environments
CAP	Common Agricultural Policy
CBD	Central Business District
CBI	Confederation of British Industry
CCT	Compulsory Competitive Tendering
CCTV	Closed Circuit Television
CDA	Comprehensive Development Area
CEC	Commission of European Communities
CFC	Chloro-fluoro-carbon
CIBSE	Chartered Institute of Building Services Engineers
CICSC	Construction Industry Council, Standing Conference
CIOB	Chartered Institute of Building
CIOH	Chartered Institute of Housing
CISC	Construction Industry Standing Conference.
CJD	Creutzfeldt-Jakob Disease
CLA	Country Landowners Association
COSLA	Convention of Scottish Local Authorities
CPD	Continuing Professional Development
CPO	Compulsory Purchase Order
CPO	Chief Planning Officer
CPRE	Council for the Protection of Rural England
CRE	Commission for Racial Equality
CSO	Central Statistical Office
DC	Development Control
DCMS	Department of Culture Media and Sport
DDA	Disability Discrimination Act

DETR	Department of Environment, Transport and the Regions
DG	Directorate-General (EC body)
DLO	Direct Labour Organization
DLR	Docklands Light Railway
DoE	Department of the Environment
DoT	Department of Transport
Dpa	Dwellings per acre
Dph	Dwellings per hectare
e-coli	*Escherichia coli*
EA	Environment Appraisal (according to context)
EA	Environmental Assessment
EA	Environment Agency (for England and Wales)
EC	European Community
EEA	European Environment Agency
EEC	European Economic Community
EHTF	English Historic Towns Forum
EIA	Environmental Impact Assessment
EIP	Examination in Public
EOC	Equal Opportunities Commission
EPA	Educational Priority Area
ERDF	European Regional Development Fund
ES	Environmental Statement
ESDP	European Spatial Development Perspective
ESRC	Economic and Social Research Council
ETB	English Tourist Board
EU	European Union
EZ	Enterprise Zone
FoE	Friends of the Earth
FSA	Food Standards Agency
FSI	Floor Space Index
FUN	Frauen Umwelt Netz (Women's Environmental Network)
GDO	General Development Order
GIA	General Improvement Area
GIS	Geographic Information Systems
GLA	Greater London Authority
GLC	Greater London Council
GLDP	Greater London Development Plan
GMF	genetically modified food
GNVQ	General National Vocational Qualifications
GWR	Great Western Railway
HAA	Housing Action Areas

HBF	House Builders' Federation
HMG	Her Majesty's Government
HMSO	Her Majesty's Stationery Office (now TSO see below)
Http:	Hyper Text Transfer Protocol
IBG	Institute of British Geographers
ICE	Institution of Civil Engineers
ICLEI	International Council for Local Environmental Initiatives
IDC	Industrial Development Certificate
IPCC	Intergovernmental Panel on Climate Change
ISE	Institution of Structural Engineers
ISVA	Incorporated Society of Surveyors, Valuers and Auctioneers
IT	Information Technology
LA	Local Authority
LA21	Local Agenda 21
LBC	London Borough Council
LCC	London County Council
LDA	London Development Agency
LDDC	London Docklands Development Corporation
LEC	Local Enterprise Council (Scotland)
LDCC	London Docklands Development Corporation
LGMB	Local Government Management Board
LMS	London Midland and Scottish [Railway]
LNER	London North Eastern Railway
LPA	Local Planning Authority
LRN	London Regeneration Network
LSE	London School of Economics
LWMT	London Women and the Manual Trades
MAFF	Ministry of Agriculture, Fisheries and Food
MCC	Metropolitan County Council
MDC	Metropolitan District Council
MOD	Ministry of Defence
MPG	Minerals Planning Guidance Note
NAEE	National Association of Estate Agents
NEA	National Environment Agency
NFU	National Farmers Union
NGO	Non Governmental Organization
NIA	Noise Impact Assessment
NPPG	National Planning Policy Guidance Note (Scotland)
NRA	National Rivers Authority
NVQ	National Vocational Qualifications
ODP	Office Development Permit
OECD	Organization for Economic Co-operation and Development
ONS	Office of National Statistics (successor to CSO)
OPCS	Office of Population, Census and Surveys
OS	Ordnance Survey
PAL	Planning Aid for London
PAN	Planning Advice Note (Scotland)
PAN	Planning Advice Note (RTPI)
PCU	Passenger Car Unit
PFI	Private Finance Initiative

Ppa	Persons per acre
PPG	Planning Policy Guidance [Note] (England and Wales)
Pph	Persons per hectare
QUANGO	Quasi Autonomous Non-Governmental Organization
QUANGO	Quasi Autonomous National Governmental Organization
RDA	Regional Development Agency
RGS	Royal Geographical Society
RIBA	Royal Institute of British Architects
RICS	Royal Institution of Chartered Surveyors
RPG	Regional Planning Guidance Note (England)
RSPCA	Royal Society for the Prevention of Cruelty to Animals
RTPI	Royal Town Planning Institute
SAP	Survey Analysis Plan
SDA	Scottish Development Agency
SDO	Special Development Order
SEM	Single European Market
SEPA	Scottish Environmental Protection Agency
SERPLAN	South East Regional Plan
SIA	Social Impact Assessment
SOBA	Society of Black Architects
SoS	Secretary of State
SPZ	Simplified Planning Zone
SR	Southern Region [Railway]
SRB	Single Regeneration Budget
SSSI	Site of Special Scientific Interest
TAN	Technical Advice Notes (Wales)
TCP	Town and Country Planning
TCPA	Town and Country Planning Association
TEC	Training and Enterprise Council (England and Wales)
TFL	Transport for London
TPO	Tree Preservation Order
TSO	The Stationery Office (successor to HMSO)
UCAS	Universities and Colleges Admissions System
UCO	Use Classes Order
UDC	Urban Development Corporation
UDP	Unitary Development Plan
UN	United Nations
UNCED	United Nations Conference on Environment and Development
UNEP	United Nations Environmental Programme
UNESCO	United Nations Educational, Scientific and Cultural Organization
VDU	Visual Display Unit
WCC	Women's Communication Centre
WCED	World Commission on Environment and Development
WDA	Welsh Development Agency
WDS	Women's Design Service
WGSG	Women and Geography Study Group
WHO	World Health Organization
WWF	World Wildlife Fund
WWW	World Wide Web

AUTHOR AND PERSON INDEX

N.B: Full names are given for famous and contemporary historical figures in the story of planning, and surname and first name initial are given for authors. Reports named after their chairmen are listed under the subject index, for example, Tudor Walters, Barlow.

SUBJECT INDEX

Reader: this index includes both specific references to topics on particular pages, and themes which run right through the book for which individual occurrences and relevant chapters are listed for guidance.